COLD AND DARK

BY
MISCHA L THOMAS

Credits

Writing, Game Design & Layout
Mischa L Thomas

Interior Art
Johan Fredriksson

Additional Art
Henrik Karppinen, Fanny Eriksson, Justin Adams

Proofing & Editing
N. Conte, Joseph Vega, Mischa L Thomas, Cecilia Hermansson

Starmap and Planetary Graphics
Mischa L Thomas

Webpage
http://wicked-world.se/

Special Thanks To
www.brusheezy.com
PowerOfCreativity, MB-ArtisticSet-III, suztv, photoshoptutorials,
Rebecca-Parker-Stock, crestfallen, webdesignerlab

www.obsidiandawn.com
http://www.obsidiandawn.com/space-photoshop-gimp-brushes
http://www.brushking.eu/, texturemate, Galaxy Set - By BLazteR,
Thomas Beal, Hitokiri147, crazykira-resources

DeviantArt
http://redheadstock.deviantart.com/journal/12379986/, http://basstar.deviantart.com/

free-brushes.com
http://free-brushes.com/2010/01/24/tech_vector_brushes.html

WICKED WORLD GAMES

MÖDIPHIÜS
ENTERTAINMENT

*Please visit the webpage for free stuff such as the OST and the ready
to play story Darker Than Most found in the quick guide.*

wicked-world.se

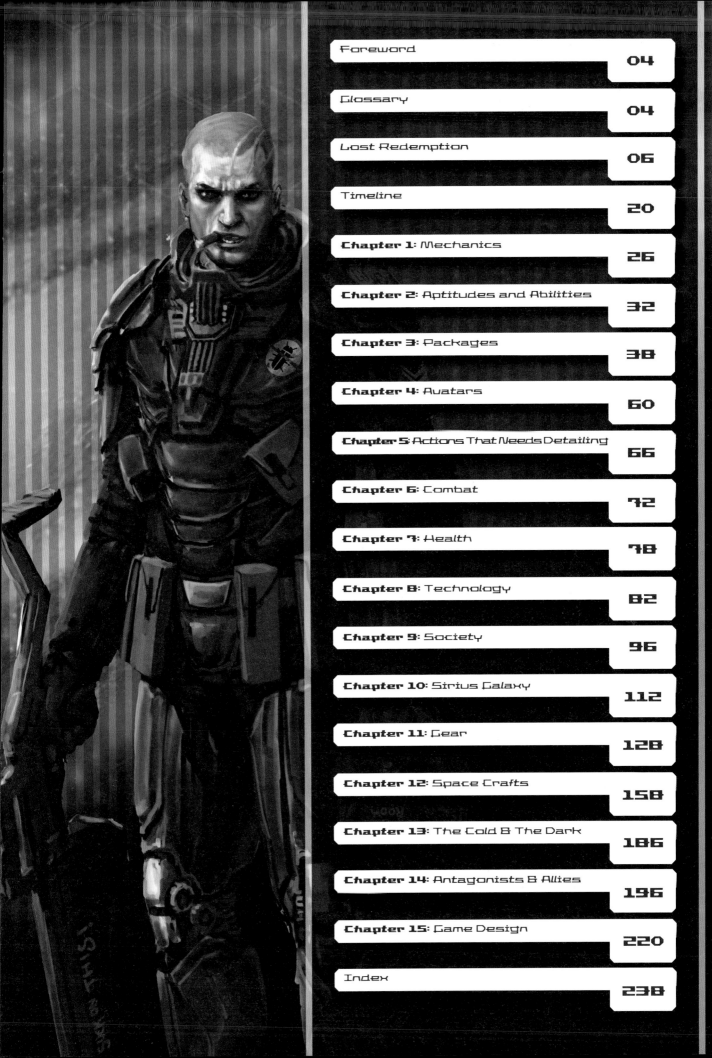

Foreword

I was about four or five years old when I had my first run-in with the *Alien* series. It was a behind the scene segment on TV and they showed parts of the scene in which Newt and Ripley were attacked by the two facehuggers in *Aliens*. As I still remember it, it obviously had an effect on me. When I saw the full movie I was nine years old. I snuck away to a friend who had it. Afterwards I was scared and thrilled. I and my friends played Colonial Marines for a long time after that. Later on I saw *The Thing*, *Alien* and *Event Horizon* when it came out.

I was about twelve when I started to play on a regular basis. Whenever we played a sci-fi RPG (with a space setting) we twisted it into another game. It ended up being an Alien series and The Thing (and later on Event Horizon and StarCraft) hybrid that had nothing to do with the game we were actually playing. Later I got more into pure horror and basically stopped playing space age sci-fi.

But then about one and a half decade after my first dark sci-fi RPG session, the game *Dead Space* came out. It was a wonderful mix of pure horror with a lot of my favourite titles thrown in. I sat down and played it through, and after I felt the urge to get my hands on a dark and gritty space-age pen and paper RPG. But I couldn't find one that popped out at me (nothing with the design and background I was looking for) and by that the Cold & Dark project was born.

I had no illusions – this game would be heavily influenced by my favourite genre specific titles. In the end, all the titles in the genre borrow heavily from each other to begin with. That the actors in Aliens had to read the Starship Trooper novel to get into the mindset speaks to that fact. Cold & Dark pays homage to all that I love about gritty, heavy and horrifying sci-fi. If you do NOT recognize themes I have seriously done something wrong.

The mechanics of the game are straight forward and use a classic foundation (basically a Value + Value = dice pool). Yes, this has been done *a lot* before but the system is simple and adaptable.

Beyond wanting to create a cool science fiction game I needed some reference material for my game design essay so writing this game was also a part of a school project for me. Parts of the game design section have been greatly inspired in its structure by the second edition of *Games Design Workshop: A Playcentric Approach to Creating Innovating Games* by Tracy Fullerton, Christopher Swain and Steven S. Hoffman. I wanted to apply the same methods used in designing a computer game and its levels when designing stories for a pen and paper RPG. After all, the essentials are the same.

But in the end my main hope is that I managed to create a game that fans of the dark sci-fi genre will enjoy.

Main List of Inspiration, Includes But Not Limited To...

Command and Conquer
Dead Space Franchise
Doom (movie)
Doom 3
Event Horizon
Firefly/Serenity
Mass Effect/Mass Effect 2
Pandorum
Pitch Black/ Chronicles of Riddick
Resident Evil Series
Screamers
StarCraft
Starship Troopers
The Alien series
The Thing (John Carpenter's)

What Is a Roleplaying Game?

"A role-playing game (RPG) is a game in which players assume the roles of characters in a fictional setting. Players take responsibility for acting out these roles within a narrative, either through literal acting, or through a process of structured decision-making or character development. Actions taken within many games succeed or fail according to a formal system of rules and guidelines."

—Wikipedia 2011
Regards from Sweden,
Mischa L Thomas

Glossary

AES: Adaptable Encounter Skin
AI: In Cold & Dark the AI is an abbreviation for Adaptable Intelligence and is a title used to describe the person managing the game (juxtaposed to Artificial Intelligence in computer games). Some call this person storyteller, game master, dungeon master, director (or whatever really).
AR: Armor Rating
Avatar: The alter ego/gestalt the player controls in the game.
BD: Base Damage
Belinium: A very energy rich crystal that is used to fuel short range ships, appliances and auxiliary systems.
BIE (Bureau of Interstellar Exploration): This branch of the GIC is responsible for exploratory space operations.
Big Black, The: Space as a whole.
Big Empty, The: Sometimes space as a whole but more often the reaches between planets and solar systems. Interstellar Space.
CAV (Caliphrian Aggression Virus): An utterly dangerous pathogen that kills and reanimates the victims. The abbreviation is pronounced like the word *cave*.
Chapter: The AI creates the stories and in order to get an overview (while playing and while designing them) the story is divided into chapters. And in turn, each chapter is divided into three levels which are even smaller pieces of the story.
Ghost Lines: A faster than light way of travel that uses (a sort of) dimensional distortion.
CIM (Clandestine Industrial Militia): A fringe group that fights the rule off the GIC using whatever means necessary.

COG (Customized Operation Gear): A collective name for a highly advanced type of upgradable nanotech supported suit, vital in the world of Cold & Dark.

Coreanium: An extremely valuable source of energy that is harvested from the molten core of planets (destroying the planet in the process). This substance is what allows mankind to travel the reaches of space (with such extent).

CSNC (Cortex Stimulation Node Cauterizations): An alternative to the death sentence, leaving the criminal as a docile, simple-minded but productive member of society.

D: 8 sided dice.

DU: Durability.

E&R (Evacuation & Retrieval): A network of rescue units that usually are the first one on the scene when a ship/station/colony is in trouble. This is a combination of the triple A and 911 of deep space. They're funded by the GIC and are not allowed to salvage wreckage.

EES: Enemy Encounter Suit

GIC (Governmental Industrial Complex): This is the ruling body of the Sirius galaxy consisting of a Chairman, Senate and political forum.

GLC (Ghost Line Calculations): This is the algorithms and equations used when travelling through the extra dimensional plane known as the Ghost Lines. The GLCs are fed into the Ghost Drive.

Grav-cuffs: A system of artificial gravity tethers working off a receiver/transmitter system. This is often used in automatic docking procedures.

HUD: Head Up Display.

IMC (Interstellar Mining Corporation): One of the largest corporations.

Infinitology: The largest religion in the C&D universe. They believe that everything in the universe is connected and that all the energies of sentient beings will end up in the *Great Stream*, a sort of heart blood of existence and only by leading a good and pure life will a person's energy grow into a strong and positive influence to the universe. Infinitologists strongly oppose the aggressive mining industry, believing that it harms the universe and in the end will harm mankind.

ISA (Interstellar Security Agency): This clandestine agency works directly under the GIC senate and chairman and handles all kinds of operations.

ISS: Internal Seal System.

ITS: Internal Tram System

JB (Justice Board): The GIC branch that handles everything that has to do with the law and due process.

LED (Law Enforcement Division): This is the main arm of the Justice Board when it comes to dealing with criminal elements.

LSA (Line Signal Amplifier): Also known as "the scare" or "scare box". This device is used to send and receive transmissions through the Ghost Lines.

MEC (Military Economic Corporation): A fringe group that opposes the GIC, similar to the CIM.

MPG: Mining Prospector Gear.

MRG (Medical Research Group): Beyond handling all medical responsibilities this GIC branch oversees DoX 2 (Department of Xenomorphology).

MSU (Military Strategy Unit): GIC branch in charge of the Consolidated Fleet, Marine Corps and all military operations.

NETSS: Nano Environmental Tactical Stealth Suit.

NFVH: Nano-Flex Visor Helmet.

NIS (Nano-Interface Screen): The most common way of displaying information and managing button controls. This is a pressure sensitive holographic nano system.

NPA: Non-Player Avatar, an avatar controlled by the AI.

OMCP (Office of Mining and Core Purification): All operations having to do with mining and core purification within the GIC is handled by this branch.

OMCP also includes the sub-branch. DoX 1 (Department of Xenoarchaeology).

PCR: Planet Construction Rig, a multi-purpose vehicle used in mining, colony construction and similar industrial work.

PNR: Polymer Nano Repair

PSD: Per Success Damage

PSG: Polymer Sealant Gun

Rippers: A deadly insect/reptilian-like alien species.

RMD (Resource Management Division): GIC branch in charge of economics and gathered resources.

SAC (Simulated Atmosphere Containment): The self-sufficient life support system used in larger ships, stations and colonies.

SCT (Standard Core Time): The 24 hour day used in the Divius system. It's used as a standard in most colonies and ships to measure work days and time.

Segment: Period of time which represents three seconds in the game world. It's often used to keep track of the action oriented parts of in-game events.

SER: Standard Exploration Rig.

SES (Space Exploration Salvagers): The biggest corporate competitor to IMC.

SRS: Scientific Research System.

SWG: Standard Work Gear.

TARGET (Tactical Armed Response Group and Explosives Technicians): The SWAT teams of the C&D universe and they work under the Law Enforcement Division, LED.

TCI: Tactical Command Immersion

TIS: Tactical Investigation System

VAC: Visual Audio Communication

VPS (Void Psychosis Syndrome): A psychological ailment of unknown origin which can affect people that are involved with deep space travel and those who are isolated from human contact when in space or on remote colonies. VPS will in the end result in paranoia, hallucinations and homicidal/genocidal/suicidal tendencies and behaviors.

VES: Vacuum Environmental Suit

VIN (Virtual Intelligence Network): The advanced computer systems employed in the C&D universe. They operate off a nanotechnological core and can emulate sentience, emotions and intelligence.

Void, The: Space as a whole but this epithet is usually thought of as having a mystical and even religious connotation.

ZGE: Zero G Engineering

Lost Redemption

"Never alone".

The words were no more than echoing whispers, like a voice wrapped in cotton. Seeley stepped out into the chilly corridor. Only the low-energy floor lights were active. Everything gleamed in a dusky luminosity that reminded her of the icy winters back home. The metal beams, bulkheads and floor grates that made up the corridors of the ship were devoid of life. She heard only the hum of the engine running on low output.

"Never alone." Seeley looked around and saw no one.

"Hello? "Where was everyone? Were they still in stasis? She couldn't remember waking up. Slowly she walked down the corridor. As she walked she heard a scraping sound coming from beneath the floor. Seeley stopped and listened. Wet scraping, gnawing, like something organic making its way through the innards of the ship. Something strangely familiar yet alien. Seeley ran.

Behind her she heard the corridor change into something living, something hungry. The ship itself turned against her. There were no turns, no doors or bulkheads and the corridor seemed to stretch out forever before her. She would die here, her flesh and soul torn away. Seeley closed her eyes and screamed. There was only an empty hush.

The strange voice sang to her. "Never alone".

500 IT, 4th of June, GIC D-class mining ship Kagetsu

Seeley opened her eyes and found herself in a new horror. She couldn't breathe. She couldn't move her arms, claustrophobia setting her heart racing. She was surrounded by titanium alloy and glass that pressed itself against her body. Painful wires were inserted into her flesh and she was underwater. Seeley kicked, tried to scream and once again she was certain that she was going to die. Then the cramped cylindrical walls gave way and the cables withdrew themselves from her body. A cascade of synthetic stem cell plasma flushed her out from her stasis tube onto the cold metal floor. She was naked as a newborn baby.

Stasis. She hated how the nightmares merged with her awakening. All around her two hundred more tubes opened. Most opened quietly, draining the fluids slowly as the cables gently withdrew from the awakening occupants. Others were

as violently expulsed as she had been. When the Virtual Intelligence Network noticed rapid panicked movements the quick-flush system ejected them fast to prevent drowning and any physical damage that could occur from the cables being jerked around inside the body. Some people, like Seeley, had a tendency to panic upon awakening.

Her body ached, she felt sick to her stomach and her head pounded. All was as it should be, then.

Those were the normal side effects of stasis sleep and lasted for about six hours. Being put into a hypothermic state and having your brain invaded by free radical-inhibiting nanites took its toll. Like the rest of the crew, Seeley grabbed a robe. The ship's VIN, named Liana, declared their status and marching orders with a lifelike female voice.

"You have been in stasis for four months and awakened according to schedule. During this period we have travelled sixty-four thousand five hundred thirty light years. We exited the ghost lines fifteen minutes ago and are now five hundred kilometres from the border of the Za´keth system. The date is 500 IT, 4th of June. The time is 21:32 SCT. Please report to your prearranged stations. Thank you."

On shaky legs Seeley joined the line of crew members heading for the showers.

* * *

Seeley had installed herself in her cabin. She had it pretty good. It was a priority cabin, twenty-five square meters with a double bed, desk and a private bathroom. She looked at the artificial window, a Nano-Interface Screen feeding off a camera on the outside of the hull. Stars drifted lazily by in the distance, and she wondered if she had visited any of the systems to which they belonged.

The integrated terminal squealed, declaring that she had an incoming call. She looked at the ID: Capt. Venjamin Elijah. Her hand touched the ACCEPT icon on the translucent millimetre-thin NIS and the weathered face of Captain Elijah filled a quarter of the screen. Stark lines etched into rough skin, his hair as iron gray as his eyes.

"Yes, captain?"

"Doctor Fujiko, I've arranged a meeting in my office." He anticipated her concern before she had time to voice it. "Don't worry; it will only be you and I and the chief of security. You know the chief and I have level six security clearance. Be here at your earliest convenience."

"I'm on my way." She ended the call. Seeley Fujiko walked out of her quarters and headed for the elevator.

* * *

Merhamet Surayyah, the chief of security, slammed her fist down on the table and made the ashtray jump, sending the burned-out carcasses of cigarettes bouncing across the surface. "Is this a goddamn *joke*!?"

"Surayyah, quiet down." Captain Elijah turned back to Seeley. "You must understand that your request seems risky at best."

Surayyah shook her head, unwilling to quiet down. "Risky at best? She's asking us to take a crew down there to get that damn colony up and running again!"

Seeley lit a cigarette and blew the smoke toward an air vent in the ceiling. "I understand that this is a rather… *unwanted* set of circumstances, but I'm only doing my job."

Surayyah seemed to calm a little; the security chief tossed back a jet black strand of hair from her eyes. "We *never* go this far out. Za´keth is one of the most remote systems in the galaxy and on top of that it's a restricted system. And then there's the fact that no one has heard a word from the colony in eight months by now. Beyond that we're operating on a skeleton crew by the order of the GIC. And *why* is that by the way if I may ask?"

Seeley really didn't know, but she guessed it was a matter of restricting information… and if something went wrong it was easier to explain the loss of two hundred lives rather than two *thousand*. Then there were other factors, ones she felt comfortable sharing. "We're looking for a specific object, not launching a full-scale mining operation. It would be unnecessary to bring a larger dig team. And as for the deck hands, with less people there's less to manage."

The captain leaned back in his chair, fiddling with his fleet emblem ring. "One of the main concerns is the safety of the crew. We have no idea what happened down there. For all we know there could have been an outbreak of CAV. Why don't they send in the Border Guards or the Marine Corps to do a sweep?"

They are not going to like this, Seeley thought before she spoke. "We have a squad of GIC Marines at our disposal. They're here on the ship."

Surayyah's calm was replaced with an intense anger. Before she could act on it the captain rocketed up from his chair, slamming both palms onto the table looming over Seeley.

"What? You brought aboard military personnel and weaponry on my ship without *notifying* me? According to GIC interstellar travel laws a civilian, or even the Marines for that matter, has to notify the captain and chief of security of a registered GIC vessel of all embarking passengers and hazardous equipment!" His face turned red, the veins in his temple swelled. "This is a crime, a crime punishable by —"

"I have special dispensation." Seeley held up a document. "It bears the official seal of the senate and authorizes me to bring aboard equipment and personnel I deem necessary to complete my task."

Captain Venjamin Elijah yanked it out of her hands and stared at it in disbelief. He clenched his teeth, practically spitting the words. He kept his voice level but his anger was palpable. "Nothing I can do, it seems. Where are these Marines of yours?"

"They're in the docking bay, on board one of the Gargon C-class ships. Their stasis was set to be terminated at the same time as ours. After their stasis shock has subsided I will give them their marching orders, and then they'll go planet-side and investigate the colony."

Surayyah shook her head. "What are you looking for? Why all this subterfuge?"

"What I'm looking for is on a need-to-know basis, and I didn't want to wind up the crew by advertising the presence of the Marines. People tend to get skittish when they think we're

going into Ripper territory. I'm sorry that I can't be more forthcoming. The same people sign our paychecks, chief Surayyah, and you know the drill. That's our government; one hand hasn't a clue of what the other one is doing." Seeley stood up. "Can I have that back?"

The captain, as if in a trance, handed over the dispensation document and shrank back into his seat. Seeley put out her cigarette and walked to the door, the heavy metal sliding open as she approached.

"You'll get your sweep, captain. And when you think about it, it's preferable that the dig team will be safe when they're on site." She left the captain's office and wondered if being an archeologist had always been this demanding.

500 IT, 5th of June, 16:30 SCT, planet-side (Terus B), Lerion colony

The sky was a swirl of gray lit by electrical discharges. The rain fell hard and heavy, wind whipping the drops into painful stings.

Terraforming in progress, Rook thought. His comm-link came alive with the voice of his squad leader, Sergeant Eva Tooms.

"Ok, Dak, breach the door. Rook, cover him and move in on point after the breach. The bio-scans showed nothing alive in there, so go in hot. If the scanners are wrong, well, just see it as the cost of doing business if a civi is wasted." Dak started to cut the door with his fusion cutter. The squad, *Tooth 'n' Nail,* had travelled on the down-low, stowing away on a ship in the hangar onboard the *Kagetsu.* Usually the Marines had a clue of what they were up against. Doing recon like this was unusual. The twelve man squad held their ground as the flame of Dak's fusion cutter sliced the steel open like a blowtorch through butter. Thirty seconds later it was done. Tooms gave Rook a nod and with that he kicked in the door and leveled his heavy auto carbine. He ran inside and covered the main corridor. It was empty and dark. No signs of violence. Tooms ordered eight men of the squad to move in. Four were left behind to guard the door.

"Use your ammoniac and sulfur markers, motion scanners and night vision. We have no idea what we're looking for here. You have the blueprints of the colony and your assigned sweep areas. Move in twos, get on with it."

Rook and Dak teamed up as usual, continuing on into the main corridor in direction of the security office. Quint and Gerick went to the south corridor, while Hellos, Spark, Bunny and Cain went to sweep the other corridors and rooms on the first floor. Just as they were about to split up, Gerick, an extremely feisty woman of Scandinavian descent, turned to Rook with a smile.

"Hey bitch, I bet you a pack of smokes that I get to bag something before *you* do on this run."

Rook smiled. "Oh, you're on!" They went their separate ways. They often made bets. They had to be casual like that at times just to cope with the stress. Dak shook his head.

"She'll probably win again."

"Yup. If there's anything to kill around here that is. But what the hell? I'll take point. Watch my back and the scanners."

"So who's doing recon on the dig site?"

"Gith."

Dak stopped and looked at Rook. "Is Gith here? Didn't see him."

"That's kind of the point. He's a scout."

The two of them continued on. Dak sighed. "Damn shadows. They make me nervous. Sneaky bastards."

"But they're the best at what they do."

"Yeah, but still… invisible snipers… just messed up, is all I'm saying."

500 IT, 5th of June, 16:38 SCT, planet-side Terus B, Lerion colony dig site.

>> Neural link online…

>> Environmental texture scans in progress…

>> Scan mode synchronized…

>> Stealth module algorithms initiated…

>> Stealth mode initialized…

The algorithms flashed on his HUD, as did the synchronisation of the texture mapping. Gith looked at his hands and rifle and watched them fade away into a translucent blur. The suit made him virtually invisible; it also deflected all known scanners and vision modes. Only a handful could handle the stealth module as it required doing constant math all while being on the move, concentrating on the job at hand. Those who didn't pass muster and manage the four years of scout training risked having a grand mal seizure or debilitating migraines if they tried to use the module.

This was a dead planet save for the mining colonists, if they were still alive. But the signature that had popped up on his bio-scan was weird. Like nothing he had seen before. Gith looked at the massive hundred meter wide circular shaft that led down to the dig site. The power was shut off so the lift was offline; it was a fifty meter drop down to the bottom. He shot his climbing hook into the stone, secured it and jumped. He fell fast, hitting the brake at the last ten meters, landing softly at the bottom of the shaft. He detached the line and swept the area with his high-powered sniper rifle.

There was nothing alive in sight. Strangely, mining tools and equipment lay cluttered all over the ground, as if the miners just dropped what they were doing and left. Gear like that was expensive; they had to have been in a major hurry if they just left the stuff out.

There were five tunnels which led into the shaft walls. Gith activated his topographical mapping system, especially installed in his COG for the mission. It revealed that the southwest

tunnel was the deepest one, the one he was assigned to scout first. Quietly he started to jog, keeping close tabs on his bio-scanner. After five hundred meters of tunnel he came into a large dig chamber and there he saw it.

Gith's stomach churned.

500 IT, 6th of June, 13:12 SCT, mining ship Kagetsu in orbit of Terus B

"Ma'am, we found eleven corpses in the morgue."

Seeley looked at the Marine before her. He was tall, muscular and looked to be in his late twenties. According to his file he was thirty-five. He had spent years in stasis moving from drop zone to drop zone and seen hundreds of battles. His real name was Jacob Chornovyl, but his call sign was Rook. It was a name given to him by his own sergeant long ago. No matter what kind of shitstorm he was ordered into, Rook moved right ahead without hesitation. Seeley was debriefing the Marines; she had chosen to talk to Private Rook, as he was the first to enter the morgue, Sergeant Tooms as she was the squad leader, and Gith, the scout who had made the astonishing discovery at the dig site. Seeley had reviewed the file of Gith as well. It was virtually empty. It said that he was a scout and that he had served the GIC for fifteen years. Beyond that there wasn't much more information available to her. Not even his real name, service number or a picture. The background of scouts were usually kept secret. Gith still had his COG on, with the helmet and all.

Seeley always felt stiff herself talking to military folk. They were so rigid and scouts usually creeped her out a bit. "Okay, all of you at ease. Have a seat." She gestured towards the chairs around the table in the security office. They all sat down. "Eleven corpses? Were you able to ascertain the cause of death?"

Tooms weaved the file over to the main NIS cube hanging over the table for all to see. "Our medic just did a preliminary exam and medical scan, so there's nothing conclusive. But seven of them seemed to have died suddenly of cardiac arrest, while the remaining four had been murdered with power tools. Nothing on the tox screen, and the records doesn't show any previous history of heart problems."

Seeley eyed through the report and decided to set up the medical and archaeological lab planet-side. She didn't want to bring the bodies or possible artefacts to the *Kagetsu* before she had conducted a thorough scientific investigation. She turned to Gith. "Describe what you found in the tunnel."

The scout cocked his head to the right. He reminded her of a reptile in that pose. As he spoke a thin vapour shot from his helmets mouthpiece valve. She wasn't certain but she had heard that it was some form of air sterilizer and temperature regulator that disguised possible traces of the breath from scanners. Gith's voice sounded metallic, distorted by the helmets microphone. "I can upload my vid-log."

"That's all good, but I want to hear you describe it in your own words. And I would like to see whom I'm talking to."

The scout sat motionless for a couple of seconds, as if frozen. It made her uncomfortable. Suddenly the nano-helmet folded itself into the suit with a quiet hiss. *A boy*, she thought. Gith looked very young, late teens maybe. He was of Asian descent but his left eye was blue and he was extremely pale. His eyes were calm and focused. She imagined the mental strength it took to do what he did. His black hair laid in neat cornrows on his head. As he began to speak she found herself wondering how old he really was. Stasis made these things hard to tell.

"To be precise, the bodies of the miners had been used to build a monument. They had been grafted together to form something that looked like a giant…bow."

An arch, Seeley thought. Gith continued.

"They had been stripped naked. I have no idea how the graft had been made. But there was no sign of a struggle and no obvious cause of death. And my bio-scanner gave off some strange readings."

So they could account for approximately fifty bodies. But where were the other two hundred and fifty? Could it be true? Was this the beginning? Seeley knew this was the place. She had found it, the first traces. She had a lot to do and there was no time to waste.

500 IT, 16th of June, 10:03 SCT, Terus B, Lerion colony, south power coupling tower

Culera frowned behind the mask of his SWG. "This is a fucking frame up! Kether calibrated this thing all wrong and we get the sharp end of the stick because it blew?" His work partner, Jeeky, laughed as she shook her head.

"Well, we *did* take the power three units higher than the work manual says."

Culera removed the service panel, trying to ignore the constant rain and flashes of the harsh atmosphere. "Hey, everyone does that. Every mining operation foreman expects us to do that to get a better output for less creds. But when it all goes south…"

Jeeky monitored her power scanner while Culera started to install the new coupling routers. She finished her partner's sentence. "We're left out in the shitstorm."

"That's almost literal in this case. Here we are, three miles from the goddamn colony in this damn terraform storm. I hate being out like this. Being away from the main hub on a back-end rock like this creeps me the hell out. We got Marines, archaeologists… shit, we're mining operation *engineers*. I have no idea what we're even doing out here."

The sound came suddenly, a sharp wet and rasping noise. Culera didn't seem to hear it but Jeeky spun around, making a startled sweep with her flashlight. Swirls in the rain, jagged rocks and crystals of obsidian were all she saw. A wasteland. Culera turned to her.

"What the fuck you doing? Can you give me some more light here?"

Jeeky turned back to him. "Thought I heard something…"

"Oh, no shit! It's a goddamn *storm*. Of course you heard 'something', you moron."

Jeeky tapped, or almost smacked, the top of his helmet with her flashlight out of frustration. "Well, I know that, you idiot. What I meant was that I heard something *weird*."

Culera sighed. "The planet is dead and the Marines did a sweep. So whatever you heard…"

Jeeky flinched as Culera's face exploded, spraying her with blood and bone fragments. She just stood there. It felt like an eternity in stunned silence, but it was probably just a split second. Culera's body seemed to rise up, but she realized that something had pierced his skull and that it was now lifting up his corpse. Jeeky fell backwards, jumped up in a panic and ran. She headed toward the sand hog. It was only twenty meters away, but she knew she'd never make it. She could hear the wet rasping turning into a growl as the abomination bore down on her. What was it? Where did it come from?

Jeeky didn't have time to find the answers. She didn't even feel any pain when something skewered her left shoulder and spun her around, yanking her off the ground. But when four bony sharp protrusions entered her abdomen, tearing through her innards, the pain was abysmal. As she screamed, Jeeky looked into its eyes, and as she was dying she realized that this monstrosity used to be human.

500 IT, 17th of June, 13:45 SCT, Terus B, Lerion colony, Colony Security (C-Sec) Office

Seeley crossed her arms as she stood at the high-end of the meeting table. Behind her a tempered panoramic window showed the barren terrain of the planet. She looked over the trio consisting of Captain Elijah, security chief Surayyah and the *Kagetsu*'s head medical technician, Dr. Natasha Bristol. Seeley cleared her throat.

"It wasn't really necessary for you to come planet-side to attend this meeting."

Elijah looked sternly at her. "On the contrary. We thought it was absolutely *necessary* as you don't seem to appreciate the severity of the situation."

She did indeed, but her work had to go on. A couple more days and she would have all she needed. She sat down as Doctor Bristol spoke her mind.

"During the short time we have been here we have lost more workers than I would like to count." Her fingers ran across the NIS and the files of personnel and incidents were projected as a free floating translucent cube in the middle of the table. "Planet-side, we have had six brutal murders. The offenders are confined to solitary, suffering from severe VPS. We have had five incidents of fatal accidents and five disappearances that might be homicides as well. Two occurred yesterday." She pulled up the file showing large pools of blood but no bodies. "About fifty percent of the colony crew is experiencing nightmares, insomnia and headaches. All classic signs of Void Psychosis Syndrome. If this is an outbreak, the accelerated rate of its spread is extreme. I have never seen anything of this magnitude. Not since the discovery of VPS back in 300 IT anyway. We all know what happened to the crew of the *Archimedes* and no one wants a repeat of history."

Surayyah nodded. "It's the same with the crew of the *Kagetsu*. We've had two murders, three suicides and six members have been put in the stockade on suicide watch. Several more are suffering from the sleep disorders and headaches. Some claim to have seen something… *alien* move about the ship. We haven't found any traces of this, though. And almost three hundred of the previous colonists are missing without a trace. What happened to them, huh?"

Elijah sighed and leaned back, looking more tired than angry. "This situation is getting out of hand. It's obvious that something was and still *is* very wrong here. Dr. Fujiko, we have heard that you have found… fragments of *something*. And the rumor is that the more you find and bring into your lab the worse things get. Don't you understand? If there indeed is a correlation between whatever it is you're having the miners dig up and the outbreak of VPS, we might be looking at a VPS outbreak of catastrophic proportions if it continues."

It had been impossible to keep the miners from seeing the dark red metallic shards, since they were the ones that dug

them up. She had monitored their work closely and collected the shards as soon as they had been discovered and brought them to her lab. Seeley only needed a few more in order to have a complete energy signature. How could she explain it to them? She couldn't allow her work to be compromised, but she did understand their concern. Things were, as Captain Elijah so eloquently had put it, "getting out of hand". She had to throw them a bone or it might be possible that they would abort no matter what authority she had on her side. Out here it would take months to contact the GIC and she suspected they would rather rotate the crew home and deal with the GIC back in the Divius system.

Dr. Bristol weaved another file over to the main NIS cube hanging over the table. "And then there's this little piece of 'artwork'." The image showed the perverted *arch* "sculpture" made out of the bodies of colonists. Seeley lit a smoke and Dr. Bristol matched her with a cigarillo as she continued.

"The autopsy showed that all of them died from oxygen deprivation. As far as we can tell, they all walked out there, removed their masks and suffocated. *Willingly*. And their tox-screens were clean. This kind of organized mass suicide is unheard of in the documented cases of VPS. We have as of yet been unable to determine how the flesh of the corpses had been grafted together into the shape. Nor why it was done or by *what* for that matter."

Surayyah locked eyes with Seeley. "This whole operation has been handled unprofessionally and with a flagrant disregard to the crew, colony and ship security. I don't care on whose authority you're here. I'm reporting this, Dr. Fujiko."

And there it was. The meeting took the turn she had expected, so she had to throw them that bone.

"What I'm about to tell you is highly classified. Sharing this information with anyone outside this room is tantamount to treason. You're not even allowed to discuss this amongst yourselves. If you wish to leave, do so now." They stayed in their seats as she had expected. Seeley nodded and continued.

"This is a dangerous situation because my work here concerns the inner workings of VPS and how we can go about ending it. There is something here that I *have* to extract and examine." This was indeed highly classified, but a highly classified lie.

"I'm willing to discuss changes in the medical and security procedures but the work *must* continue. An end to VPS? You all know this would change everything and save thousands of lives in the long run." She saw how her 'revelation' and her willingness to address their concerns took effect and once again she had them in the palm of her hand.

Seeley only needed a few more shards.

500 IT, 20th of June, 09:00 SCT, mining ship Kagetsu in deep orbit over Terus B

"Yes, of course. It's the only way. I understand… we have to bring them all there. Enlighten them. Make them part of you."

Fifth class engineer Calleigh Beryl stood on her knees in her berth. Her naked body gleamed with sweat in the candlelight. The walls, floor and ceiling were covered in circles, lines and glyphs. Chaotic by design, precise by nature.

"It's the only way, yes. For them. For you. For *us*." Her firm body relaxed, her upper body swaying back and forth, head tilted as if caressed by invisible hands. Calleigh smiled and closed her eyes, like a woman whose lover whispered to her between the sheets.

"I'm yours. I'll always be yours…"

* * *

Jin, the head engineer on shift, smiled as he saw Calleigh exit the elevator outside the main engineering bay.

"Yo, Cal. What are you doing here? Isn't this your time off?"

She returned the smile. "Yeah, I just wanted to look over the belinium auxiliary coils. I think I botched the calibration last night." Jin took a quick look at the diagnostics screen he held in his hand.

"No, it looks fine."

Cal looked around. They stood in the main corridor in front the main door to engineering. They were alone. Normally there would be a guard and several engineers doing extra check-ups. But now, with a skeleton crew and more and more crew members calling in sick, it was empty. Cal nervously shifted her stance. "Look, I just want a quick peek. I get so damn jumpy if I can't check and see it with my own eyes, you know? It's like when you can't remember if you turned off the stove, you have to go back and check."

Jin shrugged. "Sorry, but Surayyah has tightened the security. No off-shift personnel allowed. You understand. With all the weird shit going on, I can't really blame her. But I'll be glad to check it for you, hands on." Cal hung her head down, shifted her weight from one foot to the other and mumbled. Jin gave her a worried look.

"Hey, Cal? You okay?"

She mumbled incoherently. Jin came closer in order to hear what she was saying. Closer… closer… now he felt her breath on his neck, and he could hear what she was saying.

"For us… enlighten them…"

He put his hand on her shoulder. "Are you feeling alright?"

Calleigh's frenzied attack came without warning.

"For us!" she cried. At first Jin thought she was hitting him in the face and neck, but the sprays of blood made it all too clear that she was stabbing him with something. He had no strength left and slumped down to the floor as the life drained out of him. Even when all started to grow dark and blur out, his friend continued to stab him. She continued well after he was dead.

"Enlighten them… for us… for *you*…" Calleigh stood up and withdrew her bloody screwdriver from her friend's body. The thirty or so stabs had made the blood spatter all over her and the wall was covered with arterial spray. She took his access card and was about to enter the door when suddenly she stopped. Once again she tilted her head as though listening, closed her eyes and smiled.

"I will. I will." Calleigh dipped her fingers in the blood and started to adorn the walls with the holy glyphs of enlightenment.

Forty-seven minutes and two dead colleagues later, she had disengaged the backup outlet valve, reprogrammed the emergency pod protocol and brought the plasma saw down on the cardion gas regulator in the reactor.

500 IT, 20th of June, 09:51 SCT, Terus B, Lerion colony, south ridge

Rook stopped and scanned the area using IR, night vision and motion detection. It seemed dead. Dak stood next to him, sweeping to the north.

"Rook, got anything?"

"Nothing. Hell, those two mining techs that went missing are probably dead, anyway. With all the blood they found…"

Dak nodded. "True that. With the way things are going here they probably went Section 8 and offed each other or something. This run is a fucking joke. We're Marines! Leave this babysitting bullshit to the fleet or border guards! Looking for some idiots out in a mining colony isn't exactly a part of our job description."

Rook activated his helmet by the neural link and it folded itself into the suit. He took a deep breath of the thin and barely life-sustaining atmosphere. It was an awful thing for a man to breathe. No right-thinking person should be in a place like this. He pulled out a cigar and lit it as he looked out over the dark and jagged terrain. The Marine took several puffs, keeping it alive best he could. Its taste reminded him of home.

"We shouldn't be here, you're right about that."

Dak laughed. "You're a real rocket scientist. Smoking in an atmo that is way too diluted for us to even breathe? Moron. You'll pass out, man, I'm telling you."

Rook ignored him. Half the squad had been sent back to the *Kagetsu* for psychological evaluation. He had experienced the nightmares himself, and the headaches. Those goddamn headaches. Like an angry drill jacking up his skull from the inside

from patrolling area, over." Dak tried to calibrate the comm-system. He ran a quick diagnostics check.

"For fuck's sake! It's these goddamn electrical storms. Not a chance in hell we're going to get through and it's twenty minutes to base from here."

It was a bad risk to search the area without any backup or even reporting in, but Rook's bad feeling aside, the planet was *supposed* to be empty. Their own sweep indicated as much, so in the worst-case scenario they would have a crazed mining technician on their hands. "Let's go. Gear up and be ready for anything."

Dak checked his carbine, slammed in the clip and cocked it. "You're paranoid, man. If she's alive and homicidal it isn't like we can't handle her. What's she gonna do, try to smash her way through our combat armor with her wrench?"

Rook looked Dak straight in the eyes, his voice sharp. "Just be ready and don't fuck around!"

"Okay! Damn. Chill out, man! Upped your stims or what?"

They stepped out of the vehicle. Rook covered while Dak locked and secured it. They activated the flashlights on their weapons and headed for the opening, Rook on point. The cave was small, barely enough room for him to stand up straight. He glanced at the card. The coagulated blood trailed off into the darkness. Rook signed to Dak to hold up.

"Tamara Jeeky? I'm Pvt. Jacob Chornovyl from the GIC Marine Corps. If you can hear me, please respond."

Complete silence. They continued on inside. Here and there the walls were spattered with blood. The blood trail on the ground soon formed into several tracks. Dak knelt to examine them.

"These ain't human, but they don't belong to rippers either. They're human-*like*. Roughly the same size, but they only have four toes and… some kind of heel spur or dewclaw."

Rook covered them and cast a quick glance over his shoulder.

Was this a first contact situation? A new species? That would be enough reason for them to be sent in… but then again, there would have been a lot more people involved and a lot more firepower if the species was suspected of being hostile. And someone should have told them. It didn't make sense.

Dak mirrored his thoughts. "First contact situation? Something new?"

"I don't know. But we should get backup."

"I'm with you on that one. Let's — " The sound of grinding rock cut him off. It first appeared as if Dak disappeared into thin air mid-sentence, but Rook soon realized that he had fallen through the rock floor. Rook shone his light down the hole.

"Dak!"

"I'm fine. The fucking floor caved in. I landed okay."

As Rook looked down he saw that Dak had fallen at least seven meters, a bit too far for a man to just shrug it off as nothing. He had to have landed on something soft. In the

out. Dak had thought that Rook had meant the Marines when he had said that "we" shouldn't be here, but Rook had meant mankind itself. There was something about this place, something that made his skin crawl and blood freeze. During his years of service he had fought rippers, marls and cavers and seen all manner of horrors. He had met them with fearless aggression and cool-headed tactics, but now… now he was afraid. He spat out the cigar and deployed his helmet again, feeling the shortness of breath. "Let's just finish our patrol and get back to HQ."

They got back into their sand hog and continued on. Dak was driving, prattling on about some chick he had nailed on his last shore leave while Rook handled the scanners and monitors. They passed a rock face with what seemed to be small caves. Rook cycled the vision modes and scanners. "Stop!"

Dak slammed down on the brakes. "Got something?" Rook nodded and patched the image to the main monitor. It just looked like a small, out-of-focus square through the grainy night vision, no bigger than a business card but too geometrically perfect to be a natural occurrence.

"I have to focus." He fiddled with the controls and soon it appeared on the screen, clear as day. It was a bloodstained identi-card lying just in front of one of the cave mouths. It read: *Tamara Jeeky, Mining Technician*. Dak stared at it.

"Damn, didn't think we would find a thing. I'll call it in." He activated the comms. "This is unit 2 calling from patrolling area, over." Nothing but static in response. "This is unit 2 calling slim cone of light he didn't see much more than Dak so he switched to night vision. What he saw almost made him reel, but instinctively he reached for the monofilament line in his belt. When he spoke, his voice was soft and calm.

"Dak, listen carefully and don't make a sound. I'm going to lower down a line to you and pull you up."

Dak knew enough to listen to him and kept his mouth shut, though he couldn't help but look around. Then he saw what Rook saw: all around him there were bodies, but they looked as if they had been flayed and twisted into new perverted forms. The shreds of clothing indicated that they were some of the hundreds of missing colonists. Both of them had seen heaps of dead bodies before. The problem was that some of these bodies were moving, as if waking from a slumber, and it seemed to start a chain reaction.

These weren't simple reanimated CAV victims, this was something else. It was as if the human body had been rein-vented, weaponized. Rook saw Dak's grip on his carbine tighten as more and more bodies started to move. He shoul-dered his own weapon and lowered the line as quickly as he could. Guttural growls and murmurs rose around Dak in an almost deafening cacophony. As some of the bodies stood up, Dak looked at the line and then at Rook. The first mon-strosity locked its gaze at Dak and rushed him. Rook real-ized that there was no chance of him being able to pull his friend up in time.

Dak scoffed at the hordes and readied his weapon. A power-ful volley of automatic fire ripped the creature's bone-spiked arm right off, but it kept coming. Rook opened up, giving him support fire. Soon dozens of creatures surrounded Dak and even though their weapons caused a lot of tissue damage, it didn't seem to slow the horde down much. Some had spot-ted Rook and now climbed frantically on top of each other to reach him. He cut the line before they pulled him down. Dak screamed through the comm-link.

"Get the hell out of here and report this clusterfuck to HQ!"

Rook had seen it too many times, friends overrun by over-whelming numbers and ripped to pieces. Most of their inhu-man enemies used claws and bites that could penetrate the hardest shock armor. A Marine seldom died a quick death.

"Fuck off, I ain't leaving you here!" Rook sprayed bullets at the damn things. Dak screamed as his torso was slashed open, blood pouring through his armor. Rook saw a sliver of red light come on at the base of the neck of Dak's armor. He had activated his stim-injection. Dak continued through the pain. Amped up, on edge, firing volley after volley.

"There's plenty to go around, you fucking freaks! Keep the change!" Dak was overrun, his body pierced by a dozen spikes, but he was still shooting, running on stims and adrenaline. He was, in fact, dead, but his body and pain centre hadn't caught on due to the drug in his system. Rook felt a piece of himself break at the sight and he knew it could never be restored. When a member of his squad died in front of him, a piece of him died, too. He took two plasma grenades, pulled the pins and threw them down the hole where Dak was screaming in pain and rage.

What good am I, he thought, *when this is the best I can do for you, Dak? Semper fi, my friend.* He retreated toward the mouth of the cave, laying down suppressive fire toward the dozens of creatures that now swarmed up out of the ground. When his clip was empty he turned to run, sprinting just in time to catch the blast wave from the explosion below.

Darkness. Silence. Peace.

500 IT, 20th of June, 10:09 SCT, Terus B, Lerion colony, communications centre

My very own slice of heaven, Kether thought, as he poured the freshly ground coffee beans into the French press, poured the water and pressed the plunger. Kether had paid off the logis-tics officer to slip his bag of coffee beans past quarantine. He had won them in a card game; they were Guatemalan beans, generations removed from old Earth but they were *real*. No genetic engineering, no replication. The ancestors of these beans had actually grown on old Earth years before the Ripper War. Kether was something of a history buff, but now he filled his head with thoughts of the origin of the beans as a way to push away other trains of thought.

He felt guilty. If he hadn't been lazy and calibrated the coil on the fly, Culera and Jeeky wouldn't have had to go out there. Now they were gone, probably dead. He had come to hate this whole damn colony and planet. As an energy output con-troller he had been assigned on far out colonies before, but he had never been this far out. And Kether had never been in a situation where VPS had broken out like this. Murders, acci-dents, disappearances? There was something more going on here, he could feel it. Of late his sleeping hours had been filled

with incoherent images of death, pain and fear. Kether shook his head, feeling a chill run down his spine as the nightmares flashed before his eyes. He leaned back in his chair, sipping his coffee with closed eyes, pushing the images away.

He had been assigned to monitor the communications array in the comm-set control room. He was the most qualified at the moment as the array's specialist had gone nuts and thrown himself into an active plasma converter. This whole thing was completely out of control. What the hell were they doing out here anyway?

Suddenly the LIDAR went red and the proximity scanner wailed. Kether spilled hot coffee all over himself as he jumped up from his seat. He ignored the searing pain as his eyes fixed on the screens. *This can't be happening!* He tried to calibrate it, begging for the reading to be a bizarre glitch. But it wasn't.

"May Obresi save us…"

Kether hit the main evacuation alarm and ran.

500 IT, 20th of June, 10:09 5CT, Terus B, Lerion colony, medical lab

The energy patterns were identical. Seeley had put the fifteen shards into the electromagnetic manipulator. They hovered in the containment field, surrounded by different screens showing the glyphs, energy patterns and fluctuations. There might be more shards, but if she didn't find more she had to hope that the glyphs would leave her a clue on how to get the synchronisation to work. It would change everything, connect them to The Great Stream. Kendrin be blessed.

Others called them nightmares, but she called them visions. The shards spoke to her. They told her of the future. Humanity had to be ready for the change; The Great Stream could only be perfected if mankind fulfilled its destiny. If only she could grasp the final truth, the key to it all. When her employers had sent her here to collect the shards they had done so only because they believed they retained properties which could be used to increase energy outputs in reactor cores. They had been aware that those with a weak mind risked being… affected.

The cover story, which of course was a highly classified lie, was that the shards could affect and cure VPS. That was the lie she had told to the captain, the doctor and the security chief. Her employers, the GIC, just wanted money, another chance to line their pockets. But she had known all along. She had worked for so long in order to get here, to find traces of the divine. She had used the GIC to further the goals of her real superiors: the Church of Infinitology. The outer circle of the church wouldn't approve, but what did *they* know? They were merely a distraction. The inner circle, *they* knew the truth. She would deliver the salvation and usher in the new era.

Liana's automated voice sounded over the comms. *"This is an emergency evacuation order, directive Alpha-363-Omega. This is an emergency evacuation order, directive Alpha-363-Omega."*

The lights switched to a flashing blue, the corridor floors lined with green arrows which showed the shortest way to an exit as the alarm screeched. Directive Alpha-363-Omega meant "get out now and as far away from the main colony as possible". *Damn.* It would take at least five minutes to lower the magnetic fields if she followed the preprogrammed safety protocols. And *then* she had to transfer each shard to a containment vessel; she would never be able to get them out in time. But Seeley wasn't about to let the discovery of the millennium slip through her fingers. She contacted Captain Venjamin Elijah through the comm-link.

"This is Dr Fujiko. What the hell is going on?" At first she was met with static, but as she was about to hail him again he answered, his voice tense but steady. She heard screams of panic in the background.

"Captain Elijah here. You have to evacuate! Christ, my ship, the *Kagetsu*... it's coming down!"

"What are you blabbering about?"

"It's *crashing*! It's been torn apart and a large chunk has broken atmo, heading for the colony! There's something up here *with* us!" The communication broke off.

Seeley only reacted. She grabbed the fusion cutter off the table, put it to full burn and severed the cable to the electromagnetic field. With a burst of energy the shards fell. She grabbed a cloth from one of the tables and swept the shards into it.

"Damn it!" One of the shards gave her a nasty cut on her right hand. The pain was sharp, throbbing. She ignored it, tied the cloth together and ran out of the lab, hauling away the pieces.

As Seeley came out of the lab she saw mineworkers fleeing in a panic and C-Sec officers that were trying to keep the order. She clawed her way past the mob, heading for a maintenance hatch which she knew led to the mechanics bay. Seeley hoped she could scoop up a vehicle which wasn't too broken down but still out of rotation. She guessed she had a bigger chance of getting away if she didn't try to follow the rest of the mob. As she closed the hatch behind her Seeley saw a mine worker bury his hatchet in the face of a C-Sec officer, whose colleagues responded by riddling the worker with bullets. He fell in a spray of blood. The influences of the shards were strong, but it was as it was supposed to be. The weak-minded would fall first.

Seeley ran through the cold vent and came out in the mechanics bay. She grabbed a SWG from a locker and headed for a small survey skimmer. She got in, punched in the ignition code and the skimmer hummed to life. Automatically it went into hover mode, lifting a meter off the ground. She checked the system and it seemed to work. Seeley opened the door by remote and hit the accelerator. She knew where she was heading. Now she had a way off this rock. If only the *Kagetsu* wasn't completely destroyed.

Damn, her right hand itched like crazy.

500 IT, 20th of June, 10:14 SCT, Terus B, Lerion colony, southern ravine

Everything was white and noisy. A searing hum filled his ears. The whiteness formed shapes, silhouettes. As they came closer they solidified. It was every squad member he had ever seen die in front of him. Viscera hanging out of torn bodies, dead eyes staring at him, burning the guilt into his soul. Even Dak was there. Then they changed, twisted, broke and flayed. Soon he was surrounded by the monsters from the cave.

"Dak!" The monsters vanished.

Rook sat up and looked around, surprised that he was alive. He was in the back of the sand hog and it was moving.

"Are you okay, Marine?"

Rook ached all over, but his internal medical scanner showed that he only had three small rib fractures and some bruises. The automated medical system in his COG had fixed the worst of it. He stood up, slowly. Crawling up front, he sat down in the front passenger seat and cast a glance over at the scout.

"I'll live. What happened?"

Gith kept his eyes on the uneven path. "I was out scouting on foot and saw the explosion. I managed to shoot some of those *things* down and get you into the sand hog. The blast must have knocked you out."

"I owe you. What the hell *are* they?"

"A new alien species? Biological weapon? Take your pick. But they aren't our only problem." Gith stopped the hog and pointed to the sky. Rook stared. It was like a million stars were falling, drifting on a sea of blue and orange flames. It was beautiful and it was horrible.

"Is that...?"

Gith nodded. "It's the *Kagetsu*. Half of it, at least. It will impact on the colony in approximately one minute."

"Jesus. My squad…"

"The last communication was erratic, but I learned that there was a riot in the colony. The panic of the impeding crash made it tear itself apart. Not surprising when taking into account the VPS outbreak. We're four kilometres away, outside the range of the blast radius. But I doubt anyone got out. The odds are against it. I'm sorry."

Rook was a marine. He had to swallow his grief for now and deal with it later. Now he had to figure out a way to survive. The LIDAR kicked in and as he looked at the monitor he saw a swarm of moving bogeys five hundred meters away. "What the hell is *that*?"

"It's your friends from the cave. We have to move." Gith started the hog and drove through the ravine. Rook checked his gear and ammo.

"What's the plan? How the hell do we get off this fucking rock?"

"I have tried to hail the *Kagetsu* but there was no response. There *could* have been a voice through the static, but I'm not sure. I saw a landing platform some kilometres east of here. There's a short range mining survey ship there. It should be able to break atmo."

"Alright, let's do it." Rook had to concentrate on the now. He really didn't want to think about what shape the *Kagetsu* was in if they managed to get the survey ship up there. He didn't really want to think about what would happen if the *Kagetsu* was totally lost. The ground shook and the darkness lit up with a glare brighter than the Divius sun as burning wreckage annihilated the colony. The roar was deafening even from this distance.

It was beautiful and it was horrible.

*   *   *

Several minutes later they arrived at the platform. It looked much like a large, sturdy helipad with a small control room built in. It hadn't been used for months, since last the colonists were there. On top of the structure stood a B-class survey ship. It had seen better days, but as long as it could take them off the planet, Rook didn't care. They stopped the vehicle and got out. They had their weapons at the ready and moved up the stairs, covering each other.

As he climbed the last step he saw fast movement in the corner of his eye. Rook ducked, barely avoiding having his throat cut by the searing flame of a fusion cutter. Instinctively Rook used the butt of his gun and struck the attacker square in the face, sending the SWG mask flying. Gith placed the laser sight dot of his high-velocity rifle between the eyes of the fallen foe.

"Don't shoot!" Seeley gasped, blood gushing from her broken lip. She desperately took a hold of her mask, pressing it to her face so she could breathe. Rook growled at her.

"What the fuck is wrong with you? You just about got us *both* killed!"

Seeley stood up, grabbing a makeshift bag of some sort. "I'm sorry, I thought you were one of the miners. They've all gone crazy."

Gith lowered his weapon. "How did you get here?"

"I managed to get a hold of a skimmer, but it broke down, so I ran the rest of the way."

A dissonance of inhuman screams and grunts rang out from across the rocky valley. The sounds were at once human and alien, and utterly terrible. Gith turned and knelt, scanning the area through his scope.

"You two try to get that heap started. We've got a couple of minutes, tops. Bastards are *fast*. I'll be our eyes and ears."

Seeley and Rook wasted no time. Rook took out his field tool-kit and opened the door panel. It took him about a minute to reroute the circuitry, but he got the door opened. All the while, the screams grew louder, more pressing.

He turned to Seeley. "I'll check the power cells, try to get the flight computer online."

Gith gave him a quick glance, the growls growing in strength. "Hurry."

The ship was cranky and in poor maintenance, but it would run. Rook heard the first silenced shot from Gith's rifle.

"Rook, we have to get going!"

"You don't say! Doc, how's it going with the computer?" Shot after shot rang out. The creatures were upon them.

"Wait a sec… got it!"

The engines started up and Gith came running. The vile things clambered by the dozens over the platform ledge, their contorted bodies moving as a giant living mass of viscera and twisted bones. And those terrible howls and screams, they cut through the flesh like knives. Rook stared at it from inside the ship.

"Fuck *me*!" He took aim and squeezed the trigger, covering Gith. When the scout tumbled inside he hit the door button. There was a series of clanging thumps as the creatures ran straight into the hull, snarling frantically as they started to climb it. Seeley manned the controls and hit the vertical thrusters.

"Hold on!" She went straight up and then hit the accelerator, sending Rook and Gith sliding across the floor. Rook struggled to get to his feet.

"Sure you can fly this thing?"

"If you shut up and let me!"

Several creatures had climbed across the window and banged ferociously on it. A spider-web of thin cracks spread across the window and Seeley closed the blast shield, flying by using the front camera and scanners. She accelerated.

"Breaking out of atmo in four… three… two… *one*!" Fire engulfed the ship and everything shook, warning lights flashed incessantly. Words flickered red across the screens: **OUTER HULL INTEGRITY COMPROMISED.**

Quiet. Calm. The big empty.

Seeley smiled, laughing nervously. "We're okay. She's holding together."

* * *

"Holy Mother of God." Rook watched the screen and saw what was left of the *Kagetsu*. The front end had remained in orbit. The whole ship had basically snapped in half, but if the emergency sections had sealed off, parts of the ship would still have life support. It looked like the docking bay might be okay, which meant that there could be a way back home. Essentially, they had two chances of survival: either one of the C-class ships was intact, in which case they could use it to get home, or the second option was to place themselves in stasis and pray that they would get picked up. But if the stasis chambers and the ships were gone, they were screwed. There was no chance in hell that the damaged *Kagetsu* was capable of making a ghost jump.

If someone had sabotaged the engine, it seemed likely that the whole thing would have gone down, and when he thought about it the rift seemed contrived. It was as if someone had deliberately blown the ship in half, and by doing so had saved half of it from crashing into the planet.

Floating among the pieces of wreckage were dozens of broken bodies. Drifting like lost souls on the Styx, their bloated faces were frozen in pain. He looked away, afraid to see one of his squad members.

"Set us down near the rift, right on top of her."

500 IT, 20th of June, 10:34 SCT, mining ship Kagetsu, sealed main corridor

They managed to climb inside the wreck; Dr. Fujiko had used a VES suit they found in the survey ship. Their flashlights revealed blood smears all over the walls as they walked down the corridor. Everything was in disarray, but the crash hadn't caused all of it. People had fought here, died here. Had the crew flipped out the last couple of panicking minutes before the crash and torn into each other? What had caused the crash in the first place?

There was something else, too. Symbols. Glyphs traced in blood on the walls. Rook felt sick to his stomach just from looking at them. Images of the creatures from the planet flashed before his eyes, as did the very same symbols carved into a dark surface, almost glowing. He looked at Gith and saw that the scout seemed equally disturbed by the symbols, shaking his head in an attempt to get rid of whatever he saw. The good doctor on the other hand… she seemed *fascinated*, staring at the symbols with a hint of a smile on her face.

Rook had noticed a change in her when they were down on the planet. Something was increasingly off with Dr. Fujiko. He had met her from time to time for different debriefs, and each time she had become more and more absent-minded and aloof. Even her physical appearance had changed in the short time they had been down at the colony, going from healthy and quite attractive to a sickly pale, her face drawn.

He was quite certain that she hadn't `mistaken´ him for a mineworker back at the landing platform. In fact, now he was quite certain that she had intended to kill him, thinking he was alone. She kept scratching her hand and fondling that bundle she was carrying. And weirdest of all, she hadn't reacted to the creatures. After all, she was a xenoarchaeologist and if she hadn't seen the entities before she would have asked Rook about them. She scratched her hand again, and he saw that it was red, raw and bleeding. He exchanged looks with Gith. The scout was wary of her as well.

And the headache had become worse.

* * *

The glyphs marked everything. Not just the walls, but her very soul. They tried to tell her a truth. She couldn't decrypt what they wanted but they warned her. They knew. The Marines knew she couldn't leave them alive; they wanted the truth, to hide it from the world. She could feel their eyes on her. But she would be able to get away. The instruments of the Great Stream, the divine creatures which the colonist had become, were here as well. She could *feel* them. There weren't many of them yet but they *were* here. Some of the crew had turned. Was it the resonance of the shards? Or had someone from

the planet brought the blessing to the ship? She looked at her hand and saw that her flesh was rippling, something moving beneath it. Seeley wasn't scared; she just hoped that she could escape before her body became an instrument of the Stream. She had to bring back the salvation.

Everything depended on her.

* * *

Rook watched Seeley, keeping a bit of distance by walking behind her. She wasn't the same woman that had briefed him just weeks ago. It wasn't the fact that her eyes had a yellow tint now, or that the veins in her neck had blackened and swelled that made his skin crawl. It was the fact that she radiated the unpleasant and downright terrifying aura of the planet they just had left. This was obviously some form of contagion and if she was a carrier, and a VPS victim, he didn't want to risk her bringing it back. For all he knew this was all a biological weapons experiment gone wrong. Dr. Fujiko could well have been infected by her own experiment. He motioned for Gith to stop.

"Doctor, hold up."

She turned, keeping her eyes low. "Something wrong?"

"What's in the bag, doctor?"

"Nothing of importance."

Rook took a step closer. He heard familiar growls echo through the ducts. The creatures were onboard the ship. He didn't know how they had gotten to the ship but they were onboard.

"Have you *seen* yourself? You… you look *different*." He saw her infected hand rippling with mutation and starting to move slowly toward the fusion cutter.

"I don't know what you're talking about." Her voice was shaky, dropping an octave as she spoke.

In response, Rook's hand went to the grip of his shouldered weapon. Gith followed suit.

The doctor was changing, becoming something inhuman. Rook didn't care if he had to kill her, but he wasn't about to die here. Not now, not after all the shit he'd been through, but something told him that she wouldn't go down easily. Neither would her "friends".

Rook fought as he had so many times before. He fought for the partner at his side, fought for his life.

He fought for humanity itself.

+12 years: Japan sets a plan in motion which entails establishing a colony on the Moon and one on Mars shortly thereafter.

+15 years: The first colony is established on the Moon.

+18 years: The first colony is established on Mars.

+50 years: During these years the technology is rapidly evolving. As there's now a monetary interest in travelling to space for mining purposes the largest companies with a vested interest invest in space research. During this time world governments develop and build their first large mining ships in orbit. The first self-contained eco environment is created which enable a colony to be more or less self-sufficient. People are now born on the off world colonies, some have never been to Earth. Earth has suffered tremendously under the rule of mankind. Pollution and the environmental effects resulting from it were extreme.

+60 years: The mining company Roscoe Minerals lose their mining ship *The Queen* when a radical group of interstellar environmentalists (believing that we're not allowed to venture into space with the intent of exploiting it when we can't even manage our own planet) slam a high-jacked space shuttle into it in a suicide mission.

+61 years: China constructs their first armed space fighters and use them to escort their most valuable cargos.

+62 years: Japan builds the first space station with a rotating main section in Mars orbit with established gravity, the *Hiroshi*, which houses 500 miners and scientists. The station is armed and has a small squadron of armed fighters as well. All of this has been produced on Mars.

+65 years: The first ships with rotating sections are constructed and fuel efficiency has been upgraded, making it possible to travel further as the mining and use of helium 3 has been perfected. Genetic engineering has resulted in the first oxy-algae, opening the possibility for ships to have a self-contained air supply.

+68 years: USA constructs the first battle cruiser in space.

+70 years: Large veins of gold and titanium are discovered on Mars, and soon after they find oil and large quantities of helium 3 deposits. The oil means that there had indeed been life on the red planet. Smaller skirmishes between the corporations erupt on Mars, and the conflict spreads to Earth. Most major powers have battle cruisers in space at this time.

+72 years: The small skirmishes continue. The discovery of fossil fuels on Mars has led to new theoretic scientific disciplines such as xenoarchaeology and xenomorphology as the existence of alien life on other worlds seems possible.

+80 years: The world governments have lost much of their power and the major companies continue to battle each other. Spacecrafts, colonies and space stations are in multitude and the so-called *Resource War* breaks out. The corporations battle each other on Earth as well as in space. The governments try to contain the situation.

+95 years: The war has raged for 15 years, with only a year or so in-between with temporary truces. Some places on Earth have become uninhabitable after nuclear downfall from cruisers that crashed into the atmosphere. Both the Mars and Moon colonies wish to break away from the corporations and Earth. Most have been born in the colonies and claim that they have the right to them, not the earthers. Some of those in space whom wish to secede from Earth and the corporations have formed small cells which perform acts of terrorism, striking at the government and the corporations. They call themselves the OWA (Off-World Allegiance).

+100 years: All the major powers of Earth governments come together. All have tried to negotiate with the corporations (which basically run things by now) to cease fire, but to no avail. They realize that the corporations need to be stopped and that these have little to do with nationality or religious convictions. Even the monetary worth is exceeded by the escalating violence and the impeding catastrophe. In secrecy they come together and form the *GIC* (Governmental Industrial Complex), a united earthen governmental institution with joint interests. They pool their resources and start to create their army with as much secrecy as possible. While this is going on *The Doppelganger*, a large mineral hauler belonging to the Ferock Corporation, with a crew of 500, falls off the grid just outside Mars. It disappears without a trace. Most blame the OWA, but they deny any involvement.

+102 years: GIC hit the corporations hard without warning on all fronts. The war escalates to epic proportions. Millions are killed.

+103 years: The Doppelganger impossibly reappears just outside Earth's atmosphere. Before anyone has time to react it crashes into the ocean outside the US east coast. Minutes after, something alien starts to attack Florida. Humanity has its first ripper encounter and the infestation spreads fast. Within weeks humanity realizes that their internal conflicts need to end if Earth is to be saved. At first those born in space, with little interest in saving Earth don't care, but as the infestation was also discovered on a ship heading for Mars but stopped they changed their minds. The Resource War officially ends and the *Ripper War* begins.

+108 years: The Ripper War rages, but is never really won. Humanity manages to gain control of the planet but ripper presence is still strong. The rippers are a primitive species with carapace, teeth and claws that use no technology whatsoever. But their reproductive cycle is fast and they seem to be immune to gas, biological pathogens and radiation. Earth is more or less a war torn ripper infested planet with large radioactive zones. But humanity is still the ruling race. Earth starts to negotiate with the OWA concerning the independence of the Moon and Mars colonies. At the very same time the GIC starts negotiations with the corporations. Even though they're not at war with each other they still had several issues that had to be resolved.

+110 years: After two years of negotiation the GIC manages to sway the corporations to abide under their rule (somewhat more), conforming under the mining rules of the GIC. But the largest corporations have during this time come together, creating two factions. The IMC (Interstellar Mining

Corporation) on one side and the SES (Space Exploration Salvagers) on the other. OWA is resolved after the Moon and Mars colonies reach a consensus with Earth. They have to obey under most of the criminal laws of the GIC legislation but Earth no longer has any rights to their resources. They have to buy drilling and mining rights. This automatically takes away much of the power from the now two corporations, which was part of GIC's agenda all along.

+113 years: GIC is being hailed by an unknown source. Soon, in human languages, the source of the transmission explains that they are an intelligent race that wishes to establish a lasting communication with humanity. They call themselves the *Gerions*, and they also say that they have encountered the creatures that humanity call rippers before. GIC agrees to a meeting and it will take place in Earth's orbit. Within minutes a huge ship of an unknown configuration bursts out of nowhere through a strange wave of electromagnetism and a dense black cloud of smoke. The ship is permitted to dock with a GIC orbital defence station called *Willows*. One being emerges from the ship, and humanity laid its eyes on a Gerion for the very first time.

+120 years: The Gerion presence is low; they only interact with us through a few emissaries. No one gets to see them outside their bio-suits, but it's clear that they're an extremely advanced race. They never share much of their bio-tech, or any of their weapons or defence systems, but they do give us the technology needed to open and travel through Ghost Lines, as well as the gravitational cube technology and they also upgrade our fuel efficiency. They show us *Belinium* and how to mine and use this new fuel source. Earth is now badly torn up by pollution, but the belinium with its low emissions, our evolving eco enclave technology and the aid of the Gerions managed to set in motion a stabilisation of the environment. But with the ripper menace, Earth is a very dangerous and constricted place to live.

The ghost lines enable us to expand vastly. GIC declares this year to be the start of a new era, and with the boom in space travel which will ensue they declare it year 0 of the coming years of interstellar travel (IT). So effectively the year becomes 0 IT.

0–100 IT: During this time a barrage of things happens. Our ships become extremely advanced, and we master the art of terraforming. With the ability to travel through the ghost lines we find hundreds of new systems with unexploited resources. We establish mining colonies and terraform suitable planets. The Gerions shows us the Sirius galaxy, a vast one with a lot of planets having the gravity of Earth norm already. It takes time to travel there but a large portion of humanity establishes a strong presence in Sirius in 80 IT, quarantine procedures are harsh to ensure that the ripper menace don't follow us out in the black. Earth is liveable but still a warzone.

101 IT: GIC sets down on the planet RV-36 in the Sirus galaxy in the *Mal* system, having their mining ship *Kari*, in orbit. After establishing that there are a lot of useful minerals under the surface they start to dig. After four months they find something, an extremely large object covered with odd symbols. It's in the form of an enormous ring. It also has parts which

seem to be mechanical and slots which might be some kind of power inlets or outlets. They tow it onboard the Kari, transport it to a science station in the farthest region of the Mal system. Xenoarchaeologists and top physicists start to work on it. The whole operation is classified.

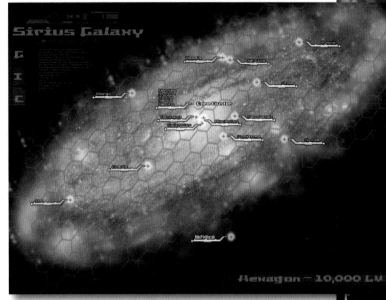

189 IT: Gerion presence is almost zero, they have withdrawn more and more as humanity reached further and further into space. During the decades that passed humanity spread, explored, discovered and mined new worlds almost obsessively. The scientists finally manage to understand the artefact they found and they started to back-engineer it, creating their own versions. It was the main siphon of a planet harvester. By drilling down to the liquid core of a planet, and then pump the hot and molten materials through the contraption (disposing a large portion of it) there was a chance that the remaining material consisted of a never by humanity seen substance. And so, still in all secrecy, they started to look for a suitable planet to test their theory.

Humanity was now travelling the reaches of space, prospecting, fighting and exploring. The ghost lines and the more or less self-contained ships seemed to grant endless possibilities; the only thing stopping us was fuel. Even with the Gerions help we couldn't make our fuel efficient enough.

191 IT: GIC had back-engineered the harvester and converted one of their largest mining ships into a harvester ship. The ship was named *Victoria*. They had chosen the planet H-09 (in the Cradle system) in the Sirius galaxy. It had a liquid core, and not much minerals. They drilled to the core, which took several weeks and then they connected the harvester unit. They began the process, which took several hours. Most of the molten magma was released into space, while the siphons caught a vestigial material. After the process they examined the hard purple and dark hued semi-glowing substance that remained. They ran tests for an entire year and in the end they discovered that it was a material with an extremely high energy content. With the right processing it could be used to fuel ships for a tremendously long time. They couldn't wrap their minds around it. The material had an energy output that seemed to be scientifically impossible. It made all other sources of energy seem inferior by comparison. But a secret like this couldn't be kept for long, and soon this knowledge spread. At this date the Gerions disappeared without a word.

200 IT: The planet harvest method was now widespread and GIC, SES and IMC used it frequently and the production of a whole new line of ships was designed. The new fuel was dubbed *Coreanium*, and battles broke out in several places over the rights to mine and harvest planets in unregulated space between the factions. However, there had been no outright war as such. Most put their military strengths in their navy fleets, the need for ground units were minimal.

205 IT: Several security forces and mining overseers from GIC, SES and IMC convened in a secret meeting without the involvement of the factions they represented. They were tired of all the regulations of mining and harvesting rights. There were always buyers who didn't care where they got the goods from. Together, they founded the MEC (Military Economic Corporation) and broke loose from their former allegiances.

207 IT: MEC started to raid mining ships and conduct illegal mining operations which they defended with deadly force.

210 IT: All new ships came with a coreanium reactor and most old ships had been converted. Depending on the size of the coreanium mainstay in the reactor, a ship could be fuelled from a year to ten years without having to change the core. Of course, this created a whole new independence among space travellers. C-class ships could now stay out for some months or so if stocked with nutrients. D- and E-class ships were fully self-sufficient with their protein pools, hydroponics gardens and completely self-contained ecosystems and could in theory stay out as long as the reactor held. The need for a home planet, colony or station lost much of its meaning. Some were born on ships, not setting foot outside it for years.

216 IT: MEC has grown and become a force to be reckoned with. They're viewed as terrorists and live out in hidden away colonies, stations and ships. They had also begun to infiltrate the GIC and the corporate scene.

220 IT: While the MEC is still going strong, a similar organisation dubbed the CIM (Clandestine Industrial Militia) was born. The information around the creation of CIM is sketchy at best, but it's believed they were formed from a large and splintered cell hailing from the MEC. The CIM employs similar methods as their sibling organisation.

230 IT: The two fringe organisations MEC and CIM are strong and through guerrilla tactics they access resources and wage small battles against each other, corporate security and GIC patrols. Even though their numbers and resources are much smaller than that of the GIC, they're still able to cause havoc due to their stealth tactics, infiltration and blitz attacks.

250 IT: An unidentified field of electrical disturbance appears, apparently everywhere. It lasted for ten minutes and during this time there was a complete communications blackout. When the disturbance was over everything seemed to function normally, but within minutes the first report came in:

The Ghost Lines seemed to be disabled. The disturbance was dubbed the *Ghost Storm*. A blackness that became known as the *Dark Rim* appeared all around the Sirius galaxy, enclosing it.

For three months the lines were down and fear and panic spread, we were now isolated and those who had been travelling in the ghost lines at the time had disappeared. But after three months the lines became active. However, our ghost navigation had been skewed and so had the efficiency of the lines. Soon it was clear; the ghost lines were unable to take us outside the Sirius galaxy. Still, most of mankind out there did not react with horror and dismay about this.

Earth was millions of light years away from the largest part of humanity, and many had never seen it, just read of it in files as "the planet where humanity came from" and it was in fact more dangerous to live on Earth than living on a ship most of the time due to the conditions on our home planet. The fact that a "home planet" as such had lost its importance showed there was no real interest in Earth. Overall, humanity was more interested in killing planets by harvesting them (after they had mined them dry) than terraforming them.

300 IT: The harvesting process had now killed off a multitude of planets. This year humanity gets to witness the first case of the phenomenon which became known as *void psychosis syndrome* (VPS). IMC science- and archaeological excavation ship *Archimedes* suddenly went to a communications blackout while in the Hardek system. When the E&R (Evacuation and Retrieval) ship *Ugly Helen* arrived two weeks later they found that most of the crew had killed each other and then themselves. Of 243 people there were 20 still alive, most quite insane, suffering from VPS. In the debriefing, seven of them were cogent enough to be interviewed. It had begun when some of the crew had reported sleeping disorders, then some had started to have nightmares. This seemed to spread and soon people started to have waking nightmares, followed by paranoia and violent tendencies. Over 200 insomniacs suffering from waking nightmares and paranoid delusions trapped in a ship in the middle of space could only lead to one thing: Extreme violence and death. Some of the survivors said that *the others* were coming and that those from the void had awakened in order to punish humanity for its sins. This was contributed to mass hysteria and extreme isolation.

304 IT: More and more of these cases were reported, seldom in such large scale, but VPS had become widespread enough to present a problem. Psychological screening became more common. The three main factions (GIC, IMC, SES) tried to turn a blind eye to the problem and weren't willing to accept that there could be any risks in leaving ships out in space for extended periods of time (this would slow down exploration which in turn would slow down mineral mining and harvesting, not that there was any real shortage).

310 IT: In secrecy a group of medical technicians (49 of them) from GIC, SES and IMC had come together and performed a study on the syndrome and dubbed it VPS. At one of the yearly summits held by the three factions four representatives from this hidden group demanded the floor. They then revealed their findings. VPS was on the rise, and there were three distinct groups susceptible to it: Crews on ships that had been out for more than six months, those who were awake and not in stasis while travelling the ghost lines and people living on isolated space stations with a small crew. Incidents on planetary colonies occurred but they were negligible. Their proof was irrefutable but no one could explain why this had started to happen in the last ten years, after centuries of deep space travel without incidents of this scale. All agreed that something had to be done.

312 IT: After two years of discussions, arguments and a lot of bureaucracy passing new laws and legislations the *Medical Research Group* (MRG) was formed. This was a branch of GIC that had the authority to step in and make executive decisions when severe outbreaks of a medical or psychological nature were in effect. The presence of psychiatric technicians on ships became more common, as did regular psych screenings of crew members in rotation.

314 IT: Having an actual home planet seemed more appealing now as VPS had popped up and with this several terraforming projects were set up, by all major organisations. It was at this point people started to realize that no one personally knew anyone that had actually been to Earth in the last 50 or so years. Last report indicated that it was still a patchwork of semi-radioactive warzones crawling with rippers, and little official information was still on file about our alien enemy. Wars, travels, a third of a millennia and several million light years had done a good job in dispersing and destroying tangible knowledge of our planet of origin.

315 IT: *The Church of Infinitology* is founded by *Elaine Kendrin*. They oppose the exploitation of the universe and the harvesting of planets, stating that it's damaging the whole of the universe, of which we are part, and it would lead to the destruction of mankind if nothing changed.

320 IT: We had managed to terraform two major planets in the Divius system. Claret and Mondus. The terraformers and early settlers were the only ones on the planet, still working on the ecosystem.

322–335 IT: A GIC survey crew discovered several alien artefacts in the Valdis system on the planet Kerrion. More would to be discovered.

340 IT: Both planets now had a working ecosystem and flora and with that the animals started to thrive. Previously,

Planet engineers at work.

mankind had mostly terraformed in order to make the air breathable, relying on temporary atmosphere processors, but now the race of man had a higher purpose. Man was creating new home planets.

360 IT: Claret and Mondus were completely terraformed, the fast rate didn't only adhere to the prime conditions of the planets and the technology. All factions had poured tons of resources into the project in order to secure the future of mankind. People started to settle down somewhat as many were afraid of spending too much time in space. With this the power of the GIC and corporations became more centralized. It didn't take long for the CIM and MEC to infiltrate the two planets in order to spy and gain access to information that was vital to their agenda.

400 IT: Claret and Mondus were now home to several billion humans and was officially the new home-worlds of humanity. Both planets were about the same size of Earth, and now had roughly the same climate as the distance from their sun was approximately the same. Still, space travel and exploration hadn't really slowed down, but many people had learned the value of spending time on an actual planet. But through the Ghost Lines new worlds were discovered and new planets were harvested.

404 IT: Some 35,000 light years away from the Divius system shuttles belonging to the SES survey ship, *The Talon,* set down on one of the many unexplored worlds, looking for minerals and the chance to harvest a liquid core. The planet was unnamed and located in the *Verbios* system. After two weeks of surveying they determined that the small planet was useless, they also reported that one of their crew members had suffered an injury in a fall. Two days after this they reported that they were taking off. Three months later they should have arrived and sent six check-off transmissions during the trip

years ago. Most of the original information of the old enemy had been lost. But the threat was real. The infinitologists said that this was just the beginning and that it was only one of the coming reactions that the universe had in store for us. *We are harming the universe and so it rightly reacts.*

411 IT: Terraforming colony E-13 on the planet Catheras in the Berion system was attacked by rippers. There were no human survivors and the planet's surface was carpet bombed by the GIC fleet. Later that same year the small scientific space station *Serendipity* in the far reaches of the Berion system was attacked. There were a few human survivors but the fleet hadn't the training needed to successfully board, sweep and rescue the personnel. All previous battles had been against human adversaries, and mostly conducted from cockpits and command bridges. GIC gave the order to blow up the station and the survivors to halt the ripper infestation.

The Arch is being discovered.

back to base. But they never reached the Divious system and not a single transmission was received. They had simply disappeared. The E&R ship that was sent found no trace of them.

410 IT: Mining colony RT-67 in the Murion system sent out a distress call, they were being attacked by an unknown alien force. The transmission was cut off. Two weeks later the GIC fleet arrived. When they landed they encountered heavy resistance by the alien forces. After sustaining heavy casualties they had to retreat as they were completely unprepared for the enemy. As most of the colonists were dead, they decided to bomb the site, annihilating all life. Footage from the attack was sent to GIC HQ and it had several clear shots of the monstrous enemy. After scanning the records they managed to find scraps of information from centuries ago. These were indeed the creatures dubbed rippers who had attacked Earth 513

412 IT: Due to the loss of resources as a result of having to bomb installations being infested by rippers, and wanting to have a real line of defence against them, the *GIC Marine Corps* were created. The fleet had tactical boarding crews and planetary assault teams, but the marines were to be trained and drilled in a different way. These men and women would be specialized in dealing with dangerous extractions, the securing of GIC property and the eradication of rippers, and any other hostile forces they encountered. The CIM and MEC suddenly had to tread more lightly.

444 IT: The rippers hadn't become a common thing, and had never been inside the Divius system, but they had attacked several colonies during the years. The marines had done a formidable job in dealing with the problem. They had access to the best equipment and the best training.

Timeline

459 IT: The first outbreak of CAV (Caliphrian Aggression Virus) is discovered. The harvest ship *Injiro* returns from its mission in the Caliphrian system under radio silence. Marines boarded the ship and were soon attacked by crazed members of the crew. They seemed extremely aggressive and capable of withstanding an enormous amount of injury before dying. The enemies were incapable of any form of communication and used simple tools, bare hands and even bites to attack the marines. In the end the marines were successful, but only after losing several of their own men. The bodies were all hauled down to the planet Peldios to the Haze settlement. When the bodies of the dead marines came to life again and started to attack people the first colony outbreak of CAV was a fact. The situation was contained by the fleet and additional marines (and all bodies incinerated) and it's unknown how CAV came to spread further. It has been speculated that it in fact laid dormant in someone only to surface later.

490 IT: During a planet harvest in the Sylvian system, on the dead planet Y-34, the crew of the core harvester *Orion* (IMC) communicated that they had found an alien structure beneath the surface. They decided to dig it up and tow it home. Some days after they had dug it up they reported a sudden epidemic of VPS in the crew. Four days after this report they had hauled the alien structure (which they simply referred to as *the arch* at this point) on board and due to the increased unstableness in the crew they decided to come home, rotating the crew and delivering the artefact. Six days later they sent a distress call. Through the static one of the now crazed crew members screamed that something from the abyss had clawed its way up and that they all had to pay. In the background there were screams of pain and panic. The crew member yelled into the camera that there were a lot worse things than rippers in the great black and that the race of man would fall. After that the transmission cut out. The Orion disappeared. This in combination with the recently discovered CAV had the Church of Infinitology saying that we had to mend our ways. They sent out even more of their pilgrims, the so-called arbiters, to help mankind to better its ways. Due to the Infinitologists open minded faith and their tactful approach to things most people had come to respect and trust them.

491–500 IT: The Gerions return, they have sent two hundred emissaries to mankind for reasons unknown and have station themselves on our new home worlds and largest ships and bases. Mankind is getting used to their presence once again, even though the Gerion refuse to say why they left or why they returned.

501 IT (Now): Several ships have disappeared during the years. Some had been infested by rippers and made into hives which the marines cleared out, while others had been found and on them there had been nothing but blood and no signs of ripper activity. Some blame VPS, MEC or CIM, while others don't have an opinion of what happened. The infinitologists say that there's something else out there, a reaction of the universe that will cast its shadow over mankind. No one really knows what's going on, but the big empty is a place of great mystery, fear and danger. There are billions of unexplored worlds and systems, and one knows where the intricate web of the ever changing ghost lines will take humanity.

Chapter 1: Mechanics

C&D is a game about dark and gritty science fiction. The big empty is a place that *should* be explored, but the dangers are extreme, incomprehensible and horrifying. In many ways the world of C&D could be a bright one, but Man will be Man. What we do and *how* we do it will decide our fate.

To a certain degree, the universe in C&D is a lonely and empty one. Sure, the cities in the core systems, especially Claret and Mondus, are shining beacons of technological advancement and civilization. But this is a society where everyone has their place and the GIC monitors every move. Only outside it, in the vast emptiness of space can one attain true freedom. Yet this, too, has its price. The great black can drive you mad, while dangers known and unknown can rend your soul and body to shreds.

There aren't dozens of civilized alien species out there in the galaxy, waiting to become our allies. There are only two known alien races: the rippers, which to those safely snuggled on the core planets are a distant threat, and the highly evolved (but probably deeply disturbed) Gerions. The rippers are a parasitic race that seems to share characteristics with both reptiles and insects. They attack without warning, without reason, using nothing other than their natural weapons. They are fearless and merciless, seeking to destroy all other life.

The Gerions are our allies, something that many quietly dispute. They have given us our most valuable technology and improved our way of life, but they keep a lot from us and none have seen them outside their horrid cephalopod-like bio-suits. What lies underneath is speculated to be even worse and we haven't even seen their home world, or know if they have one.

We have found traces of ancient and highly evolved civilizations, even more evolved than the Gerions. Some of their artifacts can be used for good, others are utterly dangerous and veritable deathtraps. All are fashioned out of the unfathomably advanced material dubbed "bio-metal". This is a living, and, according to some, sentient alloy of an unknown origin.

All the worlds we find are devoid of life, except those we colonized decades or centuries ago and abandoned. There we find genetically engineered flora and fauna. In all of this are riches to be found, fantastic discoveries to be made.

The vastness is out there, waiting…

Style and…eh…Science

When the game was developed the focus was on *style*. The aesthetic and thematic design choices we made are a mix of all those games and movies we so love (many of which had already mixed together to start with), but when doing a project such as this you always put your own touch on it. Some aspects became lighter, others darker, and hopefully it all meshed well together. Our goal was a kind of dark industrial feel. The design progressed and it *looked* cool, but then came the "science".

We haven't tried to create a scientifically probable future. Rather, we have created a set of fictional scientific realities that we have used as guidelines so that the science make sense within the context of the fictional game world and scientific set pieces. Admittedly, we put the industrial heavy feel and grittiness first.

Rusted metal, smoke and sleek, shiny nanotechnology. In some respects this sums up the feel of the world. Of course, each gaming group will add their own veneer and world description, but this is an essential part. At the same time an engineer is greasing cogs he will check the diagnostics on his Nano Interface Screen. Imagine a dirty industrial park with futuristic high tech elements and you've got the idea.

About the Game as Such

We have tried to create a comprehensible game mechanic that at its core is quite simple and fast, but leaves the possibility for advanced play. Certain things have received more attention, things that probably wouldn't make sense in another type of game (such as how long it takes to cut through or weld shut a pressure door; hey, it can save your life!). Generally we have aimed to create a system that makes good use of task resolution, but does so in support of the narrative and in benefit of suspense.

Mainly the players portray individuals that are a bit more exploratory (or maybe plain crazy) than the average person, which will lead to a lot of travels and expeditions into deep space. The milieu and its possibilities have been devised in such a way that it should be quite easy to hold game sessions. However, even though there should be enough in this book for anyone to grasp the C&D world, the game *is* aimed at players that have seen or played (and liked) at least one of the titles in our inspirational list. So, with that out of the way…

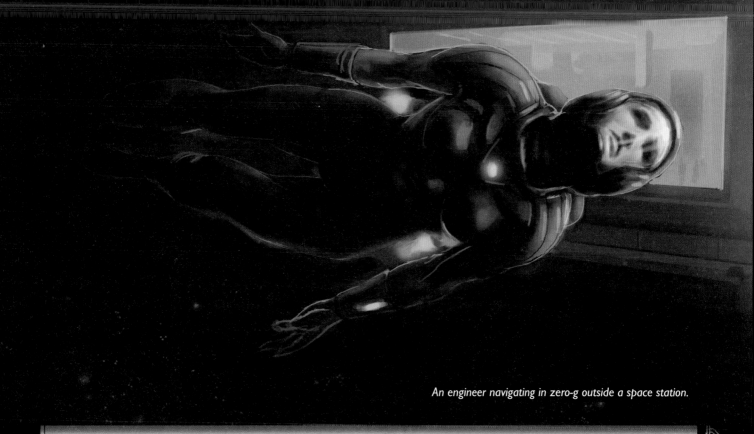

Actions

This is a broad term that is used to describe when an avatar or NPA does something of consequence to the story that involves the mechanics. Hacking a computer system is an *action*, and so is firing a gun. Actions can be of any length. Firing a gun takes but a second, while hacking a computer system takes much longer. Many actions are resolved using *rolls*.

Rolls

In order to assess if something succeeds, C&D makes use of rolls. The dice employed are eight-sided dice. These are used for every roll and are hereafter simply referred to as a "D". So "2D" is equal to two eight-sided dice.

When you want to make a roll, you combine the appropriate Aptitude with the Ability to create a dice pool, then roll a number of dice equal to the value of those numbers. When making pure Aptitude rolls, you count the Aptitude as double and make the roll. So if you have to roll your Brawn and have a score of 2, it would count as 4.

There are two basic types of rolls: Aptitude rolls and Ability rolls. If rolling for an Ability in which you have no score, you would roll the active Aptitude alone. This, however, would still count as an Ability roll and you wouldn't double the Aptitude, as you would with an Aptitude roll.

The goal is to have as many of the dice as possible to match or exceed the target number. The target number is always 7, though occasionally some *Package Bonus Features* can modify this number. Each die that comes up a 7 or an 8 is considered a "success". If the target number isn't matched or exceeded by any of the rolled dice (i.e., no successes are rolled), the roll fails.

Aptitude rolls: Aptitude × 2
Ability rolls: Aptitude + Ability

Example 1 (Ability roll without an Ability score): The scout, Gith, is driving a terrain car and he's under fire from some CIM militia. An explosion erupts just a couple of meters in front of the buggy and he has to swerve in order to avoid it. The AI decides that the Aptitude in question is Reaction and the Ability is of course Driving. However, Gith don't have any points invested in Driving, so he must use his Reaction alone, which is 3. So with that the player gets to roll 3D. He scores 4, 8 and 2, one success total.

Example 2 (Ability roll with an Ability score): Gith is a marksman and he's about to snipe a CIM guard. He has an Attention score of 3 and a Shooting score of 4. Attention 3 + Shooting 4 gives him a dice pool of 7. He scores 7,6,4,8,7,1 and 2, which makes three successes.

Example 3 (a straight Aptitude roll): Gith walks into an apparently empty room. The player doesn't state that he's looking for anything, but there's a guard in hiding. Even if the avatar isn't actively looking, there's a chance that such a thing will be discovered reflexively. The AI decides to roll Gith's Attention in order to see if he discovers the guard. Gith has 3 in Attention. When used in an Aptitude-only roll, Aptitudes are doubled, so the AI rolls 6D for Gith's Attention.

Modifiers

The difficulty of an action depends on the circumstances. When things get easier, a positive modifier is applied. This adds a varying number of dice decided by the game rules and/ or the AI. An increased dice pool also means an increased chance of success. If something is harder a negative modifier applies, which decreases the pool and makes it more difficult to succeed. Modifiers are cumulative.

If a dice pool is ever reduced to zero or less, the player still gets to roll 1D. If this roll fails, it counts as a "botch", as the circumstances are so extreme.

A dice pool can never exceed 8. When it does, every extra die is counted as a success *after* a successful roll has been made. These surplus dice have been locked. When negative modifiers apply, this "surplus" is reduced first.

Example 1 (negative modifier): *Gith is sneaking past a guard post. He has a total pool of 8 in Quickness + Stealth. But the guards are high-strung and on their toes since they received a report that there might be an intruder about. The AI decides that Gith gets a –2 to his dice pool, reflecting the guards' alertness, leaving him at 6D.*

Example 2 (positive modifier): *Having survived the rippers with a piss-and-vinegar attitude and his trusty heavy handgun, Rook sees a lone ripper feeding on the corpse of a fellow Marine. Rook levels his handgun and aims. The AI tells the player that he gets a +1 modifier because he took the time to aim. His Attention + Shooting rank is 6, but with the modifier his rank increases to 7. Rook smiles as he has the bastard in his sights.*

Example 3 (a pool beyond 8): *Gith has an Attention + Shooting score of 7, and he aims at a guard long enough to get a +2 modifier. This gives him a pool of 9 dice. The player gets to roll 8 dice and on a successful roll he gains an extra success for the surplus above 8. If he would have had a pool of 10, he would have gained two extra successes after a successful roll. If a negative modifier would be applied, the surplus dice would be the first to drop.*

Automatic and Obvious Successes

When there's no stress, an avatar can succeed automatically at an action. If the player's dice pool (including modifiers) exceeds or equals the target number, it's an automatic success (any combat action is considered stressful and thus cannot automatically succeed). The success is minimal and takes the maximum amount of time, but it gets done. If the player wants to hurry things up, he can take a chance with a dice roll. This is a mechanic that the AI can use to calibrate the flow of a story, shifting it from dice-heavy to a more narrative style when it suits the gameplay.

Then there are *obvious actions*. Climbing up a perfectly good ladder without any stress or hindering conditions can be done by anyone, even if they don't have the dice pool to pull it off automatically. Use common sense regarding obvious actions.

Example: *Operative Eric Starkwood is bypassing a lock. He has a total score of 8 for this action. Starkwood is currently in an abandoned, closed down service tunnel and there are no guards, stress or any other factors that might put pressure on him. As his dice pool more than equals the target number (7) and there's no stress, he can automatically bypass the lock. However, it takes some time since he's working slowly and methodically in order to get it right.*

Example 2: *Janice Mael, a med-tech, is trying to fix up her bioscanner after it was damaged in a laboratory accident, and it's the only one to which she has access at the moment. The device isn't too badly damaged and she has high-quality tools. However, she only has a total dice pool of 4 for the roll. But since she's in no hurry, has the right tools and the AI knows that they will need the device to move the story forward, he decides to give the avatar a +3 modifier. Since the final number is equal to the target number, 7, she succeeds.*

LED investigating a murder scene in hydroponics.

Botch

If a roll results in no successes and if half of the dice (or more) are 1s, it's considered a *botch*. In this case, the worst possible result occurs. The gun jams or breaks down while firing it, the climber loses his grip and falls, etc. The AI is the judge of what happens when a botch occurs.

Example: *Hammer is cornered by four rippers that charge him. He readies his carbine and is about to light the bastards up. The player rolls, but he scores no successes. Even worse, four of the seven dice come up as ones. CLICK! The AI says that the gun has jammed. It seems as if Hammer is about to get torn to shreds.*

Contested Rolls

Contested rolls are relevant when two opposing parties are pitted against each other. The two involved parties make a roll with the appropriate dice, and whomever acquires the most successes wins. This can also be done as an *extended contest*, where the involved parties try to accumulate the highest number of successes over a period of time. Extended contests are best used to heighten suspense with the aid of the game mechanics.

In the event of a tie, the one with the highest Ability score wins. If it's still a tie, the one with the highest active Aptitude score wins. If both Aptitude and Ability are tied, each participant rolls 1D and add their Ability score until the tie is broken.

Example 1 (contested roll): *Gith tries to hold the door shut while a CIM guard tries to push it open. Gith has a Brawn score of 2 (which gives him 4 dice, since Aptitudes are doubled when making pure Aptitude rolls) and the CIM guard has 3 in Brawn which gives him a pool of 6 when rolling. Gith rolls his 4D while the CIM guard* rolls his 6D. Gith scores 2 successes, while the guard scores 4. Gith tumbles back as the door is busted open.

Example 2 (extended contest): *Lee Wei, a freelance pilot, is flying side by side with a raider ship. Both are trying to get through to the other side of an asteroid field, but two asteroids are about to collide and only one of them will be able to make it through the closing gap; the other will crash and burn. To heighten the suspense the AI declares that the pilots will make three rolls each (instead of doing just the one). Whichever side accumulates the most successes wins. They start to roll. On the first roll, they're tied with two successes. On the second roll, Lee Wei has managed to accumulate four successes, while the raider has five. There's one roll left. Who will get through and who will crash and burn? Both sides roll their dice.*

Working Together

Up to four people can work together on a problem at the same time. The one with the highest Ability score acts as the anchor, making the roll. Each participant beyond the anchor adds +1 to the roll. Not all actions can be done together, and generally no more than four people can work on the same action at once. The AI must decide what is appropriate, as it varies depending on the situation at hand.

Example: *Senior LED officer Rorec is investigating a murder scene in a space station. He has two junior officers assisting him. Officer Rorec has a total pool of 6 in Attention + Forensics. However, since he has two assistants (both of them have a lower score than Rorec) that are skilled in the art of forensics, he gains +1 for each assistant, for a total +2 bonus. They work as a team and have a combined pool of 8 (Rorecs pool of 6 + 2), increasing the chance of success.*

> **Note on Brawn:** *When Brawn is pooled, every extra person adds +1 to the "power chart", +2 if he or she possesses a Brawn score of 4 or more. Then it's just a matter of making a normal Brawn roll, counting successes from the new level on the chart. See Actions That Need Detailing for more information regarding the power chart.*

Reduction Time

Some actions have a *reduction time* and a *base time* attached to them. Base time measures how long it takes to perform the action, while the reduction time measures how much time each success diminishes the base time necessary for the action. Then there is a *minimum time*. This gauges the minimum amount of time the action must take, no matter the result on the dice. If a minimum time isn't stated, it's counted as half the base time of the particular action (see *Actions That Need Detailing*).

The Do-Over

This rule for successive attempts at an action should be used with some care. It's never in play when executing attacks, flight maneuvers, sneaking or in any other situation where a failure will result in a direct and swift consequence, but it should apply when the avatar is engaging in something that is time-consuming and in need of some focus. This includes actions such as picking a lock, fixing an engine or performing a ghost line calculation. If the first roll fails, the player can roll a second

time, only he will get a −2 on the roll. If this fails as well, he can try a third time, but now gets a −3 penalty. After this, he's too frustrated and has to take a step back. If the action has a base time, half of this time is required as a "cool down period" before the avatar can start over with a clean slate.

> ### A Measure of Success
>
> *Every die that comes up a 7 or an 8 is counted as a success. If it's not a contested roll, one success is enough for the action to be considered successful. Additional successes (multiple 7s or 8s) indicate a greater degree of success: additional damage if attacking, reduced time for repairs and so on. Not every roll will benefit from additional successes, but most will. Just a handful of the myriad of possible situations are covered in this book, which means that you as the AI will have to come up with appropriate solutions at times.*
>
> *For example, when conducting a crime scene investigation you might decide that each success will turn up a piece of forensic evidence or clue. When conducting an interview, each success might represent an additional piece of information.*

Failures Can Be Interesting

You should always be able to imagine where a failed roll might lead. Sometimes a failure doesn't result in anything special, other than a missed shot that gets lodged in the wall or a missed chance to up the selling price in a negotiation. But at other times a failure will yield an interesting story twist or circumstance.

Example: *The rogue operative Anya has breached an abandoned underground GIC base. She is working on the security lock on an interior door. She has a gang of marls tracking her down and closing fast, so she has to hurry, meaning she can't take an automatic success. She fails miserably. The AI tells the player that Anya noticed an overgrown service hatch some steps back. She has a chance of reaching it before the marls see her, if she makes a run for it. She hauls ass and manages to dive down the vent seconds before the marls run past it, barely missing her. She lands in dirty knee-deep water. She stands up, finding herself in a wide sewage tunnel. Strange roots and vines cover the walls. Suddenly she hears a screeching hiss…and it's not from a marl. Something big is alive down there with her. The installation is an old bio-weapon lab, God knows what kind of botched, mutated military experiment might have escaped. She doesn't have to worry about the marls for now, but as she draws her SMG and sees movement further down the tunnel, she realizes that she might have been better off fighting them instead.*

The example above shows how a failure can lead to an interesting situation. The tunnel will lead to the same place as the door she couldn't get through, but the journey is far more perilous. You can plan for some of these failures but at other times you can wing it by keeping alert and concentrating on building entertaining scenes.

Sequence Zones

These are used as a means to make certain scenes more compelling and narrative. They have a time and a place where they should be used and the AI is the one who decides when they will be useful. In essence, they're a sort of macro mode which leaves much of the narration to the players (if they wish).

Sequence Zones are always connected to a physical place and physical actions in that area; in most cases predetermined things. For example, they're excellent to use when it comes to large-scale battles, stealth missions, or when you wish to speed some scenes up without taking away the suspense. They can represent everything from an area with security in place that needs to be taken down to waves of attackers trying to breach your defensive line. The zones are in the form of a circle (but can be in any form, if the AI needs to change them) and each zone has a modifier attached to it. This modifier applies to the Abilities used to pass the zone. These rolls are simply called *sequence rolls*. When a zone is successfully passed, the player gets to narrate (within the constraints of the zone that the AI has set up) how it all goes down.

The simplest way of illustrating it is to take an example which involves a stealth mission. The avatar has snuck aboard a planet harvester and he is trying to get to hydroponics without being detected, by using air ducts and access tunnels. But there are a lot of guards. Every zone represents two hundred meters or so of sneaking, and for every zone he passes the player makes a short narration: *"I can hear the two guards: they stopped at the corner where I'm standing. They talk about some strip joint in Claret City as they light up a smoke. Silently I manage to open the access hatch and slip down the vent. At the same moment I close it, they come around the corner. I crawl down the shaft."* The important thing is that the narration is in line with how the avatar operates and what the roll represents. Successfully passing a sneak zone won't end with all the guards killed, etc.

This can be very effective, as a special ops team can have different tasks in a sequence zone. One must make a Search roll to identify where the guards are from his position, while another must pass a Shooting roll in order to snipe them, and the third needs to pass a Security roll to cut the alarm and breach the door. When a roll fails, it usually means that the game moves to normal play, where the opposition makes rolls (Attention-related for discovery, combat-oriented for battles, and so forth) in order to see if the avatar is discovered or the squad injured or whatever is appropriate to the action. If the avatars manage to overcome the zone in a way that they can continue through the zone, they make a sequence roll for the next zone. It's possible to create extremely advanced zones which hold information on the number of successes needed and, if in a large-scale combat, units damaged and lost, depending on the outcome. When the *Norm* is reached, the

sequence is over. The sequence can of course end earlier, like when a stealth sequence zone goes south.

Example of Sequence Zones Chart

Example: *Gith is sneaking into a CIM base. The base is fenced and has an inner perimeter of guards, then he has to breach a door and sneak passed an additional perimeter of guards before he's in the actual base. The AI constructs the zones as follows.*

Zone 1, jump the fence and sneak past the guards: Quickness + Stealth, modifier +/- 0.

Zone 2, take out one of the guards in close combat in order to get to the door: Quickness + Close Combat, modifier +2 (the AI has decided that the guard is a bit drunk).

Zone 3, bypass the door and alarm, Attention + Security, modifier −2 (it's an unusual alarm type that Gith has never dealt with before).

Zone 4, sneak past the guards on the inside, Quickness + Stealth.

Whenever Gith passes a roll, he narrates the details of the zone to add his avatar's style and flair. He might jump up and do a split, holding onto a pipe as the guards sneak past below (I swear I've seen that somewhere…). If he messes up, the game shifts to normal mode for that zone. Maybe he has to stealthily kill a guard that he failed to sneak past, and if he fails or makes noise he has to shoot it out with the entire guard squad, effectively ending all the zones as he's discovered. If he succeeds, the game reverts to zone mode until he messes up again or clears the zones. When inside the base, the game flow is normal and will remain so until the AI says otherwise.

Life in the outer colonies can be hard but it is perfect for those who want to stay under the radar.

Chapter 2: Aptitudes and Abilities

Aptitudes

Some things you're born with, such as innate intelligence, strength or a way with people. These are the things that Aptitudes represent. If you're naturally smarter it will be easier to use Abilities that require a certain intellect. There are eight different Aptitudes: *Attention, Brains, Brawn, Clout, Cool, Gut Feeling, Quickness* and *Reaction*. The scale below gives you an insight into what the numbers mean.

Aptitude Scores

* ✶ Poor
* ✶✶ Average
* ✶✶✶ Oh, you're good.
* ✶✶✶✶ You're a credit to the human race.
* ✶✶✶✶✶ Who's the perfect specimen? *You're* the perfect specimen!

Attention

This measures a person's overall perception and represents the five senses as well as the talent to catch details. Sharpshooters and investigators alike can make good use of this Aptitude.

Brains

Logic and book smarts is the realm of this Aptitude. It is often combined with Abilities when theorizing, remembering information or finding solutions to intricate problems with multiple angles to consider.

Brawn

Brute force and toughness. Brawn represents raw physical power and endurance. How much you can dead lift, carry and how much physical punishment you can withstand is determined by Brawn.

Clout

Charisma, appeal and social influence. Clout measures a person's natural social graces, good looks or charm. Exactly how it manifests differs between individuals, but a high score in Clout means that you can get away with lies, win debates and that you have a flair for negotiations.

Cool

Cool measures willpower, focus and psychological resilience. Space is a dangerous place, and if you want to stay alive you'd better keep your head. In order to do that, you need Cool.

Gut Feeling

This is pure instinct, the capability to do guesswork and follow the good hunches. Gut Feeling is almost like a sixth sense; it might be those little hairs that stand up on the back of your neck when something is wrong or that warm tingle you get in your spine when something feels just right.

Quickness

Agility, dexterity and nimbleness can be very useful. This Aptitude makes a person quick on his feet and gives him a natural grace. Whenever you need to move fast, quietly or engage in athletic activities such as climbing, Quickness comes in handy.

Reaction

The capability to react to things reflexively and then actually act on them can keep you alive. This is what Reaction entails. Whenever there's a question about wits or a quick response to external circumstances, Reaction comes into play.

Abilities

Abilities represent skills and knowledge a person can learn. No one is born with them, but one can train, study and practice in order to gain them. Abilities very much decide what an avatar can do. Is he a good pilot, a political genius or a master of repairs?

Some Abilities are capped with either *NP (not possible)* or *SA (simple actions)*. This indicates what can or cannot be done with the Ability if the avatar hasn't invested any points. For example, the Security Ability is capped with *NP*. This means that an avatar without any points spent on the Ability is incapable of using it in any capacity. If you don't know how, it's impossible to pick even the simplest lock. Computers and Administration, on the other hand, are capped with *SA*. This means that most people not versed in the Abilities still know how to do the most rudimentary tasks for those Abilities. Simple computer searches and reading through a simple legal document would be possible, but hacking a system or forging documents would not. Science, for example, is capped with

Cassandra, a syndicator, confidently leans back as she has successfully bribed an undercover LED-officer.

NP, as it would be impossible to conduct scientific experiments or discuss extra-dimensional physics without at least rudimentary knowledge. A few Abilities aren't capped, such as Close Combat and Stealth, since these aren't divided into the same kinds of complexities (and can be utilized using the governing Ability, see *Ability roll without the Ability* above). Under *Typical Aptitude*, the Aptitude (or Aptitudes) most often used for the Ability is listed.

Ability Scores

* ✳ Amateur.
* ✳✳ You're pretty good.
* ✳✳✳ Very skilled, you can do this for a living.
* ✳✳✳✳ YYou're an expert in your field.
* ✳✳✳✳✳ Your skill is unparalleled.

Administration [SA]

This Ability lets you cut through bureaucratic red tape, grants the knowledge of which papers to file in order to get things done through the proper channels, and also entails knowledge of the law. The government and the corporations often hide their dirty operations behind facades, but they often leave a paper trail (although a digital one in many cases) and with some effort you can trace work orders, invoices and mining deeds to their point of origin, even when someone has tried to bury them. You can also spot forged documents (digital and physical) and forge documents of your own, given access to the right information and equipment.

Typical Aptitudes:
Drafting a document: Brains
Looking a document over: Attention
Forge a document: Attention
Track/create a paper trail: Brains

Athletics

Whenever you need to climb, run, jump, or engage in any similar physical activity, Athletics comes into play. This Ability shows how much time you have spent honing your coordination, nimbleness and speed. It is also vital when moving about in a zero-g environment, and without at least 1 point in Athletics you're unable to do any advanced movement in zero-g without having to make a roll.

Typical Aptitudes:
Run: Quickness
Jump: Quickness
Climb: Brawn
Swim: Quickness
Throw long distances: Brawn
Throw shorter distances with more precision: Quickness
Desperate and crazy acts, the success of which you have no real way of estimating, like jumping blindly down a shaft where there "should be" a cable some meters down if you remember correctly: Gut Feeling

Close Combat

Simply put, you know how to fight with melee weapons or your bare hands. Your fighting style is up to you to determine. The end result is the same: the Ability gives you the proficiency to defend yourself or knock someone out.

Typical Aptitudes:
Dexterous styles: Quickness
Strong-handed styles: Brawn

Computers [SA]

In the world of C&D, computer systems are everywhere. They're in ships, stations, colonies, scanners and more. Every person can use computers, but the actual Ability is needed to write programs and to hack and manipulate them. Computer knowledge is important to anyone wishing to gain access to restricted digital information and those wishing to write or rewrite system protocols.

Typical Aptitude

Trace a hacker's location: *Attention*
Hack a security barrier: *Brains*
"Spoof" a location: *Brains*
Educated password guessing (only simple ones): *Gut Feeling*
Program/reprogram protocol: *Brains*

Driving

Everyone can steer a surface buggy or a skimmer, but when the terrain gets tough, or when involved in stressful situations such as chases, this Ability is put to use. Driving can at times be the only thing standing between the avatars and death.

Typical Aptitudes:
Stunt driving (taking fast curves, jumping and ramming): *Attention*
Avoiding sudden obstacles: *Reaction*
Finding the ones you followed when they suddenly disappeared (Go left! Yes, I'm sure, turn left now!): *Gut Feeling*

Explosives [SA]

With this Ability, you can arm and disarm explosives. You're also knowledgeable about everyday chemicals and substances that can be combined and made into an explosive. The Explosives Ability also makes it possible to shape detonations (with the right equipment) and assess the blast radius.

Typical Aptitudes:
Designing a bomb: *Brains*
Putting a bomb together: *Attention*
Disarming a bomb: *Quickness*

Fast Talk

When you need to lie, negotiate or persuade someone in an informal environment where tact and subtlety aren't an issue, you can fast talk them. This Ability can be used to drop a pick-up line, haggle with a marketplace merchant or to carouse a party.

Typical Aptitudes:
Talk your way past a doorman: *Clout*
Come up with a good lie on the spot: *Reaction*
Get the sense that someone's lying: *Gut Feeling*
Make a pass at someone: *Clout*

Fringewise [SA]

If you want to buy illegal weapons, find a smuggler or get your hands on forged travel documents, you can use Fringewise. With Fringewise you know the ins and outs of the criminal world. Beyond getting your hands on illegal goods, you have some knowledge of criminal organizations and can identify groups of raiders by their ship markings.

Typical Aptitudes:
Spotting who might be a criminal in a bar (raider, fence, what-have-you): *Gut Feeling.*
Notice if someone is planning to mug you or is about to pick a pocket: *Attention*
Figuring the rudimentary hierarchy of a criminal organization after spending some time with the members (and just observing): *Brains*

First Aid

You know the basics of medical care when it comes to simple wounds. You know CPR, how to stop bleeding and how to prevent infections.

You can also set bones and handle trauma. It takes about thirty seconds to administer first aid, or a minute if the damage is severe.

Typical Aptitudes:
Stabilize a bleeding wound: *Quickness*
Set a bone or pull a joint straight: *Brawn*
Administer simple injections or set an IV: *Attention*
Treat burns: *Attention*
Stabilize fatigue trauma (hypothermia, dehydration, etc): *Brains*

Forensics [NP]

This gives you insight into the realm of criminal investigations. You can secure samples, analyze spatter patterns and reconstruct crime scenes. This Ability makes it possible to do a walkthrough of a ship or colony where atrocities have occurred and analyze the site in order to assess how it all played out. Investigators skilled in Forensics are often sent out to investigate the aftermath of VPS in order to elucidate the event. Even though scanners and technology can analyze patterns and calculate a lot of forensic data, they can never grant the most important element: the human aspect.

Typical Aptitudes:
Collecting technical evidence from a scene: *Attention*
Develop a psychological profile (requires some time and the possibility to analyze evidence and two or more crime scenes or case files relating to the offender): *Gut Feeling*
Interpret blood spatter: *Attention*
Instruct officers to properly seal off the scene, go door to door and write down witness reports: *Clout*
Do a snapshot reconstruction (how did they fight, how did the victim and assailant move, etc.): *Gut Feeling*
Quickly take charge over a fresh scene where everything is in disarray and it's unclear who is in charge: *Reaction*
Find a piece of evidence or a lead that is far-fetched, or otherwise make an almost impossible forensic connection: *Gut Feeling*

Ghost Line Calculations [GLC] [NP]

The ghost lines are capricious, dangerous but superior modes of transportation. No one in their right mind will perform a ghost jump before calculating the route. This Ability makes it possible to calculate the jump and ensure it takes the ship to its intended destination. Without calculations it's…volatile to jump, to say the least.

Typical Aptitudes:
Calculate a jump using known lanes (only available in the five core systems): *Attention, takes about a minute and the reduction time is 10 seconds.*
Calculating your own jump lane: *Brains, takes 3 minutes, reduction time 20 seconds.*
Quick-calculate a jump: *Cool, this takes half the normal time, but a failure means that your calculations are dangerously wrong.*

Interrogation/Information Gathering

When you need information from someone, the art of Interrogation is vital. Interrogation is a blend of soft and hard verbal tactics, the reading of body language and mind games. In order to make use of it, you need a form of leverage. This can be as simple as leaning on a snitch or having a person in an interrogation room. What stipulates leverage depends on the person being interrogated, what type of information one wishes to get and the overall circumstances.

Information Gathering is more subtle and indirect, using various low-key methods to glean information.

Typical Aptitude:

Reading a suspect's body language (if rather obvious) and letting it guide you to their weak spots: Attention.
Gaining a suspect's trust by relating to him: Gut Feeling
Making the suspect trip over his own words and slip up: Clout

(Information Gathering)

Read between the lines of a conversation: Attention
Subtly weave in questions in a seemingly innocent conversation: Clout
Eavesdropping on a nearby conversation and getting the gist of it in a rowdy environment (like a bar): Attention

Know-How

This Ability represents different skills, depending on who makes the roll. First of all, it measures an avatar's general education outside his field (general history, geography, knowledge of general political climate and the like). It also represents an avatar's work-related Know-How, both practical and theoretical. For example, there's no Ability for mining, geology or planet harvest procedure. But if a prospector (who doesn't have a speck in Science) wishes to make a geological assessment, or evaluate how long it would take to drill down to the core of a planet, he would use his Know-How. A Marine or operative wouldn't be able to use his Know-How in the same way as this isn't a part of their Know-How base. A Marine wishing to make an educated guess on how long his stranded squad must wait before a GIC military rescue ship arrives at their location could make a Know-How roll. In the end, it's the AI who decides how the different packages might make use of their Know-How.

Typical Aptitudes: *Varies*

Navigation [SA]

Either on the surface of a planet or in deep space, this can be a vital skill. In the vast space between ghost lines and planets it's easy to get lost. Navigation is pivotal for any pilot or driver wishing to travel to new systems or outside the charted routes.

Typical Aptitudes:

Plotting out a course: Brains
Plotting out a course to avoid GIC patrols: Attention.
Guessing which route a certain ship will take when you know their destination and who's piloting it, judging by their route (GIC, Raiders, CIM, etc.): Gut Feeling

Politics [SA]

This gives insight into the inner workings of the political power structure. Who has the most power, officially and unofficially, on Claret and Mondus? Which parts of known regulated space have the greatest SES presence? How would one political side react to a certain action by their opponents? With Politics you're privy to all these things and can assess and interpret the political climate. You can also use it to your advantage,

playing on the prejudice of one side to get them riled up and more inclined to act against the other.

Typical Aptitudes:

Making an educated guess about how a certain forum delegate will cast their vote on a specific question: Gut Feeling.
Picking out a good candidate for a particular political post or event (you have to conduct a bit of research first): Brains.
Listening at speeches and conversation amongst forum members in order to get an overall feel for areas of political interest at the moment: Attention.

Piloting [SA]

This entails the actual maneuvering of air/spacecrafts. In the world of C&D, being able to pilot is as normal as being able to drive in our day and age, but doing so under dangerous and high-stress circumstances is more uncommon. Being able to pilot when the shit hits the fan is a lifesaver.

Typical Aptitudes:

Get into firing position: Attention
Getting out of the line of fire: Reaction
Avoid a sudden obstacle: Reaction
Doing something wild and crazy (for example, zigzag inside an asteroid field to avoid followers): Gut Feeling
Catching up to/shaking off someone: Reaction
Chicken race-type situations: Cool
Firing from the helm controls: Attention

Repairs [SA]

Being able to fix something that's broken can save lives in space. A faulty airlock or a crack in the ship's coreanium reactor can really mess up your day. With Repairs, you can fix computers and busted open hulls as well as COGs, weapons or whatever else needs fixing. In the high-tech world of C&D, this Ability is quite useful and it's the bread and butter to an engineer or a gear jammer.

Typical Aptitudes:

Fix a mechanical engine problem: Quickness
Fix an electrical engine problem: Attention
Run a system diagnostics: Attention
Track and locate a power drain/surge: Brains
Find an obscure or unlikely problem in an engine or other device: Gut Feeling
Sabotage an engine and make it look like a natural error or breakdown: Brains
Create a blueprint for a device: Brains
Interpret a blueprint: Attention
Using a Nano-Matrix Board: Brains

Rhetoric

Where Fast-Talk is a quick, dirty and pushy way of getting what you want, Rhetoric is a subtle, methodical and tactful approach which doesn't ruffle quite as many feathers. Innuendo, veiled threats and the guise of sincerity make up some of the core elements of this Ability. It can be used to give speeches and to negotiate in the official arena, where tact is of the essence. It also grants the linguistics skills needed to get your message across in writing, and can be used to write such things as speeches, articles and novels.

Engineers are doing their best to keep their junker in the sky.

Typical Aptitudes:
Hold a short and spontaneous speech: Reaction
Write a longer speech: Brains
Give a longer speech: Clout
Write a news article: Attention
Write a fictional short story/novel: Gut Feeling

Scanners [SA]

Most people can look at a scanner and get a basic idea of the readout, if it's a simple enough scanner and if the conditions are ideal. More complex scanners or conditions which can interfere with the scanner or create ambiguous readings require this Ability. Scanners come in various forms. Different scanners, such as LIDARs and energy scanners on a ship and topographical mapping systems carried by miners are just a few examples.

Typical Aptitudes
Interpret anomalous readings: Attention
Calibrate a scanner to compensate for environmental disturbances (electromagnetic fields, radiation, etc): Brains
Calibrate a scanner to track/find a specific pattern within the scanner's parameters (getting a movement scanner to track objects of a certain speed or size, have a bio scanner calibrated to scan for a specific bio pattern, etc.): Brains
Figure out what kind of phenomenon might be responsible for disturbing a scanner: Gut Feeling
Hiding/Leaving the dragon tail: Gut Feeling
Chasing the dragon: Attention, each roll takes 30 seconds

Science [NP]

Physics, coreanium dispersion, advanced mathematics and similar disciplines are covered by this Ability. If you're skilled in Science, you can work out theories and perform experiments. Scientists often work on projects relating to the output and use of coreanium and how to harvest planets more effectively. They also engage in genetic engineering and the like.

Typical Aptitudes:
Remembering a piece of information: Brains
Observing a new scientific procedure and remembering the basics: Attention
Continuing another scientist's experiment with adequate notes and background information on hand: Gut Feeling.
Conducting an experiment: Brains

Search

This reflects how well you've honed your active perception. You can look for an enemy in hiding, pat someone down effectively or search a room. Anytime the avatar wishes to actively search for something, this Ability kicks in. In cases where the avatar has a chance of discovering something reflexively (the glare of a sniper scope, the click of a mine under his foot), the AI rolls their Attention as an automatic action, representing their natural perception.

Typical Aptitudes: Attention

Security [NP]

A security system can consist of something as simple as a mechanical door lock, or as complex as the computerized surveillance system of a harvester ship. You can bypass, circumvent and coordinate these systems with this Ability. Even if you're not good at computers, you can breach most systems as you don't go through the computers but hook in directly to the circuitry, wires and boards.

Security also gives insight into the theoretical and practical layout of a system (including guards, guard dogs, fences and similar things). The Ability enables you to set up these systems to be as effective as possible as well as use that knowledge to effectively infiltrate a secure location.

Typical Aptitudes:
Observe a place in order to assess the best way to plan the security: Attention
Instruct a competent team to install/place security measures according to your planning: Clout

Make an educated guess concerning possible security layouts/systems in place in an installation: *Gut Feeling*
Personally install security equipment: *Attention*
Bypass mechanical lock: *Quickness*
Bypass electronic lock: *Attention*
Bypass electronic circuitry (alarms, cameras): *Quickness*
Bypass circuitry under stress (such as when the alarm will be triggered within seconds): *Cool*

Shooting

Rifles, shotguns, SMGs and any weapon that shoots projectiles can be fired using this Ability. You can also maintain most standard weapons and have theoretical knowledge about them, as well.

Typical Aptitudes:
Shooting: *Attention*
Quick draw and shoot: *Reaction*

Stealth

Stealth lets you sneak, hide and tail someone. It can be useful in many situations. Maybe you want to tail someone in the dark alleys of the Outer Circle in Claret, sneak past a guard or hide from someone? Stealth is all about evasion and keeping a low profile.

Typical Aptitudes:
Tail someone: *Attention*
Hide: *Quickness*
Sneak: *Quickness*
Hide object/person: *Brains*

Strategy [NP]

This Ability is used to plan military operations and is also used when they're being executed. Strategy is a way to lead troops in a coordinated way in order to effectively beat the enemy. Things such as focusing the fire of a squad or setting up the best attack formation for a fleet can be done by the use of this Ability.

Typical Aptitudes:
Make an educated guess about what an enemy force is planning: *Gut Feeling*
Plan an ambush or assault: *Brains*
Make a quick and simple plan on the spot: *Reaction*

Void Lore [SA]

Void Lore consists of facts mixed in with metaphysics and rumors. Space is a very frightening place, especially in the world of C&D. With this Ability a person can theorize and make educated guesses about unconfirmed events. What does the planet harvesting process do to the harmony of the universe? What might have happened to the Cleopatra? What might VPS come from? For nonbelievers, Void Lore is nothing but legends and theology, but for infinitologists, the lore is sacred.

Typical Aptitude
Take part in a philosophical debate: *Clout*
Come up with plausible theory with a scientific slant for unexplained events that borders on the mystical: *Gut Feeling*
Insight into the creeds of infinitology: *Brains*

Xenoarcheology [NP]

All branches of archaeology are sub-categories of xenoarcheology. The discipline grants the theoretical and practical knowledge needed to find and properly excavate and preserve artifacts, structures and remains of ancient peoples. Beyond excavating objects, a xenoarcheologist is capable of investigating the objects, deciphering symbols and learning the age and meaning of discovered relics.

Typical Aptitudes:
Managing an excavation team during a dig: *Attention*
Digging out and dusting off a sensitive object: *Quickness*
Reconstructing an object: *Gut Feeling*
Deciphering alien symbols on artifacts (each sentence takes about 48 hours if possible and the reduction time is six hours): *Brains*

Xenomorphology [NP]

Simply put, this is the capability to study and speculate on the anatomy and lifecycle of alien creatures. By dissecting a body, a xenomorphology expert can (in most cases, and given some time) understand how the creature works. Ways to kill them and, if possible, communicate with them can also be determined (though not always accurately).

Typical Aptitudes:
Making an educated guess about a certain aspect of a creature's physiology after a quick glance: *Gut Feeling*
Performing an xenomorphological autopsy or vivisection: *Attention*
Cultivating xeno-bacteria or studying cellular growth: *Brains*

Chapter 3: Packages

An avatar comes from somewhere. He has a background, things he's good at and people he knows. Each player has to select a package for his avatar. Every package comes with some bonus features, set of base Abilities and Aptitude recommendations. Within the description there's a hint at a background, life views and experiences. These just describe what an avatar with this package *might* be like. This means that the player's avatars may vary greatly in personality, experiences and views from the package description.

Something to keep in mind is that a package is basically a job/ lifestyle description and the avatar doesn't have to be in that line of work anymore. The package Raider describes a lifetime as one, growing up jacking ships and smuggling. But a Raider might work as an operative nowadays (but using the Raider package). A LED-officer might make a living as a Raider. Main point being that the package represents from which walk of life the avatar comes and not necessarily what he does now. Under each package there will be some suggestions on optional variations of jobs/positions someone with a package background might go for. Feel free to devise your own.

Even though many packages hint at a background exclusive to the GIC (such as Operative, Commanding Officer and LED-Officer) the avatar might as well performed similar duties exclusively for a corporation, criminal organization or one of the fringe groups, MEC or CIM. Often he's completely freelance nowadays and this is usually suggested in the typical variations. Just see to it that the players choose avatars from backgrounds that can (at least in the end) form a functional team.

The Abilities that are capped with an asterisk or two (*) under a package are so-called "core" Abilities. These are Abilities which are vital to the package and the player has to spend the amount of points indicated by the numbers of asterisks. Two ** means you have to spend two points. The other Abilities are those that the package often has but the player is free to buy whatever suits his particular avatar. The Ability *Know-How* is never listed as it goes without saying that every package can make use of it. The exception for this is the Prospector and Medical Technician packages.

> *Note: Package bonus features never stack. For example, an Operative who now works for the Marine Corps will only get the bonus feature from the Operative package.*

Spending Credits and Start-Up Credits

Spending Credits are the amount of credits the player has to spend on his avatar before the game begins. Any leftover credits will be depleted at the beginning of the game so make the best of them. However, Spending Credits can't be spent on the COG or COG applications.

Start-Up Credits show how much cash the avatar has when the game begins and these credits can only be spent in game. If the avatar has a steady job he will of course get his monthly salary. The Salary Chart can be found in the Society Section.

Rook (Marine), Gith (Scout) and Seeley (Archeologist) on board the Kagetsu.

Arbiter

The universe and all its life forms are too complex in order for them to be random. You never could understand the belief that a one and only great God could have created it all, and even less probable it seemed that he could think and see all of creation. When you heard about infinitology as a young child you immediately knew that you wanted to learn more, and then spread that knowledge to those who would listen. Today you wish to see as much as the universe as possible. Someday you want to stare beyond the black rim and its secrets. You want to take part in those experiences that you think will enrich your life and always wished to examine and investigate strange occurrences that might bring you more knowledge of the Great Stream. You know that the infinite doesn't have a greater plan, it only reacts and you're a part of seeing to that mankind won't condemn itself by upsetting the harmony. The most important thing is that mankind one day will be able to join the Life of All.

Arbiters are the pilgrims of The Church of Infinitology. They go wherever the church tells them. They can be sent out to give aid to the needing, preside over funerals, establish orders or act as envoys in church business. In many cases they're also sent to investigate VPS, CAV and alien artifacts as these are all part of the infinite and has to be understood before mankind can find its place within the Great Stream.

Bonus Features

- **Scholarly:** *Arbiters are well versed in Void Lore. They might forget a detail or two at times but they would never be dead wrong. An arbiter can never botch a Void Lore roll because of their astuteness and they also get a +1 to all Void Lore rolls.*

- **True Believer:** *Due to their strong beliefs they get a +1 to all Cool rolls when it comes to resist the Cold (fear) and the Dark and they can never botch these rolls.*

- **Bless Endeavor:** *See Infinitology.*

Important Aptitudes: *Attention, Clout, Reaction*

Abilities: Athletics, Close Combat, Fast Talk, *First Aid*, Navigation, Politics, Rhetoric*, Void Lore**, Xenoarcheology*

Typical variations

True Arbiter: *You are sent out to act as a neutral presence and mediator between conflicting sides. Your presence is valued and your words have weight. It's a heavy responsibility and you always have to tread lightly.*

Wanderer: *You travel without a goal, only wishing to let the universe show you what it wishes. As a true hitchhiker of the stars you wish to accumulate as much knowledge as you can.*

Sheppard: *You work actively teaching your faith and providing council to those who need it onboard a ship or settlement where your religion is somewhat established.*

Spending Credits: 1000
Start-Up Credits: 500 + 3D × 100 credits

Archeologist

For hundreds of years mankind has known that there are other sentient beings out there. The Gerions live among us and the Rippers have become a dangerous part of the lives of men. Your call in life is to puzzle together the remnants of old civilizations, or groups, both human and alien. The ancient alien relics that have been found fascinates you and points to the existence of an ancient race that was even more evolved and advanced than the Gerions. The mystery of the universe just waits to unfold. There's a strangeness to it all, an eeriness that scares and intrigues you. Somehow you have felt the weight of it strengthen your will.

Archeology is a discipline that holds a lot of power and prestige. Archeologists travel all over the universe in order to search for alien artifacts and relics. Many have started up fractured businesses and work for the highest bidder, accompanying mining crews and prospectors. There's a lot of money to be made, but it's a game of chance and sponsoring is needed. There are rumors of artifacts of untold power and vast knowledge that must be unearthed.

Bonus Features
- **Strong Mind:** All interval levels of Black Resonance are counted as one less.
- **Knowledgeable:** +1 to all Xenoarcheology rolls and can never botch these.
- **Favorably Inclined:** An archeologist will always buy/sell artifacts for 20% less/more to his favor.
- **Important Aptitudes:** Attention, Brains, Gut Feeling.
- **Abilities:** Driving, Piloting, Scanners*, Science, Search, Xenoarcheology**, Xenomorphology*

Typical Variations
Artifact Dealer: You engage in the highly illegal but profitable activity of smuggling artifacts from forbidden systems. You have to be very careful as you meet and work with a lot of dangerous people.

Evaluator: You're sent out to finds in order to determine if it will be worth your employer to invest in a certain dig. It's a cutthroat business and some people are ready to walk over your dead body to keep a claim.

DoX 1 Researcher: As an employee of the GIC you follow protocol and see to it that illegal artifacts are restored to the GIC and that digs are legal. You also head up and discover many sites.

Explorer: Credits, fame, you don't care. You take the odd paid job just to finance your trips but the true payoff is the rush of making a new find! At times you work within the law but at other times you don't. Whatever the exploration requires.

Spending Credits: 4000
Start-Up Credits: 1000 + 1D × 200

Commanding Officer

The fleet wields the most awesome war machines ever known to man, and after you had seen your first war cruiser upfront you knew you wanted to be the head of one. You studied and trained hard, graduated top of the class at the cadet academy. During just a few years of active duty you rose in the ranks, and soon enough you got your officer rank and now you are one of the officers on the bridge.

Commanding a war cruiser and its supporting squadrons requires a certain mindset, skill and attitude. But you have what it takes and have gotten out of many battles victoriously. There's nothing like standing on the flight deck commanding your troops as the battle rages across the panorama. You don't like wars, but you love winning and getting your guys home in one piece.

A fleet officer often patrols the big empty and keeps things safe. They're part of the fleet and command dozens of ships and tons of hardware. The job requires a calm mind and the ability to make hard decisions. At times they're stationed in calm areas but at other times they're sent into warzones.

Their training is first class and only the best can complete the officer's training since they do wield an extreme amount of power at the helm of warships. However, the job is a dangerous one. Battles between armed ships have a tendency to end up pretty messy and explosive.

Bonus Features:

- **Commanding Presence:** Gets a +1 modifier to Strategy and cannot botch these rolls.

- **Perfect Strategist:** Gets +2 strategy points on a successful direct strategy roll.

- **Tactical Training:** Are the only ones trained in the use of the TCI battle coordinator.

Important Aptitudes: Brains, Cool, Reaction

Abilities: Administration*, GLC, Navigation, Piloting*, Rhetoric, Scanners*, Strategy*

Typical Variations

Marine Squad Leader: You didn't join the fleet but the marines and received your commanding officer training there. You head up anti-Ripper sweeper teams and see to it that you're men comes home alive.

Freelance Captain: The fleet can shove it for all you care. You struck out on your own and now command a small C-Class freighter you bought for your hard earned money. Of course you take illegal jobs from time to time. You have to take care of your ship and you have a hungry crew.

Commercial Officer: You're at the helm of a exploratory/research/mining ship serving the GIC, SES or IMC. You always take the deep space patrols, you like the quiet and the distance from your superiors. Being able to explore and act with certain latitude has always suited you.

Spending Credits: 4000
Start-Up Credits: 1500 + 3D × 100 credits

Circuit Breaker

You have never seen code, you have always seen what the code forms. Ever since your childhood you have been able to slice through whatever protective grid the circuit has been able to muster. And once you traveled out of the core systems, outside the reach of the circuit you learned that you had no problem hacking local VINs and ship subsystems. For many years you hacked for the hell of it, leaving your signature in hard to get places just to make a point but you've now realized that your talents are something that are highly valued and that you can get a shitload of cash for them. And as of late you have begun to use it to your advantage.

Working for GIC or corporate digital security seemed boring as hell so you sign up with crews that possess a more…free spirited way of looking at things. Hacking your way through a space station's docking code protocols under stress in order to obtain a valid sequence for the ship you're on so you can dock rather than be blasted out of the black is a hell of a kick.

Circuit Breakers, or Breakers, are computer wizards of the highest order. Most people believe that becoming a great hacker is about skill and experience, and to a certain extent that's absolutely true, but a Breaker has that little extra: Raw digital instinct.

To them, code isn't just code, it's a language which the computer not only uses to complete operations and run protocols; it uses it to express so much more. Breakers often claim that computers, be it a VIN or not, have an actual personality and they have good and bad days just like anyone else. And through this understanding, by listening to the digital whispers, are they capable of handling computers like no one else. They live by and for the digital experience and love it when their talents are put to the test in a high risk situation.

Bonus Features

• **Digital Affinity:** *Gain +1 to Computers and can never botch these rolls.*

• **True Hacker:** *Reduction time for hacking is counted as double.*

• **Complete Focus:** *Are not affected by Environmental Circumstance Stress while hacking.*

Important Aptitudes: *Brains, Gut Feeling, Attention*

Abilities: *Administration, Computers**, Fringewise*, Interrogation, Repair*, Stealth*

Typical Variations

ISA Tech-Head: *Working with the Interstellar Security Agency does put you on the GIC payroll but it's not like you work at some boring security section. You get to travel the galaxy hunting down CIM and MEC cells as well as handling communication and surveillance for the field agents. You're the spider in the web in the deadliest of games.*

Digital Anarchist: *You're not really a man with an overarching plan. You work for the highest bidder as long as you're hired to cause digital havoc. You want to upset the system as a whole and carve in your own chaotic mark in the digital lanes. You don't really have any love for the GIC and take on any job that might diminish the organization.*

Freelance Ship Tech-Head: *You've signed on a freelance ship. May it be a raider ship or a merc ship. While the engineer handles most of the engine repairs you look after the VIN. Your skills also come in handy during many jobs and when running hack attacks on enemy ships, disrupting enemy ship systems for an easier getaway or takedown.*

Spending Credits: 3000
Start-Up Credits: 1000 + 1D × 200

Delegate

Power is measured in money, resources, and strength of arms. But the sway over these things is decided in courts, boardrooms and by backroom deals. You have always been able to get your point across clearly and also been able to get others to see things from your point of view. And it didn't take you long until you turned your talents into a commodity.

You took a job as a delegate and you love it. Your clients send you all over the universe to broker their deals. You handle contracts, negotiations and you even appear in court at times. Multimillion credit deals stand and fall on your words.

Delegates are extremely versatile. They're like the operatives of the corporate world. They head hunt, negotiate and draw up contracts. A delegate has to be very ambitious and able to adapt. In many cases they're sent far away, without any chance of contacting their employer, and have to make hard decisions on their own. A trusted delegate wields an impressive amount of power as he is backed by the resources of his employers, acting as their voice.

Bonus Features

- **Believable:** +5 to credibility.

- **Silver Tongue:** +1 to Fast Talk and Rhetoric rolls and can never botch these.

- **Business Sense:** He will always buy/sell any merchandise or service for 10% less/more to his favor.

Important Aptitudes: Brains, Clout, Gut Feeling.

Abilities: Administration*, Computers, Fast Talk**, Interrogation/Information Gathering, Politics, Rhetoric*

Typical Variations

Corporate Lobbyist: You travel across the galaxy to strengthen the hold of the corporation you represent. You negotiate, bribe and manipulate the world around you to see to it that you open the way for corporate progress.

Travelling Escort: As a registered Escort at the Guild you have been trained in the art of seduction, rhetoric and physical pleasures. But you have discovered that your position can generate a lot of power. Pillow talk and people's dirty fantasies, combined with some social pulls and tugs make you a very effective diplomat and negotiator.

Jaded Fringe Negotiator: The crew you travel with might be first grade gunmen, aces at the helm and have the ability to fix a broken reactor with duct tape but they don't have the means to make money off the loot they steal. You negotiate pricings, deals and act as the face outward for the crew.

Spending Credits: 3000
Start-Up Credits: 1000 + 1D × 500

Gear Jammer

Thousands of people work and travel the vast reaches of space. In some cases they leave things behind, at other times they get attacked and their ship, colony or station gets blown to hell. You're there to pick up the pieces... and sell them.

You like the roads less traveled, since everything you pick up in unregulated space is yours to keep. You can be out for months and it can be a lonely existence, but come payday its all worth it. There's a certain beauty to gear jamming. The solitude, the struggle between you and the metal. Tons of hardware against your flesh, out there in the big empty. You know that this is what you were born to do.

Gear jammers are deep space salvagers. They fix up old ships, or clutter together valuable debris, and haul them back to ports where they can find potential buyers. They're simply "gear jamming".

These men and women have developed a special relationship with technology. They're experts at getting the most rundown piece of junk derelict ship up and running again, or are able to tie together massive amounts of metal as they move with ease in zero-g. They also seem to have an uncanny ability to force broken down machinery to do their bidding when the shit hits the fan. They spend a lot of time in unregulated space, scouting for things to salvage. Even though everyone knows that they're the best at what they do the general opinion is that gear jammers are crazy. And in order to do what they do they have to be a bit wrong in the head or have brass balls.

Bonus Features
- **Perfect Jury-Rigging:** *When a gear jammer jury-rigs a device or part of a device (that hasn't already been jury-rigged once and not fixed properly) there is no need to make a roll on the Wear & Tear chart when the thing breaks down.*

- **Speedy Mechanic:** *Duration for all jury-rigs are counted as being one level less complex/severe than they are.*

- **Gremlin Kick:** *Three times per story a jammer can yell, curse at and actually hit a broken down mechanical or electrical device after which it counts as jury-rigged for half the needed duration.*

Important Aptitudes: *Attention, Gut Feeling, Quickness.*

Abilities: *Athletics*, Computers, Explosives, Fringewise*, Repairs**, Scanners*

Typical Variations
Carrion: *People think you're the lowest of the low. You sit out in the black listening for distress calls, when you find one you jam it and wait for the people that sent it to die. Then the salvage is yours. You cut it up and sell the pieces at the nearest station or port.*

E&R Mechanic: *The Evacuate & Retrieval teams work to save lives and ships and respond to a variety of distress calls. You have the job of breaching the ship and getting it ready for retrieval and put together a report of the failures in the mechanics and structure in a short period of time and send it to your employers.*

Resident Gear Jammer: *You have taken up the role of mechanic and salvager on a freelance ship. You might not have the same finesse as an engineer but you can keep a bird in the sky with very little resources.*

Spending Credits: 3500
Start-Up Credits: 750 + 1D × 100

Kiru

You have always been good at fighting. Not because you were stronger or more aggressive, you won because you were alert, restrained and focused. When you were young you often found yourself protecting friends from bullies and the like. Soon you joined a local kendo and ninjitsu group in order to hone your skills. Some years later a man claiming to work with personal security within the GIC approached you. He said that his superiors had kept an eye on you and that they were very impressed. He gave you a chance to take your combat skills to a level beyond what you thought possible. Naturally you accepted and have never looked back. Now your body is your tool and with it you save lives as well as take them when necessary. You have seen some extraordinary and horrible things in your travels with your various clients as well as committed acts of both kinds. You're guided by your code and your honor.

Kiru, which roughly means "to carve" or "to cut flesh" in Japanese, is synonymous with *professional bodyguard*. There are many who claim to be bodyguards but the Kiru are the real deal. The GIC, major corporations and at times even high ranking crime syndicates train Kirus. All candidates have a natural dexterity and focus. Their training centers on close combat, even though most Kiru are quite adapt at using firearms as well. That close combat is their focus might seem odd in a world of firearms but is in fact very logical. Most establishments don't allow guns and in many environments it can be all out suicide to use one. So a person that can take on multiple opponents in close combat is invaluable. Kirus have a special bond with martial arts and are (if having a so-called Edge License) allowed to carry the weapon that has made them famous: The nano blade. A lot of their traditions and creeds are derived from the medieval etiquette of the Samurais of old Earth. To see a Kiru stride to action is both a frightening and amazing thing to behold.

Bonus Features

- **Martial Artist:** Due to their training Kirus get a +1 to all Close Combat rolls and can never botch these.

- **Perfect Strike:** A Kiru always does an additional +1 in base damage when utilizing Close Combat.

- **Lightning Speed:** Gains a +1 on their Quickness + Close Combat roll when attacking a distracted shooter when utilizing Close Combat (see Bullets vs Hoofing).

Important Aptitudes: *Attention, Quickness, Reaction*

Abilities: Athletics, Close Combat**, First Aid, Interrogation, Search*, Security, Shooting*, Stealth

Typical Variations

Assassin: *Instead of using your skills to protect and heighten security, you use them to kill and breach security. You're a highly proficient assassin working as a freelancer for the criminal syndicates or as part of a crew.*

Hired Blade: *You travel the stars, stowing away on ships. You take on a variety of jobs that require your skill-set. Bodyguard work being the most common. Only your personal honour guides you and you like being your own boss.*

Personal Bodyguard: *The ties to your employer runs deep, you were brought up together and you are fast friends as well as employer and employee. The employer who originally hired you was probably a parent of your ward.*

Spending Credits: 2500
Start-Up Credits: 1000 + 1D × 200

LED-Officer

The GIC is a machinery and all the individuals within it are cogs. However, some cogs just won't stay put and pull their weight, and this leads to a weighting down of the whole organization. You want to keep the machine well oiled and the cogs in place. And if push comes to shove, you don't mind put a bad cog or two out of commission.

Your instincts have served you well and you have always liked the shifts of scenery your work has given you. Some LED-officers just mosey on, they go on patrolling or sitting by a desk but you want to try it all. Orbit patrol, homicide division or why not TARGET? Keeping the order and the society going is a big responsibility.

LED-officers are the paramilitary police force and they're very good at what they do. They're responsible for the safety of Claret, Mondus and all GIC registered colonies, outposts and travel lanes.

LED-officers, if smart and tough enough, get a lot of opportunities to try out the variety of the LED-service. TARGET, vice, lane patrol, you name it. The best weapon they have is their versatility and instincts. There's no telling what's gonna come their way.

Bonus Feature
• **Specialized Interrogator:** LED-officers get a +1 modifier to all rolls that involve Interrogation and can never botch on these.

• **Forensic Expertise:** +1 to all Forensic rolls and they can never botch these.

• **LED-Training:** They are the only ones that have the ability to use the forensic filter array.

Important Aptitudes: Attention, Gut Feeling, Reaction

Abilities: Close Combat, Driving, Forensics*, Interrogation**, Search, Shooting*, Strategy.

Typical Variations
Stellar Forensic Technician: Freelance, corporate or GIC, it doesn't really matter. You're sent out into deep space in order to investigate violent crime. Whenever a string of murders or a murder of some magnitude occurs on the fringe you're sent out. You often find yourself thousands of light years away from the law on a ship with one or several unidentified murderers onboard.

TARGET: You might work for LED or be freelance by now but you're trained in urban warfare and explosives. Your training focuses on swift blitz attacks and strike team tactics. The skills you possess are invaluable to anyone that are in need of swift takedowns and enter and secure tactical operations.

Locator: Some years ago you left the LED behind and struck out on your own. Maybe a corporation or criminal syndicate scooped you up or you might work totally freelance. You take on missing persons cases, lost property cases and jobs that require some legwork and information gathering. There's no telling where the job takes you.

Spending Credits: 2500
Start-Up Credits: 850 + 1D × 400

Legionnaire

War. It's been your whole life. You grew up on the planet Demios in the Basala system. The GIC, CIM and MEC were everywhere, killing in the name of greed. At the age of twelve you were taken by the CIM and forced to fight the GIC. Your parents were dead and you had little choice in the matter. You saw dozens of battles and by the age of sixteen you lost count of how many people you'd killed.

During a mission your squad was ambushed and everyone was killed except you. You were able to escape badly wounded. You managed to find a dead GIC border guard. His picture in the id-card was a close enough resemblance so you simply took his uniform, gear and equipment. The GIC seldom updated their data banks out there. You called for help and were taken in by the GIC under your new identity. You fitted in there as well, sides didn't matter. Killing a man is always the same, the cause is irrelevant. At the age of twenty you had enough of the GIC so you simply took off, hitching a ride on a freighter. It didn't take long until you realized that people would pay a lot of money for the service of a skilled soldier. It seemed like every major power in the galaxy killed for money so why shouldn't you?

The Legionnaire, or lego, is a soldier of fortune. He can be hired as part of a legionnaire team or sign on with a crew for a share of the loot. What sets apart a lego from any other soldier is that he never really believed in a cause worth fighting for and in most cases he never received proper military training as such; he was forged by the circumstances of war. This doesn't mean that he's a mindless cold hearted brute, he's simply very honest about what he does. He goes to war when someone pays him enough.

Most legos do have their own code of honor, while some have none. Overall, legos have a bad rep for being merciless and greedy dogs of war. In some cases this is true but mostly they're just people trying to survive using the lessons and tools life has provided them with.

Bonus Features

- **Thick Skinned:** *A lego is very resistant to pain and count all negative modifiers due to damage or pain as one wound level less, or one negative modifier less if the pain modifier comes from another source.*

- **Saturated:** *Their bodies are extremely tolerant to stims and they're capable of taking stims five times a month without running the risk of becoming addicted and gain a +2 to resist addiction.*

- **Machines of War:** *The life they lead is a harsh one and they gain +2 to all rolls which involves endurance (running, holding their breath, etc.) and resisting toxins and pathogens. Count Severity as one level lower when using the Radiation table to determine pathogen/toxin damage.*

Important Aptitudes: *Brawn, Attention, Cool*

Abilities: Athletics*, Close Combat*, Driving, Explosives, Fringewise, First Aid, Repairs, Shooting**, Stealth, Strategy.

Typical Variations

Heavy Hitter: You specialize in being the heavy gun in teams engaging in high-end robbery and piracies. When the shit hits the fan you're there to mop up the mess.

Enforcer: The criminal gangs and syndicates' always need someone who can handle themselves in a violent situation and look scary doing it. For the most part looking scary is all you need to do but when someone can't pay what they owe you show him why he should be scared of you.

True Hired Gun: You take on jobs which have to do with all out war situations. It might be rescue ops, sabotage runs or even guerrilla warfare. As long as you get paid you keep on shooting.

Spending Credits: 4000
Start-Up Credits: 500 + 1D × 200

Marine

Rippers are filthy fucking vermin, roaches that by a fluke of nature grew bigger and a bit smarter than their smaller relatives. When you saw your first GIC-Marine Corps infomercial on the circuit at the age of six you knew you wanted to join. "GIC- Marine Corps, Been Killing Since We Were Born". The slogan stuck with you.

You joined when you were eighteen and after three years of training you were sent on your first mission: Clearing a colony from Rippers, retrieve GIC research data and rescue any survivors. The battle was fierce, you even got wounded, but nothing could beat the rush. Since then you've kept going from mission to mission. You like the feeling, the feeling of being part of something bigger and making a difference. Mankind needs a line of defense that takes on the Ripper menace head on. And you're it.

The Marines are the toughest hombres around and they know it. Marines are one of the few humans that ever come face to face with a Ripper, or a horde of cavers, and have the job of standing their ground in order to take them down. They get six weeks a year off and their contracts run for six years, not counting stasis sleep. Wherever the GIC points out danger the marines go. Often they get dropped smack down in the middle of a shitstorm. And in most cases…they love it.

Bonus Features
• **Tough as Hell:** They get a +1 modifier to withstand death, permanent damage and unconsciousness when subjected to critical hits and the target number is set at 6 instead of the standard 7.

• **Weapon Expert:** Can never botch a Shooting roll and they gain +1 to them.

• **Scanning Specialty:** Marines get +1 to the Ability Scanners when they use movement trackers.

Important Aptitudes: *Attention, Brawn, Cool.*

Abilities: *Athletics, Close Combat*, Driving, Explosives, First Aid, Scanners, Shooting**, Stealth, Strategy*.*

Typical Variations
Lifer: *The corps is your life and you have nothing else. Killing Rippers is a must and you're put in this universe to kick ass. Your squad is your family and being on your way to the next LZ is one of the best things you know.*

Soldier of Fortune: *When your contract was up you realized that if you were going to bleed you would prefer to get paid a whole lot more. As a SoF you might be part of an outfit for hire, take on illegal one man jobs or work as the source of violence on a freelance ship.*

Retired Veteran: *You have had your shares of battles and seen things no man should be forced to survive. Now you work with a freelance crew, acting as their muscle. Your looks and attitude is enough to fend off most troublemakers but those who do want to mix it up seldom live to regret it.*

Spending Credits: 3000
Start-Up Credits: 1200 + 1D × 400

Medical Technician

Medicine has always interested you, but after medical school you realized that you didn't want to be dragging your ass around in some boring hospital or medical station doing routine bed checks and administering flu shots. You decided to become a Medical Technician. It took you an extra one and a half years of studies but it was worth it.

You get to travel all over the universe investigating outbreaks of VPS, CAV and any finds that might call for Xenomorphological expertise. Of course, the job of an MT isn't exactly safe, but it's extremely exciting and you have been given the chance to unravel the medical mysteries of the void.

There's a big difference between a regular doctor and a medical technician. Medical technicians are trained to do their jobs in volatile situations such as warzones, during CAV outbreaks or as part of a rescue team responding to an emergency beacon. Only the brightest and the hardiest pass muster as they need to be both clever and physically adapt to handle the job. Many work for MRG, while others work for corporations, MEC or CIM. Some even start up their own businesses and conduct medical research and on site medical investigations for a fee on behalf of their clients.

Bonus Features

- **Expert Medical Training:** Heals +2 hit point when using First Aid or Regen.

- **Field Experience:** Three times per story a medical technician can heal 3 hit points within five minutes on a patient without the aid of any medical equipment.

- **Medical Insight:** Gains +1 to any roll dealing with their Know-How and First Aid and can never botch these.

Important Aptitudes: Brains, Cool, Quickness

Abilities: Administration, Know-How**, First Aid*, Forensics, Piloting, Scanners*, Science, Search, Xenomorphology

Typical Variations

Xenomorphologist: For whomever you work you concentrate on research revolving around Rippers, Gerions and to a certain extent mutated animals and beings. You try to derive samples, serums and analysis of these creatures that might yield important medical progress.

Psychiatric Technician: Of course you do know a lot of standard medicine as well, but you have focused your efforts on the mind. You study VPS, its effect and try to find the source of it all. You're often sent right into the middle of VPS outbreaks in order to study and calm the situations.

E&R Medic: This is the classical image the title medical technician evokes. You're sent into ships in peril to evacuate and save personnel while all hell is breaking loose. At times your orders even entail securing samples or conducting research on site.

Spending Credits: 4000
Start-Up Credits: 1000 + 1D × 200

Note: Medical technicians use Know-How whenever they perform medical work that's not First Aid. Virology, surgery, pharmacology, psychology or similar medical disciplines falls under a medical technician's Know-How.

Merc

After years in the LED, seeing the scum walk or skip bail and scurry off and jump on some cargo ship to an outer colony you'd had enough. You tossed in your shield, drank yourself miserable for a couple of months before you pulled it all together and got yourself a merc license.

Nowadays you get to hunt the scumbags down for real and you get paid well. The bastards you go after have skipped on bail, escaped from custody, or otherwise messed up big time. Since you're a merc you have the right to bear concealed weapons and a heavy shotgun if need be. Besides this you can enter private residences and other areas without a warrant if you suspect that the fugitive is on the premises.

Mercs are basically bounty hunters. Some only take legit cases and go after LED approved warrants, while others work both sides, hauling in whoever for the ones with enough creds to hire them. They're not cops, not the military but not civilians. They're simply mercs, tough as nails, relentless and they have the merc shield to prove it. Like a dog on a bone, they can chase down a profitable bounty for light-years on end.

Bonus Features

• **Combat Sense:** Being able to react quickly keeps them alive and is an instinct they have honed. They get a +1 modifier to all rolls relating to Reaction in a combat situation involving Close Combat or Shooting (using mounted weaponry or vehicle weaponry doesn't count).

• **Heightened Reflexes:** Their Reaction is counted as +1 when determining initiative.

• **Bruiser:** They get a +1 modifier to all Intimidation rolls and can't botch these.

Important Aptitudes: Attention, Cool, Reaction.

Abilities: Athletics, Close Combat*, Fast Talk, Fringewise**, Interrogation, Search, Shooting*, Stealth.

Typical Variations

Transporter: Instead of chasing after bounties as such you transport prisoners (or if you're on the shady side, kidnap victims) from one point to another. It's basically the same type of job but you usually get a steadier pay check and at times some backup from your employers.

Toe-Cutter: Not only do you track down and drag the criminals back to jail, you squeeze them dry of drugs, money or whatever else they might have, to get even more out of it. This, of course, is no ones business but yours. Needless to say, you're not that popular among the criminal elements.

Bounty-Hound: Some mercs settle to hunt small game in the core systems, but you only go after the most valuable of prey. Only large five figure bounties will do and you're ready to travel far and wide into the farthest reaches to get your hands on your mark.

Spending Credits: 3200
Start-Up Credits: 500 + 1D × 400

Operative

The visible administration and security of the GIC is impressive and grants a certain amount of safety but you know of the real threats, the ones no one else knows about. Your job is of utter importance and even if the general public would deem your methods as…questionable, you know that what you do is justified.

Many times you have no insight into the specifics of your missions. You might not know what the files you were sent to download in secrecy from the MEC contained, but you trust your superiors to put your talents to good use.

Operatives work in the shadows most of the time. Their job description can entail everything from assassinations, lifeguard duties to infiltration. In their service of ISA, they get to see and do astonishing and horrifying things. Their operations are in most cases of the utter secrecy and the general population seldom gets to see or know the dangers the ISA keeps at bay. However, living a double life in secrecy and seeing all they do without being able to tell anyone can be quite the burden.

Bonus Features

- **Infiltration Training:** +1 to all Stealth rolls and they can't botch these.

- **Security Expert:** +1 to all Security rolls and they can't botch these.

- **Perfect Bypass:** Reduction time for Security rolls are counted as double.

Important Aptitudes: Attention, Cool, Quickness.

Abilities: Close Combat, Computers*, Fast Talk, Fringewise, Interrogation, Security**, Shooting, Stealth*

Typical Variations

True Believer: You are the archetypical image of an operative. You work for GIC, MEC or other large organization and you know that they have it right. You never question your orders or ask unnecessary questions. They tell you and you do. There's nothing else.

Agent: As an agent you act a bit more open than those in deep cover. You get involved in military operations, investigations and similar endeavours acting as a liaison between the involved groups and your employer. However, in many cases you are put in place to cover things up, things you have to hide from those around you.

Rogue Operative: No one pulls your strings, and you like it that way. Black ops, wetworks whatever suits you. At times you devise your own operations, gaining access to information you can sell but a lot of times you act as an industrial spy, stealing and dealing information in the corporate world.

Spending Credits: 3500
Start-Up Credits: 1500 1D × 300

Pilot

As long as it can fly you can handle it. Being a pilot is the ultimate freedom. You sit at the helm of tons of metal capable of surpassing the speed of light. The vast reaches of space is your playground and this in itself is its own reward. Sure, you get the odd boring run of the mill job, flying a couple of delegates from Mondus to Claret, but at other times you get to fly at breakneck speeds avoiding debris and asteroids.

Many piloting jobs are tedious and repetitive, but some pilots operate with a fractured license and only their conscience guides them when it comes to taking jobs. Some own their own ship while others get paid to fly different spacecrafts. There are even some pilots that are pure mercenaries, attacking targets for a fee according to their client's instructions. Everyone can fly, but a pilot is a professional and can pull of feats in a spacecraft that others can only dream of.

Bonus Features

- **Cool Flyer:** A pilot can never be affected by environmental circumstance stress as long as he's flying and is at the helm (or if managing scanners if an Arrays Specialist).

- **Pilot Training:** A pilot gain a +1 modifier to all Piloting rolls and can never botch these.

- **Centrifuge Program:** Results rolled when blacking out is counted as two less, making a pilot much more resilient to the G-force.

Important Aptitudes: Attention, Cool, Reaction

Abilities: Computers, GLC*, Navigation, Piloting**, Repairs, Scanners*

Typical Variations

Fighter Pilot: Dogfights in the sky is your bread and butter. You never cared much for the GLC and navigation training; a short range fighter is your forte. Some fighter pilots work for the fleet or are part of corporate security escorts, while others are totally freelance and mercenary in nature.

Freelance Freighter Pilot: C-Class is your speciality, you love them. They're big but not too big. As a freelance freighter pilot you often end up piloting everything from raider ships to ships stuffed with smuggled goods. In most cases you let your gut feeling guide you on a run.

Arrays Specialist: Scanners and analysis is what you do best. You can act as a navigator, scanner expert and GLC officer. Of course, you can handle the helm quite well, but your strengths lies within navigation, GLC and scanners.

Spending Credits: 2000
Start-Up Credits: 1000 + 1D × 300

Note: Most long range pilots have a navigator that handles the main plotting out of courses and the GLCs. However, if a pilot wishes to go for long journeys all by himself he'd better be well versed in GLC, Navigation and Repairs.

Prospector

Mining and planet harvesting. These make the universe go around. Early on you wanted to be a prospector. You find the fat veins of ore and the hot pulsating cores and get a fat prospector's fee for your trouble. The actual mining is a dirty business and you're happy to leave that to the dig crews. You prospect, survey and often oversee the installment of the main mining colony and then you move on to the next job. You meet a lot of people and have seen some strange worlds in your line of work. Ripper attacks, strange artifacts and actual warzones is all part of the job when working far beyond the traveled lanes on the fringe.

The art of prospecting is a highly valued skill. There are thousands of prospectors but only a handful of really intuitive and good ones. Prospectors work and spend most of their time in really dangerous environments. They handle power tools, explosives and investigate unstable cavern systems and drill deep down into planetary crusts. All this dangerous work is often done months away from backup and without a chance of getting a message through to the employers, or anyone else for that matter, with any expediency. A lot of things can go wrong on the fringe, and only by keeping cool can a prospector survive.

Bonus Features

- **Always Calm:** *Due to being used to the worst of circumstances all prospectors get a +1 modifier when trying to withstand environmental circumstance stress and Cold.*

- **Improvised Weapons:** *They get +1 on attack rolls when using hand held mining power tools as weapons and are exempt from the penalty some of these impose when used as weapons.*

- **Geologist:** *They gain +1 to Know-How when using it to prospect and evaluate finds and can never botch these rolls.*

Important Aptitudes: *Attention, Cool, Reaction.*

Abilities: *Athletics, Know-how**, Explosives, First Aid, Repairs*, Scanners*, Search, Xenoarcheology.*

Typical Variations

Mining Operator: *The job is to establish the basic colony parameters and decide the first initial dig sites. You go in with a crew and set up shop. After the main survey team has done its job it's down to you to do the fine calibration and find the fat veins. When all is operational you go on to the next job.*

Habitat Evaluator: *There are many worlds out there that are quite liveable, those where water, vegetation and animals are found have been terraformed by humans but left and forgotten for some reason. Your job is to find these worlds and explore them. Is it suited for a mining operation, settlement or other endeavours?*

Survey Specialist: *Your job is the most basic but vital one. You get sent to a part of space and told to survey a planet. You have to go down to the surface, take samples and research and investigate them onboard your ship. The findings will act as a basis for your employers and will decide if they will start up an enterprise or not on the planet.*

Spending Credits: 2200
Start-Up Credits: 1000 + 1D × 100

Note: *Mine/planet harvesting prospecting is such a slim Ability that it hasn't been included in the actual Ability set. When making rolls in order to survey a prospector uses his Know-How.*

Raider

If you're uncle is to be believed, you were born out in the black on a C-class freight ship that your parents hijacked, all the while they were chased by the Consolidated Fleet. You don't remember your parents that much, they died when you were five as the cockpit was subjected to explosive decompression when a shot from a fleet fighter cracked it open. You managed to escape with your uncle.

The only thing you ever known was a life out in the big empty. You smuggle, steal, raid and conduct illegal salvage operations. Conforming to the GIC way of life on one of the core planets has never been an appealing thought. This is what you do best and there's no greater thrill than snagging loot right under the nose of the fleet and get away with it.

Raiders are the pirates of the void one might say. They lead a dangerous life, taking whatever job that comes their way as long as they retain their freedom. They're very versatile and their travels have resulted in a extensive network of contacts. They like it best while on a ship, not caring to much for a home on a rock somewhere.

Raiders come in all shapes and sizes, and mindsets. Some are non-violent smugglers that conduct their business with a moral code guiding them, while others are brutal cutthroats, killing off survivors on derelict ships so they can get the salvage.

Bonus Features
- **Connected:** *Twice per game session, a player of a raider can come up with a contact, or someone that owes his avatar a favor when in need. This is done in cooperation with the AI and the AI decides what's reasonable. The contact isn't added to the Resources but available during the specific session.*

- **Versatile:** *+1 bonus and a no botch possibility in an Ability of his choice.*

- **Pirate Code:** *Gains +1 on all rolls involving social interaction with other non-player raiders.*

Important Aptitudes: *Attention, Cool, Gut Feeling*

Abilities: Close Combat, Explosives, Fast Talk, Fringewise**, Piloting*, Repairs, Search, Security, Shooting*, Stealth.

Typical Variations
Pirate: *You're totally freelance and attack ships, outposts and small stations as it strikes your fancy. You sell loot to the highest bidder but for the most part you steal gear that you need to keep your ship running. The main thing is that you retain your freedom, so you seldom like to take on specific jobs from syndicates and the like.*

Corsair: *The targets you hit are always predetermined by an employer or business partner. The cut is decided before the job and you try to plan the hits as carefully as you can. You're a prudent criminal, but all kind of jobs will do as long as they're planned and come from someone with some "standing" within the criminal community.*

Smuggler: *This line of work suits you. You can run a legitimate delivery service and cash in on some extra creds by smuggling people and goods. When the heat is on, you have the opportunity to take a step back and deliver legal goods. But you know that you're a tempting target for pirates and hitters. Especially if they know that you might carry legal and illegal goods.*

Spending Credits: 3000
Start-Up Credits: 1D × 800

Science Researcher

Scientific work has probably never seen such exciting times before. Sure, all men of science most likely said that about their own time but the last hundred years has been different than all the other times. You have accesses to alien species, alien artifacts and a new dimension in the form of the Ghost Lines.

You go where the interesting research is, and where funding can be found. The universe has millions of secrets and you look to unlock them all by cutting deep into the black void with the precise edge of your craft. The Gerions biotech, the dangerous and powerful artifacts of unknown origin and the possibilities offered by nanites and electromagnetism are endless. You travel to the most remote regions of the galaxy, driven by your insatiable thirst for knowledge.

In the world of C&D there is a great distinction between a scientist and a science researcher. A science researcher is seldom stationed for long as he is more inclined to find new angles and opportunities to turn into actual science. One can say that they're the prospectors of the scientific world. They find new scientific materials and research, do the preliminary scientific work and sell the opportunity to their clients/employers. Of course, there are times when they take on more long term experiments of their own, but in most cases they sell scientific opportunities, they're the prospectors of the scientific world. Many work for companies in which case they get a monthly salary, while others operate on their own, selling the possibility of new discoveries for a fee they negotiate with their clients.

Bonus Features

- **Science Buff:** *+1 modifier to all Science rolls and can't botch these.*

- **Scientific Insight:** *Gets a +1 in Rhetoric when arguing or conveying something of a scientific nature.*

- **Versatile:** *+1 bonus and a no botch possibility in an Ability of his choice.*

Important Aptitudes: *Attention, Brains, Gut Feeling.*

Abilities: *Administration, Computers*, Forensics, Rhetoric, Scanners*, Science**, Xenoarcheology, Xenomorphology,*

Typical Variations

Aftermath Investigator: *When a scientific endeavor has gone completely awry you are sent in to find out why and if aspects of the project are salvageable. Actual reports of disasters as well as communication blackouts of multibillion research facilities are reasons that call for your attention.*

Plant: *You might be a freelance agent or a corporate spy, either way your job entails being planted for a while at a research facility under a false identity. Your job is to accumulate data and even samples of the work if possible and get it back to your clients. It's a dangerous job but the pay can be substantial.*

Artifacts Researcher: *You try to get your hands on artifacts and research their applications. However, as this is illegal in many cases you operate outside the core systems and often have to deal with dangerous environments as well as dangerous people.*

Spending Credits: 4400 + 1D × 200
Start-Up Credits: 3000

Scout

Becoming a scout seemed to be the right thing for you. Ever since you were born you had a natural aptitude for being observant and quiet. When you came of age you went through the GIC scout program and were surprised to learn that only one out of a hundred even got passed the recruiting test. For you it was so damn easy.

In the program you got some ISA training, a bit from the Marine Corp and some from the fleet, along with the stealth module algorithms. All focused on recon and stealthy long range takedowns if necessary. After three years you could be as quiet as a ghost and moved in and out of enemy territory with ease. At times you just went in for recon and at other times to tag a mark so that the fleet could bomb the crap out of it. What you see, what you report and what you mark can be pivotal in winning a war.

Scouts are not an official command of their own in the MSU, but they're not a part of the fleet, the corps or the ISA for that matter. They do have their own training facility and base of operations. Sometimes a scout is called in for a short while to be a part of a military or ISA unit. Their special training makes them more adapt at stealth, perception and sniping. Most fleet crews and marine squads have a scout or two. When they wish to have additional scouts they make a request with the MSU senator staff. Scouts are the only ones capable of handling the NETSS (Nano Environmental Tactical Stealth Suit). The mental strain of being a scout takes its toll and they have a rumor of being withdrawn and quiet. Some refer to them as shadows and think that they're down right creepy.

Bonus Features

- **Infiltration Training:** +1 to all Stealth rolls and they can't botch these.

- **Heightened Senses:** +1 to all Search rolls and they can't botch these.

- **Scout Training:** They are the only ones that can use NETSS.

Important Aptitudes: Attention, Cool, Quickness

Abilities: Athletics, Close Combat, First Aid, Interrogation, Scanners, Search*, Shooting*, Stealth**, Strategy.

Typical Variations

Sentinel: As a sentinel you're trained to work with marines and other soldiers and actually take part of the battle. You only scout ahead and give them an overview of the situation and act as their eyes and ears. When combat breaks out you often take a sniping position but have no problems with being in the thick of it.

Hunter: After you quit as a GIC scout you discovered that your abilities were well suited to hunt and track down animals. With all the mutant hybrids out there you realized that you could make a living of hunting down rare specimens for the highest bidder.

Infiltrator: Working alone is your thing, no distractions or messy entourage. You're a long range scout, often getting far behind the enemy lines where you collect data, isotope mark bomb targets or plant explosives. At times you also perform assassination jobs, freeing of prisoners of war and other types of black-ops work.

Spending Credits: 3800
Start-Up Credits: 1000 + 1D × 300

Site Engineer

You have always loved electronics, mechanics and computers. Not only have you always loved these things but you were also born with a knack to fix and understand them. You got a degree in engineering but working as one seemed way to boring. Staying on one ship or a station, or fixing broken reactor shields in Claret City, didn't really appeal to your sense of adventure. So you decided to become a site engineer.

You're shipped off all over the galaxy to different jobs. Sometimes you get to help the fleet out, or get a derelict ship going again. The money is good and you also got a special education involving advanced explosives that came with the job. Money, engineering, travels AND you get to blow things up. What's not to love?

Site engineers are not some grease monkeys or egghead types. They're smart, quick on their feet and very tough. They're sent to fix all manner of things, often in the middle of nowhere. Their job is highly dangerous as they seldom know what to expect. Their expertise in explosives lets them blow sections of hulls and separate ship segments. In many cases they're on call in a certain area, commissioned by their employer to respond to any emergency call coming from one of their ships. If the call is unspecified (just a beacon) or involves any type of engineering problem they're expected to be Johnny on the spot. Many site engineers run their own businesses.

Bonus Features

- **Technologic Insight:** Can count all repair times (not jury-rigging) as one level less in complexity.

- **Explosives Expert:** +1 to all Explosives rolls and can never botch these.

- **Engineer Training:** +1 to all Repair rolls and can never botch these.

Important Aptitudes: Brains, Attention, Quickness.

Abilities: Athletics, Computers*, Explosives*, Repairs**, Scanners, Security.

Typical Variations

E&R Engineer: As an E&R engineer you're the classic version of the site engineer. When all hell has broken loose they send you in. At times you arrive in the aftermath while you at other times show up minutes before the reactor goes critical and it's your job to fix it. You might work for the GIC, the corporation or freelance.

Engineering Executive Officer: The marines need their gear to run smoothly and you're the one who sees to that. You travel with them or other military outfits in the field, a capable soldier yourself, and you handle all the technical aspects of their job. When it comes to technical decisions you're the top dog.

Explosives Expert: You know all there is to know about explosives. Your skills involve planning all manner of jobs relating to detonations. You might travel to mining outposts, be a part of a bomb squad or you might even be the one setting the bombs in order to get your point across. You can be freelance, corporate or have any type of affiliation. You're still a capable engineer but you have devoted your learning to the art of demolitions.

Spending Credits: 3000
Start-Up Credits: 1000 + 1D × 400

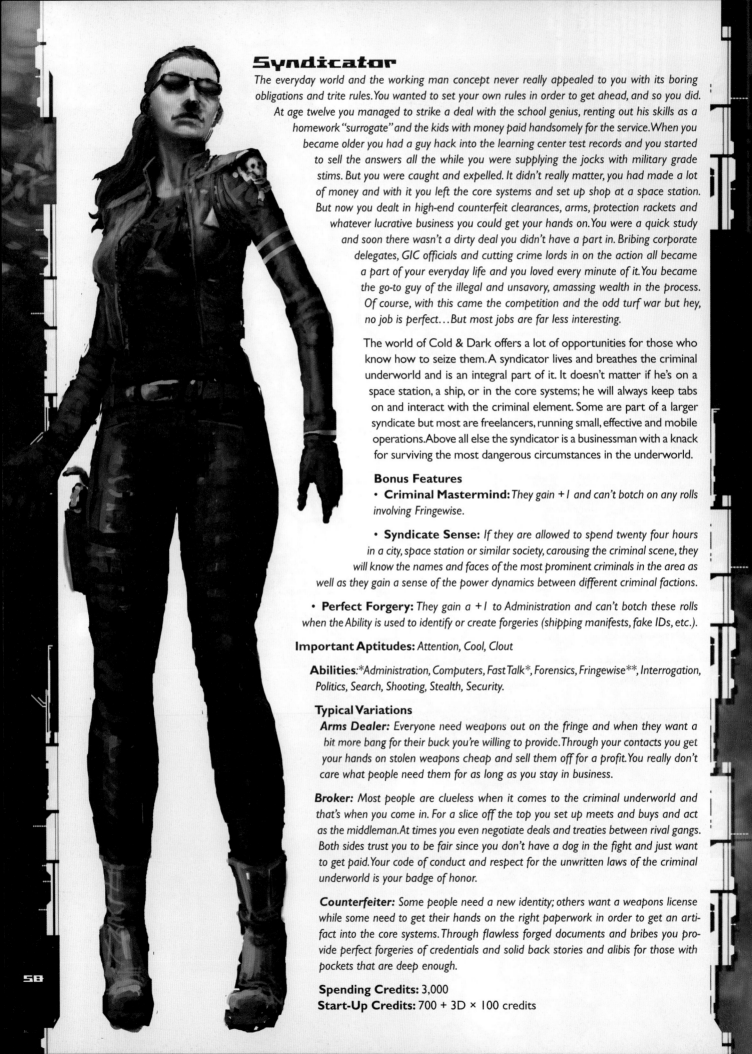

Syndicator

The everyday world and the working man concept never really appealed to you with its boring obligations and trite rules. You wanted to set your own rules in order to get ahead, and so you did. At age twelve you managed to strike a deal with the school genius, renting out his skills as a homework "surrogate" and the kids with money paid handsomely for the service. When you became older you had a guy hack into the learning center test records and you started to sell the answers all the while you were supplying the jocks with military grade stims. But you were caught and expelled. It didn't really matter, you had made a lot of money and with it you left the core systems and set up shop at a space station. But now you dealt in high-end counterfeit clearances, arms, protection rackets and whatever lucrative business you could get your hands on. You were a quick study and soon there wasn't a dirty deal you didn't have a part in. Bribing corporate delegates, GIC officials and cutting crime lords in on the action all became a part of your everyday life and you loved every minute of it. You became the go-to guy of the illegal and unsavory, amassing wealth in the process. Of course, with this came the competition and the odd turf war but hey, no job is perfect…But most jobs are far less interesting.

The world of Cold & Dark offers a lot of opportunities for those who know how to seize them. A syndicator lives and breathes the criminal underworld and is an integral part of it. It doesn't matter if he's on a space station, a ship, or in the core systems; he will always keep tabs on and interact with the criminal element. Some are part of a larger syndicate but most are freelancers, running small, effective and mobile operations. Above all else the syndicator is a businessman with a knack for surviving the most dangerous circumstances in the underworld.

Bonus Features
• **Criminal Mastermind:** *They gain +1 and can't botch on any rolls involving Fringewise.*

• **Syndicate Sense:** *If they are allowed to spend twenty four hours in a city, space station or similar society, carousing the criminal scene, they will know the names and faces of the most prominent criminals in the area as well as they gain a sense of the power dynamics between different criminal factions.*

• **Perfect Forgery:** *They gain a +1 to Administration and can't botch these rolls when the Ability is used to identify or create forgeries (shipping manifests, fake IDs, etc.).*

Important Aptitudes: *Attention, Cool, Clout*

Abilities: *Administration, Computers, Fast Talk*, Forensics, Fringewise**, Interrogation, Politics, Search, Shooting, Stealth, Security.*

Typical Variations
Arms Dealer: Everyone need weapons out on the fringe and when they want a bit more bang for their buck you're willing to provide. Through your contacts you get your hands on stolen weapons cheap and sell them off for a profit. You really don't care what people need them for as long as you stay in business.

Broker: Most people are clueless when it comes to the criminal underworld and that's when you come in. For a slice off the top you set up meets and buys and act as the middleman. At times you even negotiate deals and treaties between rival gangs. Both sides trust you to be fair since you don't have a dog in the fight and just want to get paid. Your code of conduct and respect for the unwritten laws of the criminal underworld is your badge of honor.

Counterfeiter: Some people need a new identity; others want a weapons license while some need to get their hands on the right paperwork in order to get an artifact into the core systems. Through flawless forged documents and bribes you provide perfect forgeries of credentials and solid back stories and alibis for those with pockets that are deep enough.

Spending Credits: 3,000
Start-Up Credits: 700 + 3D × 100 credits

The Kiru Lana Dharmaka armed with her custom designed two handed nanoblade.

Chapter 4: Avatars

In order to get playing, the players need to create an avatar. This is their alter ego in the game world. The avatar has a personality, a background and knowledge and skills he can use. These details are recorded on the interface, which the player uses to keep track of the avatar's stats and vitals. There are several things to record on an interface, but foremost there are two vital things: *Aptitudes* and *Abilities*.

Buying Aptitudes and Abilities

When creating an avatar, all purchases are done on a one-for-one basis up to rank three. This is true for both Aptitudes and Abilities. For example, if you spend 3 Aptitude points on Brains, you'll get an increase of 3 in your Brains score. Buying from rank 4 to 5 cost 2 points when dealing with Aptitudes. Everyone starts with one rank in each Aptitude.

Abilities work a bit differently. Buying Ability ranks higher than 3 costs 2 points per rank. So if you have rank 3 and want to buy rank 4, you'll have to spend an additional 2 points when buying Abilities. This means that it will cost you a total of 5 points to get a rank of 4 (3 points for rank 3, and 2 points for rank 4).

Buy Points
Aptitudes: 12
Abilities: 22

Derived Traits

Defense

This trait helps your avatar stay out of the way of close combat attacks and thrown projectiles. Defense is derived by adding the avatar's Reaction to his Quickness and comparing the result to the table below. See the section on combat for more information on defense.

Defense	
Quickness + Reaction	Defense
1–2	1
3–5	2
6–8	3
9	4
10	5

Carrying Capacity

With adequate and non-encumbering bags, straps and holsters to carry equipment, an avatar can carry his Brawn × 5 kg without being encumbered. Every kilo of weight beyond this will reduce his movement by 3 and every five kilos beyond that limit will inflict a −1 penalty to Quickness and Athletics.

Carrying equipment in an encumbering fashion (several weapons slung over the shoulder, dangling items tied to the belt, etc.) can cause these negative effects even if the avatar's carrying capacity hasn't been exceeded. The AI has to judge these situations on a case by case basis.

Movement

Movement equals Quickness +10 if running, or Quickness +20 if sprinting, in meters. When engaging in stealth, walking or dragging a heavy object, the movement rate is only 5 meters per segment.

Health

Health is used to keep track of your avatar's physical status. As you can see, it's divided into Fatal and Bashing damage. Under the "Scratched" health section there are five parallel dots. Fill in as many of these (in both Bashing and Fatal) as you have Brawn. Every avatar has four plus his Brawn in Scratched/Bruised hit point dots.

Credibility

This defines your social presence and endurance during negotiations, debates and similar situations. Your credibility equals your Clout × 3.

Resources

If the AI hasn't set special circumstances, every avatar has a typical living standard. They have a place to live, a couple of friends, some clothes and some everyday stuff. Resources grants things such as extra gear, contacts or financial resources. The AI has final say when it comes to resources, as some of them might change the entire dynamic of the game. A rank five in the resource Sway would work best in a game of high-end political nature where the avatars will get deeply involved. Each player can spend 7 *resource points*. The listed resources are bought on a one-for-one basis.

It's also possible to spend resource points to increase the rank of Abilities and Aptitudes. Three resource points will grant you an additional point to spend on Aptitudes, while two resource points can be spent for an additional Ability point, and finally, one resource point can be spent to gain an additional specialty.

Resource	
Resource Points	Increase
3	+1 Aptitude
2	+1 Ability
1	+1 Specialty
1	+1 Resource

Access

For starters, the avatar needs at least rank 1 in the Computers Ability in order to buy this resource. Access shows how many backdoors, hack-points and restricted systems a person can access on *The Circuit*. Why a person has this access varies. An active GIC operative may have been given clearance by ISA, while a freelance site engineer has cultivated this access illegally over the years. It also shows how well a person knows the weaknesses of any computer system. Access is used up during chapters, but replenishes during each new chapter. Each point of access burnt gives a +2 modifier to any computer roll which entails hacking, information gathering or the changing of protocols and overrides. When spending access points, automatic success is granted even under stress.

Allies

Allies are friends that you can trust to help you, and they expect the same from you. They can provide safe haven, information and job offerings. Allies are never very powerful as such, but are probably pretty average people that you know from your line of work or from your earlier days. Each dot represents an ally. The player and the AI have to work out the ally's exact details.

Contacts

With contacts you have a more mercenary relationship than with allies. Contacts are often in a position that's useful to your avatar. Crime bosses, influential delegates from the forum or maybe even a contact in ISA. But information, equipment or whatever the contact can provide isn't free. Cold cash or a favor in return of equal value is the usual deal. Contacts don't owe you a thing, and they're not your friends and they will not jeopardize themselves for crumbs. Each dot represents a single contact that you have and the AI has the final say on a contact's position of influence. A senator's aide might be okay, while a senator might be a bit over the top. Both contacts and allies can be lost and gained during play.

Economy

You might have inherited money, saved up or won the lottery. Whatever the reason you have a stack of cash tucked away that exceeds your normal means. This money can only be spent after the game has begun.

A rogue scout geared up for the field.

Economy	
* 5000 cr	
** 8000 cr	
*** 15,0000 cr	
**** 25,0000 cr	
***** 50,000 cr	

Gear

There is a large variety of special equipment available, and Gear shows what kinds of such equipment you own from the start. This gear is either specially designed or so expensive or rare that an avatar wouldn't ordinarily be able to have access to it from the start. The gear is often unique in some way. The gear listed here are just examples that can be used as guides for the AI and the player when creating their own to fit their campaign and stories. COGs are not covered under Gear.

Gear
* Rather insignificant but useful device, like a lingo sphere with ten human languages programmed in.
** An experimental gun with a nano pod which can transform normal ammunition to stun or armor piercing rounds with the push of a button before firing.

*** *Experimental A-class ship with a built-in micro VIN.*

**** *B-class civilian spaceship, complete with a built-in VIN.*

***** *C- class civilian spaceship with a VIN, RT-Drive and stasis units (no ghost drive).*

ID

You have accumulated several identities apart from your own. These documents and files are first-rate forgeries and stand up to any scrutiny. Where and why you got these documents varies from character to character. A GIC employee might have gotten them as a part of his job, while a raider probably used his contacts to obtain them. Each dot gives you an extra identity. These can be very useful at times.

Sway

This reflects your political pull in the GIC. You have a say in the halls of power and your word carries some weight. How you gained your sway varies between individuals. Maybe you bribed your way in, or just earned it the legal way. Each dot expands your sphere of sway as well as gives you a certain notoriety.

Sway can be very useful. At level one you might only get box seats for the big games in Mondus or Claret through your political sway, while at the highest level you are a factor in making decisions in war situations.

Sway can be divided into several sub-groups. The AI and the players must decide what works for them but here are some suggestions: Marine Corps, Consolidated Fleet, Church of Infinitology, ISA, LED, Raider Guilds, Kiru Guilds, Merc Guilds, General Local Sway (Xindos, Stoneshade, etc.)

The sway works similar to the GIC sway but differs in some ways. Having sway in ISA will not necessarily make anyone recognize you, given the nature of the agency. Having sway within the Raider Guilds won't make people on the street recognize you, or even other raiders if they haven't met you before, but they will know your name and heard of your escapades. The downside is that LED and some fleet personnel probably have heard of you as well. It's a fine balance and it's up to you to make it work.

Sway

* *You might have been an aide on the campaign trail; you don't have that much influence and a few people in the Inner City might recognize your face.*

** *The advice you have given has proven to be quite astute. Some people recognize your face in the Inner City and the Nimbus. A few even remember your name.*

*** *Everyone working with politics on Claret and Mondus knows your name and that your political knowledge is extensive and that your advice often hits the mark. Most people on Mondus and Claret know your face and some know your name. You might be an extremely prominent forum member.*

**** *Everyone that has access to the Circuit knows your name and face. You are very influential and even the members of the senate know who you are. You might be one of the six leading forum delegates.*

***** *Everyone that has heard of the GIC recognizes your name and face. If you're not the main envoy of a senator, you have somehow reached the same political prominence.*

Team

The avatar has one or more team members. The reasons behind why they have joined him vary just as much as the characters themselves. Maybe they're old war buddies, apprentices, or maybe they're just friends that live on his ship (if he has one) and in return they provide their aid as engineers, cooks or whatever.

Team members are Non-Player Avatars. They often have a couple of useful Abilities which are helpful to the avatar. A freelance pilot would do good to shack up with a navigator that is schooled in GLCs for example. Each dot represents a team member with a certain use (navigator, an engineer, etc.) and a narrow repertoire. Alternately, you can spend two dots for a team member that's specialized but a bit more versatile (like an ex-Marine gone navigator, perhaps with some combat Abilities as well).

Linguistics

Every avatar gets two languages for free. They're fluent in *Intra* and their own language (Spanish, Russian, English, etc.). Each dot in Linguistics gives them fluency in an additional language.

COG

This resource gives you access to a COG and some applications for it from the outset. Each level will specify how much COG equipment the avatar will have access to at the start of the game. Instead of buying an extra NAP (nano application), the player can choose to upgrade NAPs he already has in the COG. So, at level two he can choose to have a level two NAP instead of two level one applications (see *equipment* for more information on COGs)

COG

* *Pick a COG worth 3000 cr*

*** *Pick a COG worth 3000 cr, plus three NAPs, or a NETSS, or a TCI (battle or flight) with a (flight) scanner link upgrade or (battle) strategy upgrade.*

**** *Pick a COG worth 3000 cr, plus four NAPs, or a NETSS with two NAPs or a TCI (battle or flight) with a (flight) scanner link upgrade or (battle) a strategy upgrade, and a non-TCI-specific NAP (visor, array, etc).*

**** *Pick a COG worth 3000 cr, plus four NAPs, or a NETSS with two NAPs or a TCI (battle or flight) with a (flight) scanner link upgrade or (battle) a strategy upgrade, and a non-TCI-specific NAP (visor, array, etc).*

***** *Pick a COG worth 3000 cr, plus five NAPs, or a NETSS with three NAPs, or a TCI (battle or flight) with two (flight) scanner link upgrades or (battle) two strategy upgrades, and two non-TCI specific naps (visor, array, etc).*

Specialties

Every avatar also gets to pick two specialties. Each specialty represents the Ability to re-roll an 8. So if an 8 comes up on the die, it is counted as a success and then re-rolled. This means that 8s can result in additional successes. *You can only re-roll as many 8s as you have active specialties.* As a prerequisite for taking a specialty, the avatar must have a score of at least 2 in the Ability.

Specialties must be specific to a certain degree. If the avatar wants to have the Shooting Ability as a specialty, he has to specify a special maneuver or weapon. Sniping or auto-fire are examples of maneuvers that can be used as specialties. Carbines or shotguns can also be used as a specialty. This means that an avatar can have multiple specialties within the same Ability and can buy the same specialty multiple times to heighten the re-roll chance with that specialty. Re-rolled dice are exempt from botches. No more than four specialties can be active during the same roll, which means that no more than four re-rolls can be made at any one time.

Example: Gith has rifles and sniping as specialties. He's using a rifle to snipe a guard, which means that both of his specialties are active. He rolls and scores two 8s and one 7. The 8s are re-rolled since two specialties are active. The re-roll results in a 5 and another 8, one additional success. Since he has no more specialties active for the roll, the 8 isn't re-rolled but counts as a normal success.

Save Points

Each avatar begins the game with three save points. These can be spent during play in one of two ways. They can be spent to guarantee success in a crucial moment or after the fact in order to get a do-over (you have to spend the point immediately after the failure) if the avatar was killed, suffered severe damage, or fails in a way that will have a profoundly negative effect.

In cases where the player spends the point to succeed with a certain series of actions, he gets to narrate the result. Always remember that the point only can be spent in a way that's reasonable for the avatar and entertaining (ultimately decided by the AI). A player may spend a point to have his avatar (not even familiar with the Piloting Ability) crash-land a ship in order to keep everyone alive, while the point couldn't be spent for him to fly the thing in zigzag and kill off two following fighters. On the other hand, a skilled pilot might spend the save point to pull off the above action. It's all about balance, tactics and entertainment value.

Example 1 (save point spent after the fact): The operative, Eric Starkwood, has encountered a problem. While he tried to circumvent the security system on a SES lab, he failed and tripped the alarm. Guards will be swarming any minute. The player says that he wants to spend a save point after the fact. The AI approves and the game skips back to the moment just before he started to work on the security panel.

Example 2 (save point spent for automatic success): Lee Wei has a shot starboard engine, his fighter is on fire and his weapon systems are malfunctioning. His only chance is to shake off the fighter following him. They're flying through all kinds of debris. The player of Lee Wei says that he wishes to spend a save point to kill off/incapacitate his opponent by using his surroundings. The AI allows it and the player narrates how he lures his opponent into the debris, sends some of it spinning by winging it with fire and it crashes into his opponent, who loses his course and one of his engines.

Fleshing it out

C&D isn't a game that builds its stories and mood that much on personal background connected to the avatars, at least not as a general rule. But it can be good to have a grasp of the avatar's past. This makes it easier to understand his personality and views, as well as it will help the AI with the level design to a certain degree. For example, if an avatar has a score to settle with an organisation or individual this can work as a premise and motivator when playing a level. Below are some sample questions that might be helpful answering.

- Where were you born?
- Do you have any family or close friends?
- Are you religious/what's your attitude toward religion (infinitology especially)?
- If you would describe your personality with three words, what would they be?
- What's your sexual orientation?
- What's your stand on ethnicity?
- What's your take on Gerions?
- How do you view the GIC and the corporations?
- Have any opinions about MEC and CIM?
- How do you spend your spare time?
- Have any great tragedies occurred in your life?
- Do you have any enemies that you know of?

The Team

Your gaming group should sit down and decide what kind of game they want to play and the players should create their avatars accordingly. Do they want to work for the GIC, a fringe organization or totally freelance? The gaming group should also discuss what kinds of stories they want to tell in the game. Are they focusing on military campaigns, raider stories or scientific excursions? They should create avatars who can work together, which they find interesting and which have the appropriate skill-set. A simple sentence describing what they want out of the game (or a session) is usually enough and can act as a rudder for the AI. Here are some examples:

- High-end assassinations and espionage.
- Intense small squad military operations.
- Dangerous salvage operations with horror and mystery aspects.
- Political manipulation and campaigning.
- Unraveling deadly conspiracies involving corruption and murder mysteries on the fringe.

A single sentence of this nature can go a long way in crystallizing an answer to the question "What are we supposed to do in this game?"

Anchoring

The avatars should have a place they call home. Not that they need to actually live there, but it's a place to which they often return and where they have connections. Resources such as allies and contacts can be very hard to manage without a recurring location, and odds are that they will be able to keep more useful connections if they have a place to use as a base.

Creating an avatar: Step by Step

1) Consult with the AI and select a package. This will give you a framework and some direction when creating the rest of your avatar. Then decide gender and pick a name for your avatar and record 3 save points. Also figure out an approximate age, 20 to 60 is a good span when deciding age for these space travelling daredevils. This is of course real age, not counting time spent in stasis. Under "Avatar" you fill in the name you have chosen.

2) Spend 12 points on your Aptitudes, some might be more important than others depending on the package. The cost is a one for one basis. Buying from 4 to 5 costs 2 points though. Fill in your movement. Run 10 + Quickness, Sprint 20 + Quickness. Fill out your Credibility (Clout × 3). Carrying Capacity equals Brawn × 5 kg and use the Defence table to calculate your Defence.

3) Fill in the health marker dots according to your Brawn. If you have 3 in Brawn, fill in 3 of the dots and so forth.

4) Spend 22 point on your Abilities. The package stipulates that 4 points has to be spent on core Abilities. You have to buy these to a rank predetermined by the particular package as these are pivotal. This means that you have 4 core Ability points and 18 free Ability points. Buying Abilities are done at a one for one basis, but buying from rank 3 to 4 (and 4 to 5) costs 2. Also, choose two specialities, prerequisite rank 2 in the Abilities in question.

5) Spend 7 resource points. Resources available to your avatar are **Access, Allies, Contacts, COG, Economy, Gear, ID, Sway, Team** and **Linguistics** and you can also use these points to get higher scores in Aptitudes and Abilities. Record start-up gear (which you buy for Spending Credits) and calculate Start-Up Credits.

Example of Avatar Creation

1) Tess sits down with the AI and is about to create an avatar. The AI tells her that he has planned a campaign which will make use of the *Dead in the Dark* setting with a lot of conspiracy elements. Tess scrolls through the Packages and *Operative* catches her eye. She asks if it would be okay if she played a Rogue Operative. The AI happily allows it. What Tess doesn't know is that a NPA named Eric Starkwood, a GIC True Believer Operative, will become their unwilling allied and the operative connection can be used to further develop the story. Tess prints out an interface and starts building her avatar. Last time she played her avatar was a guy, so she decides to play a woman this time. The C&D universe is extremely ethnically mixed and she wants to take advantage of this to create an interesting avatar. She decides that her mother was half Spanish and half Russian, while her father was half African and half Japanese. She settles on the name Anya Mikado Cervantes. Well, at least it displays her ethnic mix to a certain degree. For a second language she chooses Japanese (all avatars gets the language *Intra* plus a family related language). So she speaks Intra and Japanese fluently. Anya is 29 years old.

2) She then has 12 points to spend on her Aptitudes (all are at rank 1 from the start). The operative package states that *Attention, Cool* and *Quickness* might come in handy. So she starts with them. Quickness really appeals to her as she already has envisioned Anya as a very dexterous avatar with a passion for martial arts. She spends 3 points and gets a rank of 4 in Quickness. She then spends 2 points on Attention and 2 points on Cool, giving her a rank of 3 in both of these Aptitudes. Now she only has 5 points left to spend. She spends one on every remaining Aptitude and ends up with rank 2 in them. Anya is now extremely quick and nimble, her level 3 in Cool makes her very stable and jaded and with a level 3 in Attention she is very perceptive and has a natural knack for firearms. She has average stats in Brains, Brawn, Reaction, Gut Feeling and Clout with rank 2 in all of them. Tess would like her avatar to have a little more Brains since she wants to be a first class hacker and she says she will spend 3 of her Resource Points right away to increase her rank in Brains with 1. The AI lets her and she now has rank 3 in Brains. Anya is turning out to be quite the elite specimen.

3) She then records her carrying capacity (Brawn × 5 kg), Movement (Run 10 + Quickness, Sprint 20 + Quickness) and her credibility (Clout × 3) and Defence (Quickness + Reaction compared on the *defence table*). She records that she has 3 save points like every avatar has when starting out.

Now she fills in her health. She has 4 + Brawn amount of hit points in the Scratched and Bruised wound levels, which gives her 6. Tess marks it so she can track it during play.

Tess now sits down with the Abilities. She has 22 points to spend, but 4 of these are devoted to core Abilities. Her package dictates that she has to spend 1 on Computers, 2 on Security and 1 on Stealth. These are Abilities that lies at the core of the operative package. Tess fills in the dots and then ponders how she will spend her remaining 18 points. She starts out by spending 2 points on Computers and 1 on Security. She then moves on and spends 1 on Stealth and 2 on Athletics. She now has 12 points left. She spends 2 on Search, 2 on Close Combat and 2 on Shooting. Now she's down to only 6 points and slows down and starts to think harder about her decisions. She thinks about what kind of operative Anya is. Which kind of clients does she take on and what kind of jobs does she do? Tess decides that Anya in most cases finds out what is of value, goes in on her own (if not in need of funding in which case she offers her service to a client, usually non-politically involved criminals) and sells the information to the highest bidder. Tess spends 3 points on Fringewise as knowing what's what is her bread and butter. She also spends 2 points on Interrogation as she deals in information a lot and finally she spends 1 on Piloting. With her high score in Attention and Quickness she makes for an okay Pilot and as she often works alone it is vital for her to be able to boost and pilot a ship in order to escape. She would have liked to invest some points in Know-How as this would have given her more insight into GIC operative procedure but she can still make rolls using the associated Aptitude and she has 3 in Brains and will rely on this in the meanwhile. Tess then records her package bonuses (**Infiltration Training:** *+1 to all Stealth rolls and she can't botch these,* **Security Expert:** *+1 to all Security rolls and she can't botch these,* **Perfect Bypass:** *reduction time for Security rolls are counted as double.*)

4) After this she can choose two specialties, provided that she has a rank of 2 in the Ability she wants to specialize in. She chooses *Bypass Electronic Circuitry* (using the Ability list rolls as a mould for specialties) as a Security speciality. Being extra good at disconnecting and bypassing alarms and cameras could come quite in handy. She then chooses *Hack Security Barrier* as a speciality under the Ability Computer. She documents the specialties on the interface. Tess looks over her avatar and is quite satisfied so far. Anya is a smart, fast and deadly security specialist and high level hacker. Pretty good operative material. She can gather information, knows her way around the criminal element and can pilot a ship in a pinch.

5) It's now time for her to spend her resource points. A player gets 7 points, Tess has however already spent 3 of her points to get an extra boost to Brains. So she has 4 left. She definitely wants a COG. Being an operative she decides to buy an Adaptable Encounter Skin (AES COG). She spends 1 point and for this she gets the COG but nothing else. Tess will upgrade it during play, at least she has the basic suit. She then spends 1 on Contacts. Together with the AI she decides that her contact is a high level Deltronix employee for whom she often has done some industrial espionage for. She then spends 1 point on Team. Her sidekick is a medical technician. She saved his life on a mission and since then they have worked together, he receives 20 percent of her earnings and patches her up when she needs it. Quite a useful guy to have around in the aftermath. She uses her last point to buy Identity. Her id is that of Taki Hitomi, a low level GIC computer technician. This will give her a reason to show up in different facilities under the guise of doing a routine (provided she manages to wrestle up the paperwork that is) system checkup and enables her to keep a low profile in general if she wants to. Tess also has 3200 cr to spend according to her package and uses it to buy some basic equipment (silenced pistol, ammo, wakisashi, lock picks, computer, bypass kit and so forth) when she's done she calculates her starting credits (which only can be spent after the game session has started) which is 1500 1D × 300. She ends up with 2700 credits in her pocket. Together with the AI Tess fills in the fleshing out list. After this Anya Mikado Cervantes is ready to be plunged into to the Cold & Dark universe and face the vastness…

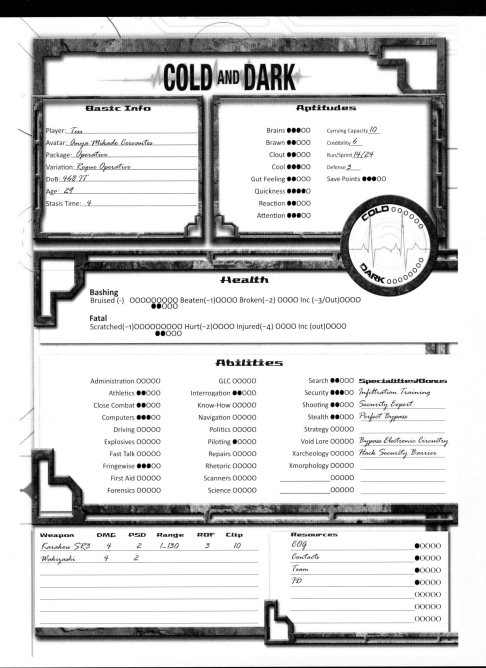

COLD AND DARK

Basic Info

Player: *Tess*
Avatar: *Anya Mikado Cervantes*
Package: *Operative*
Variation: *Rogue Operative*
DoB: *468 IT*
Age: *29*
Stasis Time: *4*

Aptitudes

Brains ●●●○○	Carrying Capacity *10*
Brawn ●●○○○	Credibility *6*
Clout ●●○○○	Run/Sprint *14/24*
Cool ●●●○○	Defense *3*
Gut Feeling ●●○○○	Save Points ●●●○○
Quickness ●●●●○	
Reaction ●●○○○	
Attention ●●●○○	

COLD ○○○○○○○
DARK ○○○○○○○

Health

Bashing
Bruised (-) OOOOOOOOO ●●OOO Beaten(–1)OOOO Broken(–2) OOOO Inc (–3/Out)OOOO

Fatal
Scratched(–1)OOOOOOOOO ●●OOO Hurt(–2)OOOO Injured(–4) OOOO Inc (out)OOOO

Abilities

Administration OOOOO	GLC OOOOO	Search ●●OOO	**Specialities/Bonus**
Athletics ●●OOO	Interrogation ●●OOO	Security ●●●OO	*Infiltration Training*
Close Combat ●●OOO	Know-How OOOOO	Shooting ●●OOO	*Security Expert*
Computers ●●●●O	Navigation OOOOO	Stealth ●●OOO	*Perfect Bypass*
Driving OOOOO	Politics OOOOO	Strategy OOOOO	
Explosives OOOOO	Piloting ●OOOO	Void Lore OOOOO	*Bypass Electronic Circuitry*
Fast Talk OOOOO	Repairs OOOOO	Xarcheology OOOOO	*Hack Security Barrier*
Fringewise ●●●OO	Rhetoric OOOOO	Xmorphology OOOOO	
First Aid OOOOO	Scanners OOOOO	OOOOO	
Forensics OOOOO	Science OOOOO	OOOOO	

Weapon	DMG	PSD	Range	ROF	Clip
Karakow SR3	4	2	1–130	3	10
Wakizashi	4	2			

Resources	
COG	●OOOO
Contacts	●OOOO
Team	●OOOO
ID	●OOOO
	OOOOO
	OOOOO
	OOOOO

Chapter 5: Actions That Needs Detailing

This section will describe some typical actions. The Aptitudes needed for an action are listed under the Abilities. The text below will give you an indication of how to handle some situations common to C&D.

Computer Systems

Whether you want to hack for information or rewrite security protocols, you will use the Computer Ability. Computer systems are divided into types, and each system type has a number attached to it. This number is used in a contested test if the hacker fails (the system versus the hacker's Reaction + Computer), and represents the system's defence mechanism (this is the defensive pool of the system). If the computer wins, it has traced the hacker. The hacker also suffers –2 on his next try as the system has upgraded itself (however, if the hacker spoofed the system beforehand, the trace and the negative modifier doesn't apply the first time he fails). The reset time shows how long it takes for the system to let its guard down again after the hacker has left the system. The AI decides how advanced a defensive system is, in order to determine the defensive pool. Usually, it runs from a pool of 3, for simple systems, to a pool of 8 for the most advanced. Simple and standard systems, found in low security municipal institutions and in home networks, seldom have a defensive mechanism of this nature. When the hacker is inside, the system does a cycle every 1–10 minutes depending on the level of security. Each cycle, a new contested test must be made. If the system wins, it locks out the hacker and only after the reset time has run out will the hacker be able to try again.

Note on computer systems: Computer systems can be used to tap into information, take control of things such as docking procedures and a variety of other systems. However, security alarms, cameras and doors are seldom connected to the overall computer system, and in most cases you must access these things directly, using security panels. Many systems are divided into subsystems, which means that there is seldom a way to take over an entire ship or space station by accessing a mainframe. For example, a ship's mainframe can be used to tap into about ninety percent of the ship's relevant information (camera feeds, propulsion systems data and the like), but can only be used to control about a third of the systems at best. And a lot of information (secure files) must be hacked into separately. First, the main system needs to be hacked and then the sub-filing system must be breached.

When computer systems are an important part of the story, you should spend some time designing them so as to make the hacking elements as compelling as possible. You can even decide that some systems are so difficult to hack that the hacker receives a negative modifier when hacking them.

Example: Operative Eric Starkwood is hacking away at the shipping manifest database on a D-class freighter. The system is a standard one, which gives it a base time of 20, minimum time of 10 minutes, reduction time of 2 minutes and a reset time of 3 (the AI went for the minimum) minutes. The AI has decided that the system is a bit beefed up; it has a defensive pool of 5 and it also does a cycle every five minutes. Eric has a total pool of 6 (Brains

Rook, Gith and Seeley on the broken hull of the Kagetsu.

Computer Systems

System Type	Base Time	Minimum Time	Reduction Time	Reset Time
Simple	10 min	2 min	2 min	2 min
Standard	20 min	10 min	2 min	3–6 min
Advanced	40 min	20 min	5 min	6–10 min

+ Computers). He scores three successes, reducing the time by a total of 6 minutes. Thus, it takes him 14 minutes to get inside the system. He downloads some information and after five minutes the system does a cycle. This means that Eric has to beat or match the system's defensive pool of 5 in a contested roll. The roll is made, but the system wins by one success. It locks him out and Starkwood can't attempt a hack until the reset time has run out, but the system probably traced his access point on the ship. He won't get another chance right now with a security force on its way, but he got hold of some of the information he was after.

Security Systems

Security systems are divided into three types, which are decided by their advancement and scale. If the bypass roll fails, the avatar has one chance to circumvent it (this counts as an environmental stress type situation). The same system is used as in the contested test made to determine if a computer discovers a hacker. Security systems have a set defensive pool, according to type.

Example: Laina is bypassing a security system. The base time for doing so is 10 minutes and the reduction time is 1 minute. This means that each success shaves off 1 minute from the base time. The player of Laina scores two successes, which means it takes Laina a total of 8 minutes of fiddling around with the system's circuitry before the door opens and the alarm is disabled.

Docking and Boarding

If a ship is big enough and has space, a smaller vessel can simply fly into its docking bay. When two ships wish to dock with each other, they can lock onto each other's outer airlock. All ships (except A-class) have an adaptable outer airlock ring. This is made from a carbon fiber polymer woven with titanium fibers and magnetic nanites. If both ships are willing to dock, these rings lock onto each other and create a sealed tunnel between the ships, roughly one hundred meters long. Docking with another ship when both ships are cooperating and the circumstances are ideal seldom requires a roll if the pilot has at least 2 in Piloting. Negative modifiers apply depending on outer circumstances (environmental stress, damaged ship, etc.), but there are two that are specific to docking.

Boarding a hostile ship often means that you need to get crew members on her hull, actually cutting through the hull or an airlock. The best way is to have someone bypass the security

of the airlock in order to avoid harming the ship, if the boarding party wants it intact. Jet packs and grappling hooks and a whole lot of danger are usually on the menu. Imagine hurtling toward a ship from another one in mid-space, hanging on by a line…

Docking

Circumstance	Modifier
Docking withtunmanned ship	*– 1*

Scanners

The difficulty in reading and using scanners varies, depending on the severity of local conditions. Successes indicate how well a person can interpret the scan. If conditions are ideal and the scanner is advanced, no roll is needed when the user has at least a score of one in the Scanners Ability. Otherwise, each rolled success represents a percentage of the available information from the scan, which becomes available to the user. The percentage per success indicates how severe the conditions are (intensity of interference). Very advanced scanners (the more detailed and long ranged, the more advanced the scanner) can take thirty seconds to a minute to calibrate, while the simpler ones just take a second or two to read.

Signal Scanners: When conditions are poor, the Scanners Ability and the system are also used when sending and receiving radio transmissions. The devices used are called signal scanners and are vital when it comes to deep space exploration. They are used to detect, jam and strengthen signals. If someone wants to jam another signal, he must first be in range and locate the signal in question. Once that is accomplished, there is a contested roll between the two scanner operators (often the navigators), Brains + Scanners vs. Brains + Scanners. For every success by which the "jammer" beats the opposition, he will jam the signal for 20 seconds. Each success by which the sender beats the jammer will give 20 seconds of sending time. During this time, the active parties can't concentrate on much other than managing the scanners. When the jam/sending time is up, new rolls are made if one party is still trying to jam another's signal.

Chasing the Dragon: This system is employed when trying to hide or leave the dragon's tail (see *piloting the ghost*). If one wants to leave a dragon's tail, every success allows it to

Security Systems

System Type	Base Time	Minimum Time	Reduction Time	Defensive Pool
Simple: Mechanical lock, simple electronic lock or alarm.	1 min	20 sec	20 sec	3
Standard: A more advanced system or electronic lock mechanism.	10 min	5 min	1 min	5
Advanced: Extremely advanced system, military grade mechanisms.	30 min	10 min	5 min	8

Engineer jury rigging in a hostile environment.

linger for another 20 seconds, and the successes add a positive modifier to the attempts of anyone that wants to follow. If the navigator wants to hide the dragon's tail, every success will act as a negative modifier to tracking attempts by others, and will shave off 20 seconds from the time it lingers (minimum 1 minute linger time). Tracking a dragon tail takes thirty seconds per roll.

> When employing the rules listed under Signal Scanners and the Chasing the Dragon section above, a negative modifier applies instead of the percentage system when affected by disturbance: Slight Disturbance −1, Bad Conditions −2, Intense Disturbance −3, Extremely Bad Conditions −4, Good Luck! −5.
>
> There are many ways that a ship can try to avoid scanners or confuse them. Powering down a ship, hiding within a highly magnetic asteroid field or slipping in behind a moon are all things that can help a ship stay off the grid, in a pinch.

Example 1: Science Officer Allison Cheng is using the bio-scanner on her Archimedes survey ship to scan an odd-looking system of caves down on the planetary surface. However, there's an electrical storm in the area which messes up the readings. The AI decides that this constitutes Bad Conditions. Cheng has a dice pool of 5 in Attention + Scanners. The player makes the roll and gets two successes. The AI tells her that she can read up to four separate life-forms inside the structure. The player has no idea of exactly how bad the conditions are and is unaware that she only has seen about 60% of what there really is to see. In reality, there are a total of seven life-forms in the caverns.

Example 2: Boris Diral is the communications and navigations officer on a deep space survey ship. The crew has just discovered a raider ship and want to blow it out of the sky before it calls for backup. Boris has a score of 5 when it comes to Brains + Scanners, while the raiders have 5 as well. Boris' player rolls the dice and gets two successes, while the raiders fail. Since each success gives 20 seconds of interference, he has now effectively jammed them for

40 seconds (roughly 15 segments). Hopefully they'll be able to blow the raiders to pieces during this time. However, if Boris was to stop calibrating the signal scanner, the raiders would be able to send.

Jury-rigging

This is the art of temporarily fixing something. Sometimes it can hold for a longer time but look a bit out of whack, but at other times a fix can only hold for a short while and actually damage the device even more, even become a danger. Jury-rigging is only done when something is so messed up that it begins to fail, but when it really needs to work. Vehicles can be jury-rigged after they have reached the *battered* level. When the object breaks down again (if not properly fixed), the AI rolls with 1D on the *wear and tear chart*, starting from the level of damage it sustained before being rigged.

How long it stays fixed depends on the amount of successes the player scores. The more successes, the longer it stays fixed. The time something stays fixed isn't measured in direct time as such, rather it's measured in duration. If a device needs to hold for a certain period, the duration show the length of time the device will hold before needing to be fixed/rigged again. Each success adds a percentage of the duration needed. This is a rather abstract system and it has been designed to deal with the extremely variable situations of jury-rigging. Jury-rigging a clutch in a car that has to run for a couple of minutes is quite different from jury-rigging a ghost drive. Remember that each new roll recalculates from the "functional time" already accumulated.

When something is jury-rigged, it counts as one or two levels less damaged than it is (roll 1D, 1–4 equals one level less damaged, 4–8 two levels). Jury-rigging can be done pretty quickly. A big problem that takes days to fix properly might take just hours, or even minutes, to jury-rig. Ultimately, the exact amount of time should be decided by the AI depending on the situation.

Example: Smash, an engineer, is trying to fix a banged-up ship. The C-class ship is at the Torn damage level and their engineering bay is out of equipment. Without at least some improvement in the propulsion system, they won't make it back in time to refill their life support. So Smash has to jury-rig the engine. The breakdown is of Problematic severity and Smash rolls his dice; he has a pool of 6. He manages to get three successes. The ship will hold up for 75% of the duration needed to get home before it breaks down again. When it does break down, the AI rolls 1D to see if it suffers even more damage. The result is 6, which means that the ship breaks apart even more, leaving it at Breached. The AI says that the problem now is Severe. The player of Smash makes another roll and scores two successes (20% of the needed time per success). This

Scanners	
Intensity of Interference	**Percentage of information available per success**
Ideal Conditions	100% with no roll if simple scanner, or with one success if advanced
Slight Disturbance	50% per success
Bad Conditions	33% per success
Very Intense Disturbance	25% per success
Extremely Bad Conditions	15% per success
Good Luck!	5% per success

Jury-Rigging

Complexity/ Severity of problem	Percentage/ Success
Slight	50%
Noticeable	33%
Problematic	25%
Severe	20%
Extreme	10%

Wear and Tear

Battered 7–8 ⟶	Torn
Torn 5–6 ⟶	Breached
Breached 4 ⟶	Smashed
Smashed 1–3 ⟶	Demolished

means that they reach their destination. Since the ship had already held up for 75% of the needed time, the additional 40% of jury-rig time accumulated was more than enough to get them into a safe port. The ship is in bad shape, but Smash is satisfied as he kept her together long enough for the pilot to get them to safety.

Repairing Things

The table below describes the levels of damage an object or device can suffer, and how long it might take to fix it. Modifiers are applied according to circumstances. Repairing ships works differently (see *Spacecrafts* for more information).

Sealing and cutting doors/ hulls

How long it takes to cut a hull or door (using a fusion cutter or plasma torch) open depends on its class. There's no skill involved when cutting a door, but a person skilled in Repairs can do it faster. Each success on a Quickness + Repairs roll decreases the time it takes. The hole cut open is enough for a grown man in full armor to pass through. Use your reason when cutting smaller holes. When a door is completely sealed, it's counted as a solid wall. If not properly sealed, it can be busted down as a door, but still requires more successes, as it is much sturdier than an unsealed door. Sealing doors takes twice as long, but has a reduction time of 20 seconds.

The Social Battle

When an avatar must get into a debate, argument or negotiation (rather than direct and unclouded intimidation) and you wish for the game mechanics to add some flavour and suspense, you can use the *social battle* system. When conducting social battles, it's important that the players and the AI really roleplay what is said, and not just roll the dice.

The actual system works as following: each avatar/NPA has their Clout times three (Clout × 3) worth of *credibility*. The party with the highest Clout is the one that goes first. If both parties' credibility is equal, roll a die and add Clout; the one with the highest result goes first. The Abilities at work are either Rhetoric or Fast Talk, depending on the situation. Each success reduces the credibility of the opponent by one, and the involved parties take turns making their point. The party who has his credibility reduced to zero first has lost the argument. Each time a roll is made, a couple of lines should be roleplayed by the players and AI. Keep in mind that a lost argument can't be won in another social battle in the same scene, but the credibility is reset for any new type of argument or negotiation. This system can be used to simulate days in court as well, in which case each roll counts as a day in court. Particularly convincing or well-supported arguments (or those that appear to be) can give an extra +1 to +4 in temporary credibility. It helps to do some research and lay some groundwork before entering court or an important debate or negotiation. The credibility system is fitting when a social situation is important and has a significant impact on the development of the story. If you want to handle a less

Repairing Things

Damage Level	Base time	Minimum Time	Reduction Time
Scraped	1 min	30 sec	10 seconds
Banged up	5 min	3 min	30 seconds
Battered	15 min	7 min	2 minutest
Torn	30 min	15 min	5 minutes
Breached*	1 hour	30 min	10 minutes
Smashed*	24 hours	12 hour	3 hours

* Spare parts and top-notch tools are required. The device is basically built from scratch, using the salvageable parts from the wreckage.

Sealing and Cutting Doors/Hulls

Door Class	Base time	Minimum Time	Reduction Time
Thin metal door.	1 min	20 seconds	10 sec
Standard metal door in a ship or colony.	2 min	40 seconds	10 sec
Bulkhead/Airlock*	2 min	1 min	10 sec
A/B-Class ship outer/inner hull.	4 min	2 min	10 sec
C-Class ship outer hull*	5 min	3 min	15 sec
D/E-Class ship outer hull*	8 min	2 min	15 sec

*Requires a plasma torch instead of a fusion cutter.

important social situation quickly, you can resolve it with a simple contested roll, disregarding credibility.

Social Moves

Staging: *By spending a point worth of credibility before the roll, the opponent will lose two extra points of credibility in addition to any successes scored.*

Cheap Shots: *These can be useful in a tight spot, but they can also backfire. On a success, the opponent loses another 3 points of credibility beyond the rolled successes. However, if the roll is unsuccessful, the aggressor loses 3 points.*

Looming: *By adding an aggressive demeanour (one acceptable to the social situation in question), you can take your opponent by surprise. All the subtleties of discourse are lost, which results in a –2 modifier. With a success, the opposing party has to skip his next roll. If the looming fails, you lose 3 points of credibility, since you've lost some ground. Each time this manoeuvre is used consecutively, another cumulative –1 penalty applies. The opposing side must be able to make a roll in-between looming attempts before the modifiers can be "reset".*

Intimidation

Intimidation is basically a contested roll. The intimidator makes the appropriate roll (an Ability or Aptitude roll, depending on the situation). The one on the receiving end makes the same roll, only substituting whatever Aptitude is involved with Cool. Intimidation is often about leverage, and in some situations it's impossible to use certain types of intimidation. Threatening a gang of street thugs that you can kill them would be quite impossible if you are a lone preppy delegate, while two GIC marines with their emblems showing would stand a very good chance of succeeding with such an intimidation. If the threatening party wins, he has successfully intimidated the victim. Very good leverage can give a +1 to +3 modifier to the roll, while bad leverage gives negative modifiers.

Slamming someone up against the wall in order to get some information: Brawn + Close Combat.

Threatening with legal procedures: Clout + Administration

Discouraging an aggressor by showing some fancy moves (flipping a knife or gun with precision): Quickness + Close Combat/Shooting

Talking someone out of using their gun in the cockpit by explaining (in every sickening detail) how it would feel to die of explosive decompression: Clout + First Aid.

Strategy

For strategy to be effective, the plan must have been long in the making and the troops involved must be privy to the information. A plan executed after a strategist's direction in this fashion doesn't require that the planner is present or in contact with the group, as long as they are well-coordinated and understand the plan. When making decisions on the spot, the commander must be in contact with his group, preferably on site with them. Filters that are in the way (such as other officers, radio, distance) make it harder for the final recipients of the orders to execute them properly. Being on site also allows the possibility of changing strategy on the fly, if needed.

There are two major types of strategy described here. It can either be used to established the best course of action in a combat-oriented situation, which is called Tactical Strategy, or it can be used to boost the performance of troops under the orders of the strategist. This method is called Direct Strategy.

Tactical Strategy: The player makes a Strategy roll and if he's successful, the AI will make him privy to strategic maneuvers available in the situation. Multiple successes will generate multiple strategies. However, the player will never be fully aware of which strategy, if any, is the ultimate one. And there's no guarantee that the plan will work. The player will simply be made privy to tactics that are possible and their best- and worst-case scenario outcomes. The execution is another matter entirely. Each success should generate a plan, or variation on a plan. This can be part of a strategic theoretical meeting, as well as quick decisions made in the field while under fire. The mechanics tie in very strongly to the *gameplay* paragraph (Choices) in the *game design* section.

Example: *The 6th squad is under heavy fire and their communication with command has been cut. Rook's player wants to make a Strategy roll as he sees no way out of their situation. As they lie behind cover and are fired upon in a corridor, the AI says that it's going to be a Reaction + Strategy roll. The player rolls his five dice and scores two successes. The AI tells him of two possible strategies. A part of the squad can provide heavy suppressive fire (spending most of their ammo) in order to provide cover for some of their comrades as they head for the steam control. If they manage to activate this, the steam will separate them from their enemies for a while and block the line of sight. This will enable the whole squad to get down to the ITS and head for the docking bay where their ship awaits. However, there's no way of telling if the scanners and visual modes of the enemies are good enough or calibrated to handle the steam. If the equipment is good enough, they will see Rook's squad through the steam, which will result in casualties and the depletion of ammunition on an unnecessary suppressive fire maneuver.*

The second alternative is that they throw their grenades at the enemy. This won't kill the entire enemy force, but it will take down a few, and it will also provide cover which will enable the whole squad to rush for the docking bay. The only problem is that there are some major coolant valves in the area. If the grenades damage them, the explosion could possibly cause harm to the main aft hydraulic hub, causing the docking bay doors to jam, which would require some time to repair. Rook's player looks indecisive. Both options have drawbacks and benefits.

Direct Strategy: This method can only be used if the strategist has at least two units (men if on the ground, ships if in the air, etc.) under his direct command. Handling direct strategy is tricky, even though the basic system is simple. While employing direct strategy, each success generates 2 strategy points. These can be assigned by the strategist to any of his units. The points basically work as positive modifiers for those to which they are assigned. However, if the strategist assigns more than two points to a unit, another unit will suffer a –1 per point exceeding the limit of two on its ally. This is symbolic and basically means that the other units are "sacrificed" to give support to the unit given the strategic bonus. Exactly how long the bonus is valid is the tricky part. In a heated battle, a strategy roll could be made every fifth segment (any surplus points will be discarded; it's impossible to stockpile these points from one roll to another), while in a larger-scale battle (such as when several squadrons of C-class battle ships are squaring off), a roll can be made every minute or every five minutes.

Example 1: Rook's commanding officer Sergeant Tooms starts to yell out orders as her six man strong squad, Tooth `n Nails, advances on some rippers. The AI rolls Tooms' Clout + Strategy and she gets two successes. This gives her four strategy points to dish out. Rook is on point, leveling his carbine. She assigns him all four. This will give the player of Rook a +4 bonus to his next attack roll (or any relevant roll, for that matter). But two of the squad members will get a –1 as they are ordered to cover Rook, exposing themselves to attack. Once Rook has used his bonus, it disappears and Tooms can't use her Strategy for another five segments (a timeframe decided by the AI, according to the situation).

Example 2: Commanding officer Arland Potowski is standing on the flight deck of his D-class heavy destroyer. He has six C-class light hunters under his command as they're advancing on their enemy, a squadron of CIM raiders. The player of Arland wants to make use of some direct strategy. Devising a plan, he makes a Brains + Strategy roll. He gains three successes, and with that he gets 6 strategy points. He gives 2 points to three of his captains, who are in command of the Osiris model C-class hunters. The AI has decided that this bonus is valid for five segments after the enemy has been engaged. Soon the dark void is filled with bursts of plasma and the tracer rounds of rail cannons.

Research

When researching a subject to learn new information using books, databases and other resources, the player makes a Brains + appropriate Ability roll for his avatar. If he is researching the history of Infinitology, the Ability Void Lore would be appropriate. If he wants to learn more about how the coreanium processing works, he would need to make a Brains + Science roll. The standard research roll (with access to the right sources of information) takes between 30 minutes to 3 hours. If the task is measured in minutes, the reduction time is five minutes, and if measuring in hours, the reduction time is twenty minutes.

Lifting and Breaking Stuff

The scale below shows how much a person can break/dead lift, according to his strength. No roll is required to manage it as long as the Brawn score matches the feat. If an avatar wishes to lift/break stuff that's above his Brawn rating on the chart,

Brawn Power Chart

1: Break a small and poorly constructed wooden box/ 40 kilos.
2: Bust a wooden chair/ 60 kilos.
3: Kick down a hinged apartment door/ 100 kilos.
4: Punch through fifteen centimetres of compact sheet rock/ 150 kilos.
5: Rip a radiator off the wall/ 200 kilos.
6: Bend a four centimetre-thick iron rod/ 250 kilos.
7: Break down a security door/ 300 kilos.
8: Rip open a sheet of metal/ 400 kilos.
+1/ + 50 kilos

he must pass a Brawn roll with a –1 penalty for every level above his own capacity he tries to lift. A human can manage to lift 2 scores higher than his Brawn normally allows. Remember, even if a person can do something physically, it doesn't mean that it won't hurt them. Punching through sheetrock will break your hand, while ripping metal will require armoured gloves, but it can be done.

Shooting Things to Pieces

Objects such as wall panels, thick glass and similar things have an armor rating and durability, just like armor does. In order for an attack to be able to break them down, the attack must have the capacity to affect the material. A small antipersonnel weapon will not damage metals and bulkheads, while a carbine might. When the durability is depleted, the object (or the area of an object) will be broken down. There are billions of objects and materials, but instead of providing an exhaustive list we have created three types that you can adapt and use on the fly. Use your judgment when deciding what kinds of attacks might damage the material types. See the *gear* section for more information on Armor Rating (AR) and Durability (DU).

> **Note:** *When the durability is depleted, it doesn't necessarily destroy the entire object. If a wall is destroyed when someone takes a sledge hammer to it, it probably means that an opening big enough for a person to slip through has been made and not that the entire inner wall has collapsed. If a hand grenade had caused the destruction, a much larger hole would probably been blown open.*

Materials

Indoors housing material (walls, doors, thick wood, furniture, etc.): AR 2–5, DU 5–20
Outer housing material (concrete, thin metal sheets, brick, thin inner ship material such as a sleeping bunk door): AR 4–10l, DU 15–25
Sturdy indoor ship materials (inner walls, bulkheads): AR 10–20, DU 25–50

Make Stuff Up, Goddamn It!

The system of C&D is very flexible and you can (and should) create your own rolls and rules whenever needed. Be sure to discuss these with the group as a whole so that everyone is on the same page with the new or modified rules.

For example, if you need to know if an avatar makes that 400 hundred meter run from the colony's airlock to the ship in the poisonous atmo before his breather runs out, you could have him make an Athletics + Cool roll with a –1 modifier for the stress, and decide he needs two successes in order to succeed. You might decide that a scientific experiment or archaeological excavation will take a month, and the reduction time on a roll is five days. As you see, it's fairly easy. Don't be afraid to expand the system. It's meant to be adapted and changed according to the needs of individual gaming groups.

Chapter 6: Combat

one with the second highest, then the third and so forth. This is called *Initiative*. However, maneuvers like hitting the deck or going on the defensive can be done at any time (this is true for all evasive maneuvers), no matter your Initiative, as long as you haven't yet acted in this segment. You can always try to avoid an attack if you see it coming. Every player declares the action of his avatar, starting with the player who goes last. It's also possible to delay an action, acting later in the segment. When everyone has acted in the segment, if the skirmish is still ongoing, the next segment begins and everyone gets to act again.

If there's a surprise attack, the one with the highest Reaction on the defenders' side gets to make a Reaction roll. If successful, he will be able to run for cover, hit the deck or dodge/duck when being attacked. So do the rest of the defenders if he has yelled a warning to his comrades. If not, they will be defenseless to the first attack.

If there's some uncertainty about who goes first (or if you need to up the suspense), you simply roll 1D for each participant, adding their individual Reaction to the roll. The one with the highest number goes first.

Time & Movement

As mentioned, all involved combatants act during a series of three second periods called *segments*. During a segment, everybody involved can complete an action that takes no more than three seconds. The movement rate of a human during this period is Quickness + 10 (with a −2 modifier to Shooting rolls if running and shooting at the same time). While sprinting, the speed increases to Quickness + 20. Trying to hit someone that sprints (if he's not running straight at the shooter) gives a −3 modifier, and the runner can't generally hit anything if trying to shoot while running at full speed. When walking, engaging in stealth or dragging a heavy object, the movement rate is only 5 meters per segment.

Anya dual wields while sliding down a cargo ramp.

Combat is handled in segments. Each segment is comprised of a three second period. Within this time, all involved parties get to perform an action. When violence erupts, the one with the highest Reaction is first to act in a segment, then the

Note: *Exact movement is only listed to use when it becomes important and the group feels that it's significant for a specific situation. Generally, there is seldom a need to keep track of exact movement and distances. This will in most cases just hamper the flow and turn an otherwise suspenseful scene into a nitpicking over exact details. The same goes for all mentioned distances when it comes to combat and movement.*

Bullets vs. Hoofing It

Pulling a trigger or throwing a knife takes far less time than running a few meters or opening a door. If you do not have the option to perform a ranged attack, and if you are standing at a distance of two meters or more from a combatant that can perform a ranged attack, the ranged attacker will be able to attack you before you can act. This disregards Reaction score. *When fitting, this rule can be bypassed as slitting the throat of a grappled hostage or pushing a button is just as fast as pulling a trigger.* If the shooter has his attention diverted from the close combatant, the close combat party is allowed to make a Quickness + Close Combat roll. If he gains two successes, he has successfully attacked the shooter before being shot (use this roll as the attack roll). This works from a distance as far as up to four meters.

Example 1: Lemi has a Reaction score of 2, while Kylia has a Reaction of 4. Lemi has a gun pointed at Kylia, who is standing three meters from her. Kylia tries to go for the gun, but even though she has a higher Reaction than Lemi, the latter gets to act first since she has the gun. Lemi squeezes the trigger as Kylia comes at her. This goes to show that even a high Reaction seldom beats a bullet. If Lemi would have been distracted, say by a sudden flash of light, Kylia would have been allowed to make a Quickness + Close Combat roll, since she stands within four meters. If Kylia had rolled two successes on this roll, she would have been able to attack Lemi up close, maybe even wrestling the gun from her, before Lemi managed to shoot her.

Brawls

For melee attacks, you roll Brawn + Close Combat or Quickness + Close Combat (depending if you use a heavy handed power style or a gracious precision style of fighting). If you're unarmed, the base damage is 3 and each success adds +1 (usually bashing). You can also grapple on a successful roll. If a person is grappled, he can try to break free using his Brawn/Quickness + Close Combat to escape the grapple. It's a simple contested test, done every segment. If the grappled party wins, he's free. However, for every additional attempt he gets −2 on his rolls to break free. If reduced to zero dice, the grappler has choked him out, or otherwise locked him in a vice grip or rendered him unconscious by pressure points. The person usually wakes up (if not just held, in which case he's still conscious) after 30 + 1D × 10 seconds after being incapacitated by a grapple. If sneaking up behind someone who is unaware and one manages to make a headlock, the victim immediately gets a −3 on his roll to get free. It's a very good way to disable guards and the like.

Reload

Discarding a clip (letting it just fall to the ground) and slamming in another takes one segment. If the person has at least 3 in Shooting, he can make a Quickness + Shooting roll with a −3 modifier. If successful, he will be allowed to fire his weapon during the same segment in which he loaded it, using the result of this roll as his attack roll. He counts his Reaction as if it were two less than it is when attacking directly after loading like this.

Putting rounds in a weapon/clip one by one is a bit more time consuming. Provided the ammunition is easy to reach (gun belt, easily accessible pocket), these are put in at a rate of one per second, for a total of three rounds per segment.

Ready/Holster Weapon

It takes about a second to ready a weapon that is easily accessible in a holster. Hard to reach weapons (like those in an ankle holster) take about three seconds to ready. If you wish to fire your weapon directly after drawing it, the roll to hit is made with Reaction + Shooting and a −2 modifier. Count your Reaction as one less when it comes to order of attack.

Dual Wield

One target: When using two weapons against the same target, the base damage of the weapons are combined as is the per success damage. One roll is still made as usual, but the attacker gets a −2 penalty.

Example: Baily levels his two heavy pistols and fires off one shot per weapon at a caver that comes hurtling towards him. Baily has a dice pool of 6, but since he has a −2 penalty, the player only rolls 4 dice. He scores one success. The base damage is normally 4, but is now 8 as the base damage of the two weapons are combined. The extra success adds another 4 to the damage (the weapons do +2 per success and this is doubled when using two guns). The damage ends up a total of 12, which is pretty high.

Two targets: When attacking two targets, the attacker suffers a −3 penalty. In a close combat situation, two weapons add +1 to defense if going on the defensive (see below), but a −1 to defense otherwise. One roll is made for the attack; those hit suffer the base damage as usual, but the damage generated per success is divided as evenly as possible among the targets. If there's only one success on the attack, only one target is hit.

From Cover to Cover

If you run from one cover to another while shooting, you make yourself a harder target. However, it's also harder for you to hit *your* target. Trying to hit someone on the run is done with a −2 modifier, but the one running gets a −3 on his attack roll. Any ranged damage that hits the runner also has its base damage reduced by −2.

Example: Rook is running from a pile of rubble to a bulkhead opening, all the while a mercenary is trying to shoot him. While on the run, Rook squeezes off a few shots at his enemy. The mercenary gets a −2 to hit Rook, but Rook also gets a −3 to hit the mercenary. However, if Rook is hit, the base damage will be reduced by −2 as he's a moving target, while Rook's damage will be unaffected if he hits the mercenary, since the soldier is a stationary target.

Hitting the Deck

If trying to avoid getting shot, the defender can also throw himself on the ground or behind cover. The standard modifier for hitting someone diving for cover is −4. If the one hitting the deck wishes to shoot, his roll gets a −5 modifier. It takes one action and a complete segment to rise from prone.

Defense in Combat

When in close combat, the avatar does everything in his power to stay out of harm's way. He ducks and parries and bobs and weaves to avoid deadly blows. In game mechanical terms, his defense acts as a negative modifier which applies to attackers that try to engage him in close combat (hand to hand or melee). It also applies to thrown projectiles, but *not* to firearms. If the avatar faces multiple opponents, his defense is counted as one less for each separate opponent beyond the first. However, defense only applies to enemies that the avatar is aware of and can see.

Example 1: Rook is tearing it up on his leave and has ended up on the business end of a knife in a bar brawl. Rook has a defense of 3. This means that his opponent gets a −3 modifier to his attacks when trying to hit Rook.

Example 2: Without breaking a sweat, Rook took out the guy and snapped the knife in two. But the guy has friends. Three of them, in fact. They gang up on Rook. As there are two additional attackers beyond one, his defense is lowered by 2. This means that his defense is reduced to only 1. Each attacker will get a −1 to his attack as Rook has a hard time keeping up with the hail of blows and kicks. He's in trouble.

On the Defensive

When an avatar wishes to do nothing other than avoid incoming attacks in a close combat situation, he can go on the defensive. An avatar on the defensive can do little besides move half his running speed and avoid attacks. This will add +2 to his defense. A player that wishes to put his avatar on the defensive must declare this before his avatar has acted in the segment. An avatar can even go on the defensive out of turn, disregarding the highest Reaction score.

Example: Realizing that he's in trouble while facing three opponents, Rook goes on the defensive. This means that his defense trait is increased by 2. The attackers now get a −3 modifier. Rook can't attack, but he might stay on his feet long enough for his Marine buddies to notice the ruckus. If he would have gone on the defensive while facing one opponent, his defense would have been 5 (original defense 3 +2 for going on the defensive).

Firing into Brawls

If you fire into a brawl and want to hit a specific person (and miss another), some modifiers apply. First of all, the shooter gets a −2 for all the movement and scuffling going on, and then he gets a −1 for each person he wishes to avoid hurting. If the roll is successful he hits his target, but if he misses, it's a fifty-fifty chance that he hits the person he wants to avoid hitting. If using a shotgun, the penalty to hit is counted as −4. In the case of an unintentional hit, re-roll Attention + Shooting. The minimum damage, regardless of the roll's result, is the weapon's base damage.

Point Blank

If the target isn't hitting the deck (see above) or running, involved in a fist fight or otherwise moving fast, a point blank shot grants a +3 modifier as well as a +2 to the base damage. The end of the barrel has to be one meter or closer to the target in order for it to count as point blank range. If a target is immobilized (sleeping, bound, etc.) a point blank shot will only miss if the shooter botches.

Called Shots & Aiming

When you shoot at a target, you generally hit the largest area on that target (the torso on humanoid creatures) if you haven't called a shot. Hitting a medium-sized target (leg or arm) is done with a −2 modifier. Targeting the head or targets of similar size incurs a −3 penalty. Anything smaller suffers a −4 penalty. Take these modifiers into account while trying to hit a target in cover (like when just the arm is sticking out, etc.).

Larger targets work the other way around. Hitting something that's double the size of a human is done with a +1 modifier, something the size of a car would grant a +2 modifier and anything bigger would give a +3 modifier. When aiming, it gets easier to hit something. Every segment spent aiming will give a +1 modifier to hit, but it's only possible to aim for fifteen seconds and while standing still.

When calling a shot at close combat range the negative modifier is counted as one less and it's impossible to aim in close combat in order to get a better hit. But remember that a person can parry the gun arm and keep the barrel away from himself at this distance, giving him the opportunity to parry these attacks like any others when in this range. This means that the target's defense is taken into account.

Range

If a target is situated within 1/3 of the weapon's total range, it's considered to be within Short range. If the target is situated within 2/3 of the range, it's considered Normal range, and beyond this it's considered Long range. Use this as a rough estimation. A weapon with a range of 60 meters would have the following ranges: Short 1–20, Normal 21–40, Long 41–60. The further away the target is the harder it is to hit it. See the range table.

Range	
Range	**Modifier**
Short	+1
Normal	±0
Long	−2

Shotgun Rules

Shots from these weapons scatter and create an arc of fire if loaded with pellets. The arc gets wider the further the pellets travel (ignoring the range table above). This results in easier hits at a distance but a reduction in damage. Therefore shotguns have three sets of damages. Each damage code corresponds to a third of the range, in the order they appear. So if a shotgun has a range of 60 meters the first (and highest) damage code would apply in the 1–20 meter range, the second to the 21–40 range and the third damage code to 41–60 range.

The per success damage gets locked after the first range. At the second range only up to three successes will count when calculating damage and at the third range only two successes will count. Any surplus damage due to extra successes is ignored. However, a +1 modifier to hit applies for the second range and a total of +2 applies to the last range.

Example: Baily has gotten his hands on a shotgun as he stalks the corridors of the CAV-infested space station, hoping to fight his way to his shuttle. He sees a caver from a distance as it gnaws away at a corpse. His shotgun has a range of 90 meters; the caver is at about 40 meters (30–60 meter range). Baily squeezes off a shot. He gets a +1 bonus because of the range as the space between the pellets widens. But no matter how many successes he gets, every success beyond the third won't add to the damage as the widening also disperses the kinetic energy of the shot, lessening the damage.

Multiple Actions

Sometimes you want to do two things at the same time, and in this case multiple actions apply. It's possible to perform three actions within a three second period. A second action will impose a −2 penalty, and the third action will impose a −3 penalty. The actions have to be physically possible and reasonable to the situation. The player rolls for every action, applying the final modifier to all rolls. Multiple actions do not allow for faster movement or reloads.

Example: Anya wants to kick a CIM guard in the groin while throwing her knife at a second guard who is standing further away. This counts as two actions, which imposes a −2 modifier. Anya has a score of 5 when using Close Combat and 6 when throwing the knife. This means that she will have a pool of 3 when kicking and 4 when throwing the knife, as the −2 modifier applies to both rolls.

Multiple Shots

When firing multiple shots, a negative modifier applies. *The modifier is equal to the total amount of bullets fired.* The ROF of a weapon decides how many shots that can be fired during a segment. If a gun has ROF 4, it means that the avatar can fire four bullets. He will get a −2 for the second bullet, −3 for the third and −4 on the fourth. The final modifier is added to the roll, as with other multiple actions, but only one roll is made. For each bullet fired beyond the first, the base damage of the weapon increases by +2 if hitting the same target. It's virtually impossible to switch targets while shooting like this, and only if people stand really close (or behind the target, coming into line of sight as the target falls) is it possible to hit a secondary or tertiary target. In most cases, this is purely a side effect or collateral damage. Stray bullets of this kind inflict base damage plus successes as normal.

> **Note:** When firing multiple shots while dual wielding, the multiple shot system works exactly the same as when using one gun, but take the modifiers involved with dual wielding into account.

Example: Anya managed to drop the two guards, but there was a third one and he's heading for the alarm. Anya has drawn her silenced Karakow SR3 handgun. It has a ROF of 3. Anya wants to pump 3 rounds into the guard in order to guarantee a takedown. Since she fires 3 bullets, she gets a −3 penalty. Anya's Attention + Shooting pool is 6; after the modifier (−3) for the multiple shots has been subtracted, the pool is 3 dice. The player only has to make the one roll for all shots. Either they all hit or all miss. She gets 2 successes. The base damage is 4 and the per success damage is 2. This generates a damage of 8. But each shot beyond the first increases the base damage by +2, and as two extra shots were fired,

the base damage is increased by a total of 4. This means that the total damage is 12! As her gun coughs out the bullets the guard goes down in a spray of crimson.

Alternate Firing Modes

Auto Fire: This can either hit one person and increase the base damage by +4, or hit five targets that stand in a cluster and cause base damage plus evenly distributed per success damage on all of them. Auto fire used in this way gives a −1 modifier and expends 10 bullets. Then one can just spray, hoping to hit something.

Burst: Increases the base damage by +2 and expends 5 bullets.

Example 1: From nowhere a ripper jumps out at Sange, a rookie boarder guard, while he is on patrol. Shocked, he simply employs his old point-and-spray tactics. He uses auto fire. He has a score of 5, but the auto fire gives him a −1 modifier, leaving him at 4 dice. He expends 10 bullets and manages to get one success. His weapon normally has a base damage of 6, but has it increased to 10 as it gets a +4 due to the auto fire. The per success damage of his weapon is 3 and in the end the ripper gets hit for 13 points of damage. After the armor has been factored in, the creature loses 9 points of damage. That's almost half of its hit points. Another volley like that and the ripper will be taken out.

Example 2: A crazed mine worker, suffering from severe VPS, has gotten his hands on a SMG and entered the eatery of a mining station during the lunch rush (it's packed). Screaming about monsters living under the skin of humans, he squeezes the trigger and sprays bullets wildly into the crowd. He covers a five meter area and there are more than five people in it but only five can be hit. He rolls and scores one success. The base damage is 4 and the per success damage is 2. Three people lose 4 hit point while two lose 5 (evenly distributed per success damage). The unarmed crowd tries to flee as the lunatic squeezes the trigger again…

Surprise Attacks

An attack staged against an enemy that's not currently in combat and who is unaware of the attack is deemed a surprise attack. The attack only fails if a botch occurs, otherwise it hits. These attacks add +1 to the base damage and +1 to the per success damage. After the first hit, the enemy is aware and can't be attacked with the same method as he's now on high alert (if he survived).

Firing Blind

If firing over cover without looking as a suppressive method, or blindly into the dark out of fear, or if firing without seeing the target or targets, it's all about chance and blind luck. In these cases the AI must decide what the odds are that a hit or several will occur. Full auto against several enemies will have a greater chance to hit than a couple of bullets fired against one target. At times there's no chance at all. The best thing to do when there's a chance of a blind hit is to figure out the approximate chance of a hit and roll 1D. If the dice comes up in favor of the shooter (hit the number/numbers that the AI chose), it's a hit and the weapon will do base damage plus one success damage to its intended targets.

A marine on stims takes on a horde of monstrosities.

Visual Modifiers

Bad lighting, smoke and similar visual obstacles can be a factor in combat (and many other situations). Thin smoke or dusky conditions might give a –1 penalty while extremely bad lighting and thick veils of smoke can give up to –2 or –4.

> **Ricochet:** *If firing weapons inside a ship or similar environment that is mainly comprised of cold hard metal, a bullet (if not using stun or "collapsible" ammo) will ricochet if it misses or penetrates a soft target. The risk of being hit depends on the size of the area and amount of bullets fired. The AI has to be the judge of this, but rest assured that most people in the C&D universe are aware of this risk and often think twice before firing a weapon in a confined area at high risk of ricochet. This information should also be available to the players. Armor piercing is very dangerous, as bullets will often penetrate soft targets on a hit, increasing the chance of a ricochet. When you decide (or determine by chance on the dice) that someone is struck by a ricochet, you have to decide the ricochet factor. A massive amount of bullets fired in a tight space will result in a high factor. The factor has the same damage as the weapon that was fired, and the factor generates a number of dice which are rolled as the Shooting Ability. Even if none of the dice come up a success, the victim(s) will still suffer the base damage if struck. So if a factor is 6 (that's a very high factor), 6 dice are rolled and each success adds an amount of damage according to the weapon. Sometimes ricochets can work to the advantage of a shooter, as when volleying bullets off a wall in order to get them to bounce around a corner with the possibility of hitting an enemy.*

Example: *In a firefight, a volley of bullets from a carbine hits the hard titanium walls in a space station and the AI decides that Rook might be hit by the ricochet. The AI declares that it's a fifty-fifty chance, as it's a rather confined space, and rolls 1D (1–4 and he's hit). The die comes up 3. Rook is hit. The factor is 3. Each success will cause the same per success damage as the carbine (3) and even if no*

successes come up, Rook will still suffer the base damage (6) of the weapon as the hit has already been decided by the fifty-fifty dice roll.

> **Note:** *When you play out combat and battles, you should make them come alive. For instance, if an avatar and a NPA are fighting hand to hand and both miss two times in a row, they don't "miss" as such and certainly don't stand still in one spot throwing slow punches in a "hit and miss" kind of way. The fight is violent, a missed punch might have been parried or avoided or actually hit but the impact was too light to cause any actual damage. Think about a dramatic movie fight. The combatants grapple, maneuver and hit their opponent in ways that don't really inflict any damage as such. A poor hit to the arm, a kick that barely hits, sliding to the side with no real impact. And make sure you take the environment into account. There are all kinds of hard objects and hindrances. Also, many fighters end up on the floor in a brutal grapple, choking and punching. A fight is as much about hindering the opponent from inflicting any real damage on you as it is about inflicting damage to him.*

Handling Hordes

There are some tricks you can utilize when using Sequence Zones to simulate larger battles, or battles where the story and mood do well with fewer details and a more epic feel (such as when holding the ground against impossible odds).

Every avatar (or allied Non-Player Avatar) that's involved in the battle gets to make a roll. It's important to decide beforehand what will happen if an avatar fails his roll. Does he suffer damage due to counterattacks, expend extra ammo or damage his equipment? You should also decide how many total successes the avatars need to defeat the enemy (or keep them at bay, or whatever fate hangs in the balance) and what each success represents. If the enemy is advancing, the avatars might only have a number of tries before they're overrun or have to escape (like when a hoard of rippers is storming them). This system can be combined with the Strategy Ability to great effect, since direct strategy successes are added to the dice pools of the people under the command of the strategist (see direct strategy rules). This system greatly reduces rolls and allows a game where larger battles are frequent to run smoothly. But keep in mind, these rules are meant to be fast and cinematic and are much less accurate and detailed. To a certain extent one can say that they toss the game balance out the window for the benefit of epic narrative.

Example: The AI decides that the four avatars in his story are going to be attacked by a large group of cavers. The cavers are at a range of eighty or so meters, while the avatars have taken up positions behind a chest-high wall. Behind them is a security door which leads into the research facility. However, the door is locked and one of the avatar's allies is bypassing the system from the inside. The door will open after six segments. The cavers (if not killed) will reach the avatars in four segments. The AI has decided that the difficulty starts at normal, as the targets are moving in a direct line toward them. Every Sequence Zone after the first will give the avatars a +1 to their dice pool as the cavers move in closer. There are about thirty cavers and the avatars are armed with auto carbines. After some thought, the AI says that each success will kill (or otherwise disable) two cavers. This symbolizes how the avatars will blast away with their weapons using full auto (expending about half a clip per segment). So If an Attention + Shooting roll results

in 3 successes, in this instance it would kill off 6 cavers (instead of inflicting detailed damage on only one or a few). If the avatars don't manage to kill them off after four segments, the combat switches to normal rules, which means they might have to face several cavers up close until the door opens after the sixth segment. If the enemies had been individuals armed with firearms, the AI could have decided that each failed roll would result in damage suffered by the avatar who failed the roll (since the enemies would counterattack at range). Also, if the enemies were heavily armored, the AI might have required two successes to disable one enemy (as opposed to two disabled enemies per one success in the above example). It's time to start rolling in order to mow down the cavers.

Each player rolls the dice pool for his avatar (Attention + Shooting). In total they generate 7 successes. This means that 14 cavers are down (2 down per success). The AI narrates how the auto fire roars across the stony dark plains and rips a fourth of the horde to shreds. The players feel confident. In the next segment, the avatars get +1 since their targets are closer. But they're not so lucky on their next attack. One roll fails, and one of the players is really out of luck and botches (his avatar's weapon jams). In total, the two remaining players generate four successes, taking down 8 cavers. They'd better step up their game or they might be overrun and killed (or at least seriously injured) by the frenzied army of cavers. The group has two more chances, but they're one gun short. Time to roll again…

Combat Quick Reference Sheet

Called Shots & Aiming

Target	Modifier
Arm/Leg	−2
Head	−3
Hand/Foot	−4
Eye/Cent	−5
Ox/Small Car	+1
Normal Size Car	+2
A-Class Ship/Elephant	+3
Very Large Target	+4
Aiming	+1/Combat Segment

Alternate Firing Table

Auto Fire: This can either hit one person and increase the base damage with +4 or hit five targets that stand in a cluster and cause base damage plus evenly distributed per success damage on all of them. Auto fire used in this way gives a -1 modifier and expends 10 bullets. Then one can just spray, hoping to hit something.

Burst: Increases the base damage on a target with +2 and expends 5 bullets.

Range

Range	Modifier
Short	+1
Normal	±0
Long	−2

Multiple Shots Table

Nr of shots fired	Modifier	Dmg Mod
2	−2	+2
3	−3	+4
4	−4	+6
5	−5	+8

Circumstance Mod Table

Conditions	Modifier
Dusk/Mist/Bad Ligthing	−1
Heavy Rain/Smoke	−3
Flashligt in Pitch Black	−3
Blizzard/Starlight	−4
Shooter is running	−3
Target is running	−2
Both are running	−5
Target is hitting the deck	−4
Shooter is hitting the deck	−5
Dual Wield − One Target	−2
Dual Wield − Two Targets	−3

Shotgun Table

Range	Modifier	PSD-lock
Short	+1	n/a
Normal	+1	3
Long	+2	2

Chapter 7: Health

In the C&D universe, violence and hazardous environments are quite common and both can be the source of injuries. Being shot, stabbed, electrocuted or subjected to a planets poisonous atmosphere can kill you in an instant. Overall, damage depletes *Hit Points* (HP).

The health system is not meant to simulate the real world in any way, but in the context of the game it's a fair and entertaining system by which you can keep track of your avatar's health. At its core, C&D is a game where brutality plays its part and the system emulates this by being quite unforgiving and harsh. One bullet is enough to stop an avatar dead in his tracks. There's a certain nomenclature attached to the health system which is as follows.

Bashing Damage: This constitutes non-fatal damage. In most cases such things as unarmed attacks cause bashing damage. Being hit by objects can also cause bashing damage at times. When an avatar has sustained enough bashing it's converted to *fatal damage*. This happens if bashing damage surpasses the wound level incapacitated.

Example: When the bashing hit points are maxed out, Rook sustains another 2 bashing damage points in a brawl. These are converted to fatal damage. Enough bashing will in the end seriously injure or kill him as it's now converted to fatal.

Fatal Damage: Everything that can seriously harm an avatar in one attack/damage incident and (or) can cause more severe wounds that takes a long time to heal is classified as fatal damage. Being shot, cut by a plasma saw or run over by a car are things that typically cause fatal damage.

> **Damage Points?:** *At times the text says that someone can sustain a certain amount of damage opposed to losing hit points. Basically this is the same thing as losing hit points. If someone sustains 5 points worth of damage he has lost 5 hit points. It's just semantics.*

Inflicting Damage

When determining how much damage an attack causes there are two damage classifications involved: Base Damage (BD) and Per Success Damage (PSD). The base damage is inflicted on the hit and is a static value attached to the weapon. The per success damage is also attached to the weapon and is multiplied by the attackers successes. Let's say that an attack has a base damage of 4 and a per success damage of 2. If the attacker scores 2 successes the damage inflicted would be 8. He would get 4 for the base damage while each success generates 2 points worth of damage. There are some damage types (accidents, explosives etc) that work a bit differently but this is the norm when dealing with most direct attacks.

Example: Anya fires her handgun which has a base damage of 5 and a per success damage of 2 and scores 2 successes. Her target sustains 9 points worth of damage. 5 for the base damage and an additional 4 for the two successes as each success inflicted 2.

HP and Wound Levels

As stated above, the overall amount of fatal and bashing damage an avatar can take before he goes down is measured in hit points. These represent the avatar's sturdiness and ability to withstand physical punishment. Mark lost hit points with an X from left to right. Every avatar has 16 plus Brawn in total amount of hit points. But these are divided into *wound levels* on the bashing and fatal scale.

While hit points are the overall "structural integrity" of the avatars body, the wound levels gives a way to gauge the effects on the body as hit points are lost. Bashing and Fatal hit points are measured on different, and for the most part, totally separate scales. Bashing and Fatal hit points are counted on four wound levels.

Bashing: *Bruised, Beaten, Broken, Incapacitated*

Fatal: *Scratched, Hurt, Injured, Incapacitated*

Each wound level comes with its own negative modifier. *The wound level which gives the most negative modifier and hindrance is the one that counts, but they do not stack and are not cumulative.* So if a person has been dropped to the Scratched wound level on the Fatal scale, and also has been dropped to the Broken level on the Bashing scale, the negative modifier on the Broken level would count.

Points per Level

Each wound level has four hit points, except the Scratched/Bruised level which has four plus Brawn amount of hit points. When the hit points have been depleted in one level the continued loss feeds into the next level and so on.

Bashing and fatal damage never effect each other as such, but when bashing hit point have been depleted continuous damage is converted to fatal. Hitting and kicking someone will indeed kill them in the end.

Healing

Bashing hit points heals at a rate of one hit point per hour, no matter what physical activities that is undertaken by the avatar. Fatal hit point takes a bit more of time and requires rest. These heal at a rate of 4 points per 24 hours when in a *medi-tank*, 2 points per 24 hours in an old fashion intensive care unit and 1 per 24 hours if just resting. If not resting it takes 48 hours per point. Healing occurs from right to left.

Healing Rates

Type	Conditions	Time	Regained
Bashing	n/a	1 h	1
Deadly	Medi-Tank	24 h	4
Deadly	ICU	24 h	2
Deadly	Resting	24 h	1
Deadly	Active	48 h	1

Grittier: *Stabilization and Deterioration*
A more advanced and gritty option demands all wounds on the Hurt and Injured (and beyond) level to be treated with either First Aid or a shot of Regen before healing properly. If damaged down to the Hurt level the hit points heals in a pace of 1 per 48 hours if resting and if the wounds haven't been treated with First Aid or Regen. Wounds on the wounded level deteriorate if not stabilized. The avatar will lose 1 additional hit point every 24 hours instead due to infection and additional wear and tear to the opened wound.

Incapacitation and Death

If incapacitated due to bashing damage the player has to pass a Brawn roll (which is not a subject to the negative wound modifier) or the avatar will be knocked out and will awake when he has regained one bashing hit point. On a successful roll he's awake but suffers a −3 modifier and can't sprint.

If reduced to incapacitated due to loss of fatal hit points the player has to make the same roll or the avatar passes out (might be crawling helplessly drifting in and out of consciousness) and loses one additional hit point every fifteen minutes due to bleeding and shock. A successful First Aid roll or a shot of regen is necessary to stabilize the individual. When reduced to zero hit points due to fatal damage the avatar is dead.

Grittier: *Hit the Ground Bleeding*
If you wish to make things a bit harsher you can have the avatar lose one hit point every hour if Hurt, and every half-hour if Injured, due to bleeding. This bleeding can be stopped by a successful First Aid roll or a shot of regen. If using this system First Aid rolls are needed in order to regain any hit points. First the bleeding needs to be stopped successfully and then a roll to stabilize the wound in order for it to heal has to be made.

Critical Hits

An attack that subtracts 10 fatal hit points in one blow can instantly kill an avatar. When this happens the player has to make a Brawn roll (this roll is not a subject to the wound penalties). Each additional hit point above 10 that is lost in the same blow imposes a −1 to the roll. If the roll fails the avatar is dead or suffers a permanent injury depending on the leniency of the AI (scratch a dot from appropriate Aptitude depending on the nature of the injury, this can be bought back with *Upgrade Points*). A successful roll doesn't mean that the avatar is unaffected; he will be dazed for 1D times 10 seconds. During this time he can only limp around and has a −2 (additional to any other modifier).

However, shots (or adequate blunt force trauma) to the head that start out as fatal and are converted to bashing as a result of wearing *shock armor* (see equipment) will still count as a critical hit as the kinetic force of such a blow is enough to affect the brain.

If 10 bashing hit point is lost in one roll a failed roll just renders the avatar unconscious for ten minutes to an hour or so.

Example: A mercenary called Slade takes a bullet and it inflicts 12 fatal hit points on him. This is a critical hit and can kill or cause a permanently handicapping injury. In order to avoid this he has to pass a Brawn roll (he has Brawn 3, giving him 6 dice to roll). As the damage is 12 he gets a −2 modifier (−1 for every point of damage above 10) which gives him a pool of 4. The player rolls but gets no successes. This means that his avatar will die or be permanently damaged…if he doesn't use a Save Point that is.

Grittier: *Let the limbs lay where they fall*
If you want to get nasty you can have different levels of critical hit tolerance for different parts of the body. The torso has 10, arms and legs 8, and the head 7. When a limb is hit and the Brawn roll is successful there's a fifty percent chance that the limb is blown off or otherwise destroyed. If the Brawn roll for the head is successful there's a fifty percent chance that the person will suffer permanent brain damage if not treated with nano-worms within 24 hours (gives a −1 to all Brains or Attention rolls in the future). Wearing shock armor (see Armor Configurations) will negate the roll for losing limbs (but it won't protect you against brain damage).

Take into consideration that the negative modifier will be sterner when dealing with limbs as the critical threshold is lower. Every hit point above 8 will impose a −1 when dealing with arms and legs and so forth.

Knocked Out

If you wish to knock someone out you have to take them totally by surprise. If you suddenly hit, shoot or otherwise attack a totally unprepared person and hit the head he'll fall down unconscious. This can be done by sneaking up on them and hit them in the back of the head or by suddenly attacking them while facing them head on. The head on approach can only be done in certain cases. Attacking someone suddenly from the front that's prepared (a bodyguard, bouncer, LED-officer or any other individual that is vigilant or have a reason to be weary of you) will not render them unconscious. However, if the person is totally relaxed by your presence (thinks he's your friend, or maybe that you're a trusted co-worker or totally harmless) he can be knocked out. A person knocked out like this is out for 2D minutes. If the attack is done from the front the victim gets a chance to roll for Brawn. If his successes are equal or surpasses the attacker's successes he won't go down and will remain conscious.

> **Stunned:** There is no real system in place which simulates when and if someone gets stunned as a result of an attack. In this, use your logic. If someone takes a shotgun blast to the chest up close, even if their armor takes the worst of it, they will probably get the wind knocked out of them. A called shot to the head with a fist or knee in an attack which generates two or more successes might also stun or daze someone. You can simply decide that the victim will lose his next action or that he will suffer a negative modifier for a segment or two due to the pain and disorientation., or employ a Brawn roll.

Sources of Injuries

There are a lot of dangerous environmental sources of injury in the world of C&D. Some is the result of a hostile atmosphere while others are the result of accidental (or even intentional) sources. A terrain can be dangerous in and of itself with pitfalls and exposed wiring.

Fire, Corrosives, Electricity and Extreme Cold

These do damage for every three seconds a person is subjected to them. How much damage depends on how powerful the source is (or how severe the exposure is). To simplify things the severity/exposure has been divided into four types: Mild, Harsh, Extreme and Incinerating. It takes a fire/corrosive about nine seconds before it starts to eat through armor if mild and six seconds if harsh. After this the individual will suffer the full damage and the durability will be diminished by the amount of damage inflicted as well. If extreme or incinerating it eats right through the armor and the effects are immediate.

Armor as such doesn't shield the wearer from cold or electricity but COGs can be equipped with insulating properties.

Sustained Damage

Severity	Armor Effect Delay	Dmg/3 sec
Mild	9 sec	3 HP
Harsh	6 sec	6 HP
Extreme	0 sec	8 HP
Incinerating	0 sec	10 HP

Falling

Falling is a pretty good way of ending up dead if the drop is long enough. If lucky something might soften the blow, such as water, cardboard boxes or whatever. The falling chart isn't measured in exact distances but instances. Armor reduces the damage by half its armor rating.

The falling system can be used to decide damage from crashes. The AI decides how severe he thinks a crash is and then pick a damage from the falling table. Crashes are more unpredictable and the damage can be deemed as bashing even if using "third story free fall" for example.

Fall Damage

Fall	Damage
Roll down a stair	1D+4 (Bashing)
Fall from the second story	1D (Deadly)
Thrown of a highway overpass	1D+4 (Deadly)
Third story free fall	2D+2 (Deadly)
Fifth story free fall	2D+4 (Deadly)
Seventh story or worse.	2D+8 (Deadly)

Radiation

In space there's a lot of radiation, everything from gamma, beta to intense UV. Then there's coreanium radiation and other manmade types. To make things simple, radiation has been divided into two measurements: Severity and Intensity. Severity decides the damage and which type of damage (bashing or fatal) while intensity decides how often the damage is inflicted. A small radiation leak can take several hours or days to kill someone while a big leak can kill within seconds or minutes. The AI has to combine intensity and severity as he sees fit depending on the situation.

The short way of writing out severity and intensity is by using a /. So if an area has a radiation of Mild/Mild it means that it has a Mild Severity and a Mild Intensity.

Radiation will often cause secondary symptoms such as blisters, sickness, vomiting and similar ailments. The exact nature of the symptoms is up to the AI depending on severity. This system can also be applied for poisons, viruses and extreme weather conditions. As a general rule, a person is incapable of healing during the exposure to this type of damage.

Example: *Operative Eric Starkwood has come across a hidden lab and an unknown pathogen has broken out and he's infected. The AI decides that the Severity is Hard and the Intensity is Mild (she sets the exact time of 3 hours since Mild intensity has a ratio of 1–6 hours). Every three hours Eric will lose 4 hit points due to the illness until he finds the anti-serum, the AI also decides that he suffers from shakes and bothersome tunnel vision (–1 to all Attention and actions that require precise eye hand coordination). If this would have been a situation involving radiation he would had the option to remove himself from the radiated area.*

Intensity Table

Intensity	Damage Rate
Slight	Every 12-24 hours
Mild	Every 1–6 hours
Concentrated	Every 10–30 minutes
Severe	30 seconds to 1 minute
Insane	3–10 seconds

Severity Table

Severity	Damage
Soft	1 (Bashing)
Mild	2 (Bashing)
Hard	4 (Deadly)
Severe	6 (Deadly)

Suffocation

A person can hold his breath for up to a minute plus Brawn × 10 seconds, when this time is up he has to pass a Cool roll every 20 seconds. Every new roll comes with a –1 modifier. A failure shows that the person has passed out and he will die within one to two minutes if not given CPR.

This rule can be used to simulate atmospheres made out of very thin breathable air. The AI can then decide that the roll is done every minute, or hour, or whatever is suitable for the situation. In these cases the persons won't die when they fail, but each failure will give them a –1 to all rolls because of the fatigue (–5 meters to their combat running speed as well per failed roll). When the negative modifier has reduced Brawn to zero the person passes out until the atmosphere mixture has changed into a more breathable one or if they're given a breather or other device to help them breathe. Their negative modifier will go away after about ten minutes after being introduced into a breathable atmosphere.

Fatigue

C&D uses a very simplified system to deal with starvation, thirst and endurance. The AI decides when an avatar starts to get tired. When they get tired the AI call for a Brawn roll. If this fails the avatar gets a –1 to all rolls. When the negative modifier surpasses Brawn the avatar needs to rest. How often the roll is done is up to the AI. Maybe one every 10 minutes if doing a strenuous task, every hour if hiking or every five minutes if pushing it to the max. How long an avatar needs to rest is also dependent on the activity. Ten to thirty minutes minus Brawn minutes is a good scale to use.

An avatar can survive three days without water or two weeks without food if he has access to water. If suffering from mild thirst or starvation the avatar will get a –2 modifier to all rolls.

If suffering severely (the last day of thirst or the last week of starvation) the avatar loses his ability to run and gets a –4 modifier. The last hours of thirst or the last day of starvation he can only crawl and is basically unaware of his surroundings. If not given fluids or food after this he will die.

Vacuum

Usually, people die from the cold, heat or radiation long before they succumb to the vacuum when subjected to outer space. However, if a human is subjected to the vacuum and there's no other environmental hazards that can kill him off, he can survive a vacuum for a short while. For every segment of exposure the avatar will sustain two points of fatal damage until he's saved or expires. He will be severely bloated after about thirty second and many of his superficial blood vessels will be ruptured but his eyes won't pop out of his head, nor will anything similarly dramatic occur. Severe (incapacitated) vacuum damage often requires a medi-tank to completely recover from. Without a medi-tank session the person will suffer a –1 from Brawn and Clout, points that can only be bought back with Ups (see *game design section*). And being subjected to a vacuum hurts…a lot.

Gravitational Effects

Take into account zero-g and different kinds of atmospheres. Gravity can affect falling for example, if the gravity in one place is higher than Earth norm, the damage of falling will increase by the amount of extra gravity, and it will be harder for avatars and NPAs to move around. If the gravity is less, falls will be much less severe. Bullets will travel further in a place where the gravity is low; while where the gravity is higher bullets will travel much shorter. Fire can free float in zero-g as long as it has fuel and it slides across surfaces and free falls. It's beautiful but extremely dangerous.

It would take a library to create an index over all the gravitational effects in regards of damage, movement, kinetic force and whatnot so this is best left to the AI. You don't have to be scientific about it, use it to create enjoyable scenes in your levels.

Explosions

These do damage according to a blast radius. Explosives are divided in the following radiuses: Ground Zero, Devastating, Destructive and Blasting. Each type of explosive has a different reach on the radiuses. The damage of C-class explosives at Blasting radius are counted as bashing as it's only a concussive effect at that range.

Explosions which cause fatal damage can't fully be countered by worn armor. All armor value is counted as half when subjected to explosives.

Example of explosive, more information can be found in the Gear section				
Explosive	Ground Zero	Devastating	Destructive	Blasting
Grenade	1–2m (8+1D)	3–4m (4+1D)	5m (2+1D)	6m (1D)

VINs

Computers are very sophisticated and can be programmed to have an array of protocols. Artificial intelligence has never been achieved, nor is there any need to develop it. Most computer systems of any significance (ship computers, main hubs, etc.) runs on a VIN (Virtual Intelligence Network, pronounced *win*). VIN systems have been designed to respond and adapt to situations that may occur and can give off the semblance of real intelligence, but in reality it's all about clever and complex programming. VINs on main hubs and onboard computers are by law prohibited to be programmed to emulate personalities in the working environment since it has been proven to distract crew members. However, when crew members are off duty and in their private quarters they may request to run a personality protocol that allows them to chat with the computer, interacting vocally as if it would be a person. On smaller vessels, or privately owned vessels, many engineers name their computers and give them a personality even though discovery by the GIC will lead to heavy fines.

VINs are incapable of making a decision that will directly kill or harm a person. Contamination, quarantine and automated decompression security procedures are controlled by a system of sub-routines that runs on pre-programmed triggers.

These systems can be accessed manually through the VIN by a human with the right access codes but the VIN can't affect these on its own in any way. This structure is used so the VIN won't risk running into logical paradoxes.

Even with the immense development of technology, the VIN core is a massive thing. The main stem is a large five hundred cubic liter cylindrical tank that contains the actual board of the VIN. This is in the form of an adaptable nano-board, that's actually liquid. It fuses, merges and diverges as the intricate calculations works on. The liquid is violet blue and luminescent, usually contained within an extremely strong titanium alloy. The built in shock absorbent material makes it extremely strong and it can even withstand a crash.

A VIN is fully capable of piloting a ship under normal circumstances (has about 3 dice and can't botch) and will alert the crew of strange scans, proximity warnings and the like. So when in calm waters so to speak the crew can play cards, work out or whatever as the VIN will tell them when they need to get to their stations or when a threat shows up. However, having a human running the scanners is much safer as the VIN only uses the rudimentary scans and is incapable of fine tuning the system or read abnormalities using instincts as a human can. After all, it's only a computer and can malfunction…

A GIC fleet commander confers with the VIN Galatea.

Nanotech

Nanites are used for an array of applications, in many cases they're used in a supportive capacity in technology. Nanites are always pre-programmed to perform a specific task, and act as a part of much larger machines. The programming of nano-technology is quite delicate and the technology has been put to good use. Dry nanotechnology is controlled and sustained by electromagnetic fields and there is no such thing as free-ranging nanites or "gray mass". The most common type of nan-otechnology comes in the form of nanomaterials and alloys.

Electromagnetism

This technology has become quite advanced and is used for a lot of things. This is something the Gerions taught us. The combination of magnetically conductive nanites and magnetic fields are used for a variety of applications. Everything from plasma tools to the so-called "grav-cuffs" use this technology and it has opened the door to a lot of possibilities. For example, it's vital in the harvesting, shaping and use of coreanium.

Genetics

Most hereditary, mutagenic and viral ailments of any significance have been eradicated and a lost limb or organ can be restored. The technology to clone individual limbs and organs has been perfected, and with the application of artificial stem cell therapy the doctors can fix most injuries. The process is quick and uses a combination of nanotechnology (nerve attachment and stimulation) and genetically engineered growth hormones. But it's not cheap, and many can't afford it. The cloning of humans is illegal but quite possible.

Artificial Gravity

The technology was provided by the Gerions but the scientists still have little knowledge as to how it actually works. The first step in the process is to manufacture crystals comprised by several different minerals. These are then cut in a very specific way and bombarded with an array of designed isotopes all the while they're subjected to several bursts of magnetism. In the last step they're coated in a titanium/wolfram/osmium and magnesium alloy. This process is extremely dependent on timing (down to the nanosecond). The end result is a silvery cube with sides that measures 11.26 cm. These are the so-called "grav-cubes". The Gerions provided us with blueprints to build the production units for these. Even though we can put them together and produce the cubes we have no idea exactly how the production unit works. However, scans have shown that the cubes generate a gravitomagnetic field and affect organic materials (including living creatures) through an advanced form of diamagnetism. So the human scientific community has a rudimentary understanding of the theoretical physics behind the technology. Basically, it's the reversal of dia-magnetic levitation but the scale and intricacy of the process is way beyond anything human science has been able to achieve.

The cubes are usually fitted in a grid (about fifty cubes per grid is necessary, a grid is formed in a square with sides of 1 meter) that is installed in the floor of colonies, ships and stations. As long as there's an electromagnetic field (which only takes a small electromagnet running on 100 or so volts to maintain) they create a gravity equal of Earth norm. Every ship designed for space travel (as well as space stations) has these as do every colony where it's necessary.

Planet Core Purification

Core purification is the official name for the process but most people call it core harvesting or planet harvesting. The ships that have been designed for this purpose have the official title of "purifiers", however the titles *core harvesters, planet harvester* or *planet reapers* are what most people call them. The PR departments of the GIC, SES and IMC prefer that their official high ranking employees (and the crew members of these ships) use the title "purifier" as it has a much more "user friendly" tone. A core harvester is basically a modified ore hauler. It has been fitted with the *core filter* and offered up some of its ore storage capacity for this. Though, newer models use a gigantic external grav-cuff array for this.

The first step is to survey the planet in order to assess if it has a liquid core. This can take several weeks. If there is ore on the planet (enough to make setting up a mining colony profitable) mining ensues. The mining can take several years and at the same time the crew digs downward towards the core in a previously surveyed area. When the mining is over a core harvester is called in. Grav-cuffs are used to remove a large piece of the planet crust over the core dig. Then the crew continues to dig manually. If the planet is small and unstable the colony is evacuated (and often disassembled) before the final stages are commenced. Powerful explosives do the rest of the job and blow away the final sediments, exposing the core. Now it's time for the core filter.

The core filter is composed of several hundred powerful electromagnetic rings filled with conductive nanites. The rings are one hundred an fifty meters in diameter. When put in use they're extended in a straight line down, held some hundred meters apart by the magnetism. This makes up a structure which acts as a tube. It's plunged into the molten core, still connected to the harvester in orbit. Then the actual harvest sequence commence. The core is pumped up through the enormous tube, fully visible as it's kept in check by the nanites and magnetic fields. The tube leads to the sifter. Approximately 50% to 80% of the core is sent into space where it cools to floating masses of hard lava rock. However, the sifter has secured the most important part. The substance which the harvest is all about: Coreanium.

Coreanium

This has become the lifeblood of the universe. It powers long range spaceships, ghost line entries, larger colonies and basically the whole of Claret City and Mondus City. It has a scientifically unexplainable energy efficiency when used as a fuel. Coreanium is an extremely dense material, approximately seventy times as dense as osmium. Coreanium in its raw form is a crystalline material which is jet-black, shifting to a glowing orange in flowing stripes as if containing a florescent liquid. Before it can be used it has to be formed into a perfect sphere. The shaping process can only be performed in zero-g. The material is heated to 5,982.3 (exactly) Celsius and shaped into a sphere by the means of an electromagnetic field. At this stage it's also divided into smaller bits depending on how large they wish to make the final cores). It has to stay heated for five days in zero-g after it has been shaped. After this it is subjected to an intense bombardment of Beta rays for twelve hours (still heated). The radiation is completely absorbed in the material and it emits no harmful radiation. Directly after it has been radiated it's rapidly cooled by being emerged in liquid nitrogen. It's left there until its frozen solid (time depends on amount). However, if the process is disturbed it can result in a coreanium explosion which is a devastating thing indeed.

When the process is complete, an inactive coreanium core immerges. It's completely harmless in this state, and virtually indestructible. It is still jet-black but it has now shifted from orange flowing stripes of glowing orange to red. When coreanium is combusted at a low rate it emits an orange to red glow. When combusted in a high rate it becomes bright blue, or white with a hue of blue.

Coreanium processing plants are located far from human colonies and space stations, surrounded by heavy security. There are about five hundred people working in a coreanium processing plant. They live on the facility and are rotated every two months.

"Coreanium is a clean and stable energy source. Its energy output and efficiency makes helium 3 look like lighter fluid by comparison…"

- Dr Darren Fujikoma, Energy Department, OMCP

The Reactor

The coreanium reactor is basically a giant led-weave polymer encased electromagnetic chamber. The core is suspended in the field. The core is then activated by a twenty thousand volt jolt. It is now active and emits a dangerous field of radiation, which is kept in check by the led-weave. When active it is capable of generating an extremely combustible gas which emits no pollution whatsoever when burned. However, the gas (cardion gas) is extremely poisonous and radioactive before it's burned. The amount of current run through the core after it has been activated decides the output. And no current results in zero output. After the core has been activated it has become a self contained system. The combustion is used to (beyond acting as a propulsion system) charge the ships spools and generators to produce electricity, which in turn is used to fuel the core and the ships electrical grid. A leak in the reactor is extremely dangerous as both radiation and gas can escape.

The core hangs very steadily in its self-contained magnetic field. If a reactor is destroyed, as by an explosion, the core becomes inactive (if not destroyed). It loses seventy percent of its remaining power life and has to be reactivated. The surface of the core becomes grey, dim and still and it emits no radiation whatsoever when inactive. This means that the core never can explode, creating a radioactive wasteland or field. But leaks in the cardion gas processing system or malfunctions in the gas cooling system can cause the cardion to go critical and explode. A short-circuit that makes the current produce excess cardion can also result in dangerous situations. There's also the possibility of replenishing a reactor core by a process called cardion assimilation. However, if a reactor has thirty percent or less of reactor life left it cannot be refueled. The reactor is hooked up to a so-called *disperser*. In turn, this device feeds of another coreanium core (dubbed assimilation nucleus). Each five percent reactor life increase in the reactor being replenished strips two point five percent of the life of the core used for this process. The assimilation nucleus has to be a core of double the size as the core being "re-fueled". An assimilation nucleus undergoes a special process which enables it to be used in this way. The downside is that this process renders it quite unstable and unable to be used in any other way (and the assimilation nucleus itself can't be refueled). Disperser stations come in the form of ships that lay in orbit or in well travelled lanes controlled by the GIC. The GIC, SES and IMC has license to own and use these commercially. The MEC and CIM also have a few. Reactors usually are refueled every couple of months or years, but the amount of ships and space station that use coreanium are plenty so an average disperser go out on calls a couple of times a week. This means that they rake in a lot of money as the customers pay a small fortune for this service. Needless to say, a disperser is escorted by heavy security.

Belinium & Capacitance

Short ranged space- and air-crafts (and ground vehicles) use Belinium fuel. As does all electronic devices that are independent of being plugged in. Belinium is a mineral that, after refined and converted into *Capacitance*, becomes a very effective fuel. It has a very low pollution output when combusted (1/100 of today's fossil fuels) and a very high energy efficiency. Capacitance comes in the form of power cells of different sizes. It can be used in two ways: produce electrical power or combustible energy. When used to produce combustible energy the rod of capacitance is actually used up. They glow blue when used, and if producing combustible energy it heats up to about 300 Celsius.

The belinium gas that is produced and the rod itself are very flammable when activated and used to produce combustible energy. Direct hits on the gas reserve or active cells can result in an explosion. When a cell has been used, even just the slightest, to produce combustible energy it can never be used to produce electrical energy.

When used to produce electrical energy the cell isn't used up. The glow of the rod gets fainter and fainter and when empty the rod looks like deep blue glass without a glow to it. However, cells used this way can be recharged if plugged in to an external power source and used again. It takes about an hour to fully recharge a battery of cells (which might have the juice to power a tank for eight hours). A cell can be recharged and used up to thirty times if undamaged. Most ground and water vehicles use electrical energy as they are independent of a combustible propellant. Belinium was one of the major sources of fuel used in space travel before discovering core purification. It's still a valuable resource and MEC and CIM have had many run-ins with the GIC and the major corporations on backwater planets, fighting for the control over the precious mineral. In its raw form belinium is a brightly blue colored crystal that can grow as high as one meter. It's

A science researcher is conducting energy efficiency research.

harvested through mining, often by mining crews using Planet Construction Rigs. These vehicles are called PCR by some, but the most common epithet among miners and work crews is the less charming *Pecker*. When harvesting belinium a very dangerous radiation runs the risk of being released. This generally happens when the mineral is harvested to quickly or if the material is cut using the wrong method, causing friction along the wrong cutting angles. Wearing radiation resistant COGs is necessary when working with belinium mining. The radiation has been a source of constant conflict as large companies and at times the GIC mine claims near smaller settlements. This has resulted in radioactive dust blowing across the habitats, causing deaths, radiation poisoning and mutations.

Plasma

Many cutting tools use plasma technology. Plasma is a partly ionized gas which is an effective conductor of electricity. The plasma is contained by electromagnetic nanites that have been programmed to keep a certain pattern when activated. The plasma is set ablaze by a charge of electricity and contained and shaped by the magnetic nanites. The actual combustion is contained within the magnetic field but the immense heat is directed outward. This system means that the tools can't ignite volatile gases or other materials (if the combustion containment chip hasn't been disabled). The density of the nanites also gives the plasma density. So what you end up with is a bright blue shaped beam of plasma with a density, edge and enormous heat. These tools are often used for mining.

Plasma technology has never been developed into weapons as such since the devices are quite bulky and heavy, which is a result of the plasma containment system. The bigger the plasma beam the bigger the device. It is possible to shoot plasma, but these "bolts" can only maintain stability for five meters before they dissipates, which doesn't make them adapted for weapon use. Only when employing electromagnetic stabilizers is plasma an effective long range weapon. But these take a lot of space and therefore only vehicles employ plasma as a weapon in this way. An active plasma tool emits a hum and a slight screeching crackling noise when used.

Gravitational Chains

Gravitational Chains, called grav-chains or grav-cuffs by most ("let's slap on the grav-cuffs" is a common phrase used), are employed in order to make docking procedures and mining

A Kiru has been hired to oversee the security of a state of the art SAC on a E-Class mining ship.

easier. Larger ships (and space stations) have grav-cuff emitters while smaller ships have grav-cuff receivers. When a small ship wishes to dock and has permission to do so (or if they have the docking code) the ship with the hangar emits the grav-cuffs while the smaller ships open its receivers. The cuffs lock on to these and then guide the ship on an automatic docking route. A small ship can always choose to disengaged, as can the hangar. But it is possible to hack and override these procedures.

The system is used to minimize accidents. It can get pretty crammed at times and some space stations are very busy. Having this system in place lets the computer keep track of all the comings and goings (under human supervision of course) and organize dockings in a safe way. It's like an automatic valet parking service.

When used in mining and construction the receivers are attached to the materials that are to be lifted and then a ship (can be in orbit or within the planets atmosphere) uses its emitters to latch on and elevate the object. While the docking emitters generate a short range field which can reach all around the ship, emitters designed for lifting requires a direct line of sight to the receivers and uses concentrated beams.

Docking cuffs are invisible to the naked eye most of the time. Occasional ripples (like heat waves over a hot object) can surround the receiving ship in small bursts. In mining this technology is used to move and lift enormous amounts of stone and minerals. This is very effective when creating the first main shaft for the core harvesting process. The expression "gravitational" is quite wrong since the system works off powerful electromagnets, but it simply stuck.

Simulated Atmosphere Containment (SAC)

Space stations, large colonies and D and E ships have a SAC. These are self-contained systems which, if not malfunctioning, can sustain a ship crew for years on end. The SAC produces air, food and recycle water. As long as the coreanium reactor is online (or ample solar energy is available) the system is on the go. The reason why only D and E ships can have these systems is due to the fact that they require some space in order to work. Of course, there are a lot more to them than the functions listed below but these are the main pillars of a SAC system.

Oxy-Algae: These genetically engineered and nanite infused algae absorb CO_2 and convert it into breathable air. The name "oxy-algae" was from the beginning a nickname since the algae produce breathable air and not pure oxygen, but the name stuck and became official rather quickly. The algae have an extremely effective photosynthesis process and they're submerged in a solution of UV florescence nanites and different nutrients. The algae pools are often located in an enclosed system running under the hydroponics garden and due to the UV the pools glow a bright violet/blue and protected goggles are needed to look straight at them up close. These pools are huge and hold thousands of tons. Larger ships also have a back-up system of air tanks and CO_2 scrubbers which can support the crew for four days if not damaged. Smaller ships relay solely on CO_2 scrubbers and air tanks. These hold much longer than four days, but this is because D and E ships only has room for a small back-up (relying on SAC) while smaller ships have much bigger (in comparison to ship size) systems as these are the only things keeping the crew alive.

Hydroponics Garden: Here they grow the so-called *adaptable greens*. This is a plant with thick moist leaves. The plant has been genetically engineered and by providing different nutrients (which in fact are produced by combining proteins with the plant itself) the plant can take on the taste and composition of most vegetables and fruits. They are highly nutritious and contain everything that the fruit or vegetable they're emulating does.

Protein Pool: Large pools of liquid protein take care of the "meat". The protein is maintained by feeding it water and adaptable greens. This protein is then treated so that it's water content, and density is changed to simulate the taste and texture of different meats. Both the greens and the protein does a good job when it comes to providing a healthy and nutritious meal but the simulation of taste and texture is only so-so, and miles apart from the splendor of the real thing.

Water Recycling: All water is recycled, but the SAC can also take in gases and materials from outside sources that has trace amount of water and filter this water out through nano-filters. All in all, and if not damaged, the water recycling is a self-contained system.

> **Note:** *Every type of contained system where breathable air is upheld by technology is highly resistant to lesser forms of contamination as the scrubbers take care of these things. So simply put, of course your avatar can smoke cigarettes and such onboard the ships, space stations and colonies. Smoke em' if you got em'!*

Stasis Sleep

When traveling for a long distance months can tick away, in order to preserve the lifespan of crew members (and on C-class ships to preserve rations and air supply as well) the crew goes into stasis. Additionally, staying awake inside a ghost line can have extremely adverse effects. When going into stasis, the crew lays down in stasis tanks. In the tank three things happen. First off, the artificially grown alkaloid metrocomexhan is released in a gaseous form (invisible to the naked eye). The metrocomexhan is loaded individually in each stasis tank,

since having a large tank of this kind of substance is a bad idea in any contained environment. Within a minute a human is put in an induced coma.

After this a concentrated swarm of nanites is released in the tank. They enter the body through osmosis. These are programmed to kick in as soon as the core body temperature goes below 36 Celsius. The tank is then filled with rapidly cooling air, which in the end reduces the temperature of the body to 1 degree Celsius. When hypothermia sets in the nanites performs one of their main tasks. They position themselves in strategic areas in the body and provide oxygen stasis, neural stimulation and other vital tasks which keep the body alive. Secondary they halt the effects of free radicals, in effect halting aging all together. This process only works when the body heat is reduced to 1 Celsius. It takes about three hours before the body is brought fully into stasis. But the actual process of waking up takes a week. The ship computer will begin the process of waking the person one week before he's suppose to be fully awake.

Waking up from stasis is somewhat disorienting and it's quite the ordeal. Imagine waking up with an extremely nasty hangover, a migraine and a bad case of arthritis and you get the idea.

Going in and out of stasis too rapidly is not a good idea. The body needs time to readjust. First off, stasis shouldn't be entered if the sleep will last less than a week (this can severely affect a person's sleeping patterns, short term memory and overall health). Secondly, a period of at least one week should pass before a person goes into stasis again after waking up. Going in too early after awakening will have the same effects as waking too early. Being exposed to early awakenings and early stasis on a reoccurring basis will in the end lead to a total organ failure and death. While in stasis a person can't heal, but on the other hand are the effects of wounds and illnesses temporarily halted as well.

> ***In Game Stasis Effects:*** *Upon awakening on scheduled time the human body is weak. For eight hours minus Brawn the person suffers a −2 modifier to all rolls due to pain and weakness. If being roused prematurely the aftereffects of the stasis will be much worse. Proximity warnings or life threatening ship malfunction can set off the VIN which in turn will jostle the flight crew from their stasis prematurely. This has the extreme adverse effects of short term but rather acute memory loss, minor hallucinations inspired by negative experiences and occasional bouts of vertigo and possible vomiting. The memory loss is very selective. It strips everything but skills and general knowledge of the world. A pilot will know how to fly and remember other flight missions, but he will be incapable of remembering his name or why he's on his current mission or any real personal details. This memory loss can last for as short as an hour or as long as seventy two hours. The memory comes back in flashes bit by bit. This is a powerful and classic tool that can be used to build your levels and chapters. The negative modifier is unchanged by premature stasis interruption and lasts as with normal awakening. Those in stasis have no need of air or nutrition whatsoever.*

Science researcher Angela Ventress is about to be roused from a month long stasis sleep.

A Horrifying Rebirth?

There are no specifics on how a person has to prepare before entering into stasis. This has been kept open for a reason. You have to decide the particulars of the stasis, how slight or gruelling is the process?

Sure, it says that the person in stasis don't need any nourishment but does his blood need to move around and does this require him to have tubes of anticoagulants and similar substances inserted into his body? Can the avatars wear clothes while entering stasis or do they have to be naked, or covered in a film of micro-proteins as a part of the process? Or maybe the stasis cache is a bit larger, containing a sludge of artificial stem cells in which the avatar is suspended during stasis. Each awakening will be like a messy and painful expulsion from an unforgiving steel womb as seen in Lost Redemption.

How you set this up goes a long way when it comes to how light or dark your game is, and as it's a part of travelling the

ghost lines it will factor in to the already reprehensive attitude most people have towards ghost jumps. You have to tweak your world details and design it until you have created a world that suits you and your gamers.

Nano-Interface Screen (NIS)

Some static keypads and displays are still used at times but NISs are the norm. These are comprised of a low current, electromagnetic field and incandescent naniets. They are set up to take on various shapes (usually a square or rectangular shape) and digital information is sent to them which provide them with color and shape data. This results in a one millimeter thin screen with projected images. These are used as gauges, keypads and screens. They can be made to look solid or more transparent. Solid objects can be run through these screens, with a pressure of only 250 grams. The screen is still maintained and undisturbed by this. Most keypads are projected so that they have a solid background (a wall, desk, etc) but screens usually hang in mid-air. The 250 gram pressure is in place for touch screen functions as it's much more comfortable and easy to be able to feel the screen when pushing projected buttons. Keypad controls (especially in ships) benefit greatly from NISs as new functions can get an added key if needed and every pad can be personally customized as the buttons can be moved around from the default settings, formatted to fit the user.

The NIS system is also used to project full free floating 3D holographic images which are extremely useful when navigating in a 3D environment such as space. The system is very well adapted at performing simulations such as engineering tests by manipulating simulated components in 3D.

Weapon Technology

Firearms are still ballistic in nature. Bullets are usually made of titanium alloys. The bullet casings hold a small amount of cold resistant nanotech supported oxygen infused gunpowder which gets the bullet moving. This composition assures that extreme cold and vacuum won't present a problem while firing the weapon. The weapon mechanism itself is also adapted to extreme environments. The barrel is mainly composed of a hyper charged magnetic coil which uses the small kinetic energy and accelerates the bullet. In effect, all firearms are *coil gun hybrids*. When fired there's a small bang followed by a short metallic "whooshing" sound.

Missiles come in many forms; one of the most effective is the plasma hybrids. These have a main plasma detonation which ignites a secondary combustible fuel and results in a powerful blast. The plasma detonation does a lot of damage on impact, actually capable of softening the metal before the secondary explosion sends out a shockwave filled with shrapnel.

Plasma and photon technology has been developed for weapons usage, but the technology requires a lot of power and room to operate and these weapons are limited to larger vehicles as a result.

The Thor model core harvester "The Pinnacle" in orbit over a prospective planet.

Terraforming/Planet Engineering

Terraforming is a process that takes a lot of money and often a lot of time. The time span depends on the individual planet's atmosphere. If the atmosphere is very hostile and far from what humans need to survive, it will take about twenty years to terraform a planet, while it could take as little as five years to shape a planet that's already close to the conditions of old Earth.

The process is basically done in two steps after the planet has been okayed. To begin with, huge atmosphere generators are set up all over the planet (ranges from 10 to 200 in numbers depending on the size and condition of the planet). Colonists stay on to monitor these. The generators produce (or recombines local gases) breathable air little by little and simulates a growing eco system that adapts to the conditions. When the atmosphere is breathable the generators are deconstructed and phase two is initiated. Phase two involves several ships that bombard the surface with enormous amounts of oxy algae, water and fauna. The colonist then sees to it that it takes hold. And this is basically how it's done. As the technology available isn't capable of changing the gravity of a planet it's lucky that there are so many planets in the Sirius system that have Earth norm gravity, or thereabouts. But in cooperation with the Gerions the research into the production of planetary gravity stabilizers has begun.

Ghost Lines

The GIC dubbed these FTL (Faster Than Light) Lanes but the term ghost lines became popular quite soon, and not without a good reason. When first introduced by the Gerions the ghost lines were thought to be a successful application of the theory of the Alcubierre Drive (a theory proposed in 1994 by physicist Miguel Alcubierre) but it soon became apparent that this was not the case.

The ghost lines have never been fully understood, the only thing the scientists know for sure is that they're extra dimensional pockets in which distances can be "skipped".

"It's like switching the gears of space. When moving in normal space everything goes on the small gear, the cog need to spin very fast in order to get anywhere. But slipping into a ghost line is like switching gears. Very little movement of the cog is needed to travel faster and further. Very much like a bicycle."

- Alessa Barkley, second grade teacher at Claret City south youth learning institute.

While traveling a ghost line it looks like hurtling down a tunnel made out of dark swirling smoke raging with electrical storms. The space in-between the tunnel walls is filled with a thin mist-like atmosphere. A quite unnerving thing about traveling in the ghost lines is the fact that colors seem to disappear. It's just not the ability to perceive color that is lost, video recording and video-logs of ghost travels sent or brought into normal space are also shown to be black and white. All ships have a ghost mode, which means that indicators which rely on color switches to symbols, clear shades of gray, voice protocols and letters. Then there's the shadow effect. All shadows cast by a living being have a two second delay. The shadow is "stuck" where it's cast and fades out after two seconds. This means that shadows will leave a fading trail on walls and floors as a person moves. These effects were the reason why the name ghost line caught on.

When a ship makes a ghost jump a jet-black cloud surrounded by an unidentified electrical disturbance appears and engulfs the ship after which it seems to dissipate, taking the ship with it. This happens about a second after the *ghost drive* have been activated. Before a jump can be made (well, it can be made anyway if the security protocol is overridden, but that's basically suicide) a ghost line calculation (GLC) has to be done. When jumping through established and plotted out lines it's a pretty simple task to do the calculation. However, if plotting out a new course and arriving at a never before known destination it's always a more arduous task. One thing that has to be understood about ghost lines is that they're not travel lanes that move the ship a distance in a direction like a road or normal space travel. They move the ship between dimensions. So a miscalculation will not result in being brought "half way there" rather it can result in being brought to the wrong system, or worse, beyond the *Dark Rim* from which no one has returned as of yet. There are many ships that have gone missing in the lines.

The actual calculations are made using the onboard computer which feeds off the ghost drive's weaver unit. The ghost drive is a device given to us by the Gerions, like most the technology they have given us we're capable of using it and back engineer it, but we can't really figure out how it works. The drive weighs about a ton. It is composed of an intricate web of nano filament wires and nano circuit boards which are tightly packed together (using nano-tube technology). The drive's core is made out of an extremely complex alloy which is kept in liquid form and suspended in a magnetic field, when activated for calculation the core splits into billions of microscopic components. The weaver unit is a highly advanced laser scanner which is connected to the ship's scanners, and transmits the calculations to the core. When the drive core splits up it actually creates an extremely complex (and without translation, incomprehensible) extra dimensional map which the weaver unit translates into mathematical calculations that can be interpreted by a human. By adjusting these calculations and running them back and forth to the weaver unit a GLC navigator will in the end (if not very unlucky) get an accurate and safe route. It is unknown how the drive's core gets a signal out to these dimensions and accurately scans them within seconds, but no transmissions can be picked up from the core as it is activated. The drive is surrounded by a cooling unit (without which it would blow up when activated) as the drive heats up to near 3,000 degrees Celsius when activated.

An established lane uses a set of algorithms and calculations already on file, but there are always small adjustments which means that even established lanes require the navigator to make calculations. Someone who wants to make a jump but has no idea how to calculate can only try to take the calculations on file, copy and paste them (four to twelve algorithms have to be combined before the drive can make a jump) and hope for the best. Using this method there's no way to tell where the ship will end up, or if it will make it at all.

The "speed" by which a ship can travel wile using a ghost line changes depending on the distance. It is unknown why these distances are the ones in place and why the "speed" seems to change violently depending on the distance traveled. The time cut off is always done according to a set multiple measured in light-years with the margin of error of 500 meters of the final destination, which makes it extremely accurate. It would be quite possible to make several short jumps, stopping and jumping repeatedly, in order to make better time but there are two things to consider. The drive has to cool down for about four hours after a jump (some ships comes with dual drives, one for emergencies) and then there's the fact that each new jump requires a new calculation which involves an unnecessary risk. But it is possible to jump with a hot drive, but the risk is that the ship blows up or ends up outside the black rim. Beyond this, the risk of VPS seems to increase if jumping in and out of the ghost lines.

A ghost jump can't be "cut short" while ongoing without consequence. The drive isn't active while traveling in the lines, only when getting in and out. So when you jump you better be damn sure you have it right and that the ship is prepped and stocked because you can't turn back in mid jump so to speak…at least not without major risks.

Before performing a jump the ship has (should) be at least five hundred meters from any objects (or tight clusters of several small ones forming one) that weighs a ton or more. This includes surfaces on planets or surrounding atmospheric gases. If these requirements are not met there's a 50% chance that the object/gases merges with the ghost drive. This can result in everything from a nuclear explosion to hull breaches or erratic jumps.

Before the Ghost Storm the ghost lines were much more effective, but this is the maximum ranges that we can travel today in one go.

Ghost Jump Chart	
Light Years	**Time**
1–500	24 hours
501–2000	2 weeks
2,001–6000	1 month
6001–24000	2 months
24,00 - 72,000	4 months

Transmitting Through the Ghosts: Radio transmissions moves faster than solid objects when traveling the lines. Any radio transmission takes between half to a quarter of the time it takes to travel. So for example, a transmission sent for a distance of 2,001 to 6,000 ly would take approximately one to two weeks to reach its destination. Most ships have a LSA (Line Signal Amplifier), which is a device that is designed to open up a small line while in normal space trough which a signal can be sent long distance. The LSA is commonly called "the scare" or "scare box" (as in not a whole ghost but a scare). This is a device separate from the main radio and scanners. When used, all other scanners on the ship using it (not affecting other ships) are jammed for about half an hour. D and E-Class ships have a separate LSA array which is insulated from the rest of the system, preventing the scanners from being jammed. If this breaks down they have to use the emergency LSA which will jam the scanners for 30 minutes as usual.

Piloting in the Ghost: It's possible to travel with other ships if they have synced up with your jump. They don't have to go the same distance but they have to be within 0,5 light years from each other. There's really no reason to sync, as they will arrive simultaneously if going the same time and to the same place. But it might be prudent to sync if raiding a ship inside the ghost line.

Two minutes after someone has made a jump there's a so-called "dragon tail" (grab on to fly with) left behind. This is actually a small dimensional rift holding the energy pattern of the ship that jumped and their ghost line. If quick enough a navigator can calculate using this and jump after the ship. The end destination doesn't have to be the same though. While inside the ghost line everything looks the same, but there is a space that the pilot can move around in. Each ghost line has a spherical space of one hundred kilometers in which the pilot can move around and put distance between himself and other ships in the same line. The "walls" of a ghost line is basically one giant electrical storm (which ship scanners will pick up on) and if going into this wall the ship blows up. So ships can have dog fights inside a ghost line. But remember that you can't flee. Once you're in the line you're in. If not doing a FMS.

The FMS: FMS simply stands for Fuck Me Sideways and was uttered by freelance pilot Christina G Ahlqvist. Back in 367 IT she was being bushwhacked by raiders while inside a ghost line. The odds were four to one in their favor. She fought bravely but she was losing and she had no where to run. She knew that activating a ghost drive within a ghost line would result in blowing up her ship. But what would happen if she put the drive in reverse, flipping the energies? She knew that this (at least in normal space) would blow up the ship as well. So she took a shot, maybe it wouldn't blow up the ship while inside a line. She calculated her last jump, reversed the energy and jumped. She ended up about five hundred light years from her intended destination (instantly), and her ship had basically ripped itself apart but she was alive. As she came out debris and chunks of her ship came flying off it. She had also ended up in the middle of a well traveled lane outside a trading station and ships had to avoid smacking into her and pieces of wreckage. The LED-officers patrolling the area had seen the whole thing and immediately hailed her. Asking what had happened and if she was okay. On their screen they got a wide-eyed Christina clamping on to the controls as if they were a life raft, staring at them franticly repeating the phrase "Fuck Me Sideways, I'm Alive!"

So when in a pinch inside a Ghost Jump one can try to do a FMS. This will hurl the ship out of the line very violently. The physics of it is unknown, but the person will end up anywhere from 200 to 1,600 light years from their point of origin or destination (Roll 2Ds and multiply the result by 100). However, the ship will take a severe beating. Roll 1D+2 and that's the amount of HIL that will be reduced from the ship (won't go beyond smashed if the ship hasn't reached lower than banged up). It's impossible for someone to get a hold of the dragon tail of a ship doing a FMS. When performing an FMS the ship is exempt from the proximity rule concerning objects.

The Social Impact of Stasis and Ghosts: Age is a relative term in the world of C&D. Space travelers who work in deep space travel for months and lay in stasis for months. A ten year career of this can result in years of accumulated stasis sleep, which means years that the person hasn't aged. The ID cards in the C&D universe contains date of birth and stasis time put in to keep track of how many years the person has been inactive.

Deep space workers seldom have a family, if they do the family live on the ship with them as part of the work crew. Deep space mining ships have schools, maternity wards and everything else needed. It's hard to have a family in port. They age and experience the months, while the one in stasis simply go to sleep and awake months later (which seems like an instance to them) and haven't aged a day. Coming home can be hard. For the person in stasis nothing has changed while they slept, but the person at home has experienced and felt a lot of things during this time. And in the end, the person in port will age much faster (in a way) than the one in stasis. This is something to keep in mind as it will have a profound impact on relationships.

No One Likes the Ghost

Ghost lines are in fact a very perilous way of travel. We activate a device we don't understand, hurl hundreds of tons worth of spaceship, and ourselves along with them, into an eerie dimension we don't comprehend. Inside it's unnatural and very unsettling. And each jump can be the last.

Ghost jumps are quite normal to those who travel the reaches, but most still don't like them. There are no game mechanics that will emulate this, but it should always be kept in mind that ghost jumping is something that makes most people a bit unnerved.

Take into consideration the scientifically proven risk of VPS in crew members while awake in the ghost, and that a lot of ships have gone missing in this strange place during the years.

This said, most prefer to pilot in normal space whenever possible if not in a hurry. If it would take a ship two weeks to reach a planet they rather take their sweet time than making a dangerous and expensive jump which would save them thirteen days. "If you can get there within two normal space months, don't bother to jump" is the general rule.

Rapid Transit Drive

Using the enormous energy output provided by coreanium, the RTD (or RT-Drive) simply accelerates a spaceship to incredible speeds. This drive is often used instead of the ghost drive when travelling within any given solar system. The upside is that the RT-Drive uses less energy than a ghost jump which means that the reactor runs on normal output. In fact, it runs on lower output than when in normal propulsion. The drive

chokes the burners, focusing them into high thrust points. The acceleration/deceleration is achieved through a series of pulse bursts and glide periods during a four day stretch. Eight days in total (four during acceleration and four during deceleration). This process has been fine tuned and refined in order to conserve fuel. After the acceleration period is over the ship cuts thrust, holding a steady speed. Overall, the acceleration/deceleration process burns less than one percent of the reactor life. Beyond this the method doesn't impose the heightened risk of VPS which is inherent to the ghost lines and there's usually no need to put the crew in full stasis, directly reducing the cost as well. The downside is that the drive can't provide faster than light travel and that travelling in these enormous speeds while in normal space imposes the risk of collision and interception. Even if a safe course is plotted there's no way of anticipating all the dangers and situations that might occur. Only ships that have a coreanium reactor can use the RT-Drive.

During acceleration/deceleration the crew has to be suspended in dampening gel inside the stasis chambers. Without this protection a human would be crushed by the force. The dampening gel is a mix of water combined with specially constructed polymers and binding nano-chains. The polymer is reusable, and the water is taken from the ships water supply. The subject climbs into the tank, puts on an oxygen mask and the tank is rapidly filled with water. After this the nano-chains and polymers are introduced and they turn the water into a gel within one minute. When deactivating the nano-chains collect the polymers and resend them to their deposit inside

the stasis tube, after this the water drains and is recycled into the ship's supply. Overall, it's an efficient and low cost process.

The crew in the gel are simply put into an artificial coma by the use of metrocomexhan (unofficial name for this state is metro-coma), the same as stage one of the stasis process. This requires that nutrients and fluids are being pumped into the crew as their bodies are still up and running so to speak. But as the metabolic rate is lowered by the metrocomexhan and as a result of the lack of movement a human only needs one tenth of his regular nourishment and oxygen requirements. A low electrical current along with micro-vibrations in the gel stimulates the muscles and the bones of the occupant in order to hinder atrophy. While in this state a human still ages normally. The healing rate is slowed down (half of the normal healing rate) due to the changes in the metabolism. If travelling for extended periods the crew is put into stasis as when travelling the ghost in order to preserve rations on C-class ships but also in order to preserve the lifespan of the crew. It only takes a minute to be jostled from the metro-coma. Waking up from this state imposes the same aftereffects as waking up from stasis, but the effects only lasts an hour and however violent the awakening is there's no memory loss or similar side-effects. Metro-coma does not protect crew members from the adverse effects of the ghost lines like full stasis does.

When the ship is in transit and not accelerating/decelerating the crew is free to walk around as there's no physical danger. But most stay in their tubes in order to conserve resources and being awake for months, especially on a smaller vessel with little human interaction, can have adverse effects on the mental stability of an individual. Usually a handful, sometimes just one or two, crew members are awake to check on things, rotating a fresh watch crew after only a couple of weeks or so. The policy of keeping a few crew members awake has been put in place for safety reasons. It is impossible to steer while using the RT-Drive and the VIN is only so effective when using its scanners and warning systems. It's very prudent to have a watch crew that performs regular long range scans using the LSA and LIDAR, giving them at least a slim chance to decelerate in time if they see an unmoving high-risk object in their path four or more days beforehand. Even though the ship moves at an incredible speed, it's not impossible for other ships to intercept it using well placed missiles or even mines if they managed to calculate where the ship is going to be at a certain point and if the attackers are within range. Also, space pirates are known to buy RT-Drive routes for mining and trade ships from corrupt employees and ghost jump ahead, awaiting the arrival of the unsuspecting vessel.

The deck holding the SAC system of D and E-Class ships use several security measures in order to ensure the safety of the SAC while the RT-Drive is accelerating/decelerating the ship. The entire SAC-deck is suspended in a giant gravity swing with a lot of room to manoeuvre. The whole section moves during the four day period of acceleration/deceleration in order to compensate for some of the force, as well as sending gravitational shift waves throughout. This, in the combination with secure shielding around all the pools and hydroponics, and the fact that the adaptable greens have been genetically engineered to withstand the RT-Drive way better than natural plant life, makes it possible to subject a SAC to these forces. A human would however die in this environment while accelerating/decelerating.

Most systems have plotted out travel lanes, how safe they are often depends on how far out the system is. Most pilots and navigators start the deceleration a bit early, bringing the ship to a halt a day's worth of travel using normal propulsion from the intended destination. When travelling in these speeds it's quite unnecessary to work with tight margins.

RT-Drive Only Ships

Some companies buy ships with the intent of only using them within a solar system. These ships often handle cargo or missions which aren't that time sensitive. Prison transports, planet to planet ore hauling and crew rotation within the same solar system are examples of such operations. These ships are bought without a ghost drive which reduces the cost by thirty percent and they also get a ten percent reduction on all coreanium cost such as disperser services. This enormous reduction is more a question of a GIC tax reduction on ship price and coreanium than the actual manufacturing cost being brought down. The GIC makes it easier to buy and maintain these ships for civilians as a ship without a ghost drive is easier to keep track of. RT-Drive only ships are limited to C and D-class ships. In order for these ships to travel to faraway systems they dock with a larger ship that have jump capabilities or tag along in a ghost net. A lot of smaller outfits buy a

RT-Drive only ship, get jumped to the system where they're supposed to operate and start hauling their goods within the system. When their contract is over they get jumped to the next job. The jump fee is 5,000 for C-class ships and 10,000 for D-class ships, one way. Don't have the cash to jump? The jump-vendors won't care.

Medical Care

The technology has done amazing progresses due to genetics (see above) nanotechnology and stem cell research. Cancer, MS, Parkinson, Alzheimer, AIDS and all those other illnesses that plagued the 22th century are all but eradicated and curable. There are only a few incurable diseases left in the galaxy. But the most infamous and feared is the Caliphrian Aggression Virus (CAV, often pronounced *cave*). And of course people still suffer from the odd cold and mild flu. The basics of healthcare are still the same but the organization and technology has vastly improved. Beyond the astonishing ability to cure most illnesses, there are three major additions to health care technology which are worth mentioning. They're all variations of the same technology: Nanotechnology and artificially grown stem cells.

Regen

This has been a godsend, especially to the military. The regen comes in the form of an injection, which when injected straight into the wound will stabilize and heal it somewhat within thirty seconds. The artificial stem cells and nanites combine efforts and restructure the damaged area using nutrients within the solution. This process can close up knife cuts, bullet wounds and even grow back damaged parts of organs. But it can only be used in moderation, after which it actually can harm the body instead. Regen cannot heal or repair any form of brain damage.

Neuro-Worms

These are about one centimeter long and have a diameter of one millimeter. They're brightly blue colored and have one objective and that is to heal brain damage. The worms are injected into a small drilled up hole (if the damage hasn't exposed the brain that is) in the skull. From here they move around carefully in the brain tissue and restores damaged parts, even rebuilding entire sections.

Medi-Tank

Every hospital and well supplied medbay has a medi-tank. The tank is only used for emergencies when the damage is extreme. The injured person is submerged in a viscous reddish solution of nanites, artificial stem-cells and oxygen enriched nutrients. These encase the body and start to reconstruct the damaged area. The nanites can apply pressure by which they can reset bones and then graft and heal them. A person can come in to the hospital with several broken bones, and severe organ damage and walk out perfectly healthy just some days later. A medi-tank is necessary if replacing lost limbs and organs.

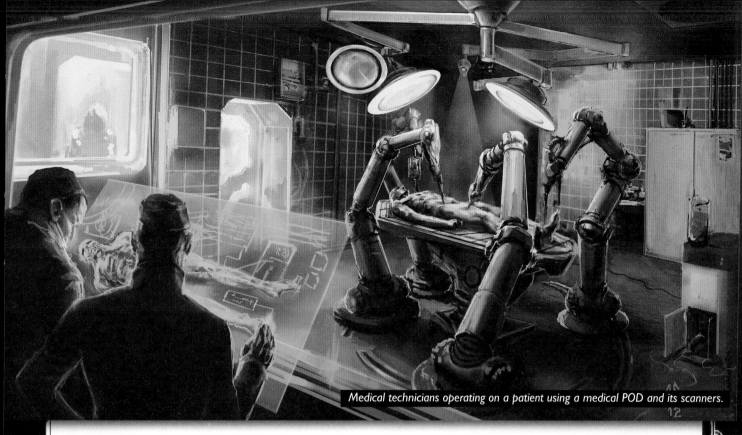

Medical technicians operating on a patient using a medical POD and its scanners.

COGs

COG stands for **C**ustomized **O**peration **G**ear and has become a vital part of everyday life and space exploration. From the beginning people used a lot of equipment that they carried around, but naturally it would be much smoother if most of the gear could be fitted and incorporated into a single unit. And with that the COG was born. There have been several versions of a COG unit, but the last twenty or so years there has been a standard model in use.

The basic COG comes in different template forms depending on the usage. Different work groups have their own customizations. For example, those working in an engineering capacity have interlinked tools while most military personal have flak plates and weapon links installed. However, there are many standardized COGs that corporations lend to their employees. The employees can buy these out and all upgrades they have made to them on their own are theirs to keep if they quit and don't buy out the COG. COGs are a very common sight and are very important pieces of equipment involved in space exploration and mining.

Powering the COG

Generally speaking, you don't need to keep track of the power supply of a COG. The suit recharges itself whenever it has access to one hour of ample sunlight or when the user moves around in an environment which uses grav-cubes for half an hour. The COG is designed to use sunlight to recharge its power cells as well as siphon current through the mag-boots through the electric grid used by the grav-cubes. It's also possible to physically plug the COG into any electrical grid available on a ship, solar power array or other facility with access to power.

A COG works for 48 hours before it needs to be recharged. After 48 hours without power everything will go offline, except the repair system, HUD and vital systems such as heating. These will remain active as long as the avatar can move around for at least four hours out of a twenty four hour period as it is recharged by nanogenerators woven into the absorption fibers. This works off a piezoelectricity system which converts kinetic energy into electrical. COGs that have shock armor installed will lower the movement of the user by 5 and give him a −2 to all Athletic rolls when running in low energy mode. This is due to the failing of the Ionic Polymer Metal Composite (IPMC), which when active generates artificial muscle activity, compensating for the weight of the shock armor.

> *The Etiquette of COGs: COGs are basically worn when in use. People who use them don't wear them as clothing but only as a part of their job. Pilots wear their COGs (if linked) when behind the helm, engineers use them when working in an environment that requires them and so forth. So basically, people wear COGs when they need to use them. Off shift flight crew or military personnel won't wear them on the ship.*
>
> *COGs are prohibited in most social locales such as bars, restaurants and the like. It's the equivalent of wearing a full army get-up (with helmet and all), construction gear with all the tools or a flight suit complete with the helmet and mask. Space harbor bars and some space stations allow them as there are a lot of travelers. But they are a common sight on the streets as LED-Officers wear them as a part of their job. It takes about 10 seconds to put on a COG if in a rush.*

Chapter 9: Society

In the Divius system's main hub GIC runs a pretty tight ship. Most travel lanes are marked and ghost line entries and exits have to be reported and done in one of the many space docks in the *ghost jump yard* (affectionately called graveyards). The *LED* units patrol all the known routes, and perform routine controls outside these lanes as well. But the further one comes from the core the less the law applies as the GIC presence declines. Whenever a large GIC colony, or station, pops up the GIC presence increase. As it can take months to travel to certain destinations there are a lot of backwater colonies which are run by local criminals as if they were their own private fiefdoms. The odd GIC patrols in these areas are often paid off as they have little choice as they're months from any significant backup.

Structure of the GIC

The GIC is the organization which runs things in the world of C&D. They legislate, uphold laws and regulate space and grant mining and planet harvesting licenses to corporations.

The GIC is a democratic institution which consists of a senate led by a chairman. Every ten years a new chairman is elected by the people and every forth year the people get to elect new members of the senate, of which there are six. Most decisions are discussed and voted on in the senate and they have monthly meetings. The vote of the chairman counts as two, which grants him a bit of leverage. The chairman is also considered to be the commander in any war situation and have the power to command the entire Consolidated Fleet and Marine Corps. Voting for proposals and legislations is the norm but in war times the chairman has complete control and the senate acts as a supportive think tank.

Half of the senate is always positioned in Mondus City while the other half spends most of its time in Claret City, as does the chairman. One of the senators have the position of vice chairman and he is by law required to live and work out of Mondus City, as are his two other senators. This is done so that if one of the planets is attacked, and the chairman or vice chairman is killed, the other can hold together a functioning government and military structure. Vice chairmen are elected every forth year in conjunction with the senate election. Of course, there are hundreds of other positions and people involved in the senate such as vice senators, resource management division, military strategy unit, the justice board and many others. The current chairman is the thirty nine year old Miaku D´Charnas. She has been in office for two years and is the youngest person in history to have been elected leader of the galaxy.

Senators and Departments

There are six major organs of the GIC: Resource Management Division, Military Strategy Unit, Medical Research Group, The Justice Board, Bureau of Interstellar Exploration and Office of Mining and Core Purification.

Each senator that goes up for election comes from a background (or at least tries to convince the voters of this) that makes him suitable for one of the six institutions. Each senator acts as the chief supervisor over one of the six governmental branches. They oversee the dispersal of resources, argue for increased budget if needed and keep up the structure of their branch. At the monthly meetings they report to the rest of the senate and the chairmen. These organizations are massive and a senator naturally delegates most of the work and only handles the key issues and the most important bits that needs to be taken care of.

Every month the so-called Forum is convened. Here the senators (or their representatives) convene and meet up with three hundred representatives of the people. Forum delegates vote on issues and legislations and argue for their needs and demands. They have no direct power as such, but how they vote and what they say act as a guide for what the common man on the street thinks, wants and needs. The forum election is done in clusters, several local delegates run for the position, six are chosen by the people and these six then hand picks forty nine (often predetermined already) forum members.

Bureau of Interstellar Exploration (BIE)

BIE is responsible for the planning and execution of exploring and mapping out new frontiers. They search for resources and alien artifacts. They investigate which planets that are candidates for terraforming and plan and execute GIC colonization. The BIE work closely with the OMCP and report when they have found a new mining site or core harvest opportunity.

Subdivision - Department of Xenoarchaeology (DoX 1): Every ship BIE send out has at least one scientist and one academic from this department on board.

Department of xenoarchaeology isn't fully accurate since DoX 1 has a lot of other scientists assigned to it. Physicists, chemists and similar researchers are attached to this institution as well. Their mission is to look for, excavate and examine alien artifacts and structures. Their finds are reported directly to the branch senator who in turn reports to the chief council of ISA. The ISA council will give a recommendation as to how to handle the find based on the data. Is it dangerous, where should it be transported and which level of secrecy should be attached to it? All divisions, private citizens and corporations are by law required to report any such finds to DoX 1. However, many disregard this in hopes of profits or new technology. The penalty for such a subterfuge can range from a steep fine if the thing found is minute and of no real value, to twenty-five years in prison if the artifact was dangerous, valuable or otherwise significant.

Senator: Elijah Naverepadjuhn

Interstellar Security Agency (ISA)

This organization isn't a part of the six divisions but work directly under the chairman and the senate. In extreme cases the chairman can exclude the senate (except the vice chairman) when discussing sensitive information and operation specifications with the ISA.

ISA has a direct insight into all military operations of any magnitude. These are reported from the chairman to the chief council of ISA. This is so that they can have the opportunity to decide if a particular situation should be handled by them or require the presence of their operatives in some capacity. If they think that something is worth investigating or important enough to launch an operation they file a recommendation with the chairman.

The chairman always has a liaison from the chief council of ISA close by. He sits in on the monthly senate meetings and report back to the council who then file a report to the chairman and vice chairman with an assessment if there's a security issue. As ISA has access to the chairman and the senate they're privy to everything that goes on within the official structure. They do have plants here and there in the branches so that they can get the heads up on things that might not get reported. They also take care of senate and chairman security.

ISA run covert as well as official operations. When ever they've got the ok from the chairman they can start their operation. The chairman grants them a certain amount of latitude depending on the nature of the operation. Those of the highest rank represent the senate itself when they have been granted the authority on a mission and have a clearance to take over all GIC personnel and access the most classified of files when on a job. If given the clearance by the chairman, an ISA operative even has the right to order around a senator. But then again, ISA conducts their own operations that neither the chairman nor the senate

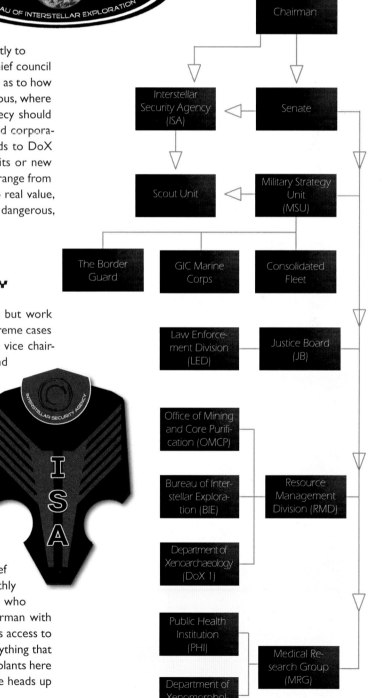

are aware of from time to time. Within an organization which has a "need to know basis" policy, corruption and power mongering of a more personal or fanatical nature is hard to avoid.

Justice Board (JB)

The Justice Board handles the laws, prisons and courts. They oversee the rights of the individual and are the main line of defense standing between criminals and law abiding citizens. The organization is composed of lawyers, administrators, judges and prosecutors. They often work with the OMCP and RMD when it comes to mining and core harvest rights of companies. JB also handles the LED.

Subdivision - Law Enforcement Division
(LED): This is the arm of the Justice Board. LED officers patrol the streets, investigate murders, keep tabs on organized crime and handle the everyday order in society. There are a lot of branches within LED such as uniformed patrols, homicide investigators and TARGET (**T**actical **A**rmed **R**esponse **G**roup and **E**xplosives **T**echnicians) and many more. LED is charged with the control of larger cities and the regulated space surrounding important planets. Larger (and official) GIC colonies, ships and space stations have a small LED team that keep the order.

Senator: Stina Lagerkrants

Medical Research Group (MRG)

This group has the responsibility of looking for dangerous pathogens and VPS. When they first started out they were a group that only focused on special cases, but these days they're also responsible for the general health.

In medical emergencies when a dangerous pathogen or an outbreak of VPS has occurred the senate appoints military resources to MRG containment and investigations teams if necessary. In these situations the operation is under MRG jurisdiction and the MRG are considered to have the highest rank until the senate or the chairman says otherwise.

A lot of the work they do is considered classified and they often coordinate with ISA in joint ventures. ISA and MRG are known to squabble over jurisdiction. ISA is never comfortable when they have to obey MRG and the door swings both ways. The senate and the chairman decide how an operation is to be classified. In many cases, also when MRG is working with the military, is the operation split into several stages of jurisdiction. The actual breach of an infected colony is under military jurisdiction (following containment procedures of course) while the on-site investigation and operation is under MRG jurisdiction, and when it finally comes to the cover story and the final decision on how to handle the aftermath ISA steps in. The senate never informs the public of outbreaks and VPS incidents if not absolutely necessary. Only about ten percent

of the VPS incidences reach the general public, and seldom the worst ones. The senate sees no meaning in "upsetting" citizens. Most of these tragedies are set up as "reactor failure, mining gas explosions" or "crashes".

Subdivision – Public Health Institution: Simply put, the PHI runs the general hospitals and handles everyday medical care (including dental) and ambulance services. Healthcare is paid for by the general taxes and medical care is administered without cost and there's no need for insurance. The GIC wants its citizens to be healthy and provided with high-quality care. However, some treatments do cost the patient. Re-growing limbs is extremely costly and this is only done if the person has a limb care plan package (which runs them about 5,000 credits a year) or if they have the means to pay directly. But the PHI does re-grow organs which without the patient wouldn't survive and this is free as it goes under the "humane treatment act" which is put in place to guarantee a certain quality of healthcare for the citizens. But health care isn't very high quality or reliable in many of the outer colonies as these have a hard time getting supplies.

Subdivision — Department of Xenomorphology (DoX 2): They focus on researching rippers and Gerions and alien pathogens. When new pathogens of an alien origin are found DoX 2 get to work on it. They also study the best way of handling rippers and study their life cycle and the most effective way to kill them.

Senator: Dr Svetlana Boraski

Military Strategy Unit (MSU)

Every military action and strategic positioning of defense outposts is planned by the MSU. This branch is responsible for military research, tactical planning and oversees the Consolidated Fleet and the Marine Corps. Their different departments always have at least one ISA liaison that has total insight into the operations and projects. The core of the MSU is run by the joint commanders, which consists of twelve members. These are the brightest and best of their fields (weapons research, defensive and offensive tactics and strategy). The MSU have hundreds of departments and subdivisions of think-tanks and researchers but whatever weaponry they come up with, or whatever strategy they choose to employ, there are three well known external resources that make use of them.

Consolidated Fleet: The fleet is an old institution and was from the beginning the only military force that the GIC needed. Most of their military actions off Earth were won and lost in the void. The fleet had army tactical ground and ship breach teams on board. When supported by a well coordinated fleet this was enough. But after the interstellar ripper infestation, things changed. Today the fleet is just that, a fleet which sole purpose is to patrol and conduct their business in the air/space. Their onboard ground team was cancelled the day the GIC-Marine Corps were created. Nowadays the marines take care of the ground and breach teams, which have created a bit of rivalry between the two institutions since the GIC-Marine Corps were created in 412 IT.

The fleet is a force to be reckoned with as they command the GIC armada. They patrol the borders of space, transport the marines to their destinations and keep watch, always looking into the darkness in hopes of being ready to stop the next threat before it reaches the rest of mankind.

GIC Marine Corps: Even though this group only has about a hundred years of history they're rightfully known as the toughest military unit that has ever existed. From the beginning they were created to board space stations and ships, and breach colonies that had been infested by rippers. But nowadays they handle any military operation of importance. They're an elite group specialized in handling rippers, violent outbreaks of VPS and they are sent in to handle special threats. Where space ends and the planet, colony or infested ship begins the job of the GIC-Marine Corps commences. The corps got a hard time at its inception from the fleet that more or less heckled the "rookie" organization. But what the fleet didn't realize was that the corps had a whole different angle and training. The corps proved their worth and nowadays they heckle the fleet back, saying that they're not much without their ships. Bar brawls between the fleet and the marines are not an uncommon sight. However, when the shit hits the fan they got each other's backs, even though they don't skimp on the un-pleasantries even when cooperating. Of course, not every fleet member and marine dislikes each other but it's a common thing, especially among rookies.

The Border Guard: These men and women have gone through basic training and are the most common type of soldier. They usually have a standard two year contract (a marine contract runs on for six). The border guard patrol outposts, smaller colonies and engage in larger scale battles where expertise isn't needed in

the same degree and they represent the "run of the mill soldier". This organization was created due to the increased need for military presence at mining colonies and other outpost as a result of increased ripper infestations and raider activities. This is another reason why the fleet has a problem with the marines. The border guards were originally formed from the onboard strike teams of the fleet after the corps was created. Now they represent the general army of the GIC.

Senator: Gorman Elkins

Office of Mining and Core Purification (OMCP)

When a possible GIC mining or purification site has been spotted by BIE the OMCP moves in. They send in surveyors and a small crew to evaluate the site and then send back a report to the RMD of estimated costs, projected return of investment and time table. When and if mining or core purification begins the OMCP spearheads the operation. They estimate needed security and also handle the transportation of the ore, minerals and raw coreanium. In short, OMCP is the heart of the GIC mining and planet harvesting operation.

Senator: Josephine C Kempler

Resource Management Division (RMD)

One could say that this is the nerve center of the GIC. RMD manage and siphon all the resources that go through the GIC. With the guidance of the senate the RMD calculate and administrate the resource needs of the GIC commonwealth. They point and the OMCP runs off to mine and harvest. When the resources have been amassed the RMD review the budgets of the GIC division, the needs of the commonwealth and, with the go from the senate, they administer them according to their deductions. They also handle the taxes (the GIC imposes a twenty-five percent tax on incomes).

Senator: Chen Lin Lau

The Corporate Structure

In a world where the resources are spread across accessible star systems for whoever has the patience, manpower and funds to find them, the power and wealth that can be amassed by a single corporate structure is virtually limitless. The economic and judicial system is a very complex one, but it can be broken down into three simple forms of corporate structures.

Franchised: These are the behemoths of the corporate world. They have the funds (now basically run on a self-sufficient

payment system because of their vast revenues) to buy planetary mining and harvest rights. These corporations are enormously wealthy and has just about (and sometimes more) as much juice as the GIC. These corporations do have some side interests other than mining and planet harvesting, but they concentrate on these two endeavors.

Splintered: These are a common form. Someone had an idea for a restaurant, car mechanic shop or clothing line and started a company. Some have mining licenses and in most cases they don't sell the finds, they use the material in their production to cut costs. These come in every size and shape, from the fast food vendor on the corner to the multi billion credit weapon company. These and the franchised are registered on the stock market. It costs 10,000 C to register a splintered company.

Fractured: When a splintered or franchised company needs some outside expertise they hire one of the fractured companies. Usually there is only one sole owner and he is hired to do a job within his expertise. The payment to him from his clients has to be legit but here ends the responsibility of the client. Who the fractured company hires and how they pay for this and gets their job done isn't something that the client has to take responsibility for (as long as they are unaware of illegal actions). This has led to an extremely shadowy world of these fractured sub-contractors. Even raiders often have a *fraxnse* (pronounced "frack-sense", an abbreviation of *fractured license*, a registered document one needs in order to open and run a fractured company) in order to launder money and gain access to an actual legitimate job if need be. It takes two thousand credits, and a credible business plan in order to get a fraxnse. GIC has tried to change this system to minimize the seedy element but it's a hard thing as the fractured companies have become an extremely important part of the economical system. The franchised and the splintered companies are working against such a change in political debates, but most people believe that they're also working against it by other means behind the scenes.

The Various Companies
There're millions of companies but here the top three of the franchised and splintered corporate structure will be given a quick overview. These are those that are the most prominent and have left their mark in the galaxy. There are of course a lot of rumors about many of them, ranging from illegal planet harvestings to the testing of alien weapons technology on remote colonies. But if any of the rumors are true is another matter.

Franchised
Interstellar Mining Corporation: IMC is an extremely wealthy company and their main interest is mining and planet harvesting. Of course, they have several subsidiaries in the form of splintered corporations which they have merged into their fold. Their secondary interest is the development of terraforming equipment and they also have a substantial amount of military R&D contracts under MSU.

CEO: Jarla Imarco

Space Exploration Salvagers: The SES does have several mining and harvesting sites as well, but their main interest is alien artifacts and the back engineering of these. SES has been quite successful in this and has adapted or managed to simulate the function of several artifacts. One of their biggest successes is the very useful translator, *lingosphere*.

CEO: Kazim Bin Asud

Girshaw Amalgamated: This corporation has only existed for ten years and during that short time the company has managed to become the third largest in the galaxy. They managed this by snagging a lot of lucrative mining and harvesting contracts. They have their fingers in a lot of pies and no one has really got a good grip of them yet.

CEO: Lain Takashi Girshaw

Splintered
Deltronix: Deltronix is the most lucrative of all the splintered companies as they were the ones who integrated parts of suits into a specific frame and gave it a name: COG. They're the largest manufacturers of COGs, COG add-ons and parts. This has made them extremely successful. The COG technology has made working in space a lot safer and effective and for this everyone has Deltronix to thank.

CEO: Zachary Bloom

Ishimoto Systems: Due to their extremely innovative thinking and their cutting edge R&D department Ishimoto has managed to become the most successful company in whole Sirius when it comes to computers and VIN systems. About sixty percent of all VIN's in service come from Ishimoto, which is an extremely high number. They do have other interests, such as their own line of ground vehicles and class A and B air and spacecrafts.

CEO: Reiko Yamamoto

Ladus Mark: This company has become extremely successful as it's the biggest manufacturer of all ranges of spaceships. Ships and parts for them is their main interest. About forty percent of all ships in service have been manufactured by Ladus Mark, and about eighty percent of all the other ships have Ladus Mark parts in them straight out of the shipyard. Needless to say, the revenues accumulated from their military subcontracts with the Consolidated Fleet are astronomical.

CEO: Willow Chernekov

Freelancers & Guilds

There are a lot of freelancing teams in the world of C&D who live outside the law. Many of these groups are members of a suiting guild. The guild takes ten percent of the income but in return they can offer shelter, safe houses and connections. High ranking members of the guilds are extremely powerful individuals. If a team has joined a guild they better pay-up and play it straight. Guilds can also provide jobs. Any job provided by the guild has a set pay which already has been negotiated by the guild and the client. Teams taking on these jobs will receive 35 percent of the pay. This is standard and non-negotiable. It's just the way it is. A botched guild job can put some real dents in a team's reputation. Beyond the MEC and CIM, the different guilds are one of the greatest threats to the power of the GIC.

These are the major guilds. Pirate Guild, Lego Guild, Merc Guild, Covert Guild, Prospector Guild, and the Free Guild. The names of these guilds are pretty much self-explanatory, except the Covert and Free Guild.

The Covert Guild deals with groups specializing in assassinations, in industrial espionage and political manipulation. The Free Guild isn't specialized and deals in pretty much everything. On the downside the jobs they provide aren't always tailored to members as they can spread themselves to thin at times. The Escort Guild is the only legal one and they go about their business quietly and in peace.

Law

When millions of light-years and beyond is to be governed by a government the law can often be hard to implement. A city is hard enough to manage, a country harder. Imagine managing a galaxy.

The GIC tries its best to bring the law and the justice system to all the dark corners of the galaxy. But out on backwater colonies and small terraformed worlds the law is quite…flexible at times. In some places it's basically nonexistent. When a patrol only swings by every six months or so for a quick look there's not much stopping people from breaking the law. However, most places have individuals that have a sense of justice and they often set up a makeshift law enforcement system, which sometimes holds up quite well. These law men more or less abide by the GIC but often skip a few steps in order to dish out their own brand of justice. Sometimes they're very humane and at other times they're cruel. There are basically three names for these types of "officers of the law": Regulators, Marshals or Sheriffs.

The death penalty is still in effect but is mostly used in the marines or the fleet as a way to deal with traitors. But the traitor has to have done something off the charts in order to get executed. Desertion isn't enough but selling secret battle plans and launch codes to those outside the MSU would be something that most definitely would lead to the death penalty. The most common means of execution is by firing squad or by "spacing" (shot out an airlock while still alive). Violent and sexually driven repeat offenders (rapists, pedophiles, murderers) are "cool burned". Cool burning (official name *cortex stimulation node cauterizations*, or *CSNC*) is a precision nano-surgical procedure in which the different parts of the brain were the lust for these crimes has manifested in the individual is burnt. The memory of the person is burnt as well. The criminal is left very docile and has no recollection of what they have done and are physiologically incapable of ever feeling the urge again. But the procedure causes damage to the short term memory system, sexual drive (a zero libido) and the learning and coordination system. The individual is only capable of handling quite simple tasks which they were capable of performing before the cool burning. They can run simple computer system checks, drive or fly taxis, assist in engineering tasks and so forth. After the procedure they're put in stasis, flown to a place far away from the people who remember them or the crimes they committed and put to work. They are highly suggestible and find themselves content in the work situation they're put in.

Piracy (as in shanghaiing a spaceship) is a quite common crime. There are a lot of raiders out there and they attack whatever they come across and sell the goods. Sometimes they do contract jobs, stealing and kidnapping from ships selected by an employer for whatever reason. Until recently, the penalty for piracy was death or cool burning. The Chairman of that time (Rachel Zerganov) had deemed the crime especially heinous as an attack on any ship in space risked the lives of every one on the attacked ship. One little tear in the hull could kill every passenger. But the current chairman D'Charnas has changed the punishment. Nowadays the crime is punished by thirty years of work camp prison. Only if someone dies as a result of the crime can the guilty parties (everyone on the pirate ship who participated in the coup) be sentenced to death or cool burning. D'Charnas instituted the change as pirates didn't risk anything extra by shooting a hole in the hull of the ship, killing everyone onboard, and take the payload. Today they can risk the death penalty or being cool burned if they kill anyone. Of course, if one person dies they can kill the rest to get rid of witnesses. But the mortality rate connected to victims of pirates has gone down significantly after the new legislation.

Another crime which can be punished with cool burning is trespassing on a coreanium processing plant with the intent of sabotaging. The same goes for unregistered and illegal coreanium processing.

Prospecting Laws: Mining without a license is a crime. Steep fines to three years in jail, additional to the fines, can be the result. Not including the GIC, only franchised and splintered (with its business plan and structure leaning toward the mining industry) are allowed to apply for mining rights. Franchised get access to entire planets (and harvesting rights) while structured gets a time bound license (usually one year from the first dig, not including the establishing of a mining colony) to mine a site and can't get harvesting rights. The license itself is costly and then the GIC takes eight (mining fee) percent of whatever they find, plus income tax (all and all they take thirty three percent).

Salvaging Laws: Ships and debris that are found in regulated space are the sole property of the owner (company, private person) to whom it belongs. This only holds up if the logs and/or registration number/logos can be established and traced back. If the wreckage is found in unregulated space, it's finder's keepers. However, the one salvaging it has to have a salvaging license. A private person has to have a fraxnse in order to apply for one. This license is more expensive than the actual fraxnse and is purchased for 5000 credits. It has to be renewed every year for the price of 1500 credits. If someone without a license finds debris and reports it, the salvager that shows up is required by law to pay the one who reported it with a 10 percent finder's fee. And of course, if the ship is found with onboard survivors the wreckage has to be reported to the GIC and is not eligible for salvage. If whole ships are found they are seldom sold as a whole but rather hacked up and sold for parts. Selling these is a hassle. First of all you need a salvage sales license which cost 10,000 a year, and then you need time, contacts, logistics and storage. Because of this most salvagers sell their findings to a broker who does an estimate of what he will get for the parts and gives the salvager twenty five percent of this. Of course, the salvager has to pay full tax on this as well if going by the law, so basically the salvager gets one eighth of the profits when all is said and done.

Weapon Laws: Due to the danger of raiders, rippers and possible CAV outbreaks, it's legal to carry firearms. Those whom have been convicted of violent crimes or severe sexual crimes are not allowed to carry or own a firearm. The firearm has to be carried openly (in a holster visible to the naked eye). The license only includes pistols and heavy pistols. When visiting larger cities such as Claret or Mondus City or a ship, space station, or colony located in a non-life sustaining atmosphere, weapons are confiscated on arrival and given back on departure. Only the facility/transport security personnel are allowed to carry firearms in these locations (if not having special dispensation, as being a marine on duty or an ISA agent). In order for the weapon to be legal, it has to have been bought in a legitimate gun store (with an official GIC registration).

Most establishments (bars, stores, etc) have a no weapon policy and all weapons are checked in at the door and given back when exiting the locale. Carrying a weapon without a license can give up to six months in prison. Carrying a concealed registered weapon gives a 500C fine and also results in the license being revoked for a year. Each new offence adds 250C and six months to the suspension.

Sexual Trade: In order to legally sell sexual services the sex worker has to go through the Escort Guild and become listed. It's not everyone who can get in. It takes a certain panache. The schooling period is two years during which time the escort to be learns everything from seduction to rhetoric and details about different sexual preferences. The escort is then free to work, choosing his/her own clients. Once a year (not counting stasis) they have to get a medical and psychological examination and can be subjected to random controls. No illegal drugs are allowed. Escorts are exempt from taxes, paying ten percent to the guild who in turn pays taxes to the GIC. Listed escorts are in most cases a rather respected line of work. According to surveys, fifty-five percent of the citizens of the core planets see it as an honest and respected line of work. Illegal prostitution is still about, and in many cases these people fare pretty bad as they can't make official complaints when being harassed by pimps or beaten up or raped by "clients". Also, there are many who engage in illegal prostitution to support drug habits.

High-Tech Option: Every gun has its registration number etched into the hammer, which leaves its mark on the casing. Each gun also leaves a specific electromagnetic imprint on the actual bullet and casing. The barrel leaves this imprint and the actual field is powered by the kinetic energy of the bullet. These magnetic signatures can be read and translated into a registration number, giving the information on where the gun was bought and by whom. Then of course, for a couple of bucks and some connections one can get a hacked gun, with no imprints whatsoever. This option makes it a lot harder to carry and use firearms illegally and should be discussed with the gaming group.

Merc License (Msense): Mercenary is nowadays synonymous with bounty hunter. In order to become a merc the individual *"cannot have been convicted of a violent crime that was committed for personal gain or as a result of a personal flaw and/or committed without moral guidance or to an extent which is deemed excessive"*. In other words, bank robbers, psycho killers and wife beaters can't get a merc license, but someone who beat their girlfriend's attacker to a pulp or shot an armed burglar dead as he tried to enter the persons home, could get a merc license. And of course, those without a rap sheet could get one to.

A merc is allowed to arrest criminals on the run if GIC has put out an official bounty. They also have the rights to enter civilian homes if they have reason to believe that the perpetrator is on the premises. Mercs are allowed to carry a SMG or shotgun in addition to their handgun and are also allowed to pilot a ship armed with rail-cannons. It requires a fraxnse and these cost 5000C per year.

Edge License (Edgesense): This is the license carried by Kirus. It allows them to get paid for their services as bodyguards, grants them the legal right to purchase a nano-blade and to carry it on their person in establishments that normally don't allow weapons. These establishments are limited to official places such as civilian bars, stores and stations. Many GIC and corporate establishments has the right to bar the use and carrying of the weapon on their premises. It's collected and returned as the person leaves. An edgesense is given after completed Kiru education. It is without cost but can be revoked if the Kiru is found guilty of severe violent crimes.

Note: The laws are in many ways very similar to the laws of most western countries in our day and age. Murder, robbery, assault, rape and similar violent crimes are illegal, as is smuggling, forgery and theft. Only crimes that might be unique (or more common, such as flight piracy) or treated special in the C&D world are mentioned. The AI is instructed to use common sense when it comes to the law and the punishment of crimes. Same goes for drug use. Alcohol is legal, but all other recreational drugs are illegal.

Ethnicity

Ethnic groups are still very relevant, and almost more so now. Humanity has lost its original home world, but still has a strong sense of belonging. Most religions and traditions are intact. However, racism has diminished severely due to the presence of aliens such as the rippers and the Gerions. In broad strokes, one can say that racism has gone down about sixty percent. This, and the fact that traveling has gone to a whole new level, has lead to a massive increase in mixed relationships and mixed religions within the same relationship. Names are often quite colorful. A name like Murimoto Tasjlinkov De Luca is not that uncommon. More than names and skin color your primary language and the traditions you grew up with weighs in when others size you up and determine your ethnicity.

About ninety percent of humanity is at least bilingual. Intra is the language spoken everywhere in the Divius system and beyond by humans. It's a combination of Spanish, Mandarin, English and Japanese. Parents that know Intra are required by law to teach this to their children, second to their own language. Many grow up knowing three or four languages. Intra, their father's language, their mother's language and a fourth language as language studies is a standard in most education institutes. However, there is another form of "racism" present. People from the core systems who are bigots tend to patronize colonists from the fringe and vice versa.

Religion
Religion still exists and is quite widespread even though practicing religious groups have gone down. New religions have popped up and some branches of old ones have more or less disappeared. The religious groups that believed in the creationism that rebuked evolution have basically died out. It's impossible to say what happened to those who stayed on Earth, but those who followed into space are all but dead. They knitted together in tight groups and refused to be part of the benefits gained by genetic and artificial stem cell research. In the end, due to the wish to keep their bloodline free from any manmade genetic alteration, they ended up being the only group still susceptible to cancer, Huntington's, MS and all the other illnesses that the rest of mankind had been rendered immune to, or that there was a cure for. But there are still creationists left.

In 314 IT The Church of Infinitology was founded by Elaine Kendrin. It has only existed for roughly two hundred years, but it has managed to become the most widespread religion among mankind during this time. About forty percent of mankind practice some form of faith actively; thirty percent of those who practice their faith are Infinitologists. Hundreds of new religions have been born, but only one of them has become an important part of everyday society.

Church of Infinitology
Infinitologists (Infinits for short, Infinit singular) believe that every particle of the universe is connected. And not only that, they perceive the entire universe as a single living being. Sentient beings that are of flesh make up the flesh, blood and organs of the void. Creatures that have mastered bio-tech and integrated their bodies with it are of a higher order and constitute the nerves and the impulses. And those whom have left their bodies behind and managed to become pure energy

The Church Of Infinitology
Embrace The Life Of All

and one with the universe have become a part of the thought process. They have truly joined the Life of All.

Infinits are not hypocrites (well, no more than your average Joe) and they're fully aware that even though beings might have become elevated to a higher state, they can still be in the wrong and in the need of guidance. Infinits don't struggle for perfection, only for unification and harmony.

Even though they believe that the universe reacts to the actions of sentient beings, all sentient beings are responsible for their individual actions. A human is a part of the universe and if a human is wronged she will react, still part of the universe. But she can still choose how to react. The Church of Infinitology has amassed a great deal of trust from the GIC since their arbiters often have acted as mediators in tough situations without any ulterior motive.

One big difference between infinitology and many other religions is the fact that they don't believe that there's a reason behind everything. They see no reason for an innocent child to become sick and die, or try to find meaning in accidents that kill hundreds. This only happens because the universe is in fact a cruel place for beings that haven't reached the state of pure energy. Also, as sentient beings it's the duty of infinitologists to react to these events and try to make a difference. When someone dies horribly for no reason other than chance you will never hear an infinit say "The universe has a plan for us all, even this is part of a bigger plan that we cannot comprehend and you can find comfort in that.".An infinit is more likely to say "The universe can be as cruel as it can be beautiful, but you can only react to what has happened. Will you be crushed under the weight of sorrow, or will you harden and grow, enabling you to one day react in a way that may spare others the sorrow your loss has instilled in you?"

When a sentient being dies his essence is splintered, transferred and assimilated into the *Great Stream*. The Great Stream is what lies between life and death. Here all the energies that wait to become injected into a physical being linger. New energies are sometimes added from other parts of the universe. Only when a race as a whole has evolved will the stream start to change and pour the essences into a higher evolved state. Thus, the infinitologists do not believe that one and the same person will be reborn or that they will end up in a paradise. When you die, you as a person and your thoughts will truly end. But if you have done good in your life by helping the universe and the species of man to get closer to harmony by reacting in such a way during your life that you helped others, your essence is purer as it runs down the stream and mixes with it. Even if it's just a little, this will make the stream and those born of it as a whole, purer and stronger which will move the race as a whole toward joining the true core of the Life of All.

As they believe the universe to be an organism that reacts, they also realize that when parts of its body turn against it, like tumors if you will, it will react and fight it. Infinitologists believe that mankind's exploitation of the universe, such as the extreme mining and planet harvesting, has turned us into such a cancer. VPS and CAV are reactions to this, the universe regards us as an illness and its immune system is ridding it from us. If we don't better our ways we will be wiped out. So they struggle to mend, heal and help humanity to understand this. Their wish is that we stay in the Divius system (or wherever system people choose) since there's no need to travel using coranium as we do, and without the extreme travels the alternate fuel sources available to run cities and on surface technology, we wouldn't need coreanium.

This means that a true infinit tries to do as good as he can while alive so that the race as a whole can benefit. They follow ten creeds in their work. They don't follow the words blindly but try to follow their meaning.

The Creeds

1) Accept the inevitable such as certain death and defeat, but a thing is only inevitable after you as a being have reacted fully and until you're incapable of reacting. When pain is plaguing the inevitable you should mend it in any way you can, but only if the one suffering has so ordered.

Meaning: Never lie down and die and give up. It's in the nature of all sentient beings to struggle for survival and fight adversity. But in this, they're not above mending suffering. They believe in euthanasia in the case of the terminally ill (which is extremely rare in the day and age). But they only give their aid in this if the person in question have undergone several psychological screenings, concluding that they're in a state of mind clear enough to take such a decision. There are occasions where they have done so anyway (as when someone is dying from a mortal and painful wound without any chance of getting help and beg for death).

2) Help those in need wherever and whenever you can.

Meaning: If you can help someone in a reasonable fashion, or if you're otherwise truly needed, you should help. Helping someone commit crimes for personal gain wouldn't be reasonable, but aiding someone in duress would be.

3) Sentient life is sacred and lesser life is not to be mistreated. In the interest of protecting life, you should try and hinder those whom slake life for no other reason than gain, selfishness or malice.

Meaning: Infinitology is a faith that condemns violence as such. They often act as intermediaries between parties in conflict since both sides trust them not to act against the other. But an infinitologist also understands the necessity of conflict. It is an inevitable part of evolution. All beings of the flesh engage in it. But infinits themselves would never start a conflict. But they can engage in violence to protect those in need as they know it to be a necessity. They would never harm or kill a known murderer after the fact because the person *might* kill again. But they would have no trouble shooting the same person dead if he's in the act of killing another. If you ask an infinit if he believes in the death penalty he would say "Only if the guilty party is killed as he's in the act of committing his next murder". And no, they're not allowed and do not justify the entrapment of killers using lures in order for an infinit to do a "righteous" kill. Infinits respect all life, but only according to evolution. They have no problems eating the meat of a lesser being as this is natural, but they would never torture an animal. Neither do they wear real leather or furs (if not necessary for some reason) as there really is no need with so many alternatives to wear.

4) When you are dead you're gone and your essence joins with the Great Stream, hopefully making it purer. So you have one life as you and therefore enjoy it and leave a legacy of kindness and helpfulness behind. But when enjoying it, do not do it in a way that may harm others or in a manner that will lead you to neglect your duties.

Meaning: The individual is gone when he's dead. He will never be seen again. His personality, memories and thoughts will forever be gone and if not, as if caught somehow, they've not joined the stream. In death the life essence goes through The Joining, the process of becoming a part of the collective consciousness of The Great Stream. Infinits believe that they have one life as themselves. There's no heaven or reincarnation of the soul (they don't even believe in the soul as such,) and the one life you have as the sentient being you are is to be spent wisely, but not without joy. They may drink, have sex and gamble if they so wish. But they may never drink themselves stone drunk, gamble away all that they have or engage in similar behavior. And also, they are not allowed to enjoy themselves in a way that harms others, mentally or physically. For example, they could drink and become tipsy and have sex with a registered escort but they wouldn't be allowed to get shitfaced and get it on with a street prostitute.

5) Strive to teach others the ways of your faith, but do not force it upon them. Neither should you be hostile or damming towards the religious ways of others.

Meaning: Even though an infinit thinks it's profoundly damaging to a sentient being to follow a religion which takes away the responsibility from the individual (its God's will, the devil led me astray, I kill in the name of God, etc.) he will never condemn the religion as such or forcefully try to convert others. And an infinit seldom preach to outsiders, they hold monologs and dialogs. They often ask people why they believe what they do, or not believe in anything if that's the case. But if asked they answer truthfully about their views on other religions, but they are in most cases tactful.

6) Do not participate in actions that will harm the universe or the stream if you can avoid it, but the protecting of sentient life is of vital importance.

Meaning: Infinitologists strive to hinder the excessive mining and planet harvesting that goes on. But in doing so they would never harm sentient beings. The Church of Infinitology doesn't own a single ship with a coreanium reactor on board. Infinits travel by hitch-hiking from planet to planet or simply by booking a flight to where they're going. But in most cases they do hitchhike as this doesn't support the coreanium industry in the same manner. Not even in this are they hypocrites, and do understand that all the core planets use this fuel and they use it as well by just living there. This is why most infinitologist live on smaller worlds which uses alternate fuels or travel from planet to planet by hitchhiking, not having a home as such.

7) Never shield yourself behind your faith or the universe for this is not our way. Our faith is such that you are responsible for your actions and such that you have to deal with and overcome adversity.

Meaning: Ultimately you're responsible for your actions. Only if affected by an illness or other outer circumstance that you truly have no control over may this change. Otherwise you have to ask the big questions, act in a manner that the church and you can be proud of. You have to work hard in order to make sense of things and to lead a good life. There is no ultimate answer, only the willingness to find answers to really hard questions which will lead you further on your path. There's no inborn sin spawned from another entity or dimension, there's only you and what you do is only your responsibility. You cannot use your faith to justify greed, malice or any other selfish cause of action.

8) Embrace your emotions as they often can lead you through difficulty but still you have to be careful how you act upon them.

Meaning: We feel things and this is a double edged sword. Emotions lead to the most wonderful and most horrible acts known. Infinitologists are aware of their emotions and use them, but they also try to control how they act upon them. Vengeance, anger and jealousy often lead to the breaking of the other creeds which cannot be allowed. So they try to be careful on how they handle things emotionally. As they, like the rest of the universe, can only react they wish that their reactions are meaningful and are of value, not spawned of angry or vengeful impulses.

An arbiter has a chance encounter with a Gerion while investigating a derelict ship.

9) Possessions and wealth should never go before the sentient being or the universal harmony as a whole.

Meaning: Infinitologists never search for worldly possessions. They get what they need from the church and whatever payment they receive goes to the church. There are different positions within the church but whatever the position no one makes more money than the rest. Most of the money the church makes goes to charities and medical and energy sciences which could benefit mankind.

10) Your body is your own to govern and should be treated with respect. How a person chooses to treat his body is up to him and so are the consequences.

Meaning: Infinitologists are prone to take good care of their bodies; an overweight infinitoligst is a rare sight indeed. This creed also extends to choices individuals make in regards of medical and sexual decisions. They do not condemn abortions. Neither do they condemn sexual preferences which don't harm others. When it comes to abortions they only approve of those done early on before a sentient being has evolved. But they do not judge or in any way try to stop people from making their choices, they simply tell them (and in doing so they're prohibited to use any form of scare tactics or "guilting") how they see things. The new life is neutral and in one way it doesn't matter if it lives or dies since its essence hasn't been affected in any way. It might grow up to benefit the universe and then again it might not. Basically they discuss the possibilities while being as neutral as they can. But only if the pregnant woman has asked for advice in the matter.

The Creators and Foci

Infinitologists don't believe in a god as such but they do believe that a higher intelligence created man, or at least the circumstances making it possible for man to become what he is today. Infinits simply call this higher intelligence The Creators. They believe that The Creators have ascended to pure energy. Alien artifacts and relics found are considered by the church to be of the utter importance as they are convinced that these objects indeed was crafted by The Creators before they ascended.

It might seem strange that a religion that doesn't believe in any form of god that actually communicates or influences its worshippers pray, but infinitologists often pray. It's their belief that the power of the human will alone can cause change or favorable circumstances. Everything is connected, even the energy locked inside human beings and it's just a matter of directing it. Infinitilogists have created a systems of symbols they refer to as *the five*. The system makes use of five different foci. They use these as a mental focus when they pray. Each foci have a specific property. When praying the infinit choose a foci depending on what he wants to influence with his prayer. The foci and their names were devised by Kendrin and according to the *Archive of Origin* (commonly known as The Archive), a book describing the faith and its history, Kendrin was given the names in a dream the night after she had touched an artifact she bought in the a market place of Xindos station. During the last hundred years the five have also been given faces in the form of idols bearing their symbols. This greatly increased the popularity of the church as the idols were something people easily could relate to and recognize.

Akal

The foci of Akal influences dimensions in the void and is often used to bless space travel and ghost jumps. It symbolizes the greatness and power of the void. This is the favored foci of pilots and devout ship crews.

Camran

This is the foci of truth. It is used to influence restoration of order among people and the finding of perpetrators. It's often used by LED officers who are believers.

Cadaar

Cadaar is the foci of the evolutionary struggle all biological creatures endure. It's used to influence violent situations. Prayers to Cadaar are often ones of peace, wishing to hinder unnecessary violence. However, many soldiers do the opposite, praying for their aim to be true.

Obresi

Obresi influences entropy and is one of the most common and popular foci. It's used to bring order out of chaos and to affect randomness. Basically, it's the foci of luck to many and more than one gambler has the foci around his neck.

Perli

The human will and capabilities is the domain of Perli. This foci influences healing and self-improvement, as well as the improvement of others. People who have great regrets often use the foci in order to become better people as it helps them stay on the straight and narrow.

Bless Endeavor

An educated and official arbiter has the ability to bless an endeavor. An endeavor is measured as a specific part of a larger undertaking. It can be a specific battle, an important negotiation or an infiltration attempt limited to a specific location such as a base or ship.

During a story, an arbiter can make a number of blessings equal to his rank in Void Lore and the blessings can affect a number of people equal to his Clout times two plus church sway. It takes about five minutes and the arbiter invokes the influence of the five foci and asks that the universe will grant the devotees favorable reactions. After, those blessed will get a +1 modifier to all rolls they make while partaking in the endeavor in question. And only one blessing is allowed per endeavor.

There are some requirements that must be met in order for a blessing to work. The avatars that are being blessed has to be true believers, they have to have one of the five foci symbols or idols (or the Archive) on their person (necklace, tattooed, painted on their armor etc.) and they have to be in the same physical place as the arbiter during the blessing and be aware of the blessing. It can be argued that it's all a placebo effect but on the other hand it does work for the believers so it doesn't really matter.

Example: The arbiter Emma Berdio is performing a blessing before a battle. She has Clout 3 and church sway 2 which means that she can bless eight people. The squad of marines in front of her has six members so the blessing can affect all of them. However, two members are not believers. Emma blesses the entire squad and during the coming skirmish (the AI decides the blessing will last for the breaching of the caver infested colony) the believers will get a +1 modifier to all their rolls. The two unbelievers will just have to do without.

Sayings and proverbs of the church

Kendrin be blessed
Embrace the Life of All
By the Great Stream
Mend the mind, heal creation
May the age of purity come
The Joining awaits us all
Creation is divine and the divine is creation
Walk in harmony
In the name of Kendrin

Corruption

All ruling bodies throughout history have had its share of corruption in different scales and the GIC is no different. ISA and MSU are (in certain circles) rumored to have a "shadow department" which conduct illegal experiments without the knowledge of the chairman or the senate. Experimenting with ripper DNA on humans, trying to breed psychics and whatnot are typical rumors. Some rumors even say that they're working with the Gerions.

Something that is true however is that the further you come from the Divius system the worse and more obvious the corruption becomes. Many GIC commands that have been separated from their superiors for to long and been far out during this period have often gone a bit renegade, bullying colonies and settlers. Due to this, GIC have a bad reputation on the fringe. Even though they try to make the world a better place (an endeavor that's subjective at best), the widespread area they cover has lead to a lot of corruption and outright war crimes that are hard to keep track of. Being stopped by the Consolidated Fleet or a LED-patrol is usually nothing to worry about when in the Divius system or when close to a core planet in another system, but if far from any of these you can get bullied around for no reason or even raided by them. A well placed bribe might however work, but this is always risky. And of course, the large companies often try to get their lobbyists into positions of political power.

CIM and MEC

Even though they've been a factor in the society for almost three hundred years, very little is known about them. What is known is that they harvest the odd planet and mine ore illegally. In many cases they also attack corporate and GIC ships.

CIM and MEC waged war on each other for the first hundred years, after that they called a truce (this is unknown to anyone outside the organizations at the moment) as they were beset on all sides by enemies. The last twenty years or so they have begun to exchange information and the odd favor.

During the last ten years, both MEC and CIM have started to have other motives than sheer greed. They have begun to question the entire authority of the GIC and the corporations. Most people on the core planets have a decent life (but extremely controlled) but those on other worlds often have it scarce, living under the boot of a local criminal or corrupt Consolidated Fleet commander. They want to change things.

They are divided into small cells all over the galaxy and they work through infiltration, terror attacks and covert operations. Effectively, they have formed a sort of resistance that wants to give more power and rights to the people. They often have a high interest in gaining access to GIC and corporate labs and research facilities as they want to get their hands on new weapon technology as well as information on genetic engineering, artifact research and other experiments that are kept from the people. Their structure and methods really make it hard for the corporations and GIC to deal with them. The GIC often runs anti MEC and CIM infomercials on The Circuit. The two fringe organizations respond by hacking info nodes at times, sending out a short burst of info that hits The Circuits screens in the homes of the people, spewing propaganda back.

The Independence Movement

A lot of self-sufficient colonies and systems outside the core have begun to question why the GIC should lay claim to them. They want to secede from the GIC and strike out on their own. However, the GIC won't budge. The movement isn't really official or organized but it's heading that way. The CIM and MEC has started to take an interest in the movement. If they can get it organized there's a chance that the Sirius galaxy will be plunged into all out war. Here and there one can find messages scrawled on walls "The Independence War Is Coming".

Claret and Mondus

These two planets were the first we settled down on in the system and are the most developed. They had a gravity of Earth norm and they were ideal for terraforming, even containing water frozen deep within its surface. It was about two hundred years ago mankind became more centralized and the majority moved to these two planets, leaving smaller colonies. Today, Claret is home to five billon people while Monuds houses four billion.

The planets are not divided in any form of counties or regions, only sectors but people are extremely centralized and most live within the walls of Mondus- and Claret City. The concept of a rural lifestyle isn't something that's particular popular or widespread on the two planets. People band together for reasons of safety.

Mondus and Claret City are gargantuan masses formed in cylindrical shapes surrounded by high walls. The two core cities are built upward, higher in the center and lower in the *Outer Ring*. The *Inner City* is the nerve center where all the political and economical decisions are made. Here the forum is located, the senate and all important corporate headquarters. Surrounding the Inner City lies the *Nimbus*, luxury homes situated high up where the rich and famous lives. After that comes the *Ribbon*. The majority of people live here and its considered to be the middleclass area. Closer to the Nimbus means higher middle class and the outer areas of the Ribbon which is close to the *Outer Ring* is considered the lower middle class. The Outer Ring is a combination of slums and production units. A lot of mined ore gets shipped here to be refined, vehicles are built and food is grown. Many people work here, but only the poorest actually live here. In rough figures there are about a thirty percent unemployment rate among the city population, and about two thirds of these people live in absolute poverty (overall pretty acceptable numbers). Just outside the Outer Rings lies the *Perimeter*. This is the two hundred meter high wall that surrounds the city and is patrolled by LED and the Boarder Guard. There's not a savage world waiting beyond the walls, as such, but their have been reports of the odd ripper, CAV victims and the like, so most people just don't venture outside, there's no need and it's quite unnecessary.

CIM commander Motoko Whistler leads an offensive against the GIC Border Guards.

The cities of Mondus and Claret also have three levels. Sky, Midpoint and Below. Sky is up on high, being higher up also indicates how much money you have. Below is a fog riddled system of power stations and sewage, all over the city. People in their right mind don't venture down there. LED does the odd patrol just to keep an eye out. Below came to be when the cities were built. A lot of things got left behind and forgotten after the main build up and nowadays no one cares that much. Below runs under all of Claret and Mondus and the rumors speak of both Cavers and all kinds of inhuman individual banding together down there. When workers have to go there they often do so armed and in the company of a LED TARGET team. Due to the structure, crime rate differs from area to area and can get pretty high out in the Outer Ring.

The weather is very much like that of old Earth. The cities on both planets have been built on the southern part of the western hemisphere, giving it a year around warm weather and moderate rainfall. Roads connect the different levels, and there's a lot of flight traffic as well but only registered taxi flights, LED and GIC official crafts are allowed to fly in the city and only A-class flying crafts are permitted for civilians outside the flight docks.

GIC tries to keep tabs on their citizens and on the streets and in the air they have surveillance cameras. The Inner City is riddled with them, the Nimbus is packed, the monitoring of the Ribbon is so-so and the Outer Ring is basically unmonitored and then it picks up again at the perimeter with pretty good security and surveillance. It also happens that they place cameras in more out of the way colonies at times just to get an overview of things.

> **Info:** It's illegal to harvest planets in any of the five systems actively used by man. With so many planets out there it would be unnecessary to destabilize the systems we use.

How People Live

Most city folk don't go much further than Claret and Mondus, or from their settlement. Space travel is extremely common, but the attitude towards it is not the same as before CAV and VPS, and for a good reason. It has always been dangerous but with VPS, CAV and increased ripper activity the common folk have settled in during the last one and a half century. Sure, many travel the five systems in their work, which also can be quite dangerous but those who go outside these systems voluntarily like deep salvage crews, are often a certain type of individual.

Site engineers, travelling arbiters, prospectors and the like are a certain breed with an innate drive to explore, discover and experience. Everyday people look upon these as crazy, heroic, mad or adventurous. Most people in the cities have never seen a ripper other than on *The Circuit* (see below). And CAV and VPS is something *almost* mythical. GIC likes to keep it that way and often use a lot of restraint when broadcasting the news. They want people in the cities to know that it's dangerous to leave them, but they don't want them too scared. So if a site engineer spins a tale to city folk of a CAV infested derelict ship and of the engineer team's captain trying to blow up the whole team by forcing the engines to reach critical mass since he was afflicted with VPS, they will raise an eyebrow in disbelief.

Economics

In the five systems (or anywhere GIC has a strong presence) credits (creds, C or cr) are always good. These come in three general forms. Cash (bills and coins, or the sphinxes which are five by three cm oval metal plates made out of platinum, titanium with traces of coreanium dust) cred chip (a small chip which is pre-tanked with a certain amount and usable by anyone or locked with a code which is entered on payment) or account transfer which entails a card that transfers the money from your local bank. Stocks work pretty much as they did on old Earth and Galatea (see below) handles the stock market.

Far-out colonies and places (that have little or no contact with any of the five systems) usually have their own barter system. However, money works perfectly well when meeting people who will travel back and have their home base in any of the five systems as they can spend them when they get home (if the situation isn't such that they need something else desperately at the moment).

Credits

Sphinxes	Bills	Coins
1000 cr	500 cr	1 cr
3000 cr	100 cr	50 cents (1/2 cr)
5000 cr	50 cr	
10.000 cr	25 cr	
	10 cr	

Salary

The list below will show some typical (after taxes) monthly salaries for steady income (and legal) jobs. If not otherwise stated these salaries are based on the premise that the GIC is the employer.

Marine Corps (free limb care package health plan): 2500 per standard mission and 3500 per life threatening mission (sustaining critical damage).

Medical Technician: 2500
Site Engineer: 2200
Commercial Deep Space Cargo Pilot: 1900
Operative: 2600
Scout: 2400
LED-Officer: 1700
Kiru: 2000
Arbiter: 1400 (stipend+500 for each child the arbiter has.)
Archaeologist: 2400
Border Guard Soldier: 1600
Commanding Officer (as per assignment below)
Consolidated Fleet: 2600
Border Guard: 2000
Cargo Ship: 2100
Mining Ship: 2300
Core Purifier: 3300
Delegate: 2400
Gear Jammer: Only works in the private sector
Merc: Only works in the private sector, bounties run from 500 to 20,000.
Prospector: 2100 + finder's fee

The Show Must Go On

So how do people live and how do they stay entertained? It's quite similar to that of the entertainment of old Earth, some things are just a bit jazzed up. Telecommunications in the five systems, such as radio signals, phone calls and the like, goes trough The Circuit. This is a huge network connected to the most all encompassing VIN to date, Galatea. The Circuit is used for everything from simple data searches, watching movies to the handling of billion credit transfers. It's hooked up to everything.

When it comes to sports there are still some classics around such as baseball, basket and hockey. But a lot new ones have popped up due to the possibilities of electromagnetism. *Slide Sphere* being the most popular of the *emps* (Electromagnetically Powered Sport). Two teams, ten players per team, slides across a huge metal bowl on electromagnetic shoes, flinging a hard rubber ball with a metal core, also powered by the magnetism, with lacrosse like instruments which are fitted to their arms with gauntlets. On each side there's a goal and well, it's about scoring as much as you can. The game is played in three matches, each fifteen minutes long. If there's a tie it's decided by sudden death, five minutes each until there's a winner. Injuries are quite high as the players can reach speeds at a hundred kilometres an hour and the ball can reach almost five times that if thrown in the right way, using the power of the magnetism.

There are gyms, bars and strip clubs and the music is quite similar to that of old Earth and most music from old Earth is still accessible. The entertainment will of course adapt to technological access, wealth and the like, but in essence: Man will be man.

The Other Places

There are a lot of backwater settlements and mining colonies and space stations out there. Some are mapped out and act as outposts while others have been long since forgotten. The technology level shifts enormously. Some places that have been forgotten for two hundred years or so has a strange mix of technology, riding horses, firing black powder guns while still siphoning power from the damaged coreanium reactor on their since long broken down ship.

Often, strange religions and customs have evolved. Remember, the human race have been travelling the ghost lines for almost four hundred years, and the first two centuries the lines were even more effective so there can be civilisations that has evolved undisturbed without any knowledge of the outside universe for several hundred years. There might even be places that live as in the days of the 1800-hundreds of old Earth, their origin perhaps cast away or hidden by the ruling body. In in-between colonies the tech level often results in a "technological rustic charm" as put by chairman D´Charnas after visiting Stoneshade and its outskirts. In some places you can walk into a shaggy brick and wood building, get a rye whiskey served on a bar put together by two by fours while still paying with a cred-chip and watching the news in 3D on the latest NIS.

Gerions and Us

The Gerion presence is minute. Most of them spend their time in Claret or Mondus City, and they always have at least ten representatives in each of the other four core systems. In general, Gerions don't mix with the population as such. Their emissaries have access to entire private floors in the upscale buildings of the Inners City and also have a dozen or so ships in orbit. Most people never get to see a Gerion in person, even though they often see them on news broadcasts on The Circuit.

Gerions often like to sit in on political meetings, but they have never interfered or had an opinion. They even sit in on senator meetings at times. Some exploration and mining ships, and even military crafts have housed Gerions who have wished to follow them in order to observe. In these cases they have one of their own ships docked in the crafts hangar in which they stay.

Gerions get a lot of leeway as they're the reason why mankind can live the way it does. They provided the ghost lines, grav cubes, electromagnetic technology and a lot of other tools which without mankind would be quite lost. But even so, there are a lot of suspicions and rumors flying around. Why did they disappear for centuries? Why have they never shown what they look like underneath their bio-suits, or never allowed a human inside one of their ships? They clearly have superior technology compared to mankind, why not share more? And why do they refuse to discuss their home world? All-in-all there is a sort of hidden suspicion and tension on the human side of things. Then there's the fact that they look…well, very alien and some might even say frightening by human standards. What the Gerions think or feel (if they indeed feel anything) when it comes to humans is so far a mystery, beyond their official outlook that has become such a well known Gerion quote: "*As an old and advanced race it's or duty to provide, as an old and wise race it's our duty to help you survive.*"

Chapter 10: The Sirius Galaxy

Flight computer initialized.....))

Standby for navigational instructions.....))

RTD Screens and Navigation

The RTD Screens will show how many days it will take to travel between planets when using the RT-Drive. It is up to you as the AI to decide in which position the planets are when the avatars calculate their trip, as this will decide how long it will take. The travel time includes the acceleration/deceleration process. A successful Brains + Navigation roll will reduce the time it takes to travel as the navigator calculates and programs in slingshot events, planetary star orbits and the optimal thrust vector. Each success will shave off a certain amount of time. The exact time it shaves off depends on the total distance. If it's a hundred day trip each success might shave off twenty days while rolls made for a forty day trip might shave off five days per success. It's impossible to reduce the travel time to less than two thirds.

LOGGED BY: Divina Larkin
DATE: 501 IT, 6th of June
STATUS: Freelance navigator

The Sirius galaxy is massive. It's approximately 180,000 ly wide and 20,000 ly thick and has about 800 billion stars and somewhere around 500 billion systems. Even with the technology we haven't explored a tenth of it. The Sirius galaxy ends with what is called the Dark Rim. This is as far as the ghost lines will take us. Those whom have ventured beyond this have never been heard from again and no one knows why or how the physics of it works. Looking out at the dark rim is unnerving. There's nothing but blackness. No stars, no life, nothing in sight. This appeared when the ghost storm hit. Probes have been sent and they just go black and never return. Those who have stared into it and travelled close to it for to long are said to be struck by instant VPS. The Gerions have never commented or answered any questions regarding the dark rim. It might be that they don't know, or they might know more than they like to share...

Mankind as a whole is concentrated in one system with heavy interest in four others close to Divius (Hardek, Murion, Berion and Valdis). There are of course several far away systems that we harvest, but these four are close to Divius which makes ore hauling faster.

The systems here are the ones made public by the GIC. Thousands of system are only available to the GIC and corporations and there is no official number as to how many dead systems the core purification has created. Only those working on deep space missions (which per capita is pretty low) ever travels beyond the core systems. The discovery of new systems has to be reported to the GIC and the information is considered classified. Failure to do so (or to sell non-standardized starmaps) is considered a criminal offence and can result in steep fines or imprisonment. The GIC claims this structure is in place to protect society from rippers and dangerous pathogens (so they don't run across another CAV situation with a new virus I guess). I can't talk about them but I know for a fact that there are myriads of systems out there.

This map is in standard format but my notes will give you some extra insight at times. And speculations and theories aren't illegal last I checked.

Sirius Galaxy

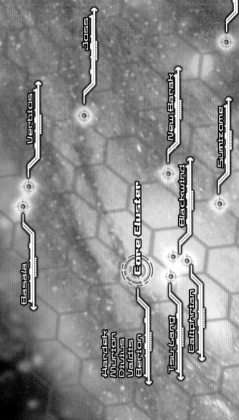

Rykos

Sylvian

Joss

Verbios

New Barak

Basala

Blackwind

Sunizone

Core Cluster

Zd'Whet

Hardek
Murton
Divus
Valris
Barton

Tsurlang

Caliphan

Merax

Eradle

Wal

Hexagon = 10,000 LY

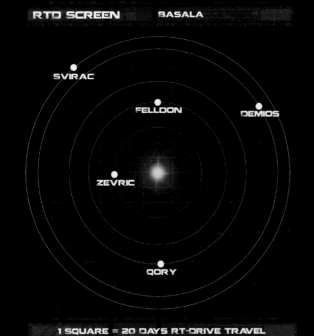

SVIRAC

FELLDON

DEMIOS

ZEVRIC

QORY

1 SQUARE = 20 DAYS RT-DRIVE TRAVEL

Basala

Planets: Svirac, Demios, Felldon, Zevric, Qory

System Information: This system is extremely dangerous but still alluring. It was discovered 457 IT and soon there after surveys made it clear that all the planets were about Earth norm gravity and had a lot of mining potential. The GIC and corporations set up shop, but soon CIM and MEC followed and several skirmishes ensued. In 497 IT the system was infected by ripper presence. Felldon and Zevric were hit heavily. However, as these planets basically were mined dry they were all but abandoned. There are still the odd Border Guard and mining outpost around. These two planets are partly rocky desert worlds with only about 3 hours of sunlight per 24 hours. There is some flora and fauna (and water) as a result of terraforming. But there are still rich deposits of minerals and belinium around as well as loot found in the form of abandoned colonies (vehicles, drill rigs etc). But one has to be careful as rippers are about as well as zones filled with belinium radiation.

The other planets are active mining operations plagued by skirmishes. There are no cities, only large but movable colonies with the exception of the subterranean settlement CryoCore on Svirac. All planets have a working (but somewhat unreliable) satellite system capable of supporting GPS and telecommunication capabilities when on the surface. The space in-between is filled with debris from different hostile encounters and a crafty (and illegal) salvage crew can make a bundle.

Three explorers stumble upon an archeological find.

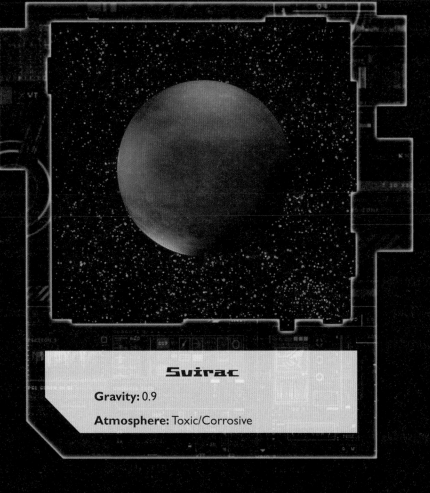

Svirac

Gravity: 0.9

Atmosphere: Toxic/Corrosive

Qory

Gravity: 1.2

Atmosphere: Suffocating

Berion

Planets: Mallick, Delos, Catheras, Gellos

System Information: Delos and Gallos are sti
being mined and holds several settlements and
cities. Mallick is made up of several mining co
onies and vehicle/ship (A,B and C-class) pro
duction facilities. Mallick has about three millior
people that live in the so-called Steeple. The
Steeple is a gigantic complex that reaches 2
kilometer above surface and 1 down. The mair
tower (the structure running the height and
depth above and under ground) has a diameter
of 500 meters. A fifty story circular sprawl sur
rounds it. The structure is one giant industria
facility owned by the GIC, SES and IMC. They own
isolated sections, share others and rent some to
other industries. The planet gravity is Earth norm
but the atmosphere is mostly methane and the
gigantic station supports itself by several SACs
The Steeple is not just a large industrial build
ing, it holds a city core and living quarters for
all the families living and working there. Severa
tram systems connect the various sections

The planet Catheras is off limits and set in quar
antine by GIC since the ripper infestation and
carpet bombing back in 411 IT. It's rumored
that several GIC research facilities are on site.

Blackwind

Planets: Memphi, Adelva, Stoneshade, Cekos

System Information: Blackwind is known to be a
cutthroat system. Memphi and Adelva are unin
habitable planets that have been mined dry, but
they often serve as a meeting spot for smug
glers and drop offs. Stoneshade is a settler
planet that never got to be a real city. There
are about one million people scattered across
a small mountain range divided into smaller set
tlements, the largest being named Stoneshade
after the planet. The GIC presence is low, and
the tech level is rather low as well. However
even though the settlers live a simple life farming
and raising cattle, some raiders have made this
their base of operation. Due to the small and
corruptible outposts of LED-officers and Border
Guards it's quite easy for criminals with half a
brain to set up shop here. Cekos is made up
of small mining colonies that mine and refine
Belinium. There are a lot of small fractured com
panies that manage these operations but the

rumor is that these are just a cover for the MEC or CIM (maybe both) that use the rather modest Belinium
production to get a foot in the system. Between Cekos and Stoneshade lies the Slate, a trading outpost
space station with a population of about ten thousand people. This actually belongs to the GIC but is to a
large degree neglected and greatly influenced by different criminal elements

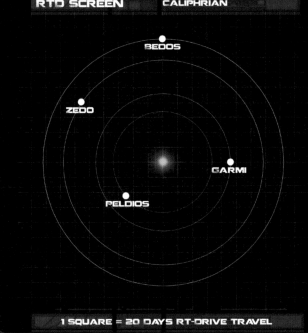

BEDOS

ZEDO

GARMI

PELDIOS

1 SQUARE = 20 DAYS RT-DRIVE TRAVEL

Caliphrian

Planets: Bedos, Zedo, Garmi, Peldios

System Information: This is a small but ominous system and is recognized as the origins of CAV. Since the CAV was discovered the whole system has been deemed restricted so we can only base our knowledge on the files pre-dating 459 IT. Bedos was originally a mining planet with ore smelting capacities but when several alien artifacts and ruins were discovered in 458 IT sections of the planet became restricted by the GIC in cooperation with the SES.

Zedo had been terraformed into a jungle planet back in 134 IT and left untouched, only used as a recreational hunting world filled with bizarre (genetically engineered) animals. In 449 it was rumored that traces of a primitive colony of people had been discovered. The rumors said that this was the relatives of a ship's crew that crashed in the jungle some three hundred years ago. The people now live on as tribesmen cut off from civilization. But there is no confirmation that any of it is true. Garmi was a mining world that delivered its ore to Bedos. It's believed that the SES and GIC are conducting excavations and experiments involving the alien artifacts and ruins and are trying to find the source of CAV. Peldios has been swept clean of CAV and is still a working mining planet.

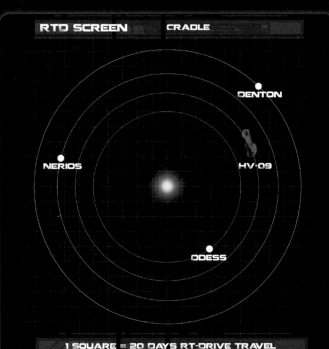

DENTON

NERIOS

HV-09

ODESS

1 SQUARE = 20 DAYS RT-DRIVE TRAVEL

Cradle

Planets: Denton, Nerios, Odess, HV-09 cluster

System Information: Cradle is a pretty far out and empty system. Denton, Nerios and Odess are of little value and quite uninhabitable. The Cluster is the debris left after the first core harvest. It resembles a large asteroid field. However, there are rumors that several artifacts have been found on Denton and Nerios but as far as we know there is no GIC or corporate activity in the system. Many ships have disappeared and the VPS ratio seems to be off the scale. Basically it's a ghost system that most people stay away from.

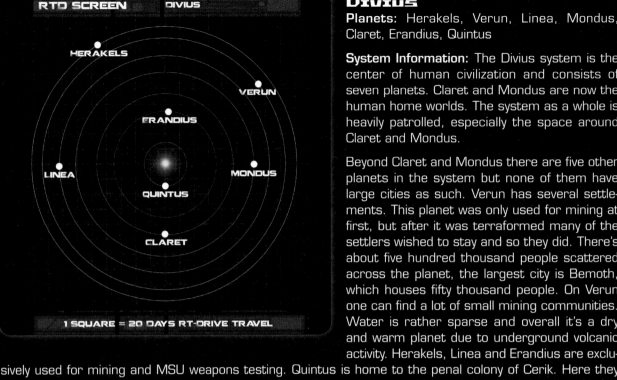

Divius

Planets: Herakels, Verun, Linea, Mondus, Claret, Erandius, Quintus

System Information: The Divius system is the center of human civilization and consists of seven planets. Claret and Mondus are now the human home worlds. The system as a whole is heavily patrolled, especially the space around Claret and Mondus.

Beyond Claret and Mondus there are five other planets in the system but none of them have large cities as such. Verun has several settlements. This planet was only used for mining at first, but after it was terraformed many of the settlers wished to stay and so they did. There's about five hundred thousand people scattered across the planet, the largest city is Bemoth, which houses fifty thousand people. On Verun one can find a lot of small mining communities. Water is rather sparse and overall it's a dry and warm planet due to underground volcanic activity. Herakels, Linea and Erandius are exclusively used for mining and MSU weapons testing. Quintus is home to the penal colony of Cerik. Here they keep those few lifers that they for some reason haven't executed or cool burned. It is said that the place is a cover where they keep ISA agents that gone renegade and other traitors that they can't execute or cool burn as they sit on valuable information. Other rumors say that there's a secret GIC lab on site where they experiment with alien technology, no one is sure. Getting to it is hard since the surface temperature reaches 800 Celsius daytime, during nighttime it drops to 60 degrees. The atmosphere contains a mixture which a human can breathe if fitted with an SWG. A day lasts for 13 hours while the night only lasts for one hour due to its extreme rotation. The facility (whatever kind it is) is located underground for obvious reasons.

Hardek

Planets: Merik, Gesalion, Rilk, Erandus, Dregas, Faveli

System Information: The planets Merik and Rilk are terraformed and contain several cities. Each planet house about two billion people. They're pretty much self-contained and the way of life is quite similar to that of old Earth. While Claret and Mondus rely more on cloned animals and industrial managed eco systems to provide the vegetables Merik and Rilk rely on actual farming. Some work in the cities while others work on the countryside. But the cities and farming communities are no more than a few miles from each other and the outer communities are patrolled by the Border Guard. GIC wants to be able to contain a ripper or CAV infestation quickly on the odd chance that it would appear.

The other planets are made out of smaller mining colonies and Border Guard outposts, as well as the odd farming enclave.

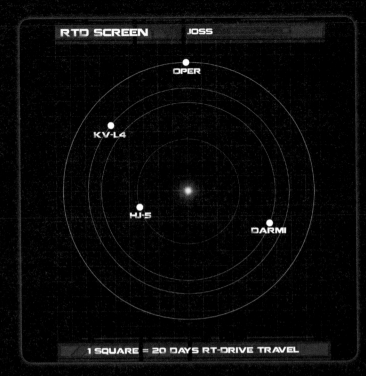

RTD SCREEN   JOSS

OPER

KV-L4

HJ-5

DARMI

1 SQUARE = 20 DAYS RT-DRIVE TRAVEL

Joss

Planets: Oper, KV-L4, Darmi, HJ-5

System Information: Joss was declared a dead system in 498 IT after Oper and Darmi had been harvested while KV-L4 and HJ-5 had been mined dry. However, Dox 1 and Dox 2 found several structures of unknown origin on KV-L4 and HJ-5 soon after. As these structures were believed to be of the same configuration as many of the more harmful artifacts they decided to shut down access to these two planets for the safety of the public and set up two research centers. The Fleet has had some trouble with illegal salvage crews. There is still some leftover equipment on the planetary surfaces which could fetch quite a good price.

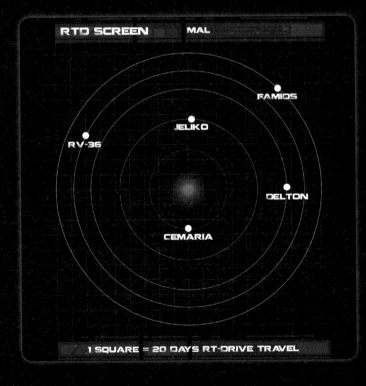

RTD SCREEN   MAL

FAMIOS

JELIKO

RV-36

DELTON

CEMARIA

1 SQUARE = 20 DAYS RT-DRIVE TRAVEL

Mal

Planets: RV-36, Jeliko, Delton, Famios, Cemaria

System Information: It was in this system, on planet RV-36, the artifact that laid the groundwork for the core harvester was discovered. This planet has been restricted since then. It's unclear exactly when, but the GIC put it under lockdown. According to rumors one of the largest artifact energy research facilities is located on the planet. It is heavily guarded and intruders are said to be blown out of the sky on sight.

Jeliko and Delton are rich with belinium and annexed by the GIC. Most of the ore is in all likelihood shipped to RV-36 and used to produce energy. Famios and Cermaria are both surrounded by electrical storms. They are rich with minerals and belinium. However, due to the remoteness of the system and the safety issues involved when flying through the electrical storms, no company has deemed it worth setting up shop in the system.

Locked & Loaded: A Boarder Guard outpost is mobilizing in order to conduct a sweep in the southeast sector on the planet Rilk.

Merik
Gravity: 1.2
Atmosphere: Breathable

Rilk
Gravity: 0.9
Atmosphere: Breathable

Claret
Gravity: 1.0
Atmosphere: Breathable

Quintus
Gravity: 1.3
Atmosphere: Suffocating

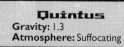

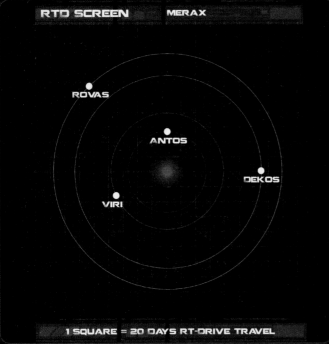

ROVAS

ANTOS

DEKOS

VIRI

1 SQUARE = 20 DAYS RT-DRIVE TRAVEL

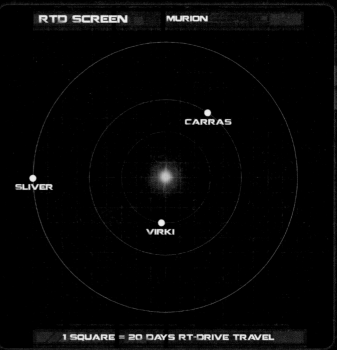

CARRAS

SLIVER

VIRKI

1 SQUARE = 20 DAYS RT-DRIVE TRAVEL

Merax

Planets: Rovas, Dekos, Viri, Antos

System Information: Very little is known about this system as it was discovered 498 IT and recently became a part of public records. According to rumors there are artifacts, minerals and liquid cores. The terraforming possibilities are excellent as every planet seem to possess Earth norm gravity (or thereabouts) as well as frozen water deposits. The negotiations for different rights are ongoing between the corporations and GIC. The MSG has also begun plans for a ripper sweep of the planets now when the orbital surveys has been completed.

Murion

Planets: Sliver, Carras, Virki

System Information: Sliver and Carras are combined mining and farming planets with smaller outposts and colonies scattered about (a settlement usually house a population ranging from 1000 to 50,000). These two planets are quite busy and have several large orbital stations and shipyards that are filled with travelers. Many come here to restock, sell goods and meet as the system is the closest when coming from the unexplored vastness surrounding Merax, Cradle and Mal. The small jungle planet of Virki is MSU territory and off limits to civilians. It houses many of their training facilities and research labs.

GIC survey team setting up a temporary geological station on Rovas.

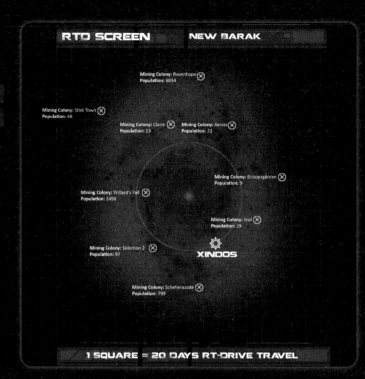

Mining Colony: Ravenhope ⊗
Population: 6834

Mining Colony: Stint Town ⊗
Population: 46

Mining Colony: Claire ⊗
Population: 13

Mining Colony: Xerxes ⊗
Population: 72

Mining Colony: Biskopsgården ⊗
Population: 9

Mining Colony: Willard's Fall ⊗
Population: 2498

Mining Colony: Krol ⊗
Population: 29

Mining Colony: Solomon 2 ⊗
Population: 97

XINDOS

Mining Colony: Scheherazade ⊗
Population: 799

1 SQUARE = 20 DAYS RT-DRIVE TRAVEL

New Barak
Planets: Asteroid/Debris Belt/Nebula

System Information: New Barak is basically a system consisting of a sun and a large quantity of asteroids, debris and clouds of gases. Many of the asteroids are rich in ore and belinium and have built in mining colonies with hundreds and at times thousands of workers living in them. In the middle of it all lies Xindos, a large space station with a population of about 150,000.

Mining rights are divided between several corporations and the GIC. New Barak is known as a cutthroat place with a lot of shady characters and deals. This is the kind of place you come to when you want to disappear or hide from the GIC. The GIC are officially running things in Xindos but the criminal organizations run rampant and corruption is everywhere.

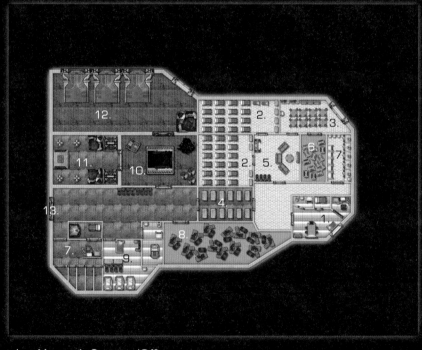

Typical Small Mining Module

Mining colonies are often composed of several modules, which are hooked up to a common reactor, SAC and additional residential area with larger private living quarters for those who have families. Small colonies may be limited to a single standalone module. These depend on supply ships which come by every four months as they don't have a SAC.

1. Manager's Quarters/Office
2. Mineworker Sleeping Quarters (bunk beds)
3. Mess Hall & Kitchen
4. Personnel Lockers
5. Lounge Area
6. Food/Nutrient Supply
7. C-Sec Office, Officer Quarters and Containment Cells
8. General Supply Area
9. Medical Bay
10. Engineering Bay
11. Power Station & Main Colony Shaft (connects to the SAC and Reactor Hub).
12. PCR Mechanics Bay and Staging Area.
13. Airlock/ Main Colony Access Corridor

1 SQUARE = 20 DAYS RT-DRIVE TRAVEL

RYKOS

Planets: LV-237, Baldos, Old Marl, Sellis

System Information: The system was discovered 289 IT and was initially thought of to have potential as a mining resource. But the ore soon dried up and due to several disputes between IMC and SES as to who had the harvesting right the GIC stepped in. The harvesting rights were never granted. The GIC and the corporations withdrew from the system in 293 IT. However, some of the mining colony crew stayed behind. There have been very little contact with the far away system but according to rumors the colonists found a rich vein of belinium (or knew that it was there all the time) which they used to build up their colony and equipment. The mining process resulted in radioactive downfall which mutated many of them and today they are believed to live as savage mutated raiders. They're said to venture out through the lines at times, travelling the ghost for months only to raid small colonies for their resources and women as a way to reproduce after which they return. The GIC pays little attention to these rumors and no one (at least officially) has travelled to the system in over fifty years. Common folk who spread the rumors simply call these savages Marls.

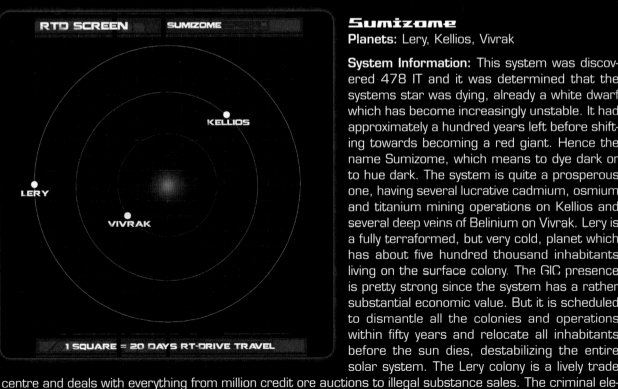

1 SQUARE = 20 DAYS RT-DRIVE TRAVEL

Sumizome

Planets: Lery, Kellios, Vivrak

System Information: This system was discovered 478 IT and it was determined that the systems star was dying, already a white dwarf which has become increasingly unstable. It had approximately a hundred years left before shifting towards becoming a red giant. Hence the name Sumizome, which means to dye dark or to hue dark. The system is quite a prosperous one, having several lucrative cadmium, osmium and titanium mining operations on Kellios and several deep veins of Belinium on Vivrak. Lery is a fully terraformed, but very cold, planet which has about five hundred thousand inhabitants living on the surface colony. The GIC presence is pretty strong since the system has a rather substantial economic value. But it is scheduled to dismantle all the colonies and operations within fifty years and relocate all inhabitants before the sun dies, destabilizing the entire solar system. The Lery colony is a lively trade centre and deals with everything from million credit ore auctions to illegal substance sales. The criminal element has a strong hold on the colony, as does the GIC so things are pretty tense. That MEC and CIM also have a finger in the pie doesn't exactly help. Violence and bombings are not uncommon.

Sylvian

Planets: Y-34, Mefune, Hathos

System Information: In 490 IT the ship Orion sat down on the planet Y-34. They found an alien artifact they referred to as the Arch. Soon after the crew experienced an onset of VPS and they left. Save for a desperate last (and very confusing) emergency transmission the Orion was never seen or heard from again. DoX 2 set up a research facility on the planet. It's patrolled by the Consolidated Fleet and Border Guard and only those with the proper GIC clearance are allowed access. Mefune and Hathos are inhospitable planets with a harsh atmosphere. They do have some mining potential and short term mining licenses are granted. There are several larger mining colonies on site on both planets.

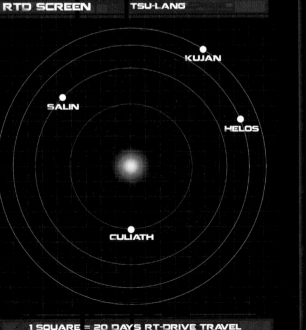

Tsu-Lang

Planets: Kujan, Helos, Salin, Culiath

System Information: All the planets are terraformed and have a lot of belinium and ore scattered across them. Tsu-Lang is an extremely destabilized system and war between GIC, (with corporate funding and aid) CIM, and MEC has raged for about 100 years. A myriad of skirmishes over resources are spread across the system. All planets have a couple of large colonies and the terrains vary between desert, deep pine forests and snowy mountains. There are a lot of remote (and possibly forgotten) military outposts. A lot of places are filled with radiation, mutated animals, traps and old motion activated turrets. It's a place of great danger but also one of great opportunity.

KERRION

LIDA

BECK

ASENDOR

PROPERIS

1 SQUARE = 20 DAYS RT-DRIVE TRAVEL

Valdis

Planets: Kerrion, Asendor, Lida, Beck, Properis

System Information: Valdis is one of the core systems and highly developed and home to the rich and famous. Asendor is the central planet and has a population of about three billion. Most live in Oneda, the largest city. Asendor, Lida, Beck and Properis have a collective population of 12 billion. All the worlds are beautifully designed terraformed works of art. On them you can find all manner of terrains and animals and a wide range of hotels, resorts and housings. Valdis is heavily patrolled by LED and patrons are thoroughly screened. However, large sectors of Kerrion is off limits as they contain artifact digs and alien ruins. The city of Markel on Kerrion holds a large museum of artifacts and dig history as Kerrion was the first planet where humanity discovered alien artifacts.

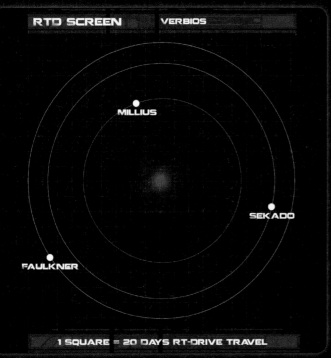

MILLIUS

SEKADO

FAULKNER

1 SQUARE = 20 DAYS RT-DRIVE TRAVEL

Verbios

Planets: Faulkner, Sekado, Millius

System Information: This system is strictly off limits and the GIC has poured vast resources into patrolling this area. The official explanation is that the whole system is unstable due to the presence of several electrical storms. However, long range scans indicate that there is neither. The history file shows that the SES ship The Talon, sat down on an unknown planet back in 404 IT in the Verbios system never to be heard from again. Whatever happened to them, it happened in the Verbios system and not for whatever reason the GIC says. We have no information on the value or resources of this system.

Za' Khet

Planets: Unknown

System Information: The existence of this system was meant to be classified but a breach in GIC security resulted in a small information leak. As of yet there is no more information on the Za'Khet system other than it has been deemed restricted by the GIC and that it's closer to the black rim than any

Veteran GIC prospector Ivan Surito DeNovi.

Chapter 11: Gear

The gear listed here should be sufficient to run your game. Keep in mind that illegally obtained gear often comes at a higher price; usually, the price increases by anywhere from × 1.5 to × 5. However, if the item is hot and the fence is in dire need of getting rid of it, the price can go lower than the legal price. The NIS ammo display most firearms have can be switched off at any time as to not become a tactical disadvantage (giving away position in darkness, etc.).

Pistols

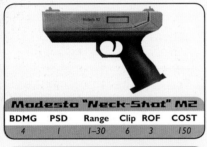

Modesto "Neck-Shot" M2

BDMG	PSD	Range	Clip	ROF	COST
4	1	1–30	6	3	150

Jako Hornet

BDMG	PSD	Range	Clip	ROF	COST
2	2	1–20	7	2	180

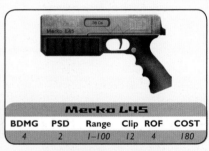

Merko L45

BDMG	PSD	Range	Clip	ROF	COST
4	2	1–100	12	4	180

Karakow SR3

BDMG	PSD	Range	Clip	ROF	COST
4	2	1–130	10	3	700

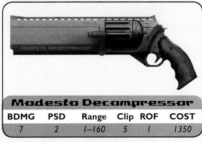

Modesto Decompressor

BDMG	PSD	Range	Clip	ROF	COST
7	2	1–160	5	1	1350

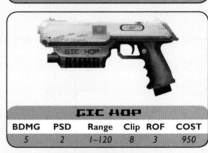

GIC HOP

BDMG	PSD	Range	Clip	ROF	COST
5	2	1–120	8	3	950

Built in laser sight

CSD (City Self Defense)

BDMG	PSD	Range	Clip	ROF	COST
3	2	1–60	6	2	800

SSD (Settler Self Defense)

BDMG	PSD	Range	Clip	ROF	COST
3	2	1–70	8	3	550

Deltronix P.454

BDMG	PSD	Range	Clip	ROF	COST
6	2	1–80	7	2	1500

GIC 50P

BDMG	PSD	Range	Clip	ROF	COST
4	2	1–80	15	3/B	650

Op-Lang 9

BDMG	PSD	Range	Clip	ROF	COST
5	2	1–80	8	4	900

Merko I Palmkill

BDMG	PSD	Range	Clip	ROF	COST
4	1	1–40	10	2	200

Wivelex HG .50

BDMG	PSD	Range	Clip	ROF	COST
5	2	1–70	10	2	1000

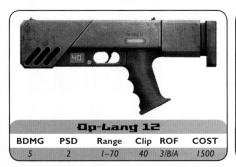

Op-Lang 12

BDMG	PSD	Range	Clip	ROF	COST
5	2	1–70	40	3/B/A	1500

GIC SOP MR

BDMG	PSD	Range	Clip	ROF	COST
4	2	1–150	30	3/B/A	780

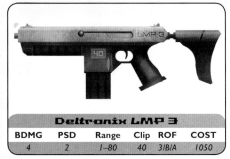

Deltronix LMP 3

BDMG	PSD	Range	Clip	ROF	COST
4	2	1–80	40	3/B/A	1050

Karakow TSMG

BDMG	PSD	Range	Clip	ROF	COST
6	1	1–90	30	3/B/A	900

Jako MHawke

BDMG	PSD	Range	Clip	ROF	COST
3	2	1–100	50	3/B/A	780

Karakow TSMG with silencer, laser sight and stock.

Shotguns

Jako Widenet 12

BDMG	PSD	Range	Clip	ROF	COST
5/3/1	2	1–60	15	2/B	980

Merko Staggerwalk

BDMG	PSD	Range	Clip	ROF	COST
7/5/3	2	1–40	6	2	1350

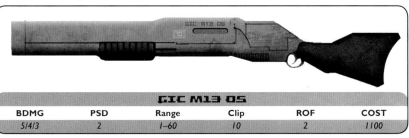

GIC M13 OS

BDMG	PSD	Range	Clip	ROF	COST
5/4/3	2	1–60	10	2	1100

Karakow SG 2

BDMG	PSD	Range	Clip	ROF	COST
5/4/3	2	1–60	10	2	1100

Merko Staggerwalk Tactical, 8 Shooter. +500 cr

Merko Staggerwalk Shorty 4 Shooter. –500 cr

Rifles

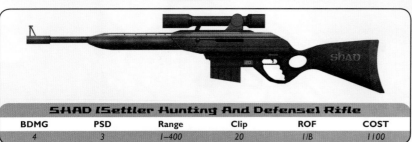

SHAD (Settler Hunting And Defense) Rifle

BDMG	PSD	Range	Clip	ROF	COST
4	3	1–400	20	1/B	1100

Deltronix Scoutspear

BDMG	PSD	Range	Clip	ROF	COST
7	3	1–1500	10	2/B/A	6700

Devor Lane SM 3

BDMG	PSD	Range	Clip	ROF	COST
6	2	1–3000	15	3	6700

Wivelex HSS .50

BDMG	PSD	Range	Clip	ROF	COST
5	3	1–2500	18	1/B/A	4600

EBC Bolt Hawk

BDMG	PSD	Range	Clip	ROF	COST
8	2	1–700	8	2	2950

Carbines

GIC Marine Corps M17

BDMG	PSD	Range	Clip	ROF	COST
6	3	1–300	50	1/B/A	4000

Karakow CM3

BDMG	PSD	Range	Clip	ROF	COST
7	2	1–250	40	1/B/A	3500

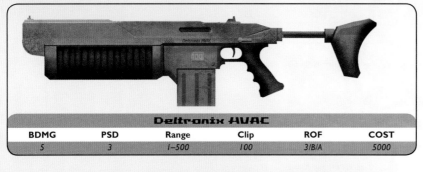

Deltronix HVAC

BDMG	PSD	Range	Clip	ROF	COST
5	3	1–500	100	3/B/A	5000

HAC

Spreadshift AC .50					
BDMG	PSD	Range	Clip	ROF	COST
8	2	1–200	30	1/B/A	4500

HAC (Heavy Auto Cannon)

The HAC is a large caliber, rapid fire, anti-personnel weapon (C-class weapon, see Spacecraft Chapter for more information on weapon class). It has a two hand grip and requires that the shooter has a Brawn of 3 or higher. It weighs fifteen kilos. In order to enable the shooter to use one or both hands for anything else while armed with the weapon it comes with a support harness. The harness allows the user to free up one hand or lock the weapon in a vertical position horizontally over the chest area, freeing up both hands. The harness can be discarded with a push of a button (takes one segment) if need be, but using the weapon without the harness (or a support on which to rest it upon) imposes a –2 on the Shooting rolls.

Being armed with the a HAC makes it impossible to sprint or crawl and move in any constricting area (such as smaller air ducts) and it also imposes a –2 on Close Combat rolls, relevant Stealth rolls and to all Athletic rolls. It retracts –3 to Defense (if the Defense score drops below zero as a result of being armed with the HAC the negative is counted as a positive modifier in favor of those attacking the shooter in close combat due to his bulk and slow movements). The only firing mode it has is full auto volley, which expends 25 rounds per every squeeze of the trigger (segment). The HAC is capable of hitting up to twelve separate targets that stand within ten meters from one another. Focusing on one target adds +4 to the base damage as normal auto fire does. If using the sequence zone system, Handling Hordes, a HAC user receives an additional +2 successes after a successful roll, enabling them to cut down more enemies. Marine squads, if the terrain allows it, usually have a couple of men designated "Sweepers" who carry a HAC.

HAC (Heavy Auto Cannon)					
BDMG	PSD	Range	Clip	ROF	COST
9	4	1–500	500	Spec	21,000

Close Combat/ Projectiles

Close Combat	BDMG	PSD	Cost
Knife	2	2	30
Combat Knife/Large Knife	3	2	50
*Plasma Saw/Drill	6	2	350
Axe	5	2	25
Fusion Cutter	3	1	150
Scimitar/Broad Sword/Katana	5	2	500
Wakizashi-Short Sword Machete	4	2	250/50
Nanoblade (see description)	5	3	2000
Large Wrench/Pipe	3	1	n/a
Stun Baton (bashing)***	3	1	150
Simple Projectiles			
Spear	3	22	n/a
Slingshot	2	2	n/a
Bow	5	1	150
**Crossbow	4	2	200
Bolt Gun	4	2	250

*This weapon is slow and clumsy and results in a –1 penalty when used as a weapon.
**Takes two combat segments to reload.
***On a hit, this weapon has the same effect as stunner ammunition. See below.

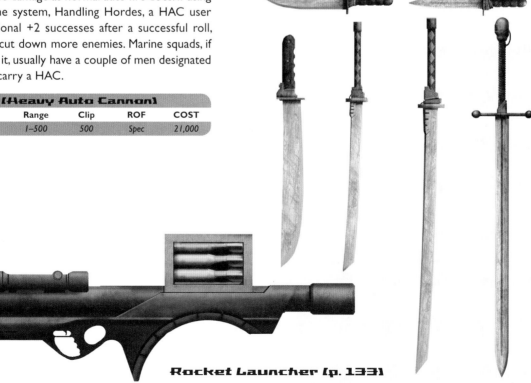

Rocket Launcher (p. 133)

The Nanoblade: *This weapon is a formidable piece of technological engineering. In essence, it's composed of a high-tensile memory metal induced with an automated nanite repair and sharpening system. It reconstructs itself after every cut, remaining as sharp as a scalpel at all times. The core of the sword is comprised of a electromagnetically controlled high-density liquid metal. This core can be controlled by a neural link in the COG, or by simply holding the sword in ones' bare hand. By shifting the weight of the core, adapting it to each stroke instantaneously, the user is able to maximize the damage of the cut. However, only a kiru is capable of using the weapon in this manner. When it comes to resisting corrosives, the self-repair system counts as a level three shield and the sword has a durability of thirty. The nanoblade is a weapon which takes a kiru to master. Those not versed in its ways have their base damage and per success damage reduced by −1 (4/2). A kiru wielding the nanoblade may make a called shot with a −2 modifier against an opponent wearing armor. If the kiru scores two successes or more, the armor rating counts as half and the damage is counted as fatal, even if the opponent is wearing shock armor. Nanoblades are illegal to own without an edge license.*

Ammunition

To make things simple, ammunition is listed by type of weapon, instead of per specific weapon. There are also different types of ammunition.

Light Pistols
Empty Clip: 15
100 bullets/shells: 30

Pistols/Heavy Pistols
Empty Clip: 20
100 bullets/shells: 35

Shotguns
Empty Clip: 20
50 bullets/shells: 35

Rifles
Empty Clip: 30
50 bullets/shells: 50

Carbines
Empty Clip: 40
100 bullets/shells: 100

SMGs
Empty Clip: 25
100 bullets/shells: 35
Full COG mag: 70

HAC Ammo
Empty Drum: 100
100 Rounds: 250

"Collapsibles"

These add 10 credits to the price of the ammunition, and all armor rating is counted as +2 against the attack. After the initial hit, the bullet pulverizes, removing any risk of ricochet. Most security forces on ships and space stations use collapsibles as standard ammunition. They do have access to normal ammunition, as well.

Stunners

Stunner ammo is only effective against unarmored targets or targets wearing armor no thicker than absorption fibers. Hitting unarmored parts of an otherwise armored target will also do the trick, but only if the area hit is big enough (a hand wouldn't do it, but hitting the arm would stun the target).

These bullets are basically globs of conductive gel which is infused with a powerful current. Upon a hit that strikes the head or torso, both the kinetic energy and the electricity will stun the target. If hit, the target must pass a Brawn roll with a −2 modifier. If the roll fails, he will be rendered unconscious for $1D \times 10$ seconds. If he passes, he will get a −2 on all his rolls and have his movement reduced to half for a duration of ten segments. If hit in other parts of the body, the target will only suffer the negative modifier and reduction to movement and will not be rendered unconscious.

Roll the damage as normal, but the damage counts as bashing. Stunners only have one-third of the weapon's normal range, as the bullets are propelled with much less force in order to be kept intact. Most security teams and LED officers have one gun (usually a pistol) which is loaded exclusively with stunners, in addition to their normal weapon.

Stunners are very effective when one wants to take out a target without causing permanent damage, and very handy when it comes to crowd control. Stunners that hit the head of a target have a fifty percent chance of doing fatal damage, and the lawful users are prohibited from aiming for the head when using this ammunition for crowd control and non-lethal interventions. These go for normal cost and are very popular among security personnel working in low-risk areas.

Armor Piercing (AP)

AP rounds count the armor rating of a target as −3. If the armor rating is 3 or less after the reduction has been taken into account, the damage inflicted is counted as fatal even if the target is wearing shock armor. However, AP rounds don't affect the classification of weapons when it comes to shooting or damaging vehicles. This ammunition is highly illegal for civilians and costs three times as much as standard ammunition. AP is the standard ammunition used by the Marine Corps. AP cannot be loaded into a shotgun.

Weapon Accessories

Compensator

A compensator reduces some of the kick presented by weapons. The compensator is attached under or on top of the barrel and somewhat increases the size of the weapon. When installed, it reduces the penalty of multiple shots by one and gives a +1 bonus when firing burst fire and auto fire.
Cost: 300

Laser Sight

All negative modifiers imposed when making called shots or shooting at moving targets are reduced by two when using a laser sight. In order get this bonus, the shooter must be standing still (but can, however, shoot from a moving vehicle if the shooter himself is still). A laser sight becomes ineffective after seventy-five meters, as the shooter has a hard time seeing the dot.
Cost: 300

Silencer

This can be attached to most weapons (even shotguns), except carbines. Anyone standing further than twenty meters from a burst or single shot (auto fire requires fifty meters of distance) must make an Attention roll. If all else is quiet, they need only one success, and if there's some noise in the area, they need two successes in order to identify it as actual gunfire. If there's a lot of noise about, or if the person is otherwise occupied, he will need three successes to even hear it. Silenced light pistols can be used without detection as close as five meters from someone, using the above rules. However, the range is reduced by a quarter and the weapon's length increases by one-fourth as well.
Cost: 200

Accelerator Boost

This rectangular box is attached on either side of the gun barrel. It's a bit bulky and increases the overall size of the weapon. However, the electromagnetic enhancer increases the range of the weapon by one quarter.
Cost: 1000

Scope

Works by the same principle as a laser sight but isn't affected by range. Otherwise, the same bonuses and rules apply, except that the target must be at a range of at least ten meters for the scope to be effective. Scope and laser sight bonuses don't stack; only one can be effectively used at a time.
Cost: 500

Heavy Weapons

Here are examples of heavy weapons with explosive capabilities. As you can see, there are two numerical values displayed within each blast radius. The first shows the blast radius (measured in meters) in each range (Ground Zero, Devastating, etc.), while the value within parentheses shows the damage within the specific blast radius.

Grenade Launcher

These pump-action grenade launchers can be attached to SMGs, Shotguns and Carbines. They can hold four grenades at a time. The grenades have the same blast radius and damage as the thrown versions. However, these grenades are formed as projectiles. They can be thrown as well by removing the protective top cover and pressing down the detonator. They have a three second delay but have none of the fancier options (see below) that the thrown versions have.

Before firing, the user can choose between two settings: Delay or Impact. The delay option activates the three second delay after firing, giving the user the option to bounce grenades off hard surfaces in order to get at enemies, while the impact option makes the grenade explode upon hitting a solid object with any significant density. They have an effective range of 100 meters. There's also a stand alone grenade launcher. It works exactly as the attached version but carries a drum magazine which holds ten grenades. This verison weighs five kilos.
Cost (attachement): 1200
Cost (stand alone): 3400

> **Hitting the spot:** All grenade and rocket launcher attacks that hit with only one success are counted as ending up within the Blasting radius. Sometimes, circumstances dictate otherwise, such as tossing a grenade inside a small room with the target, which would make the range end up at Ground Zero or Devastating by default. Each success will "upgrade" the damage radius affecting the intended target. So for example, two successes would make the hit end up a Destructive one, while three successes would make it a Devastating one, and four successes would bump it up to Ground Zero.

Heavy Weapons							
Weapon	Ground Zero	Devastating	Destructive	Blasting	Range	Cost	Class
*Rocket Launcher	1–5m (10+1D)	6–10m (8+1D)	11–15m (6+1D)	16–20m (4+1D)	1 km	6000	C
**Grenade	1–2m (8+1D)	3–4m (4+1D)	5m (2+1D)	6m (1D)	Brawn × 10	100	C
**Plastique (TTN)	1–2m (10+1D)	3–4m (8+1D)	5m (4+1D)	6m (2+1D)	Brawn × 10	70/125g	C
**Thermal Rods	1–2m (8+1D)	3–6m (6+1D)	7m (4+1D)	8m (3+1D)	Brawn × 10	70	C
**Blasting Caps	1–2m (1D)	n/a	n/a	n/a	Brawn × 5	70	C
*** Plasma Grenade	1–2m (Incinerating)	3–4m (Extreme)	5m (Harsh)	6m (Mild)	Brawn × 10	150	C

*Rocket launchers take six seconds (two segments) to reload, and the rockets themselves cost 1500 apiece. There is also the option of buying plasma hybrid rockets. These cost 2500 each and do the same damage as the normal missiles, but armor is counted as two less against them. Plasma missiles of this size don't count as E-class weapons, like those employed by vehicles, but as C-class weapons. The box magazine takes four rockets.

** The range on these weapons show how far they can be thrown by a person. Throwing with some accuracy is done with Attention + Athletics.

*** When a plasma grenade explodes, hot blue plasma spatters within the blast radius. The plasma burns for two segments and sticks to everything. Plasma grenades don't have any real blasting power, as the shell is made out of plastic polymer. They are mainly anti-personnel weapons.

Grenades of the C&D universe: Plasma and fragmentation grenades in the world of C&D have several functions. They can be timed to go off three seconds after the pin has been pulled, or they can be set to go off up to an hour afterward. The actual pin also acts as a detonator, which can be used to remotely detonate the grenade from up to a distance of hundred meters. All grenades also come with a micro-coat of "attachers"; these can be used to fasten the grenade to any surface (and it sticks about as hard as if it was fastened with a strong magnet). The grenades also have a proximity setting and can be set to go off when something comes within one to six meters. In other words, grenades are very versatile. A grenade weighs 0.5 kilos.

Armor Configuration

There are two types of armor configurations: Lean and Shock. Lean is a more flexible type of armor which allows for higher maneuverability and less bulkiness. This, however, has a price. Lean armor doesn't absorb any kinetic shock from high-velocity projectiles. Damage from firearms (or another high-velocity projectile) is reduced, but it counts as fatal damage, while the armor rating is halved (round down) when reducing damage from falls.

Shock armor is made out of more armor plating. It can take one hell of a beating, but it's heavier and bulkier. Every point of shock armor rating imposes a −1 to movement (this is not applicable to shock armor in COGs). Also, every point of shock armor rating above five gives a −1 penalty to all rolls which involve actions requiring bodily nimbleness and agility. Most Athletics and Stealth rolls (and many Quickness-related rolls) will suffer. If using Stealth to hide an object or using Quickness in a security bypass roll, it wouldn't be an issue, but if sneaking, climbing and jumping, or other similar activities, the negative modifier would apply. Shock armor converts most kinetic fatal damage into bashing damage, as well as reducing it. But no armor protects against environmental hazards such as fire or corrosives.

COG armors have two numbers attached to them within parentheses. This is the maximum AR (Armor Rating) an armor of that configuration can have when installed into the COG: For example, Lean (6), Shock (3) simply means that the COG in question can have a maximum armor rating of Lean 6 or Shock 3. Also take note that COG armor can only have one of the two configurations, Lean or Shock. It's impossible to have both. It's also impossible to have more than one armor installed. In other words, you can't stack armor in attempts at gaining ridiculous amounts of armor rating and durability.

Example: A border guard is shot by a CIM commando and the bullet inflicts 12 points of damage. However, the guard is wearing a flak suit which has an Armor Rating of 7 and a Durability of 25. This means that the damage is reduced to 5 as the Armor Rating was subtracted from it. The Durability is also reduced by 5, leaving it at 20. Also, since the armor was of the Shock configuration, the damage is converted from fatal to bashing. When the Durability is reduced to 0, the armor is worthless. If the guard instead wore a Lean armor with the same numerical values (AR 7 and Durability 25), the damage taken and the Durability lost would have been the same, but the damage inflicted would have been fatal, as Lean configuration don't convert the damage from fatal to bashing.

SWG (Standard Work Gear)

The SWG is a four-piece suit consisting of a jacket, pants, mag-boots and a gas mask. The suit is made out of absorption fibers. The suit has several pockets and placement for tools and weapons. The gas mask has an atmo-breather, which supplies the mix needed to breathe in a low-oxygen atmosphere. As long as the atmosphere has the equivalent of 25% breathable air, the atmo-breather provides the user with fully breathable air for eight hours before it needs to be refilled. It filters the ambient gases, changing them while supplying its own mix, which makes it ideal to use during the early stages of terraforming. The SWG also comes with a shoulder flashlight, comm-link and a mask camera that can record up to three days of material and stream the feed to HQ.

There is no HUD in the full-facial gas mask, and gauges are located on the left forearm. The SWG is a common sight and they are used by miners, engineers and security personnel alike. Companies use them as often as possible, as they're cheaper than a COG. The SWG can keep the user warm in temperatures as low as −90 degrees Celsius, but it isn't any better sealed than your average outdoor clothing and can't help a person survive in a vacuum.
Cost: 900

COGs

NETSS – Nano Environmental Tactical Stealth Suit (Scout, restricted)
EES – Enemy Encounter Suit (Marines, Merc, Raider)
SER – Standard Exploration Rig (Arbiter, Delegate, Raider)
SRS – Scientific Research System (Archaeologists, Science Researcher, Medical Technician)
TCI – Tactical Command Immersion (Pilot, Commanding Officer, Raider)
ZGE – Zero-g Engineering (Site Engineer, Gear Jammer)
AES – Adaptable Encounter Skin (Kiru, Operative, Raider, Merc)
TIS – Tactical Investigation System (LED)
MPG – Mining Prospector Gear (Prospector)

COG Setup

All COGs have a number of slots that can be fitted with a certain type of equipment. Each type can be fitted with a variety of equipment depending on the design specs. COGs are very tough, but the technological and structural balance within these systems is a delicate thing. It's a matter of energy consumption, room and equipment coordination. An engineer might be able to fix and make minor changes to a COG given the right tools, but to upgrade them for real, adding new equipment, a nano-matrix and the right components are needed. Some upgrade types are only available to specific COG types. If this is the case, these will be listed within parentheses after the upgrade description. Below is described the standard setup of every type of COG, followed by a quick overview of COG types and add-on equipment.

The basic configuration below makes the COG work from the get-go. Beyond this, some COGs (like the NETSS) comes with some extra features built in as well. Those extra features are standard (and don't hog any slot space).

Nano-Flex Visor Helmet (NFVH)

Flashlight

UAC

Flashlight

Camera

Camera

Solar Power Array

Mag-Boots

Breather

Solar Power Array

Ionic Polymer Metal - Augmented Brawn

NavComp

Capacitance Cells

Nexus

ISS

Interwoven Shock Armor

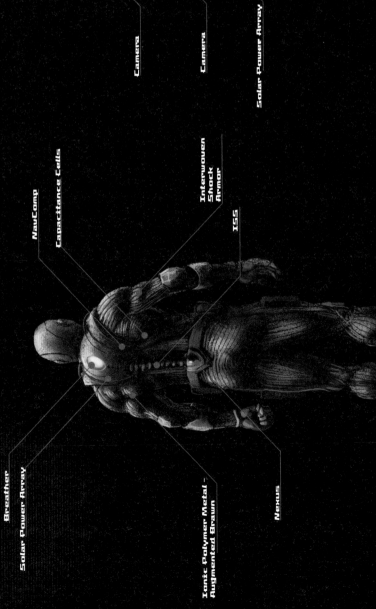

Upgrading the COG

Anya has come across some credits and she decides that it's time to upgrade her COG. As an operative Anya wears an AES which is well adapted to her line of work. The first thing she wants to upgrade is the armor. At the moment she has the standard Lean armor. The AES can be upgraded to a Lean 6 armor or a Shock 3 armor. According to her COG specs each armor rating takes up 2 of the shell slots. In order to get a Shock I armor she has

to configure the COG and looks under the Shell armor option. This cost 1500 credits. Each additional Armor Rating will cost her 1000 cr as it is Shock armor (800 if lean). She spends 2000 cr. When all is said and done she has spent 3500 credits and maxed out her armor option. She now has a Shock armor rating of 3 and this takes up 6 of her 10 shell slots. This means that she still has some Shell slots left if she ever wants to buy a shield of some sort.

Tess, the player of Anya, decides that the next step is to get some high-tech optics. So she springs for a level two IR in the Visor options. The standard IR cost 1,750 credits while the upgrade cost 650. The IR takes up 2 of her 10 slots in the Visor per level. The level 2 grants her a +1 bonus when relevant while using the IR. Now she has burned an additional 2,400 credits, so in total she has burned 5,900 credits, it's getting expensive and her cash is

beginning to run out. She spends another 1,000 credits to buy × 2 magnification. This takes up another 2 slots in her Visor. Anya is almost out of credits and Tess decides that her avatar will need the rest as walking around money during the mission. For now, she ends her COG upgrade shopping spree.

VES (Vacuum Environmental Suit): This suit is no more than one and a half centimeter thick and has a "one size fits all" configuration (adaptable absorption fibers). When it's put on, it adjusts to the wearer's size and comes to a slim fit. It's over this that the rest of the COG is fitted. The suit comes complete with a NFVH, which is connected to a breather. On its own, the suit has an armor rating of 2 and a durability of 30 (Lean armor). When Shock armor is installed, these ratings are ignored and you only count the ratings of the new armor in question. However, if buying Lean armor, it's a matter of upgrading, starting at armor rating 2 and adding to it. Wearing extra armor on top of a COG will severely encumber the wearer.

Of course, it comes with a powerful flashlight attached to the left side of the chest. The flashlight is detachable and even comes with a dimmer. A smaller flashlight is built into the helmet.

The suit has a built-in self-contained heating system which keeps the wearer warm in the reaches of space. When it comes to pressure, the outer shell can withstand a pressure equal to that generated at 200 meters depth of water in standard Earth gravity.

The "Normal" space suit: The normal space suit is basically a VES with an air tank on its back (-1 to all Quickness related rolls) and has no upgrade possibilities. The normal space suit only costs 1000 credits and most ships have several of these scattered about for emergencies or everyday work. They also sport mag boots. Those who can't afford to have COGs simply have to make do with these suits. The air tanks cost 100 credits and have an air supply of six hours.

Breather: This five-by-thirty centimeter tube connects to the NFVH and can be used to breathe. It is usually installed over the left shoulder blade on the COG. The breather is a delicate system which combines nanotech with biotech to create a CO_2 scrubber and a network of oxygen saturation cells. The breather only provides the user with 60 seconds worth of air supply on its own, but when it's used in an oxygen-rich environment (or connected to an air tank), it replenishes itself at a rate of 10 seconds worth of breathable air every 20 seconds. This sleek unit only weighs three kilos (two when empty) and is easily connected to one's NFVH. Of course, it is possible to connect an air tank to the COG when in need (see the air tank penalties above). The small size is necessary for the contained system, though minor upgrades are possible. If recharging it by siphoning air from a tank, the breather will drain a whole twenty minutes worth of air from the tank due to its saturation needs (it will actually vent out a large portion as part of the process). Of course, it comes with a timer which is linked to the HUD. A breather is used as an emergency air supply. Those 60 seconds can give you the time you need to get out of an environment that suddenly has been deprived of air.

Nano-Flex Visor Helmet (NFVH): This helmet consists of three main parts: the front armored inner glass visor which covers the face, the protective metal visor and the back-end shell. The back-end shell (everything except the visor and glass of the helmet) rests inside the actual visor when the helmet isn't in use. In this stage, the helmet is a front mask that's usually kept in a protected pocket on the outer side of the left thigh of the suit. When the helmet is needed, the back-end structures itself with a push of a button, making the helmet ready to wear.

NFVH can't be "dismantled" while someone wears it. When worn, a nano-seal connects it to the rest of the suit, closing it shut. The helmet has a built-in gasmask and atmo-breather as well. For an additional 500 credits to the COG price, the NFVH can come interlocked with the suit's collar, building itself up around the head and face of the user on command using nanotechnology. This is very effective and it takes about three seconds for the helmet to deploy in this manner. The command is a mental one; the suit responds via the neural interface.

The NFVH also comes with a HUD (Heads-Up Display). Through this, the wearer interacts with most of the COG functions. The HUD is an interface filled with different icons which are controlled through voice and/or eye movements (the user can choose which at any time), and supported by a neural link. Switching modes and using scanners and other features which are connected to the COG is done totally handsfree.

NavComp: These tools are vital parts of any expedition. First off, the COG comes with a gyro gauge. The user can manually set what is up and what is down when in zero-g, or go by gravity when this is available. This is used to keep track of direction and is also a good tool to employ while deep underwater. There is also a compass, which naturally is only useful on a planet with a magnetosphere. The nav-tools come with a built-in distance meter. This can track and measure the distance of ten objects at the same time, but only if they are in line of sight and no more than 2000 meters away. If the object ever falls out of sight (if the user turns his head, for example), the distance can't be measured until he looks at the object again. Schematics and maps can be uploaded to the NavComp. Lastly, there's a beacon tracker. Beacons have different frequencies, and if the user has access to the beacon, he can home in on it. This gives him the distance and direction of the beacon. Most D- and E-class ships have multiple beacons in place (bridge, engineering, medbay, etc.), to which the crew of the ship has access. This is a very useful thing in an emergency, as the crew can use these to navigate when the ship systems are down and when explosions and similar events have "reconfigured" the layout of a ship or station. When boarding a ship or station, it's a good thing to sync up to their ABN (Automated Beacon Network). Some places have an open ABN policy which syncs automatically with any COGs that come onboard, while other places (such as secure ships and stations) require a sync-code. It's possible to get access to this by unlawfully plugging into the ship's terminal system and hacking for the code if it's restricted.

VAC (Visual Audio Communication): The VAC system features a small camera mounted on the NFVH (which can film in all the spectra installed in the visor), internal and external microphones, earphones and a comm-link. The system can be used for normal radio communication, but the user can also send his video feed to whomever he wants. This allows members of a team see and hear what the other members see and hear at any time, which can be pretty useful. The built-in comm-link transmitter has a range of 10 kilometers, but can be routed through any transmitter within this area (if the user has the right codes, accesses and frequencies). This can also act as a beacon which allows teams to track members, and the bridge on a ship to keep track of the crew members using a NavComp.

The beacon function can be shut down or set to any frequency, according to the wish of the wearer. The VAC also allows COG wearers to send NavComp information such as schematics, maps and any files on store in the nexus to one another.

ISS (Internal Seal System): In a hostile environment, the tiniest of tears in the COG will kill you. Whenever the COG is breached, the nano-fibers will instantly (as fast as the hole is made) seal it, protecting the wearer from environmental conditions such as a vacuum. This system is shut down when half of the COG's durability has been lost, as the damage is too much for it to handle and a Polymer Nano Repair (or other means) are needed to seal tears.

Nexus: The nexus is a nano-board-based computer. It keeps track of all the COG functions and displays them on the HUD. The actual computer is about as big as a shuffle puck and is located in the lower spinal area of the suit, encased within a titanium alloy casing. The nexus also contains a COG status interface, which lets the user keep track of damage the COG has sustained, and it also includes information on what components/tools are needed to fix it. It has a storage space of five terabytes, in which the user can store any information that's being routed to his COG. In the front of the COG, in the belt so to speak, there is a memory chip slot. This is often used as a backup system when the COG is out of range of a remote upload point, and when the user wants to backup collected data when his memory bank is getting full. The nexus can be set on different loops, for example recording every information feed for 24 hours before recording over it, effectively acting as a black box in the suit.

Mag-Boots: These can be activated at any time and can be used to walk on anything metallic, such as the hull of a ship, or the metallic floor of a ship or station when the gravity is off. The boots are not strong enough to allow the user to walk up walls or ceilings if the gravity is more than half of Earth norm gravity, and it's impossible to sprint when the boots are activated.

COG Slots and Features

All COGs have five different categories of equipment that can be fitted with devices which take up slots. Every COG has ten slots available in each one of these categories. What differs is that each type of category equipment takes up a different amount of space, depending on the function of the COG. An Enemy Encounter Suit can fit more weapons and armor than a Nano Environmental Tactical Stealth Suit can. Many pieces of equipment can only fit in certain types of COGs. The amount of slots a device takes up is listed within parentheses by the device in the different COG descriptions. These are the following slot categories:

Arrays: These describe placements for scanners, tools and weapons.

Augmentations: These give different boosts and also contain the kinetic unit.

Expendables: Things as extra air, nutrients, and extra energy sources are fitted here. Often, an Array requires a certain amount of Expendables slots as well. If someone fits an SMG into an Array slot, the ammo will take up Expendables slots.

Shell: Shell-type equipment is comprised of external protection such as armor or radiation shields.

Visor: Shows the number of vision modes and digital add-ons that can be installed. It also handles a few internal add-ons and external helmet scanners.

Managing Upgrades

Most components in a COG can be upgraded. The main feature (Array, Expendable, etc.) has both a base cost and an upgrade cost. Upgrades are done in levels. All COG features begin at level 1 upon purchase. In order for an avatar to make an upgrade (or in order to install a new device), he must have access to the correct nano-application (often called NAP). A NAP contains the nanites needed to make the upgrade or install the device. The NAP and the COG must be placed inside a nano-board matrix, often referred to as a nano-board or nano-matrix.

There are some things that must be explained before understanding how the upgrade system works from a game mechanical point of view. The actual NAP (the upgrade or new device before it has been installed) costs 25% less if the user has his own nano-matrix and the ability to upgrade it. If he uses a store to make the upgrade, he pays full price.

Cost: This is the cost for the actual feature (scanner, SMG, etc.).

Upgrade Levels: This tells you how many levels the feature has. All devices start at level one. At this level, they gain no bonus. The device works the same as its non-COG counterpart. Upgrade bonuses are only added when buying levels beyond level one. So if a device grants +1 to a certain roll per level, the avatar has to buy it up to level 2 before this bonus applies. If he bought it to level 4, he would gain a +3 bonus, as the first level doesn't provide a bonus. There are some exceptions to this, but these will be explained in the device Descriptions.

Upgrade Type: Some upgrades only cost creds, while some also require additional slots. When they require additional slots, each level takes up a cumulative amount of slots. So if a feature requires 2 slots and has a slot cost of 2, each upgrade level will require an additional 2 slots.

Upgrade Additions: This will simply tell you what the upgrade does.

Upgrade Cost: Here you will be able to see how much it costs to upgrade the device.

Notes on COG devices: Most COG devices have a handheld equivalent. The devices on the COGs work exactly the same as these, but the devices used for the COG are much more expensive and upgradable. Also, they're much sleeker and actually integrated into the COG. It's impossible to dislodge a device without breaking it, as it's a part of the COG as a whole. At times, there will be slight differences to the devices installed in COGs, in which case they will be described in the device listing.

Nano-Board Matrix

This device is vital when it comes to upgrading and fixing COGs. The nano-matrix is a rather big device. It's about the same size as a kitchen table but is a completely solid bench.

When the COG is placed on the top slate, the matrix's screens activate. Here all the statistics and data from the COG are displayed. Fixes and upgrades can be performed by placing NAPs and calibrating the COG through the matrix. Each upgrade or fix has a base time of 30 minutes and a reduction time of five minutes (using Brains + Repair). However, fixing durability only takes about thirty seconds. Failure on these rolls only indicates that the engineer can't sync the NAP to the COG at the moment, and he's free to try again. The NAP won't be spent or rendered useless when the engineer fails, only if he botches.

A nano-matrix only contains the tools and software needed to fix and upgrade a COG, but durability packs and NAPs must be bought and installed separately. So if someone wants to upgrade their COG, they have to buy the NAP (which contains the actual upgrade) and then place it inside the nano-matrix.
Cost: 200,000

Durability Packs

These are used to restore lost durability to the COG, and can either be used to refill the Polymer Nano Repair (PNR) or fed into a nano-matrix in order to refill the COG's durability directly. Every point of durability has a cost of 100 credits, and the largest packs contain 10 points worth of durability.

Circuitry

Circuitry shows how well the slotted equipment on the COG holds up when the COG gets banged up. This is rated at a level from one to eight. Every device that is interlocked with the COG has a circuitry rating. The rating equals the level of the device times two. So a level three array would have a circuitry of 6. In other words, high level devices can also withstand more punishment.

Then the actual COG has a circuitry rating as well. This starts out at rating 1 and can be upgraded, for a price. The main circuitry is very important, as it determines how well everything from the VAC to the nexus holds up under stress. These devices can also fall apart, potentially leaving the wearer in a dangerous situation: being without a HUD makes it impossible to use a lot of the equipment, and being in space without the heating system of your VES means "corpse-sicle".

COG Main Circuitry Price Range

Upgrading from 1–2: 1000
Upgrading from 2–3: 2500
Upgrading from 3–4: 4000
Upgrading from 4–5: 5500
Upgrading from 5–6: 7000
Upgrading from 6–7: 9500
Upgrading from 7–8: 12,000

Whenever a COG loses 7 points worth of durability, a circuitry roll is made. The AI must decide which device (a scanner, the HUD, etc.) is hit. If the roll fails, the chosen piece of equipment is broken. This will temporarily render the device in question useless and reduce its level by one. If the level is reduced to zero, the device is broken and must be replaced. If the COG main circuitry is reduced to zero, the COG is

irreparably damaged. The devices can still be used, but a new COG must be acquired.

Example: Rook has taken a heavy hit and his COG loses 7 points of durability. The AI tells him that his IR (level 2) might break down. Rook's player makes a circuitry roll for his IR NAP. Since it is level 2, he gets to roll 4 dice. He doesn't score a single success, and the AI tells him that the level of the IR NAP is reduced to 1 and that it's taken offline until he gets a chance to repair it.

> **Note on Device Failures:** A good way to handle device failures in the middle of an intense scene is to make a note of the number of rolls required and make these rolls after the scene, if you think the rolls will disturb the flow of the combat. It's a bit more lenient of an option, as the equipment won't fail during the combat.

Price of COGs

Most COGs cost 3000, but the Standard Exploration Rig only goes for 1,000. The actual upgrades and devices are, in many cases, more expensive than the actual COG. However, the TCI and the NETSS are much more expensive, as they have special functions. The NETSS costs 8000. The information on the extra price involving the TCI can be found under that specific COG further down on this list, while stealth module upgrades are listed under the NETTS.

AES – Adaptable Encounter Skin
Used by: Kiru, Operative, Raider
Armor Configuration Available: Lean (6), Shock (3)

Due to the need of versatility and stealth, the AES has a very sleek design. All arrays are folded as close to the body as possible, and the helmet is so sleek that it more resembles a pull down mask with a small visor and a gas mask attached. Due to its sleek design, many NAPs take up a lot of slots.

Arrays: Atmosphere Scanner (3), Chemical Scanner (3), Energy Scanner (3), External NIS (2), Fusion Cutter (3), Grappling Hook (1), Ground Penetrating Radar (3), Medical Bio-scanner (3), Mineral Scanner (3), Movement Tracker (1), PSG (3), Radiation Scanner (2), Signal Scanner (2), SMG Gauntlet (3), Tactical Bio-Scanner (1), Titanium Blade (1), Viral Analyzer (3).

Augmentations: Reaction (2), Brawn (5), Kinetic Unit (4), Quickness (2), Speed Run Kit (2), Weapon Link (3), Vehicle Link (4).

Expendables: Ammo (2), Breather Upgrade (2), Drugs and Injectors (4), Extra Capacitance (1), Flair Launcher (2), Fusion Fuel (3), Jet Boots and Fuel (4), Nutrients (2), PNR (3)

Shell: Armor (2), Corrosive Shield (3), Electrical Shield (3), Heat Shield (2), Radiation Shield (3)

Visor: Bridge Terminal (3), Diagnostic Screen (3), Internal Medical Bio Scanner (3), IR (2), Low Light (2), Magnification (2), Sulphur/Ammonia Marker (3), Topographic Mapping System (4), Ultrasound (3), UV (3), X-Ray (3)

EES – Enemy Encounter Suit

Used by: Marines, Raiders
Armor Configuration Available: Lean (10), Shock (10)

Mainly, this suit is designed to get the shit shot out of it. Its design is adapted to carry as much armor as possible. When fully loaded, these are the bulkiest but hardiest COGs around. They can withstand a lot of damage and have been designed to make room for equipment suited to fighting rippers.

Arrays: Atmosphere Scanner (3), Chemical Scanner (3), Energy Scanner (3), External NIS (3), Fusion Cutter (2), Grappling Hook (2), Ground Penetrating Radar (4), Medical Bio-scanner (2), Mineral Scanner (3), Movement Tracker (1), PSG (3), Radiation Scanner (3), Signal Scanner (3), SMG Gauntlet (1), Tactical Bio-Scanner (2), Titanium Blade (2), Viral Analyzer (3)

Augmentations: Reaction (3), Brawn (2), Kinetic Unit (6), Quickness (4), Speed Run Kit (3), Weapon Link (2), Vehicle Link (4).

Expendables: Ammo (2), Breather Upgrade (3), Drugs and Injectors (3), Extra Capacitance (1), Flair Launcher (3), Fusion Fuel (3), Jet Boots and Fuel (5), Nutrients (3), PNR (2)

Shell: Armor (1), Corrosive Shield (1), Electrical Shield (4), Heat Shield (4), Radiation Shield (3)

Visor: Bridge Terminal (4), Diagnostic Screen (4), Internal Medical Bio Scanner (2), IR (4), Low Light (4), Magnification (4), Sulphur/Ammonia Marker (1), Topographic Mapping System (4), Ultrasound (3), UV (3), X-Ray (3)

TIS – Tactical Investigation System (LED)

Used by: LED – Officer, Merc
Armor Configuration Available: Lean (7), Shock (4)

When it comes to both tactical charges and pure investigation, the TIS is the way to go. It balances combat readiness with room for scanners and arrays needed to do the job. It's a sturdy but rather streamlined design. This is the only suit that features the Forensic Filter, which makes it invaluable to LED-Officers.

Arrays: Atmosphere Scanner (3), Chemical Scanner (3), Energy Scanner (4), External NIS (2), Fusion Cutter (4), Grappling Hook (5), Ground Penetrating Radar (4), Medical Bio-scanner (4), Mineral Scanner (4), Movement Tracker (3), PSG (3), Radiation Scanner (4), Signal Scanner (2), SMG Gauntlet (2), Tactical Bio-Scanner (2), Titanium Blade (3), Viral Analyzer (4)

Augmentations: Reaction (3), Brawn (4), Kinetic Unit (4), Quickness (4), Speed Run Kit (3), Weapon Link (2), Vehicle Link (3).

Expendables: Ammo (3), Breather Upgrade (3), Drugs and Injectors (4), Extra Capacitance (1), Flair Launcher (4), Fusion Fuel (4), Jet Boots and Fuel (5), Nutrients (5), PNR (4)

Shell: Armor (2), Corrosive Shield (4), Electrical Shield (3), Heat Shield (4), Radiation Shield (4)

Visor: Bridge Terminal (3), Diagnostic Screen (4), Internal Medical Bio Scanner (3), IR (3), Low Light (2), Magnification (3), Sulphur/Ammonia Marker (4), Topographic Mapping System (4), Ultrasound (3), UV (3), X-Ray (3)

> *In game terms, the forensic filter gives a certain amount of re-rolls on failed dice when using the Ability Forensics to investigate a crime scene. It starts out with one re-roll, but it can be upgraded for up to four re-rolls. This dramatically increases the chances of success and of getting better results.*
>
> ***Upgrading the Forensic Filter:*** *The filter start out at level 1, which simply gives it one re-roll. Each additional level ups the circuitry by 2, like in all other NAPs, and grants an additional re-roll. The filter is integrated into the TIS and takes no slot space. Each level costs 2,000 credits.*

> ***Forensic Filter:*** *The forensic filter uses a neural link to stimulate the memory of the user and connect this processing to the present scene. This promotes what is called "Rapid Crypto-Amnesia Processing", or R-CAP. Minute details which the investigator might have missed are directly put into context and brought up on the HUD as suggestions. LED-Officers have been specially trained in its use, as it takes a particular analytic and instinctive thought process in order to make the neural link work with the computer.*

MPG – Mining Prospector Gear

Used by: Prospectors, Miners
Armor Configuration Available: Lean (7), Shock (3)

This suit is extremely hardy and configured to withstand the stress of mining and prospecting in a hostile environment. The suit has a sturdy design with a ridged, exoskeletal look.

Arrays: Atmosphere Scanner (2), Chemical Scanner (3), Energy Scanner (4), External NIS (3), Fusion Cutter (3), Grappling Hook (4), Ground Penetrating Radar (2), Medical Bio-scanner (4), Mineral Scanner (1), Movement Tracker (3), PSG (3), Radiation Scanner (2), Signal Scanner (3), SMG Gauntlet (4), Tactical Bio-Scanner (5), Titanium Blade (5), Viral Analyzer (4)

Augmentations: Reaction (4), Brawn (3), Kinetic Unit (2), Quickness (5), Speed Run Kit (5), Weapon Link (4), Vehicle Link (3).

Expendables: Ammo (4), Breather Upgrade (1), Drugs and Injectors (4), Extra Capacitance (1), Flair Launcher (2), Fusion Fuel (2), Jet Boots and Fuel (4), Nutrients (2), PNR (2)

Shell: Armor (2), Corrosive Shield (3), Electrical Shield (3), Heat Shield (3), Radiation Shield (2)

Visor: Bridge Terminal (4), Diagnostic Screen (3), Internal Medical Bio Scanner (2), IR (2), Low Light (2), Magnification (3), Sulphur/Ammonia Marker (4), Topographic Mapping System (2), Ultrasound (2), UV (3), X-Ray (2)

NETSS - Nano Environmental Tactical Stealth Suit
Used by: Scouts
Armor Configuration Available: Lean (5), Shock (2)

COGs are extremely advanced pieces of technology, but the NETSS are considered to be an even more sophisticated COG. Only those with scout training can use these effectively. The entire outer skin of the suit is covered with environmental 3D nano-scanners and NIS. The information scans the physical environment and sends data to the HUD as mathematical algorithms and to a neural link as impulses. Using the electrical impulses and the mathematical algorithms the scout can, by using extremely rapid eye commands and neural linking, basically "copy paste" the surroundings and transmit them to the NIS, effectively rendering himself translucent.

The nano-skin also disposes of smaller foreign particles which land on the suit, so as to not disturb the stealth process (so dust, spray paint and similar substances won't stick to the suit).

While the stealth mode is in use, the scout is constantly concentrating on the process. It has been shown that a computer (even a micro-VIN) is incapable of calculating the stealth information properly. Computers do math perfectly, but they miss that human element of instincts and creativity which makes the stealth mode possible. So the computer and the scout cooperate in the process. A large portion of the scout program consists of mental exercises and mental stress training. People who don't have the scout training can't use the stealth module. Just trying to interpret the constantly flashing algorithms gives most people a headache, while also imposing a −3 on all actions without even gaining the benefit of the stealth module. When the module is activated, the scout seems to fade away, becoming a transparent blur.

The stealth module extends and can cover an object that he holds (about as large as a suitcase, which is enough for the sniper rifle). It also covers smaller objects he carries, such as his sidearm or other light equipment he has close to his body. Needless to say, scouts travel light. The stealth module algorithms take IR, UV and all other kinds of spectra into account. It even fools ultrasound, motion detection and LIDAR. Others will be unable to use different vision modes to penetrate it. However, decloakers can be used to temporarily disrupt the module and render the user visible.

Upgrading the Stealth Module: The module can be upgraded, and each upgrade adds one extra stealth mode activation per 24 hours, plus an additional four minutes worth of stealth time. The module starts at level one and, like most other NAPs, it has four levels. The circuitry works exactly the same as for other applications. Each level costs 6,000 credits to upgrade.

Arrays: Atmosphere Scanner (3), Chemical Scanner (4), Energy Scanner (4), External NIS (4), Fusion Cutter (4), Grappling Hook (3), Ground Penetrating Radar (4), Medical Bio-scanner (5), Mineral Scanner (5), Movement Tracker (3), PSG (4), Radiation Scanner (4), Signal Scanner (2), SMG Gauntlet (4), Tactical Bio-Scanner (3), Titanium Blade (3), Viral Analyzer (4)

Notes: *The stealth module can be activated for the scout's Cool × 10 minutes at a time. After this, he needs to take a fifteen minute break as his mind is incapable of upholding the calculations; he can't even try to sustain it since all information becomes jumbled up in his head. A level one stealth module can only be switched on and off four times per 24 hours, but this (and the duration of the stealth) can be upgraded. If he cuts the stealth mode short, he must still rest his head for fifteen minutes because his concentration and mental preparedness have already been put out of balance. So yes, shutting down stealth after ten seconds would result in a fifteen minute break. If the scout is rendered unconscious, the stealth mode ends. Whenever a scout loses more than 6 hit points (fatal or bashing) in one blow, he must make a Cool roll. If this fails, the stealth mode ends.*

It's very hard to go by any exact set of rules when it comes to the stealth module. How hard it is to see someone using it depends a lot on the circumstances (standing against a wall or out in the open for example). But as a general rule, the one using the stealth module gets +5 to his stealth roll when it comes to staying out of sight (and in most cases when using stealth in a sequence zone). If someone tries to discover an individual using a stealth module and the scout is standing still he gets a −5 modifier to his Attention + Search roll on top of any other modifier (darkness, mist, rain, etc.). Trying to hit someone in combat who has activated his stealth mode (granted you see them already) is done with a −3 modifier (on top of everything else). But if the scout is in active combat, actually fighting against targets that are attacking him, he gets the same negative modifier since he has to concentrate at the stealth mode and focus on active targets. However, if sniping unaware targets or engaging targets who don't have a bead on him, he does not suffer the penalty.

Whenever a scout falls out of sight and has his stealth module activated (and if he has multiple ways to go) the individual looking for him has to make an Attention + Search roll with a −3 modifier to see where he went. If the durability of the suit ever goes below 15, the stealth module is put out of commission until the durability is brought above 15 again.

Augmentations: Reaction (4), Brawn (5), Kinetic Unit (5), Quickness (3), Speed Run Kit (3), Weapon Link (3), Vehicle Link (4).

Expendables: Ammo (4), Breather Upgrade (3), Drugs and Injectors (3), Extra Capacitance (1), Flair Launcher (4), Fusion Fuel (3), Jet Boots and Fuel (5), Nutrients (2), PNR (4)

Shell: Armor (2), Corrosive Shield (3), Electrical Shield (3), Heat Shield (2), Radiation Shield (3)

Visor: Bridge Terminal (3), Diagnostic Screen (4), Internal Medical Bio Scanner (3), IR (2), Low Light (2), Magnification (1), Sulphur/Ammonia Marker (3), Topographic Mapping System (3), Ultrasound (1), UV (1), X-Ray (2)

SRS – Scientific Research System

Used by: Archaeologists, Science Researchers, Medical Technicians

Armor Configuration Available: Lean (4), Shock (2)

When undertaking a scientific endeavour, the SRS is the way to go. This COG is designed to be fitted with scientific scanners and tools while remaining sturdy. As the scientific occupations that use the SRS often land the wearer in some hot water, it can take quite the beating if configured correctly.

Arrays: Atmosphere Scanner (1), Chemical Scanner (2), Energy Scanner (2), External NIS (2), Fusion Cutter (4), Grappling Hook (4), Ground Penetrating Radar (3), Medical Bio-scanner (2), Mineral Scanner (3), Movement Tracker (2), PSG (3), Radiation Scanner (2), Signal Scanner (2), SMG Gauntlet (4), Tactical Bio-Scanner (4), Titanium Blade (3), Viral Analyzer (1)

Augmentations: Reaction (4), Brawn (4), Kinetic Unit (5), Quickness (4), Speed Run Kit (4), Weapon Link (4), Vehicle Link (3).

Expendables: Ammo (4), Breather Upgrade (3), Drugs and Injectors (3), Extra Capacitance (1), Flair Launcher (3), Fusion Fuel (4), Jet Boots and Fuel (4), Nutrients (3), PNR (3)

Shell: Armor (2), Corrosive Shield (3), Electrical Shield (3), Heat Shield (4), Radiation Shield (4)

Visor: Bridge Terminal (4), Diagnostic Screen (4), Internal Medical Bio Scanner (2), IR (3), Low Light (2), Magnification (3), Sulphur/Ammonia Marker (4), Topographic Mapping System (4), Ultrasound (4), UV (3), X-Ray (3)

TCI – Tactical Command Immersion

Used by: Pilot, Commanding Officer, Raider

Armor Configuration Available: Lean (6), Shock (4)

The TCI has been designed to act as a coordinator of tactical information as well as a battle suit. Squad leaders as well as fighter pilots can make good use of this, as it can be directly plugged into a cockpit and also used as an on-site command center when it comes to sending and receiving information. The COG can be used as it is, or one of two special customizations can be installed.

TCI flight coordinator customization: The wearer of the flight coordinator has the choice of eliminating some scanner options altogether in exchange for a link sync, which will allow him to sync with the onboard scanners of ships. The installment options for ship scanner sync and the slot spaces are the following: Bio Scanner (2), Energy Scanner (1), Environmental Scanner (2), LIDAR (1), LSA (2), Signal Scanner (1). Each ship scanner sync eliminates the corresponding COG installed scanner. The LIDAR and LSA options eliminate a scanner each (of the player's choice) from the COG. The levels and upgrades work a little differently than for other scanners. Here the user gains a +1 bonus at level one and the fourth level only adds to the circuitry rating. The level system for the TCI flight coordinator looks like this:

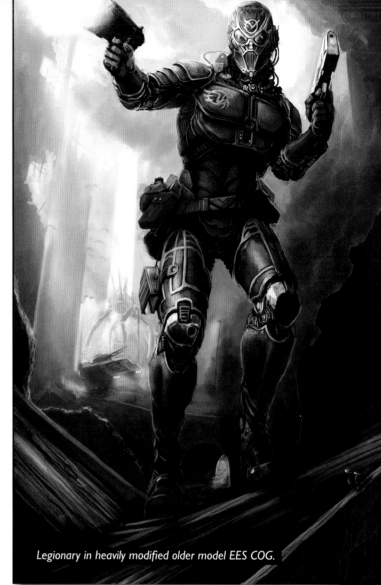

Legionary in heavily modified older model EES COG.

Level 1: +1 to relevant scanner/function
Level 2: +2 to relevant scanner/function
Level 3: +3 to relevant scanner/function
Level 4: Only adds to circuitry

There's also the possibility of installing a targeting sync link, which eliminates three visor options. In return, it gives +1 per level to all rolls involving the ship weapon systems which are a part of the ship's targeting system. Upgrading this feature works exactly the same as upgrading the above scanner sync. These links and sync options really give a pilot/navigator an edge while in his ship. This COG also has a special vehicle link configuration. When the augmentation Vehicle Link is installed, the modifier applies to Handling, Speed and Acceleration, which means there's no need for multiple links (the cost and the upgrade levels work exactly as the normal Vehicle Link though). A pilot in a customized ship wearing his TCI can perform the most astonishing feats. The cost for the scanners is 800 credits higher than normal when buying them and 400 credits higher when upgrading. The LSA and LIDAR cost 3,200 to buy and 900 to upgrade while the weapon sync costs 4,400 to buy and 1,500 to upgrade.

TCI battle coordinator customization: This system has been specially designed to effectively coordinate large-scale attacks and the organization of squadrons and platoons, both on the ground and in the air. At level one, this device grants the user +1 to all Strategy rolls and 2 strategy points he can spend per 24 hours. These are the result of the coordinator, which analyzes the field and the situation constantly. The TCI battle coordinator has four levels. The levels work exactly the same as with the flight coordinator, but grant different bonuses:

Level 1: +1 Strategy, 2 strategy points/24 hours
Level 2: +2 Strategy, 3 strategy points/24 hours
Level 3: +3 Strategy, 4 strategy points/24 hours
Level 4: Only adds to circuitry

The cost for this option is 3,500 credits and the upgrades cost 2,200 per level. It's impossible to have both the TCI battle coordinator and the flight coordinator installed.

Arrays: Atmosphere Scanner (3), Chemical Scanner (3), Energy Scanner (3), External NIS (3), Fusion Cutter (2), Grappling Hook (3), Ground Penetrating Radar (4), Medical Bio-scanner (3), Mineral Scanner (4), Movement Tracker (3), PSG (3), Radiation Scanner (3), Signal Scanner (1), SMG Gauntlet (3), Tactical Bio-Scanner (3), Titanium Blade (3), Viral Analyzer (4)

Augmentations: Reaction (2), Brawn (4), Kinetic Unit (4), Quickness (2), Speed Run Kit (3), Weapon Link (3), Vehicle Link (1).

Expendables: Ammo (3), Breather Upgrade (2), Drugs and Injectors (2), Extra Capacitance (1), Flair Launcher (3), Fusion Fuel (3), Jet Boots and Fuel (3), Nutrients (3), PNR (3)

Shell: Armor (2), Corrosive Shield (2), Electrical Shield (2), Heat Shield (2), Radiation Shield (2)

Visor: Bridge Terminal (3), Diagnostic Screen (2), Internal Medical Bio Scanner (3), IR (3), Low Light (3), Magnification (3), Sulphur/Ammonia Marker (4), Topographic Mapping System (3), Ultrasound (3), UV (3), X-Ray (3)

SER – Standard Exploration Rig
Used by: Arbiter, Delegate, Raider
Armor Configuration Available: Lean (6), Shock (3)

This is the most common COG available. It has no specialty as such and is designed to be as versatile as possible. Even though there's nothing special to it, and despite the fact that most installments take up the same amount of space, it's the most widely used. This is due to its price. All upgrades and installments have a 25% price reduction.

Arrays: Atmosphere Scanner (3), Chemical Scanner (3), Energy Scanner (3), External NIS (3), Fusion Cutter (3), Grappling Hook (3), Ground Penetrating Radar (3), Medical Bio-scanner (3), Mineral Scanner (3), Movement Tracker (3), PSG (3), Radiation Scanner (3), Signal Scanner (3), SMG Gauntlet (3), Tactical Bio-Scanner (3), Titanium Blade (3), Viral Analyzer (3)

Augmentations: Reaction (6), Brawn (6), Kinetic Unit (4), Quickness (6), Speed Run Kit (4), Weapon Link (4), Vehicle Link (4).

Expendables: Ammo (3), Breather Upgrade (3), Drugs and Injectors (3), Extra Capacitance (1), Flair Launcher (3), Fusion Fuel (3), Jet Boots and Fuel (3), Nutrients (3), PNR (3)

Shell: Armor (2), Corrosive Shield (2), Electrical Shield (2), Heat Shield (2), Radiation Shield (2)

Visor: Bridge Terminal (3), Diagnostic Screen (3), Internal Medical Bio Scanner (3), IR (3), Low Light (3), Magnification (3), Sulphur/Ammonia Marker (4), Topographic Mapping System (3), Ultrasound (3), UV (3), X-Ray (3)

ZGE – Zero-G Engineering
Used by: Gear Jammer, Site Engineer
Armor Configuration Available: Lean (7), Shock (6).

Barring the EES, this is one of the toughest COGs ever made, and it beats all the others hands down as it is mainly adapted to withstand hostile environments. Engineers and gear jammers tend to form a special relationship with their COG, sometimes even naming them.

Arrays: Atmosphere Scanner (2), Chemical Scanner (2), Energy Scanner (1), External NIS (1), Fusion Cutter (1), Grappling Hook (2), Ground Penetrating Radar (3), Medical Bio-scanner (4), Mineral Scanner (3), Movement Tracker (3), PSG (1), Radiation Scanner (1), Signal Scanner (1), SMG Gauntlet (3), Tactical Bio-Scanner (3), Titanium Blade (4), Viral Analyzer (4)

Augmentations: Reaction (5), Brawn (5), Kinetic Unit (3), Quickness (4), Speed Run Kit (4), Weapon Link (5), Vehicle Link (4).

Expendables: Ammo (6), Breather Upgrade (3), Drugs and Injectors (4), Extra Capacitance (1), Flair Launcher (3), Fusion Fuel (3), Jet Boots and Fuel (2), Nutrients (2), PNR (2)

Shell: Armor (2), Corrosive Shield (2), Electrical Shield (1), Heat Shield (1), Radiation Shield (1)

Visor: Bridge Terminal (3), Diagnostic Screen (2), Internal Medical Bio Scanner (4), IR (3), Low Light (3), Magnification (3), Sulphur/Ammonia Marker (4), Topographic Mapping System (4), Ultrasound (4), UV (3), X-Ray (3)

Arrays

Atmosphere Scanner
Cost: 1,500
Upgrade Levels: 4
Upgrade Type: Creds
Upgrade Additions: Each level increases the range by 10 meters and gives +1 to the scan roll.
Upgrade Cost: 800/level

Chemical Scanner
Cost: 1,700
Upgrade Levels: 4
Upgrade Type: Creds
Upgrade Additions: Each level increases the range by 10 meters and gives +1 to the scan roll.
Upgrade Cost: 700/level

Energy Scanner
Cost: 2,000
Upgrade Levels: 4
Upgrade Type: Creds
Upgrade Additions: Each level increases the range by 10 meters and gives +1 to the scan roll.
Upgrade Cost: 700/level

External NIS
Cost: 900
Upgrade Levels: 4
Upgrade Type: Creds
Upgrade Additions: Only adds to the circuitry.
Upgrade Cost: 200

Fusion Cutter
The fusion cutter extends from the COG glove of the chosen hand and can be used normally. Keep in mind that the actual fuel for the cutter falls under expendables and it would be a total waste of space to invest in the cutter without also buying the fuel.
Cost: 900
Upgrade Levels: 4
Upgrade Type: Creds
Upgrade Additions: Each level gives +1 to the Repair roll when using the device.
Upgrade Cost: 300/level

Grappling Gun
The polymer tether is actually woven from liquid polymers inside the COG when the grappling gun is shot. The tether reverts to its liquid form when pulled back in. The grappling gun is usually positioned as a gauntlet, virtually invisible, as the hook morphs itself into shape upon activation and only then does it show.
Cost: 1,000
Upgrade Levels: 4
Upgrade Type: Creds
Upgrade Additions: Each level adds room for an additional 20 meters worth of polymer tether
Upgrade Cost: 500/level

Ground Penetrating Radar
Cost: 2,300
Upgrade Levels: 4
Upgrade Type: Creds
Upgrade Additions: Each level grants a +1 modifier to rolls involving the scanner, such as Xenoarchaeology, Scanner and Search rolls whenever feasible.
Upgrade Cost: 900/level

Medical Bio-scanner
Cost: 3,200
Upgrade Levels: 4
Upgrade Type: Creds
Upgrade Additions: Each level grants a +1 to the scanner roll.
Upgrade Cost: 1000/level

Mineral Scanner
Cost: 2,200
Upgrade Levels: 4
Upgrade Type: Creds

Upgrade Additions: Each level grants a +1 to the scanner roll, increases the range by ten meters and adds another one cubic meter to the amount of material that can be scanned.
Upgrade Cost: 900/level

Movement Tracker
Cost: 1800
Upgrade Levels: 4
Upgrade Type: Creds
Upgrade Additions: Each level grants a +1 to the scanner roll and increases the range by 25 meters.
Upgrade Cost: 600

PSG
Cost: 800
Upgrade Levels: 4
Upgrade Type: Creds
Upgrade Additions: Each level add +1 to any Repair roll involving the PSG.
Upgrade Cost: 300

Radiation Scanner
Cost: 2,300
Upgrade Levels: 4
Upgrade Type: Creds
Upgrade Additions: Each level increases the range by 10 meters and grants +1 to the scan roll.
Upgrade Cost: 800/level

Signal Scanner
Cost: 3,000
Upgrade Levels: 4
Upgrade Type: Creds
Upgrade Additions: Each level grants +1 to the scan roll.
Upgrade Cost: 900

SMG Gauntlet
This small SMG is placed on the top of the forearm. A COG can only sport one gauntlet application (titanium blade, SMG and Grappling Gun) per forearm. Use the GIC SOP MR template when it comes to damage, ROF and range. The ammunition for the SMG is a separate matter which goes under expendables. Buying the SMG gauntlet without adding the ammo would be pointless.
Cost: 1,800
Upgrade Levels: 4
Upgrade Type: Creds
Upgrade Additions: Adds +1 to the Shooting roll.
Upgrade Cost: 600

Tactical Bio-Scanner
Cost: 3,600
Upgrade Levels: 4
Upgrade Type: Creds
Upgrade Additions: Adds +1 to the scan roll and also increases the effective range by 25 meters.
Upgrade Cost: 900

Titanium Blade
This 30-centimeter jagged titanium blade comes in the form of a retractable gauntlet setup. It's ideal for close combat. The blade has a base damage of 4 and 2 damage per success.
Cost: 700

The Border Guard is testing out experimental jump packs.

Upgrade Levels: 4
Upgrade Type: Creds
Upgrade Additions: Only adds to the circuit rating.
Upgrade Cost: 200

Viral Analyzer
Cost: 2,200
Upgrade Levels: 4
Upgrade Type: Creds
Upgrade Additions: Increases the range by 10 meters and also adds +1 to the scan roll.
Upgrade Cost: 1000

Augmentations

Aptitude augmentations add +1 to the Aptitude in question at level one. Some of the augmentations have (+1) listed after the number of upgrade levels. This means that an avatar can buy a fourth level in order to max out his circuitry rating in the device, but the upgrade doesn't add another bonus.

Reaction
Cost: 4,000
Upgrade Levels: 3 (+1)
Upgrade Type: Creds
Upgrade Additions: Adds +1 to Reaction.
Upgrade Cost: 1500/level

Brawn
Cost: 4,000
Upgrade Levels: 3 (+1)
Upgrade Type: Creds
Upgrade Additions: Adds +1 to Brawn.
Upgrade Cost: 1500/level

Kinetic Unit

The kinetic unit is a grav-cuff transmitter with a range of five meters. It shifts the gravity, creating a contained field which can be moved by hand. This gravity field surrounds the object and the shift of gravity amplifies the movement of the user, acting as a kind of gravity servo engine. The unit lets the person manipulate objects that have a grav-cuff receiver (and is within the proper weight class). The objects can only be moved at a speed of ten meters per three seconds, and thus the kinetic unit is mainly used to lift heavy objects such as crates and components. Engineers make great use of this, since most heavy engine parts (and even ITS trains) and connectors have these receivers. This lets an engineer manipulate heavy objects in confined spaces without assistance or the hassle of using clumsy equipment like forklifts. It also lets them manipulate dangerous objects like large power couplings.

At the first level, the kinetic unit is capable of lifting objects that weigh up to a ton. Most ships don't assign specific codes to each and every one of their crate and equipment receivers, but it sometimes happens, and in this case the engineer must get his hands on these codes before he can manipulate the objects. If the manipulation becomes dicey, an Attention + Athletics (if moving crates or similar object) or an Attention + Repair (if dealing with engine parts) roll is required. The engineer can twist and turn the objects as he pleases (about 90 degrees per combat segment), provided he passes the manipulation roll. The unit is located in both gloves and forearms of the user (and does not interfere with gauntlet devices), and using it requires the full attention and both hands of the user. If standing still, the user can free up one of his hands for a short while (such as when he needs to press a button or perform a minor task).
Cost: 3,200
Upgrade Levels: 4
Upgrade Type: Creds
Upgrade Additions: Each level increases the weight limitation by 1 ton and also adds +1 to manipulation rolls.
Upgrade Cost: 1,200

Quickness
Cost: 4,000
Upgrade Levels: 3
Upgrade Type: Creds
Upgrade Additions: Adds +1 to Quickness per level.
Upgrade Cost: 1,500/level

Speed Run Kit

This adds a small gravity shift to the running motion, effectively accelerating the movement of the legs without any extra effort on the part of the user. At first level, the movement increases by 7 and a +1 is added to all Athletics rolls involving running (such as when chasing someone or being chased). This bonus also applies to Athletics rolls made to perform running jumps. Additionally, each level adds +1 meter to the distance a close combatant can attack a distracted shooter at under the *Bullets vs. Hoofing It* rules.

Cost: 3,500
Upgrade Levels: 3
Upgrade Type: Creds
Upgrade Additions: Level 2 adds another 7 meters to the movement and +1 to the Athletics rolls, while level 3 only adds an additional +1 to the roll.
Upgrade Cost: 750

Weapon Link

All firearms (modern, factory-made ones, at least) have a sync option. When a COG has a weapon link installed, the user can basically sync it to any weapon. This requires that he has access to a nano-matrix and it takes about five minutes to install it and sync it to the COG. The weapon link can only support one weapon at a time, so additional synced weapons require additional links.
Cost: 2,900
Upgrade Levels: 3
Upgrade Type: Creds
Upgrade Additions: Each level adds +1 to all Shooting rolls involving the synced weapon.
Upgrade Cost: 800

Vehicle Link

This works off the same principle as a weapon link, but syncs the user up to a ship or ground vehicle. Most ships have a link system, but in many cases it's locked. If locked, the pilot (or someone else) must hack the system before the pilot can sync up. If synced to a ship already, the pilot will sync up with the system the same second he steps aboard. If not, the sync process takes about ten minutes. As with weapon links, this device can only support one link at a time. The bonus is added to either Handling, Acceleration *or* Speed rolls. It's possible to wear three links to get bonuses to all three stats.
Cost: 5,700
Upgrade Levels: 2
Upgrade Type: Creds
Upgrade Additions: Adds +1 per level to Pilot/Drive rolls involving the linked vehicle.
Upgrade Cost: 2,000

Expendables

Ammo

This expendable starts out with a capacity of fifty. The ammunition is situated in a flat, streamlined box magazine on the underside of the forearm. Reloading the magazine takes a while if done manually. There is, however, something called a "COG mag". These are the same size as the clip on the COG. When placed directly on the clip, it briefly merges with the clip, refills whatever bullets are missing and disconnects, requiring two segments to reload. These contain fifty bullets and are discarded after use, as they become worthless when emptied. A full COG mag has a cost of 50 credits, +10 per every twenty-five additional bullets.
Cost: 500
Upgrade Levels: 3
Upgrade Type: Creds/Slots
Upgrade Additions: +25 shots per upgrade
Upgrade Cost: 700/level

Breather Upgrade

All COGs have a breather installed, which is considered to be level zero and contains sixty seconds worth of air. This upgrade heightens the effectiveness of this device.
Cost: n/a
Upgrade Levels: 3
Upgrade Type: Creds
Upgrade Additions: Each upgrade adds 20 seconds worth of air.
Upgrade Cost: 1,000

Drugs and Injectors

Auto-injectors can be invaluable in a sticky situation. These are positioned inside the COG and the drugs are injected directly into the COG wearer whenever he so commands. The device can hold one dose at level one. Filling it up is a simple matter of pushing a vial of the desired injection into a protected slot near the nexus, in the small of the back. An injector can be combined with an internal medical scanner in order to administer regen, stims or NRC should certain circumstances arise (critical hits, extreme mental strain, unconsciousness, etc.).
Cost: 1,350
Upgrade Levels: 4
Upgrade Type: Creds/Slots
Upgrade Additions: Each upgrade adds an extra vial slot.
Upgrade Cost: 450

Extra Capacitance

This is used as a back-up system when devices in the COG are about to be broken or destroyed. This feature gives a number of expendable points which can be spent in order to boost any circuitry temporarily. The points are spent whenever a circuitry roll is about to be made (if the player so chooses). Each point will give a +1 to the circuitry roll. When bought, the backup system can hold 1 point worth of capacitance. To refill it, the avatar must buy COG power cells, a special type of power cell made out of COG-adapted and condensed capacitance. A COG power cell costs 200 credits.
Cost: 2,300
Upgrade Levels: 5
Upgrade Type: Creds/Slots
Upgrade Additions: +1 capacitance slot per level.
Upgrade Cost: 1,200/level

Flare Launcher

The flares are fired from slots just under one of the shoulders in the COG. At level one, the flare launcher holds three flare (+1 flare per additional level). The COG uses normal flares when in need of a refill.
Cost: 900
Upgrade Levels: 4
Upgrade Type: Creds
Upgrade Additions: Each upgrade adds 1 flare.
Upgrade Cost: 400/level

Fusion Fuel

This gauntlet unit holds fifteen minutes of cutter fuel. Fuel takes about fifteen seconds to replenish at a fusion fuel station, which can be found in any well-equipped mechanic garage or engineering bay.
Cost: 1,000
Upgrade Levels: 3

Upgrade Type: Creds

Upgrade Additions: Each upgrade adds an additional five minutes of fuel time.

Upgrade Cost: 600

Jet Boots and Fuel

These small jets are concealed within the boots of the COG until engaged. They're not very powerful and are only useful in a zero-g environment. The jets are positioned parallel to the outside of the lower legs and can be rotated 360 degrees. The jets are capable of propelling the COG wearer at a speed of twenty-five kilometers per hour in a zero-g or underwater environment. At level zero, the jets hold fuel for one minute of use. Each burst counts as three seconds worth of fuel. Refilling the device is done by using a ZGJ (Zero-G Jetpack) station. These can be found in most airlocks in C-class and larger ships, and it takes about a minute to refuel. A station contains 15 refuels.

Cost: 3,300

Upgrade Levels: 4

Upgrade Type: Cost

Upgrade Additions: Each level adds 15 seconds worth of fuel.

Upgrade Cost: 700

Nutrients

This highly nutritious solution can save a person's life. The liquid is actually contained in the COG itself and a straw can be flicked out within the helmet. When installed, there's room for two liters of nutrient, which can keep a person alive for five days without the need for any other liquid or nutrients. To refill it, the avatar simply buys a nutrient pack and connects it to the COG, transferring the solution. As with many other expendables in a COG, it's the actual space and administrating device for which the avatar pays.

Cost: 950

Upgrade Levels: 3

Upgrade Type: Creds

Upgrade Additions: Each upgrade adds one extra day worth of nutrients (0.5 liters).

Upgrade Cost: 300

PNR

COGs can't regain durability by the use of a PSG and need a nano-matrix for this. But the PNR (Polymer Nano Repair) is a built-in nanite protocol, an actual expansion of the Internal Sealant System. This is an internal repair system that can refill

the COGs durability. When bought, the system contains 5 durability points which can be spent to replenish lost durability in the field. In order to refill it, the avatar needs to put the COG in a nano-matrix. The cost of loading this system is the same per durability point as the cost of regaining durability for the COG using the nano-matrix.

Cost: 3,200

Upgrade Levels: 5

Upgrade Type: Cost

Upgrade Additions: +5 durability points per level.

Upgrade Cost: 750/level

Shell

Armor

There are two prices listed under upgrade cost. The first is for Lean armor, while the second shows the price for Shock armor.

Cost: 1,500

Upgrade Levels: 9

Upgrade Type: Creds/Slot

Upgrade Additions: +1 AR per level

Upgrade Cost: 800/1000

Note on Shields: Shields can never protect an avatar from the worst of effects, and in many cases they can only protect the wearer (and the COG) for a limited amount of time, depending on the severity of the damage.

Each level corresponds to a level of severity, according to the source and shield. The shield negates any damage inflicted by the source for a certain amount of time (depending on the shield). The most powerful shields go up to level three, which means that no one can be completely protected from the most severe levels of hazardous environments.

Each shield level will provide an amount of protection against the type of hazard it is designed to handle. If the damage levels are higher, the protection is deducted from the damage.

When an avatar is subjected to a severity that's higher than his shield level can handle, he will lose the amount of hit points (and by that, COG durability) listed for that severity, minus the level of his protection. The protection of shields also deteriorates from exposure to the hazard in question. How long

Fire, Corrosives and Electricity Shields

Shield Level	Protection	Severity	Damage
1	3	Mild	3
2	6	Harsh	6
3	8	Extreme	8
		Incinerating	10

Radiation

Shield Level	Protection	Severity	Damage
1	1	Soft	1
2	2	Mild	2
3	4	Hard	4
		Severe	6

this takes depends on the hazard and will be stated under the shield description. This deterioration is temporary and will be restored after a certain time. Each time the shield deteriorates, it counts as one level lower, reducing the protection it offers.

Example: A level 3 fire, corrosives and electricity shield grants a protection of 8. If it's hit with an extreme severity, which inflicts 8 points worth of damage, the wearer and the COG would be unharmed. If it was subjected to the incinerating severity, the wearer would suffer 2 points worth of damage, as the incinerating severity inflicts 10 points and the level three shield offers a protection of 8. If this shield deteriorates once, it would count as a level 2 shield, and if it deteriorates a second time, it would count as a level 1 shield, and if it deteriorates a third time, it wouldn't offer any protection until restored.

It takes a shield five minutes to regain a deteriorated level as the nanites rearrange themselves and reset. As shields are composed of a thin layer of nanites programmed to protect the material from certain conditions, this application can break apart just like any other device as the units containing the program suffer damage.

Corrosive Shield

The shield deteriorates one level every ten seconds of exposure (every third combat segment).
Cost: 2,200
Upgrade Levels: 3
Upgrade Type: Creds/Slot
Upgrade Additions: Increases the shield level by one step per level.
Upgrade Cost: 1,000

Electrical Shield

The shield deteriorates one level every thirty seconds of exposure (every tenth combat segment).
Cost: 1,700
Upgrade Levels: 3
Upgrade Type: Creds/Slot
Upgrade Additions: Increases the shield level by one step per level.
Upgrade Cost: 800

Heat Shield

The shield deteriorates one level every thirty seconds of exposure (every tenth combat segment).
Cost: 1,500
Upgrade Levels: 3
Upgrade Type: Creds/Slot
Upgrade Additions: Increases the shield level by one step per level.
Upgrade Cost: 700

Radiation Shield

The shield deteriorates one level every ten minutes of exposure.
Cost: 2,000
Upgrade Levels: 3
Upgrade Type: Creds/Slot
Upgrade Additions: Increases the shield level by one step per level.
Upgrade Cost: 700

Visor

Bridge Terminal

This is a built-in terminal, which the avatar can control through his HUD.
Cost: 1,600
Upgrade Levels: 3
Upgrade Type: Creds
Upgrade Additions: Each upgrade gives a +1 to any roll using the bridge terminal.
Upgrade Cost: 600

Diagnostics Screen

The access cable for this device (if there's no remote jack in place) is positioned in one of the gloves of the COG and is three meters long. All the relevant information is projected onto the HUD.
Cost: 3200
Upgrade Levels: 4
Upgrade Type: Creds
Upgrade Additions: Adds +1 to diagnostics rolls when using the device.
Upgrade Cost: 700

Forensic Filter

TCS – Tactical Investigation System only
Cost: —
Upgrade Levels: 4
Upgrade Type: Creds
Upgrade Additions: Adds +1 to the re-roll die (see forensic filter).
Upgrade Cost: 1,800/level

Internal Medical Bio-Scanner

Cost: 1,900
Upgrade Levels: 4
Upgrade Type: Creds
Upgrade Additions: This grants +1 to all First Aid rolls to those who are privy to the patient's information. Also, the person must have at least 1 dot in the Ability First Aid (or be a med-tech) in order to gain from this bonus. The device also transmits accurate medical data in detail to the wearer. It records blood loss, location and severity of injuries and adrenaline level.
Upgrade Cost: 450

IR

Cost: 1,750
Upgrade Levels: 4
Upgrade Type: Creds
Upgrade Additions: Gives +1 to any Search or Ability rolls that benefit from infrared scans (such as searching for a source of heat).
Upgrade Cost: 650

Low-Light

Cost: 1,000
Upgrade Levels: 4
Upgrade Type: Creds
Upgrade Additions: Only adds to circuitry.
Upgrade Cost: 400

Magnification

This vision mode plugs in to all others, so for example if the COG has IR, it grants magnification to that vision mode as well. It won't bypass the limitations of a vision mode. X-Ray will only see as far as it does, but the magnification can still zoom in on objects within the range. Magnification in the COG does not act as a scope and can't be used while firing a weapon, but it can grant bonuses (according to the AI) on other Attention-based rolls, and can be used to scout like a pair of binoculars. At level one, magnification starts at ×4 zoom.
Cost: 1,000
Upgrade Levels: 4
Upgrade Type: Creds
Upgrade Additions: Each level adds another ×2 magnification level, so at level 3, the maximum magnification could be set at ×10.
Upgrade Cost: 350

Sulphur/Ammonia Marker

Cost: 2,800
Upgrade Levels: 4
Upgrade Type: Creds
Upgrade Additions: Only adds to circuitry.
Upgrade Cost: 750

Topographic Mapping System

Cost: 1,500
Upgrade Levels: 4
Upgrade Type: Creds
Upgrade Additions: Each level adds +1 to Navigation rolls that make use of the device.
Upgrade Cost: 600

Ultrasound

Cost: 2,800
Upgrade Levels: 4
Upgrade Type: Creds
Upgrade Additions: Each level adds +1 to all Search rolls that might benefit from the ultrasound vision mode.
Upgrade Cost: 750

UV

Cost: 2,200
Upgrade Levels: 4
Upgrade Type: Creds
Upgrade Additions: Each level adds +1 to all Search rolls that might benefit from ultraviolet vision mode.
Upgrade Cost: 800

X-Ray

Cost: 4,500
Upgrade Levels: 4
Upgrade Type: Creds
Upgrade Additions: Each level increases the range of the X-Ray by five meters.
Upgrade Cost: 1,000

Durability Upgrade

The durability of the COG can be upgraded by as much as 15 points. Each point costs 1000 credits. It might be a bit steep, but it's often worth it as the whole COG becomes more resilient to damage. Every three points upgrade will also increase the amount of points that must be lost before a device is in jeopardy by 1.

Security Gear

Lock Picks

A set consisting of ten picks and three tension wrenches. These thirteen tools are enough to open most mechanical locks. The picks come in a small and sleek carbon fiber case.
Cost: 50

Electronic Lock Bypass Kit

This kit contains the tools needed to remove the panel on most alarms and electronic locks, a small handheld security controller and cables and connectors needed to hook the circuits from the lock up to the controller. The user then hacks the lock by decreasing, increasing and rerouting the power, which if done correctly will open the electronic lock. Security is the Ability used.
Cost: 400

Placement Bridges Pack

Placement bridges are used to remotely control things as doors, alarms, cameras and locks. A placement bridge connected to a door panel can be used to remotely control the object. The most common way to control the device is by a *bridge terminal*. A placement bridge pack comes with 10 bridges. They're about as big as a matchbox and contain four thin wires that are about a meter long, which are used to connect it to the device. When the panel is put back in place, the bridge is hidden and no one will be the wiser. However, the placement bridge can be hacked remotely, as it is a remote controlled device. The hacker must first have found the frequency (often using a signal scanner). Bridge packs can be reused if uninstalled and taken back. Basically, only simple on/off commands can be issued using placement bridges. If there's no interference, the transmitter/transceiver has a reach of two and a half kilometers. Repairs or Security (in combination with Attention) are used to install the bridge, depending on the circumstances.
Cost: 100

Bridge Terminal

This looks like a twenty-centimeter long iron rod from which you can pull a NIS (this is called a D-NIS configuration, D for Deployable). The terminal is exclusively used to monitor and control devices tapped into with placement bridges and *loop bridges*.
Cost: 400

Loop Bridges

These are exclusively used to remotely send up to four feeds of data from one point to another. The user must choose what information the loop bridge will send when installed. For example, data from a certain scanner, to surveillance cameras and the reactor status might be streamed. Of course, the bridge must be installed physically (like the placement bridge) into the device, terminal, or system which handles the information and can be hacked in the same way as a placement bridge. The loop bridge has the exact same design and size as the placement bridge.

The name, loop bridge, comes from the fact that the device can store and loop up to one terabyte worth of information and loop it indefinitely. The looping takes up a slot of information feed but is very useful. If you both want to loop *and* view a video feed, it would take up two out of the four feed taps. It has the same transmitting/receiving range as the placement bridge. Repairs, Computers or Security (in combination with Attention) are the Abilities used to install these, depending on the circumstances.
Cost: 200

Engineering

PSG (Polymer Sealant Gun)
The PSG is a hand held gun-like device which contains adaptable polymers. It can be used to temporarily seal smaller tears in equipment such as armor and weapons. It has enough polymers in it to restore 20 points worth of durability. The polymer comes out in the form of a paste, which hardens within five minutes or so. If using it to fix other materials, you can count on having to spend 5 points of polymer for every 10×10-centimeter gap you need to fix. The polymer only holds for a couple of days, and is only a temporary solution used to keep things from falling apart in emergencies. This tool can't be used to fix the durability of COGs.
Cost: 250
Refill Batch: 25

Fusion Cutter
A handheld cutter which can be used to cut steel or weld it shut. It has 15 minutes worth of fuel in it.
Cost: 200
Refill Batch: 20

Engineering Belt
A belt containing all the lightweight tools needed to perform engineering tasks and make most repairs (no scanners or fusion cutter, though).
Cost: 350

Diagnostic Screen
This D-NIS device can be used to tap into computers, engines and most any other system. Most systems have a diagnostics jack or remote access node (ten meter range, direct line of sight), which is designed to sync up with the diagnostic screen. The engineer must have the diagnostics code specific to the system (that particular engine, computer, pulley system, etc.). If not, it must be hacked. However, not all systems are locked in this way.

When tapped in, the user gains access to all relevant information (outputs, anomalies, data flow speed and such). By reading the information and rolling Repair (and a suitable Aptitude), the engineer can determine what's wrong with the system (or just make a routine start-up check before takeoff, if on a ship). All ships have such a system directly linked to the main computer, and this information can also be accessed on several terminals (always one or more of these in engineering) if one has the code. The diagnostic screen can come in handy

when the computer system is on the fritz or a power drain has taken out the local terminal. An engineer must identify a problem before he can fix it.
Cost: 680

Bolt Gun
This is basically a huge nail gun. It has a drum magazine containing eight monofilament-tipped high-tensile titanium alloy bolts, about thirty centimeters long. When the tip of this gun is pressed against a surface, the safety catch opens and allows for a bolt to be fired. The bolt rotates in high-speed as it's fired. This is used exclusively to attach hull squares, effectively patching up hull breaches.
Cost: 1,000

PCA
Most computers come in the form of a D-NIS configuration and are called Personal Computer Agents. The NIS slides out to about thirty centimeters long and ten centimeters wide, and the key/screen portion of it can be configured as the user sees fit. They are sleek and powerful and there are all sorts of extra NISs that can be bought: larger screens, keyboards, game spheres (a spherical NIS into which gamers put their hand, and control the game by hand and finger movement; some newer ships have actually begun to put this interface in use). The PCA has a transmitter which can be used to access the circuit if in proximity to circuit towers or satellites, and it can also be used to dial up other computers directly, and comes with a camera as well. Almost everyone has one, even if they're not into computers. The PCA acts as a home entertainment system, workstation and phone. Most have one with multiple upgrades that never leave their homes, and one less expensive one they keep on them for access and communication purposes when out and about. Hackers have it good, as all they need to hack something can fit inside their pocket. PCAs all have a standard ten terabyte micro drive (can be upgraded to five times that with ease). Memory chips are bought to copy and hold information. These are about the size of a business card, but one millimeter thick. The actual memory core is only the size of a pinky nail, but the extra size is added so that it's easier to keep track of them. The smallest hold fifty gigabytes, while the largest hold one terabyte. There are three types of PCAs and the quality of them influences the Computer roll.
Cost: 500 (poor, −1 modifier), 1000 (standard, no modifier) 2000 (excellent, +1 modifier).

Scanners (Handheld)
Unless stated otherwise, all handheld scanners come in the D-NIS configuration. When the text describing the scanner says that a roll for Scanners is needed, use the example rolls under the Ability Scanners to come up with the appropriate Aptitude. All scanners have a memory chip slot which can be used to save reads and transmit them to other mediums. Additional information on how much information is divulged when using scanners under different conditions can be found in the section *Actions That Need Detailing*. These D-NIS devices weighs 0.5 kilos.

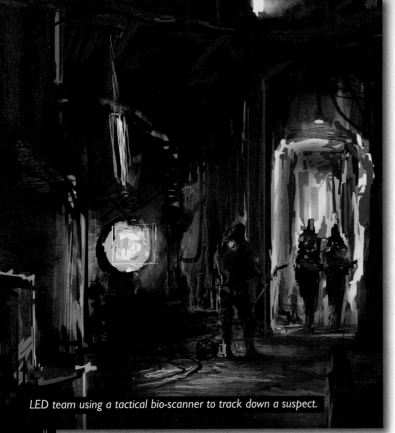

LED team using a tactical bio-scanner to track down a suspect.

Atmosphere Scanner

These scanners take a sample of the air within a ten meter radius and also measure the gravity and temperature. It can give the exact percentage of known atmospheric gases and substances. If confronted with chemicals, viruses or other substances which it is ill-equipped to identify, it will usually give a percentage but quantify the substance as unknown. Since most atmospheres where humans (or any other living being or organic material) exists have an amount of bacteria or other substances, such as air freshener (where humans live), cigarette smoke or the like, a small percentage is always expected to come up as unidentified. If there is higher than three percent of unidentifiable substances in the air, one should probably make a chemical and viral scan in order to be safe.
Cost: 500

Tactical Bio-Scanner

Bio-electrical energy given off by living organic creatures can be detected with this device. It gives off distance and approximate height/depth of the creature in a three dimensional space. It has a range of 200 meters (spherical scan) and gives information in two second bursts (almost like a radar). Getting exact numbers and size of the life forms, especially if they're standing close, requires a roll for Scanners of varying difficulty. Keep in mind that some artifacts might give off a reading (see artifacts).
Cost: 900

Chemical Scanner

As with the atmosphere scanner, this can take a sample of the air within a ten meter radius. It can't give a percentage of the air to substances/gases ratio, but it can separate all the different elements and identify them (if they're something which has been encountered by modern science and catalogued). However, it does give a ratio, which at least gives a scale to indicate the amount of the substances relative to each other. The scanner can be used to lock on a certain substance, using the substance density as a homing beacon. This is very practical when searching for the source of a substance emission. If the density is low, a Scanners roll (determine an appropriate base time) can be done to determine how long it takes (and if they manage) to find the source. Of course, substances can be sampled and put directly into the scanner as well. It can also be set to warn when the levels of a certain chemical (can hold six different chemicals in this warning "pattern") goes up or down in density. This is used to warn work crews when chemical levels rise to a dangerous density.
Cost: 780

Energy Scanner

It can be extremely handy to measure energy and the strength of energy fields. This scanner does just that. It scans a 100 meter radius and gives an indication of what kind of energies of an electrical/combustible nature are in the area. It measures their ratio in output and strength. This can be used to locate power drains, surges and magnetic fields. It can also be used to pinpoint exactly where on the other side of the bulkhead the aft trust cooling valve is located, by measuring the downward spiral in combustible energy. A trained engineer can scan an engine and directly determine the capacity at which it's running. As with the chemical scanner, this scanner can be set to scan a specific type of energy, using the energy itself as a beacon. Someone who can handle scanners can measure the energies, but without some background involving Repairs, they will have a very hard time determining exactly what the different energy spikes and slopes indicate.
Cost: 650

Forensic Filter

This is a stand-alone forensic filter which is worn as a pair of goggles. It works exactly as the COG version but isn't upgradable.
Cost: 1,300

GPR (Ground Penetrating Radar)

This gadget can detect hollows and shapes through surfaces up to three meters thick. The GPR must be held a maximum of two meters from the ground and the user looks at the screen while walking. Only one meter can be seen at any one time. When something pops up, the user must make a roll for Scanners in order to determine if it's just a natural density/hollow or something they're looking for, whatever that may be. To determine exact details, it's possible that other Abilities might be put to use (Explosives if looking for mines, Archaeology if on an excavation or Forensics if looking for a body, etc.). Without these rolls, the user can determine that something's definitely there, but they can't determine what. It's impossible to track moving objects (like a moving enemy behind a wall), as moving objects make the whole scan come up blurred and distorted. The user must walk slowly and pay close attention while using the GPR.
Cost: 460

Medical Bio-Scanner

This is exclusively used to scan living creatures and is the equivalent of an MRI, CAT scan and all other (x-ray, heart rate, etc.) non-invasive tests. It's possible to make a quick scan which only gives heart rate, temperature and respiratory frequency. This takes about ten seconds as the doctor slides the scanner from the patient's head down over his torso. To get all the information, the patient must lie down and the user has to slide, calibrate and re-slide the scanner over the patient. It's almost impossible to find anomalies without a medical background.

Cost: 1,000

Mineral Scanner

The user points the scanner at a rock face (or a pile of rock or any collection of stone or metal) and calibrates the amount through the screen (maximum one cubic meter). The scanner will reveal the percentage of metals, rock type and minerals (and compositions containing these) within the block. Everything shows up as geological diagrams, so those without a prospecting background have little use for the information. The scanner has a range of ten meters and can be used to take samples from two meters deep into a rock face. The scanner can also be set to search for a specific mineral/composition and picks up its resonance if it's within ten meters. It can be calibrated to concentrate on the highest possible density/ratio of the material (used the same way as a chemical scanner in this regard). Electrical storms, magnetic interference and certain types of radiation can interfere with this type of scanner. The prospector's Know-How comes into play if a mineral composition is so unusual that it needs to be interpreted. Materials not of a base mineral nature shows up as unknown.

Cost: 700

Movement Tracker

With one-second pulses, this tracker shows moving objects. When they stop, they're undetectable by the tracker. The distance, speed, approximate size and level in a three-dimensional space can be determined by the tracker. By interpreting the scans, a person can differentiate between a ripper, human or CAV victim with a Scanner roll (this requires some experience). A place where there is a lot of movement will confuse the scanner, as will creatures moving close together. So at times, the exact numbers, speed and distance can be hard to determine. The scanner has a range of one hundred meters. Keep in mind that the tracker doesn't distinguish between living or dead moving objects, so a factory floor with robotic arms will indeed set it off. It can (and often is) calibrated to track things over or under a certain size. It can track things as small as a mouse and as big a signal as can fit the screen.

Cost: 650

Radiation Scanner

This works exactly as the chemical scanner, but scans for radiation.

Cost: 400

Signal Scanner

This can be used to scan for radio signals. It has a range of five hundred meters (but can pick up any signals being transmitted through the area). There are hundreds, if not thousands of radio signals flying about a ship, and probably millions in a city. Information such as the device used, frequency and such can be of huge help. The device can track the source of a

transmission or receiver. It can be set to come online as soon as it picks up a certain signal.

Cost: 900

Viral Analyzer

This is similar to the chemical scanner in function (ten meter radius), but is focused on detecting viruses. It has data on all known viruses and bacteria programmed into its memory. When confronted with one it doesn't recognize, it will simply state that it has found an unknown biological agent. This device can be programmed to scan for sub-strains within a virus. If a sample is taken from an area or infected individual, it can be compared to other strains in order to determine if they come from the same main strain, and how many generations they're removed by mutation. In this way, the analyzer is effectively able to track pathogens to patient zero, or from patient zero to the infected. However, to scan an area or patient takes about five minutes. A sample of the area can be taken and processed for five minutes after one has left the area, but the processing requires the active participation of someone with a medical background (though a Scanners roll is used).

Cost: 950

Exploration

Emergency Beacon

This is about as big as a pack of smokes and is a standard personal emergency beacon. It sends a pulse signal every five seconds on the four standard emergency frequencies when activated. It has a range of ten kilometers and is good for a week. Emergency teams use it to home in on the position and come to the aid of the ones in need. The beacon has solar cells and three hours worth of sunlight equals twelve hours worth of pulse signals. So with access to solar power, it can send indefinitely. Beacons can be tracked using a signal scanner.

Cost: 150

Jetpack

The jetpack fits on the back or on an air tank and is used to move around in zero-g. It works by the same principles as the jet boots, but has 20 minutes worth of fuel. However, it takes about one minute to strap it on and all rolls involving Quickness when not in zero-g are done with a −2 penalty, due to the bulkiness.

Cost: 1,400 (a refill of the fuel cost 300).

Nav-Beacon

Working on the same basic principle as the emergency beacon when it comes to size, range and energy, the nav-beacon (called "nav" or "navs" when plural) is placed to secure and track nav-points when there's no GPS available, which is the case on all unexplored worlds and most mining planets outside the core systems. The navs are set to a predetermined frequency or frequencies (if the need to switch arises). They can also interlink with each other if in range (10 km), effectively building a network which can be tracked by ships in low orbit and personnel on the ground. This is ideal when scouting out an area and building a map.

Cost: 50

Glow Stick

Snap it and shake it to induce the chemical reaction, which produces a faint glow for up to 6 hours. They're abut twenty centimeters long and are a very reliable source of light in an emergency.
Cost: 4

Heavy Duty Flashlight

Sleek but water- and vacuum-proof. It has a battery life of 72 hours.
Cost: 45

Light Beacon

This is a fifty centimeter-long carbon fiber stick with a sharp, serrated and screw-threaded metal alloy bottom end. It has a light which can be set to blink red, blue, green or yellow. It blinks every five seconds and is good for about a month (and also has solar cells that work on the same principle as the beacons above). These are set down firmly in the ground and used as visual markers. They have slots for up to four beacons and come with a built-in VAC, which features a slowly-rotating IR/low-light camera. The light beacon contains a powerful antenna which can transmit information up to a distance of twenty kilometers. All other beacons jacked into it will have access to this range, as well, as they feed off the antenna. These are a very common sight, and the most usual way to deploy nav-beacons.
Cost: 120

Solar Power Unit

This unit comes in four cases (often bundled together), which contain a five by five meter solar cell blanket, power grid and six power outlets. It can funnel solar energy directly as well as store it. It can store a maximum of two-day low-output power (three hours of strong sunlight gives six hours of use). It can power a small heat grid (enough to heat up a tent holding four and which is big enough to stand straight in), some low-light lamps and about four smaller devices (such as handheld scanners). It can't be used to fuel devices while charging.
Cost: 1,700

Flare

Push the button and a bright red flare will come out of the thirty-centimeter pipe. It will fly about hundred meters up, deploy a parachute on the way down (if not removed) and burn for anywhere from thirty seconds up to a minute.
Cost: 15

Nutrients

A nutrient bar weighs one hundred grams. A bar always has a simulated taste (chocolate, vanilla, pizza, etc.) but the result is, in most cases, awful. A single bar contains every bit of nutrient a grown man needs to survive for 24 hours. He will be hungry, he will be dissatisfied and his blood sugar will complain, but he won't starve. If living exclusively on these for more than three days, the person will get a –1 to all rolls involving Cool, as he's worn down. Beyond this, a person can go through his entire life living off these things (as long as there's water about).
Cost: 8 (refilling a COG nutrient pack costs 60 credits)

Smart Polymer Starch Tent

These come in all shapes and sizes. Basically, they come in backpacks, and they look like a large bar of solid carbon with a digital button pad in the middle. When placed on the ground and the combination punched in, the material configures itself into a tent (of whatever size the user has bought). It takes about one minute for the tent to be assembled. The tent has little strength and can't harm anyone when folding itself up or down. If interrupted, the code must be punched in again, and if nothing is stopping the tent from folding up or down, it will do so. The pikes attached to the tethers still need human hands to hammer them down into the ground for stability, though. The tent is sturdy and can withstand fierce conditions. If undamaged, it can be set to completely seal and it has an entrance which can be configured to function as a one man airlock. This feature is only available if the tent is large enough to hold four people or more. The four-person and larger models are large enough for a grown man to stand up straight.
Cost: 300 for a two man tent; 30 credits are added for each increase in size (per extra person), to a maximum of a ten-person size tent.

Polymer Tether 50m

Very strong line that holds up to three metric tons, but can be cut like any other rope.
Cost: 6 per meter.

Grappling Gun

This is about as large as an SMG and holds a thin (can take five hundred kilos) polymer tether line with some elasticity (for those falling and grappling situations) and a strong motor. At the end is a hook. The gun can be set in different modes. It holds a distance meter and can be set to fire a certain distance. It can also be set to fire and attach differently. Harpoon setting works best on stone, wood and similar materials, where the hook penetrates and deploys barbs in the material in order to get a solid grip (when pushing the right button the barbs detach, loosening the hook). Then there's the magnetic function, which is used to attach itself to metallic surfaces, and the third function is pure grapple, which deploys four hooks that can latch on to things. The gun comes with a standard 50 meter polymer tether.
Cost: 750

NavComp

This works exactly as the NavComp in the COG (see above), but comes in a D-NIS configuration.
Cost: 250

Topographic Mapping System (TMS)

A TMS sends out a pulse which has a reach of 2000 meters. The pulse needs about thirty seconds to scan an area, during which time the user needs to remain still. It disregards moving objects but will give a pretty accurate topographical map of the area, with distances and everything. Rolling for Scanners can be necessary at times, if there are a lot of moving objects, sandstorm or other disturbance. As do most devices, it comes in a D-NIS format. The TMS also comes with a beacon tracker, which has a 20-kilometer range. This means that an explorer can map out an area and get the beacon nav-points to show up as an overlay on his 3D map. This map can then be transmitted to anyone who also has a beacon tracker and access to the beacon frequencies.
Cost: 750

Short Range Probe (SRP)

The SRP is a very effective tool. It's a spherical device, slightly larger than a tennis ball, weighing a little less than a kilo. It can be programmed to move in a certain direction, or to scan as much as possible of a certain area before returning to the beacon. The probe hovers and uses a gravity shift field, a technology provided to humans by the Gerions. The shift field basically works as a reverse grav-cube, an effect only possible to achieve with smaller objects. The SRP shifts gravitomagnetic fields to achieve propulsion. It's capable of moving ten meters above ground at a speed of twenty-five kilometers per hour.

The SRP contains several scanning units, though each unit is only capable of scanning five meters in every direction, thus enabling it to scan everything within a sphere of ten meters. The scanners contained within the SRP are the following: Bio-scanner, energy scanner, atmospheric scanner, radiation scanner, laser based close range topographical mapping system and signal scanner. The scanners are only rudimentary and can only give off four results: Negligible, Faint, Notable and Strong, though the topographical mapping system is thorough.

It has a battery life of fifteen minutes, but if it has ample sunlight it can recharge itself, which only takes five minutes. It will return to its beacon (a specific PCA, COG, ship or whatever it has been programmed to return to) after it has performed its preprogrammed scan. It's very useful, as it can be sent into a cavern system, derelict spacecraft or colony and feed the user a 3D map which includes all the distances and scanner results marked out.

Cost: 400

Optics

These come in the form of binoculars, goggles and scopes.

IR

This shows everything in the infrared spectrum, which means it's dependent on varying degrees of heat to be of much use.
Cost: 700

UV

The user can see through the ultraviolet spectrum. He will be able to pick up radiation, and substances that react to UV (as they emit a small amount of UV as well).
Cost: 390

Low-Light

As long as there's a small amount of light, the user will see in darkness and gloom without a problem. The image is greenish but very clear.
Cost: 700

X-Ray

These are only good for thirty meters, but can see through most materials, except for lead and coreanium. The distance can be set (so you don't have to see through five walls and thirty people at the same time) to make things easier, but it's very confusing and quite impossible to distinguish other features on people than their bone structure, length and whatever equipment they're wearing. It's very hard to tell one person from another. An active x-ray might show up on radiation detectors and scanners.
Cost: 1200

Magnification

This can be installed in a pair of goggles, scopes and binoculars. They usually range from ×2 magnification to ×10. All can be set to whatever magnification you have installed, from ×1 to the highest magnification allowed by the device.
Cost: 50/ per magnification

Sulphur/Ammonia Marker

Rippers have no body heat to speak of and don't show up on IR. The alien's dark-colored and spotted exo-skeleton makes it very adept at hiding in space stations, ships and similar environments, as they blend right in among the bulkheads, tangled cables and machines. This filter reacts to sulphur and ammonia and makes these glow a faint blue. This gives a +2 when trying to spot a ripper in hiding, but gives −2 to all other Attention-based rolls. Keep in mind that gunpowder contains sulphur, and anywhere from thirty seconds to a minute after gunfire (at least a couple of shots or a burst of auto fire), the surrounding area (five meters or so) will come up bluish, actually giving the Marine −2 to track the ripper during this time. It's prudent to use the filter wisely.
Cost: 900

Ultrasound

Basically a sonar, this sends out an ultrasound wave. It brings up a computer-modulated 3D rendering of the environment. It's all presented in grayscales, but the ultrasound visual mode can be quite handy. It can see through smoke and darkness and is completely independent of ambient heat or object heat. However, it can't make out texts or be used to read anything that isn't carved into a surface, or painted with a thick paint, as it only can see 3D objects. Reading something on a screen is thus impossible.
Cost: 900

Mining Tools

Most of these tools can be used as weapons, and some can be jury-rigged to function differently when in a pinch. All plasma tools are loaded with a plasma cell. These come in different shapes and sizes: about as large as a cigar box for the smaller applications, and as big as an attaché case for the two-handed tools. These contain propane mixed in with capacitance. Each plasma device is good for six hours of work with a fresh plasma cell. Plasma cells have an AR of 4, so they can take a few dings, but a gunshot will rupture it and there's a 3-in-8 chance that it will blow up if this happens. There is, of course, the odd low-tech tool such as a normal pickaxe or small handheld drill, as well.

Plasma Drill

A fifteen-kilo drill which uses plasma and can cut through just about anything, given enough time. It requires a two-hand grip to maneuver.
Cost: 800

Plasma Saw

This looks very much like a large chainsaw, but instead of a saw blade, there's a flat iron bar. This is actually the magnet which will keep the plasma in place. When in use, a thin sheet of plasma surrounds the magnet. It weighs about 15 kilos.
Cost: 700

Thermal Caps

These are the most commonly used explosives; they're about the size of a stick of dynamite and are colored brightly yellow with a red tip. The red tip must be unscrewed and the button beneath pushed for them to be activated. After this, a blast rod (about five centimeters long and five millimeters in diameter) must be inserted. The blast rod can be hooked up to timers or remotes. The rod gives of a small blast, which ignites the thermal cap. On its own, a thermal cap is quite safe. Only other explosions in combination with fire can set them off. So they can burn or be shot without going off. If burning hot *and* shot… well, keep your distance.

Cost: 25

Plastique

Tribelium TetroNitrox is the most common plastique around (often referred to as TTN). This substance needs blasting rods or another, smaller direct impact explosive to be detonated.

Cost: 25/125 grams

Blast Rods

These are bought separately and their function is described above. The rods cause 1D8 fatal damage and have a 1.5-meter blasting radius.

Cost: 15

Plasma Torch

Basically, this is a flamethrower and is used to melt sheets of ice when mining or to cut through thick metal, like heavy blast doors or outer hulls. It has a two-handed grip, weighs almost twenty kilos and consumes a lot more plasma than your average plasma tool, as it actually disposes of the energy in a much more radical way. The plasma torch is good for twenty-five bursts of blue heated plasma fire, or can be used to douse an area continuously for one minute. It has a reach of ten meters. The fire damage is counted as Extreme. When set to the cut/weld mode, it only has a one-meter reach but it can be used continuously for ten minutes.

Cost: 1200 (a full tank costs 120)

Sample Drill

This is a titanium alloy diamond-head drill which must be placed on a trident, and it can drill five meters down into solid rock or a mineral bed. The drill is hollow and it takes rod-shaped sediment samples, each thirty centimeters long. The drill weighs two hundred kilos and is run by remote by an operator after it has been placed.

Cost: 5,000

Sample Cases

These are hermetically-sealed sturdy cases which can be carried like a suitcase or a backpack. They have room for ten sample rods, which fit in small automated grippers within the case. The temperature in the case can be set to everything from 200 degrees °C to −150 degrees °C if the sample requires it. It has one hundred hours of energy for temperature regulation. It can be directly plugged into an energy source, in which case it will hold the temperature and recharge. It takes fifteen minutes to fully recharge. It's also possible to just switch the power cell.

Cost: 300

Cryo Spray

At times it's necessary to cool down materials, and this device is used for those occasions. It's as big as the plasma torch but douses the intended object with liquid nitrogen. It has a range of ten meters and has the same capacity as the plasma torch. The main difference is that the cryo spray cools things down and uses a tank of liquid nitrogen instead of a plasma cell. The freezing damage is counted as Extreme.

Cost: 1,400, (a full tank costs 150)

Isotope Marker

This can be used to mark minerals, rocks and metals with different harmless irradiated isotopes. The device looks like a small gun and the user simply puts it against the surface and marks it. The marking device can separate the different isotopes, and the user can attach different names and numbers to the different markers, as well as scan markers from ten meters away using the same device. There are also larger markers which can mark mounds of material. These require a two-hand grip. The markers are used to catalogue materials so that they go to the right destination/cargo hold.

Cost: 340 (large version 1,000)

Medical Gear, Drugs, Research

First Aid Kit

This kit holds everything that you need in order to treat most non-fatal wounds. A successful First Aid roll will stop bleeding and stabilize a wound. If lacking a first aid kit, using ad-hoc equipment, the medic gets −2 on his roll. A first aid kit is good for about five treatments and comes in a 20 × 15 × 7 centimeter box.

Cost: 50

Portable Research Station

"Portable" is stretching it, but it does fit in five large suitcases. There are three types of stations: Medical, Archaeological and Scientific. The kits can be plugged into a power source, run on solar power or use the internal power cells (which last for 72 hours and take five hours to fully recharge). The kit contains the basic tools needed to conduct research within the branch, and static scanners as well. The kit is good for about five thorough research endeavors (a month's worth of research each). After this, the kit must be "filled up". A real lab is far superior and there is only so much these stations can do, but they're pretty versatile and should be able to provide a researcher with tangible data, which will tell him if a certain project is worth pursuing in a real lab or not.

Cost: 10,000 (filling it up costs 1,000)

Regen

This is a revolutionary drug with the ability to accelerate tissue regeneration. The drug is a combination of nano-tech, biotech and pharmacology. The vial is ten centimeters long and has a diameter of 1.5 centimeters, and fits in most auto-injectors (the standard drug vial size). Regen is a viscous red and clear liquid. When injected directly into a wound with precision, it begins to regenerate the damage. The drug affects the body chemistry, adds the necessary proteins and releases a batch of nanintes which reassembles the damaged area. Thirty seconds after injection, the wound has stabilized and the recipient has regained 4 hit points. If not performed by a medical technician, or if the user has less than a rank of 2 in First Aid, the injection will be imprecise and only 2 hit points are restored.

Regen takes its toll on the body, causing the metabolism to go into high gear. Thus, it can only be used effectively twice per twenty-four hours, and four times per week. Using it more than this will actually harm the person, causing the loss of 2 hit points (which are healed normally) and also imposing a −1 to Brawn for a month.

Cost: 350/vial, and requires medical license and medical facility authorization (medbay on a registered ship will do).

Stims

This is a combat drug used by a large number of military personnel. Stims are injected and consist of a clear green liquid. It stimulates the adrenaline gland and the production of endorphins, and amps up the activity in the amygdala. The individual becomes on edge and prone to more aggressive and territorial behavior. Due to this, stims are illegal, but many Marine squad leaders look the other way. The user gets a +1 to all Brawn-related rolls, gains 7 temporary hit points and can count all pain modifiers as if one wound level lower. The effects last for two hours.

After the main effect has ebbed, the user will of course lose his temporary hit points. If they were lost due to damage, this damage will not affect the user after the fact; temporary hit points go first and are basically used up as if they were a kind of durability. The user also suffers a −1 to Brawn and Cool for four hours after the stims has worn off. If an individual takes stims while stims are already in his system, the person gains an additional +3 temporary hit points gets a total of +2 to his Brawn. However, he must pass a −2 Cool roll or become highly aggressive, running into combat without any regard for his own safety, ignoring orders. If a third dose is given while under the influence, the person will attack everything living in sight until he is knocked out or killed and he will remain in this state for two hours.

Stims are also quite addictive. If taking stims more than three times within a month (time in stasis does not count), the person must pass a Cool roll with a −1 difficulty. Every additional hit beyond this imposes an additional −1 to the roll. The user has to stay off the stims for one month before this penalty disappears. If he fails the roll, he has become addicted. He will need at least one stim a day, or else he suffers a −1 to Brains and Brawn and also becomes highly aggressive, antisocial and jumpy. He also suffers a −1 to Cool rolls when trying to withstand the Dark. A stim addict needs help and won't quit otherwise. Cold turkey is the best way to go. The user will suffer bouts of violent behavior and possibly be prone to self-harm as well. This lasts for about a week. During this time, the user is often kept on sedatives and/or in restraints. After the week, they still crave the drug but are calm. After a month, they are fully detoxed. They will still crave it, but can in most cases keep off it. A former stim-user will always have to make a Cool roll whenever injecting a stim. If he fails, he will fall back into his old habits. Stim addicts who are injecting on a daily basis seldom live more than two years, often

suffering brain aneurisms and similar afflictions as their brain is completely fried. Most die sooner, as they get mixed up in violent confrontations and crimes. Athletes also use stims to get better results, and this is of course illegal as well. Stims are used within health care at times, to aid the immune system in fighting off severe infections and for certain types of physical therapy. Stims are often used to get the heart going again if a patient suffers from cardiac arrest.

Cost: 300/vial, and requires medical license and medical facility authorization. Stims require the medical facility to be a GIC-registered one, or a GIC medical authorization.

NRC (Neural Relaxation Compound)

NRC dampens the effects of trauma and shock as well as soothing the temper. The user will get a +1 to all Cool rolls that involve withstanding the Cold and the Dark, and both of these are counted as two levels less while on the drug (see The Cold and The Dark section). The effect lasts for four hours, and during this time the person also suffers a −1 to Brains and Reaction. Two doses will render the individual unconscious for 1D × 10 minutes. This drug counters the effect of stims, but it requires double the dose. So in order to get rid of one dose of stims, two doses of NRC must be injected, and in order to sedate a stimpack user completely (if he has taken only one dose), it requires three doses of NRC. The effect of this drug kicks in fully after about 5 seconds.

More than four doses per week will create an addiction after a failed Cool roll. The addicted will need two doses per day, and without them, he will get a −2 to Cool and count his Cold and Dark as one level higher (this will lead to a constant level of at least one in the Cold and the Dark, leaving the individual filled with anxiety).

Cost: 5/vial and requires prescription by doctor. NRC can also be bought as pills and is a very common drug among the middle class, whose habit is fed by their doctors.

Neuro-Worms

These are injected into the brainstem upon severe injury and can heal brain damage. Not all patients can be helped or saved using this technique, but most are completely restored. Memories, however, cannot be restored if the damaged part is the memory section. Keep in mind, they can only fix *brain damage*, not miraculously restore the brain of someone who got his brain blown out by a clean gunshot to the head. They are injected into the brain stem, after which the individual must heal. In game terms, these can fix "permanent" damage caused by critical hits to the head that the avatar has survived.

Cost: 500/vial, and requires medical license and medical facility authorization (medbay on a registered ship will do).

Medi-Tank

This marvel of medical science weighs about three hundred kilos when it's empty and about seven hundred when filled. It can restore lost limbs, mend critical injuries and regenerate lost organs. But it's expensive. The fluid inside must be replenished, and when bought, it contains ten units. Units can be programmed to perform certain tasks but are used up in the process. One can't just strip a dying person and throw them into the tank; a trained doctor/medtech must program and calibrate the machine (using Know-How). This takes about ten minutes and a failed roll wastes half (round up) of the units that were to be invested, and the doctor has to start over. When the doctor has successfully calibrated the patient's genetic profile to the machine, and programmed in the extent of his injuries, he can only wait until the person is healed up. Anyone submerged in a tank will be kept somewhat stable for at least half an hour. If the doctor hasn't managed to program in the damage and DNA profile by then, the person will start to bleed again and must be moved to surgery for traditional treatment. **Cost:** The machine itself costs 150,000 credits, while each unit costs 5000 credits.

Medi-Tank	
Trauma	**Units**
Healing normal damage (per 4 HP restored per 24 hours).	1
Fixing a critical hit that is causing permanent damage to a leg.	3
Fixing a critical hit that is causing permanent damage to an arm.	2
Fixing a critical hit that is causing permanent damage to the torso.	4
Fixing a critical hit that is causing permanent damage to the stomach.	4
Regenerate an arm.	7
Regenerate a hand.	5
Regenerate a foot.	5
Leg	7
Regenerate a large amount of skin.	3
Regenerate eyes/fingers/ears/tongue/teeth	3
Regenerate a major organ (not the brain)	10

Medical Pod [Med-Pod]

These are a common sight in medical bays, as they are effective and come at a reasonable price. The med-pod is basically a surgical table combined with a surgical robot and high-powered medical scanner. It can be used to stabilize a patient, diagnose him or to perform advanced surgery. It even has a limited capacity to restore tissue through artificial stem cells and can restore 10–20% of lost tissue in a body part. This means that it can be utilized in order to reattach limbs and even parts of organs, if the severed part is saved and if the tissue damage isn't too severe. Also, the severed limb/tissue can't be in a state of decomposition. The pod is fully capable of replicating human skin and is extremely useful when it comes to treating burns and superficial damage.

In game terms, it requires a successful Attention + Know-How roll (medical technicians and doctors only). If successful, the pod restores five hit points to a critical hit and reattaches a severed limb, if possible. The base time is four hours and the reduction time is thirty minutes. If using old-fashioned methods (plain scalpel, pliers and retractors and no med-pod), the base time to perform surgery is six hours and the reduction time is fifteen minutes.

The pod also grants a +1 bonus to any medical scan roll and a +1 to a medical technician's Know-How roll when performing

surgery. It comes with enough expendable materials (scalpels, sutures, anesthetics, etc.) to perform twenty surgical procedures. Three people can cooperate when performing advanced surgeries, using a NIS interface.

Through voice commands and the internal NIS interface it's possible for an individual to perform surgery on himself (not recommended unless there is no other choice). This, of course, requires that the individual is conscious. Local anesthetic is somewhat effective but can't completely stave off the pain caused by procedures such as amputations, skin grafts and internal organ repair. The AI should make Cool rolls for any individual who performs major surgery on himself in order to determine if the patient gains Cold as a result of the trauma of being awake while cutting into his own flesh. The +1 bonus for performing surgery is not applied when used in such a manner. The machine weights half a ton.
Cost: 10,000 (refill 300/procedure max 20)

Communications/ Surveillance/Forensics

Micro Reconstruction Camera [MRC]

This is a handheld camera which contains high definition digital optics as well as ultrasound-emitting nanites. In combination, these can be used to "film" an area and create a 3D version of it, either on a 2D NIS or a full-blown 3D NIS. Of course, it also picks up sound. This can be used to film an area of one hundred cubic meters. When wanting to cover a larger area, the cameraman usually moves in sectors, pasting the areas together later into a bigger whole. Everything the camera films can be viewed in 3D, so a cameraman usually takes five minutes per sector in order to be sure that he managed to snap up everything. The NRC is too energy-consuming and bulky to be installed inside a COG, but it's an invaluable tool, used in the entertainment industry as well as within surveillance and forensics. Most crime scenes are filmed using this technology, which allows the investigators to review the crime scene as many times as they wish. As it's nanites that perform the scan, the data is actually so detailed that the investigator can order the program to flip through a book, or he can ask it to search through cabinets.

All the chemical analysis, DNA samples, fingerprints and other material collected by the on-site investigators is added to the reconstruction, which lets the investigator command the program to bring up all this information during his virtual investigation. Of course, if something was missed (not properly filmed or analyzed) in the actual crime scene, it won't show up, which still makes some good old-fashioned gumshoe tactics invaluable. And keep in mind, the MRC only creates a 3D scan and makes no analysis whatsoever. The nanites are incapable of giving any medical data on people. They will flow inside cabinets, drawers and in between the pages of a book, but will never venture inside any material. There are a lot of safes, walls of high-end housings and secure areas that use a Nano Barrier. These consist of nanites that counteract those of the MRC. Filming a safe protected by a Nano Barrier won't give the scoop on the interior.
Cost: 4000

Handcuffs
A pair of strong titanium alloy handcuffs.

Cost: 50

Decloakers
These are devices used to counteract the NETTS. They come in three forms: static, expendable and dynamic. All decloakers have a rating that goes from one to four. If the rating is equal to or less than the circuitry rating of the NETTS stealth module, a contested roll is made. If the decloaker wins, the scout becomes fully visible. If the rating, however, is higher than the module's the scout has no chance and becomes visible. The number of dice used by the decloaker is equal to the rating × 2. So a rating 3 decloaker would use 6 dice when discovering a scout.

The existence of these devices is classified and they're extremely hard to come by for the common criminal. The price listed is the price you pay for them, if using the proper channels. On the black market, the price goes up significantly and most fences wouldn't touch this kind of equipment with a ten-foot pole, as it's way too dangerous.

Static: These look like small radar arrays and are two meters high. They have a range of 200–500 meters and have a rating that goes from 2–4. Whenever a scout comes within range, the contested roll is made. If the scout wins, a new roll is made after three combat segments, so the scout had better hurry out of the area. If the decloaker is successful, the scout is visible until he leaves the range of the device or disables it.

Cost: Standard rating 2 costs 5000, and each extra rating adds another 2500. Every extra 50-meter radius costs 500.

Dynamic: These look like a shotgun microphone and have a rating of 2–3. They are handheld and have a scope of 90 degrees and a range of 50 meters. They work the same way as the static versions, but the operator must track the scout manually, even after he has managed to decloak him. If he loses him for more than two combat segments (Attention + Scanners vs. the scout's Quickness + Stealth), new contested rolls must be made, if the operator gets the scout in the line of sight of the device again.
Cost: 1500 for a standard rating 2. A rating of three costs 2000.

Expandable: Basically, these are grenades which send out a decloaking field spanning 10 meters from the point of "detonation" (a fast static field of bluish electricity). They have a rating that goes from 1–3. If the decloaker is successful, the scout is visible for three combat segments.
Cost: 150 (rating 1), 200 (rating 2), 300 (rating 3).

Services/Wares
Below are some examples of everyday services. These are based on prices in the core systems.

Docking Fees:
Planetary/space station docking fee per 24 hours.

C-Class: 100
B-Class: 30
A-Class: 20

Communications Unit/Comm-Link
This is an advanced headset walkie-talkie. It has about fifty frequencies and a range of 10 kilometers. The signal can be routed through communications antennae and satellites, like all other types of communication, in order to be effective in long-range situations.
Cost: 75

Cell Phone
A simple cell phone which relies on local cells for sending and receiving calls. Larger colonies, stations and all major cities (and larger, well-organized ships) have local cells which will let the user call others within the grid and send voice messages or texts trough the LSA, if the installation has one.
Cost: 10

Services
These are core system prices. Outside the core systems, or on the fringes of them, prices vary depending on supply and demand.
Glass of beer: 4.2
Long Drink: 8
Dinner in restaurant (low rate/mediocre/luxurious): 6–7/13/90
Six pack of beer: 5
City cab: 5
Flight Ticket, Within Atmosphere: 100
Flight Ticket, Nearby (24h or less) Outside Atmosphere Destination (moon, station, etc.): 200
Flight Ticket, Interplanetary RTD Jump While In Metro Coma: 1000 (+100 per day if awake)
Sports tickets: 90
Night club entrance: 10
Escort per hour: 200–1,000
Lap dance: 10–20
Monthly tram card: 40
Newspaper: 2
Monthly gym membership: 67
Pack of smokes: 4
Massage: 56
Haircut: 30
Set of average clothes: 120
Set of upscale clothes: 600
Set of extravagant clothes: 1500
Crappy hotel per night: 40
Average hotel per night: 80
Good hotel per night: 140
Luxury hotel per night (triple the price for a suite): 350
One room apartment (poor/nice) per month: 250/400
Two room apartment (poor/nice) month: 400/800
Three room apartment (poor/nice) month: 600/1000
Four room apartment (poor/nice) month: 900/1200
Five room apartment (poor/nice) month: 1000/1800
Fully fuel A-class ship: 500
Fully fuel B-class ship: 800
Fully fuel smaller ground vehicle: 80
Fully fuel larger (tank, rig) ground vehicle: 120

Chapter 12: Space Crafts

CRAFT ID: E-Class Core Purifier
CRAFT NAME: Dante
DATE: 11th March, 500 IT
LOGGED BY: Willow Sarapedro, Site Engineer 1st Grade.

Hi sis, I finally made it! I'm aboard an E-class core purifier, the largest class of starships in the entire universe! In class we only got to see specs of these and fixed them through simulators. C-class is the largest I've ever seen before this. I can hardly explain the awesomeness of it! I know you don't have the same interest in ships as I do and that you have no idea what the classes entail, but before I go into the details of the Dante, I'm going to break it down for you. You have to excuse me if I get a bit technical, but I want you to have an idea of how these things are dummied up. Oh, keep in mind that the range of the A- and B class ships only shows the propulsion range. In space, if going in a straight line for any length of time, most pilots simply employs a quick propulsion thrust and then glide in the vacuum, basically running on low output mode.

A-Class: These ships only have room for one to eight people and they can operate inside an atmo as well as outside. They're seldom longer than five meters. Of course, you have seen a couple of them. The crop duster papa uses on the farm is an A-class (although a dinged-up one that's incapable of space flight). A-class crafts that are designed for atmospheric flight only have a range of 1000 kilometers, and those equipped for space flight have a twelve hour air supply and a range of 10000 kilometers. A-class never has any cargo space, just small storage areas. A- and B-class use capacitance as fuel, and all ships (of any class) which are designed for space travel have a blast shield which they can deploy in order to protect the main window.

B-Class: These are much larger and can be up to thirty meters long. They usually have a two-man crew, a pilot and a co-pilot. As with the A-class, they can operate inside and outside atmo. B-class ships always have grav-cubes. They have a range of 25000 kilometers and a three day air supply.

C-Class: Well, sis, these can be considered the lightest class of the real starships. They have a coreanium reactor and a ghost drive (as is true with the following classes as well). They're seldom less than forty meters long; usually they range from sixty to one hundred and fifty meters in length.

C-class ships usually have two to four decks, counting engineering, and up to eight decks if it's a large passenger ship. These can work in an atmosphere as well as in space. The range depends on the reactor life, but they can usually run for years on end if maintained properly. These can have a crew ranging from three to as many as a hundred, depending on the size and nature of the ship. Most cargo and ore hauling ships of this nature usually end up with five to twelve crew members. They also come with a small engineering bay, usually located in the belly of the craft, with small service tunnels (basically crawlspaces) leading to the thrusters. When fully stocked, these ships have enough air, food and water to sustain a crew of fifteen for up to four months, and of course they have stasis tanks like all ghost line-capable ships. If you go through the ghost lines and stay awake without stasis for too long, you'll go crazy. All C-, D- and E-class ships also come with a RT-Drive.

D-Class: These beasts are at least two hundred and fifty meters in length and have a minimum of three decks, but usually have four or five (up to fifteen, if it's a passenger cruise ship). However, these ships can be as long as five hundred meters and have ten decks even if not a passenger ship. This size is common with large military crafts and mining ships with ore hauling capabilities. The size is a must as these ones have a SAC (hope you remember my explanation of the SAC in my earlier mails). The SAC takes up an entire deck on its own.

Whenever the length of these ships exceeds three hundred meters, they have an ITS (Internal Tram System). There are two types of ITS. Most D-class ships make use of the light system, which is composed of an open cab that can take six to twelve people. Usually, they're placed on the middle deck, and they usually have two tracks. The second type is mostly used on E-class, and is basically an enclosed tram system using small train cars with room for up to forty people. The ITS runs on an electromagnetic monorail, but the speeds generally never exceed forty kilometers an hour for safety reasons (but it can go much faster, about eight times as fast if you take off the service panel, disconnect the VIN switches and tap into the acceleration circuitry).

The number of crew members on a D-class differs depending on size, but the minimum needed to safely operate one for a short while includes one pilot, a co-pilot, navigator, two engineers and two SAC certified science officers. Cargo ships usually never have more than twelve crew members, while passenger ships (including cooks, medical staff, sanitation and a full operations crew) go from one hundred people on the smallest ones up to two thousand for the largest ones (as these require a lot more personnel to manage). But ships always have a purpose, and a mining ship might have as many as an additional four thousand miners onboard heading for their site, slumbering away the months. The largest D-class ships have room for ten thousand people in all.

Most D-class ships comes with a bar or two, a sports center, stores and similar things that the crew can enjoy while out in space for months. Some even have small greenhouse parks set up in observation decks. On passenger cruise ships, entertainment facilities can be found in abundance, very much like on those trans-ocean cruises we went on when we were little, down on the planet. And of course, D-class and beyond can't operate within an atmo and are usually built in orbit or near a spaceship engineering station.

E-Class: Wow, I can hardly talk about these goliaths of the void without becoming excited! They range from eight hundred meters to as long as two kilometers! The minimum crew to safely operate one is one hundred (but they can, like all other ships, be flown by a single individual provided the conditions are ideal). The number of crew members differs widely depending on size and purpose, but the largest of these ships can have up to thirty decks and sustain up to twenty thousand people without a hitch. As you have never seen one with your own eyes, I understand that the size is hard to fathom.

Oh, shoot! I just got a call. We have a leak in one of the coolant valves down in the aft exhaust processing unit. Have to go to work. I'll send this now and hopefully I'll be able to send you another one before we jump on the 13th, and I'll tell you more about the Dante. If not, you'll hear from me when I rotate back into the Divius system.

Have a good time, sis, and don't let papa work you to the bone. If you mind your studies and hone your medical interests, you might become a medical technician one day. Who knows, we might work together.

With love, your big sister, finally out on the great adventure.

CRAFT ID: E-Class Core Purifier
CRAFT NAME: Dante
DATE: 12th March, 500 IT
LOGGED BY: Environmental Safety Officer, 5th grade

Hello. You requested my personal overview report of the Dante's safety layout before we shipped out, but you can only have a preliminary report as we have a lot to do at the moment. I'll get right to it. Like all ships from the C-class and up, the Dante only has one main window and that's up on the bridge. Having more than one window on larger ships (and space stations) is suicidal. About two centuries ago, a lot of large ships and stations had windows all over, mostly for show, which turned out to be a deadly mistake. When a window is broken, the whole ship, if not closed off properly, could be subjected to explosive decompression. These days, the main window on the bridge has three security measures. Firstly, they have one outer blast shield which is activated when there's a high risk of collision, one between the two armored windows, and one inner containment shield. All blast shields are made from five centimeter titanium alloys. All three will automatically close if one of the windows is damaged, and they must be manually opened. This is not possible if both windows have been punctured; if this is the case, you would have to go in and reroute circuitry and hack the protocol. It takes from one to five seconds for the blast shields to close, which will lead to a period of decompression.

Other windows can at times be found in different observation decks. These have one outer blast shield and these decks always have an airlock that must be secured before the blast shield is opened. This airlock will automatically seal if the window is broken and if the blast shield isn't in place. However, working on a ship isn't as depressing as it seems, window-wise. Multiple wide-angle cameras on the outer hull feed into window-paned monitors. Interspersed throughout the ship's interior in areas adjacent to the outer hull, these monitors grant the illusion of windows. This is an excellent solution that doesn't put the crew at risk.

Firing weapons inside a C- to E-class ship seldom puts the hull integrity at risk (however, the windows might be susceptible to damage). The hull is just too hard and thick to be affected by small-arms fire. But there are a lot of other dangers involved, such as damage to vital gauges, electronics and other sensitive components. Of course, ricochets are always a danger. Firing titanium slugs inside what is basically a metal box made out of even harder metal can turn a couple of bullets into a meat grinder. This is why security personnel on ships, colonies and space stations have access to "collapsibles", bullets which break apart into a fine powder upon impacting materials of certain densities, mitigating the risk of high-velocity ricochet.

Ships and Vehicles

Vehicles have 8 Hull Integrity Levels (HIL). There are three repair times listed. Ships of classes A, B and C are measured on the same time scale when it comes to repairs, while classes D and E have their own repair times. Due to their size, it takes much longer to fix them up. Alas, the reduction time remains unchanged. The AI must decide what happens if a repair is cut short. Depending on the time invested, a level or two might have been restored, or perhaps the modifier changes in favor of the avatar due to the groundwork invested. The listed modifier applies to Piloting rolls when flying the damaged ship.

> **Note:** Class D and E ships are so large that they are divided into sections, D ships into two sections and E into three. Each section has its own HIL. If you blow the aft of a D ship, it separates from the front, which then acts as a solitary unit and vice versa. The same goes for E ships; the difference is that the middle unit can sustain crew as well in an E ship. The sections can't fly or maneuver on their own, though.

Where on the ship does the hit land?

If you need to randomly determine which section is struck, you can use the table below. This will give you a rough hit location. Roll 1D.

Hit Table

Result on 1D	Section
1	Nose
2	Front Starboard
3	Aft Starboard
4	Front Port
5	Aft Port
6	Belly
7	Upper Deck
8	Main Engine

It burns, oh my God, it burns!

When a hit is so hard that it shaves off three or more HILs, or if the ship is down to Battered or below when it's struck, crew members may be hit. **Cold & Dark** only uses a loose indication system to determine how many crew members that are affected, as the number of crew on a ship differs.

Usually only those in the damaged section of the ship will get hurt, but short-outs, flying debris and leakage can affect other sections of the ship. An overload in a power spool in engineering can result in a control panel blowout on the bridge.

Roll 1D in order to determine the amount of affected crew members (apply modifiers as you see fit). Use this system to get a general overview of how badly the crew suffers.

As a note, avatars should never die as a result of this table, but they can be seriously injured. Killing off avatars using a random table isn't a good way to handle suspense.

Reactors and Coreanium Cost

The cost of reactors and the use of dispersers depend on two things: reactor size and power life. C-, D- and E-class ship reactors vary in size, and there are basically three power life options when purchasing a reactor: 3 years, 5 years and 10 years. When purchasing a new ship, the standard reactor life is usually 3 years for C-class, 5 for D and 10 for E. The table below shows the cost of a new reactor core, as well as the cost of restoring a used core. Cardion assimilation takes about one minute per each restored percentage.

> **How long is a percent?:** This table gives a rough estimate of how many days of normal propulsion (including all systems) corresponds to one percent of the reactor life. The lifetime of reactors isn't precise. Their lifespans may be much shorter than this estimate, which is calculated using average speeds without factoring in the more extreme speeds, maneuvers, damage or jury-rigged quick–fixes. Such things have a tendency to eat up the coreanium at an alarming rate. On the other hand, using the RT-Drive barely uses 0.2%, as the ship mostly glides. You don't have to make an accounting exercise of it, simply use the table as a guide (p.162).

Ghost Drives

Ghost Drives require a reactor for power. A brand new one costs 100,000 and only C-, D- and E-class ships are capable of having one. Each jump, depending on the distance, burns off a certain percentage of reactor life. The table below shows percentage of reactor life burned per distance zone jumped, according to the size of the ship. Most people try to get their hands on a reactor with at least five years worth of juice if they intend to jump a lot. Commercial ships which only travel in normal space usually have a three year reactor and an RT-Drive.

Casualties

Result on 1D	Crew casualties per section
1	No one
2	A couple fall down but are unscathed.
3	As above, but those affected sustain 1D bashing damage.
4	More than half fall or are banged up, sustaining 1D bashing damage.
5	½ of the crew in the section sustain 1D fatal damage, while the other ½ sustain bashing damage.
6	½ of the crew sustain 1D+3 fatal damage.
7	½ of the crew is grievously injured (incapacitated and bleeding out), ¼ is dead and the last ¼ sustains 1D+5 bashing damage.
8	Only ¼ survives, but they suffer 1D8 fatal damage.

Hull Integrity Levels

HIL	Modifier	Repair Time Per Class	Effects
Scraped Reduction Time: 5 min	—	A, B, C: 30 min D: 1 h E: 2 h	—
Dinged Reduction Time: 5 min	—	A, B, C: 1 h D: 2 h E: 3 h	—
Banged Up Reduction Time: 30 min	—	A, B, C: 18 h D: 1 day E: 2 days	—
Battered Reduction Time: 2 hours	-1	A, B, C: 18 h D: 1 day E: 2 days	A bit unsteady, there might be a gust of smoke or two.
Torn Reduction Time: 6 hours	-2	A, B, C: 2 days D: 3 days E: 5 days	Now it really starts to affect the steering, and the gusts of smoke are more intense, followed by strange and unsettling sounds. If you're really unlucky, there might be some serious short-outs and small fires. This can temporarily affect some of the systems, taking out scanners, some weapons and similar things.
Breached Reduction Time: 24 hours	-3	A, B, C: 5 days D: 1 week E: 10 days	Thick smoke, blown out electrical systems and bigger fires. Whole systems might be put out of commission until fixed and the hull might be breached, which in turn will lead to the need to seal off parts of the ship, if flying in space. At this level, the ship might only run for a couple of days.
Smashed Reduction: 48 hours	-4	A, B, C 10 days D: 2 weeks E: 3 weeks	Nearly all systems are down, and if you're still alive, you must put out several fires and secure the air recycling system within an hour or you're toast. You really need to dock and fix your ship!
Demolished	-6		You're royally screwed! You're dead, or will be if you don't find a place to crash land. Abandoning ship is a good idea. In other words, your ship is now scrap metal.

3 Year Reactors		Percent per Ghost Jump		
Light Years	Time	Percent: C-Class	Percent: D-Class	Percent: E-Class
1–500	24 hours	1	1,5	2
501–2,000	2 weeks	1,5	2	2.5
2,001–6,000	1 month	2	2,5	3
6,001–24,000	2 months	2,5	3	3,5
24,001–72,000	4 months	3	3,5	4

5 Year Reactors		Percent per Ghost Jump		
Light Years	Time	Percent: C-Class	Percent: D-Class	Percent: E-Class
1–500	24 hours	0,5	1	1,5
501–2,000	2 weeks	1	1,5	2
2,001–6,000	1 month	1,5	2	2,5
6,001–24,000	2 months	2	2,5	3
24,001–72,000	4 months	2,5	3	3,5

10 Year Reactors		Percent per Ghost Jump		
Light Years	Time	Percent: C-Class	Percent: D-Class	Percent: E-Class
1–500	24 hours	0,1	0,5	1
501–2,000	2 weeks	0,5	1	1,5
2,001–6,000	1 month	1	1,5	2
6,001–24,000	2 months	1,5	2	2,5
24,001–72,000	4 months	2	2,5	3

How long is a percent?

Reactor Life	1% Equals
3 Years	11 Days
5 Years	18 Days
10 Years	36 Days

Other sources of reactor life drain: All manner of things can cause a reactor to lose power. Sabotage or damage on the Breached level or beyond which affects the reactor can cause the voltage to increase, causing excess production of cardion gas which the emergency system will vent out. A reactor can hemorrhage as much as a maximum of four percent every hour. Damaged ghost drives which still work might also require a lot more power to initiate a jump. A badly damaged but jury-rigged ghost drive might require as much as 10–15 % of the reactor life in order to make a jump.

Class of Weapons

There are four classes of weapons. Some vehicles are immune to certain types of weapons. You can't really harm a battle carrier with a SMG.

A: Melee weapons and unarmed attacks.

B: Light anti-personnel firearms (everything up to a carbine).

C: Heavy anti-personnel weapons (rocket launcher, grenades).

D: Anti-vehicle weapons (rail cannons, plasma cannon). The damage of a D-class weapon counts as double when it hits a living person, and heavy weaponry (firearms such as rail cannons) can hit up to five to ten persons standing close together with one volley. All body armor is halved against D-class weapons.

E: Heavy plasma cannons, heavy photon cannons, missiles and accelerated photon cannons (these basically pulverize/vaporize soft targets).

Damage Handling Levels (DHL)

Vehicles can have one of three Damage Handling Levels: Immune, Vulnerable and At Risk. Each DHL holds a weapon class or classes and shows how the vehicle holds up against weapons of those classes. For example, a tank is immune to class A and B weapons and this will be listed under "DHL Immune" on a tank.

Immune: Only under special circumstances can the vehicle be damaged by this kind of weapon when intact.

Vulnerable: The vehicle's armor is counted as double against these weapons, but damage that penetrates results in a −1 HIL (and only −1, no matter how much damage penetrates armor).

At Risk: These weapons can really cause a lot of damage. All the damage that penetrates armor reduces the HIL by one.

If a vehicle has an asterisk (*) after a weapon class, it means that the Damage Handling Level can be bumped up one level against that weapon class if the shooter gets a lucky hit (such as hitting the windshield or something important and unprotected). So if a vehicle is Immune against class B weapons but the B has a *, a hit from a B-class weapon could be considered a hit from a weapon class to which the vehicle is Vulnerable, if the attack hit a vital spot (tire, windshield, exhaust vent, etc.).

Turning Speed

During combat situation or another stressful situation, the turning speed of the ship can come into question. The turning speed is in place to give an idea of how much more maneuverable small ships are in contrast to the larger ones. The table below gives an approximation of ship class turning speed,

Reactor and Disperser Refill Cost

Reactor Class	Life: 3 years	Life: 5 years	Life: 10 years	5% (3 year)	5% (5 year)	5% (10 year)
C	200,000	300,000	500,000	6,000	9,000	15,000
D	300,000	600,000	900,000	12,000	18,000	27,000
E	1,000,000	1,500,000	2,000,000	30,000	45,000	60,000

measured in segments. An A-class fighter can just cut thrust and spin around on its own axle in a heartbeat, while this would be devastating for a much larger ship. As a general note, you shouldn't use turning speed when it's uncalled for, but it will be vital when several smaller ships engage larger ships, since maneuverability is the only advantage the smaller ships possess. A successful Cool + Piloting roll with a −2 penalty adds an extra 45 degrees to the turn in a tight spot.

Turning Speed

Ship Class	Segments	Degrees
A	1	360
B	1	180
C	1	90
D	2	45
E	4	45

Blacking Out: Whenever you deem that a pilot is pulling off a crazy move which has the potential to subject him to a high amount of g-force, you should call for a blackout roll. Avoiding several attackers using multiple actions, turning the fighter 180 degrees while flying at full speed, or pulling up on a really tight vector to avoid a collision are maneuvers that can cause a blackout. You roll 1D; if it's severe, you can add a modifier (ranging from +1 to +3). The number by which the result surpasses the pilot's Brawn is the number of segments he's affected by heavy G-force. The first segment, he's totally blacked out. During the remaining segments, he is extremely groggy and suffers a −3 modifier to all rolls.

Example: Jenny Zhuda has pulled off a crazy spin to avoid a volley of plasma and it's time to see if she blacks out. Jenny has Brawn 2 and the AI rolls 1D. The result is a nasty 5. This means that Jenny will black out for one complete segment and be groggy for an additional two, during which she suffers a −3 modifier.

Missiles

Type	Ground Zero	Devastating	Destructive	Blasting	Range	Cost
Fragmentary Missile	1–5m (10+1D)	6–20m (8+1D)	21–30m (6+1D)	31–40m (4+1D)	50 km	5,000
Heavy Frag Missile	1–5m (13+1D)	6–25m (10+1D)	26–35m (8+1D)	36–50m (6+1D)	150 km	9,000
*Plasma Hybrid Missile	1–10m (10+1D)	11–40m (8+1D)	41–50m (6+1D)	51–60m (4+1D)	50 km	12,000
*Heavy Plasma Hybrid	1–15m (15+1D)	16–40m (12+1D)	41–50m (10+1D)	51–60m (8+1D)	150 km	15,000

*All plasma hybrid missiles count the armor rating as two lower on a direct impact and also count as E-class weapons.

Cannons

Type	Base DMG	DMG Per Success	Range	Clip	Weapon Class	Cost
*Light Rail Cannon	5	2	150 km	250	D	25,000
Rail Cannon	6	2	170 km	150	D	50,000
Heavy Rail Cannon	7	2	250 km	100	D	75,000
**Plasma Cannon	8	2	80 km	50	D	100,000
Heavy Plasma Cannon	9	3	100 km	25	E	150,000
***Photon Cannon	7	3	n/a	25	E	175,000
Heavy Photon Cannon	8	4	n/a	25	E	200,000
****Accelerated Photon Cannon	15/10/8/6	5	n/a	—	E	Unknown

* All rail cannons fire volleys consisting of between 10 and 25 rounds and are basically automatic weapons. The clip only shows how many volleys that can be fired, instead of showing the exact number of rounds fired. All other weapons fire a single "round". This system is used to make it easier to keep track of vehicle combat.

**A ship's armor rating counts as two lower against plasma shots. Plasma has a rather short range, even in space, since the plasma dissolves after a while.

*** Photon cannons run on capacitance. It is possible to run them off the reactor, but they have a tendency to eat up a lot of energy.

****The accelerated photon cannon (also known as the GiGi, or Genocide Gun) is an extremely powerful experimental weapon which feeds directly off the ship's reactor. It can only be installed in D- and E-class ships and is about one hundred meters long. It requires massive amount of power to fire and it will basically hog the ship's power. After firing, all scanners, targeting systems, handling, speed and acceleration stats are counted as giving a −4 modifier, and the ship will run on low power mode. This will last for one minute after firing. The cannon must cool down for (10 minus 1D) minutes before it can be fired again. The Blast radius for the cannon is as follows: Ground Zero: 0–1km, Devastating: 1.1–1.5km, Destructive: 1.6–2km, Blasting: 1.7–2.5km.

The damage listed in the chart shows the damage inflicted at the different blast radii. All photon canons have an unlimited range and only stop when they hit something.

Note on Range: Most weapons fired in space can, in theory, travel in a straight line until they hit something or until they're caught in the gravity of a larger object (except plasma).

Ship Weapons

These are cannons and weapons systems that weigh anywhere from hundreds of kilos up to several tons or more. Plasma weapons are often used in ships, as many ships have room for them and they have proven to be highly effective. Photon canons are also used in ships. These are huge and require a lot of power, but are extremely reliable and powerful. When it comes to clips (we chose to use that term in the ship weapon charts as well) for these weapons, they cost a tenth of the original weapon's cost. Generally, it's illegal for civilian and commercial ships to have any kind of weapons. Commercial D and E ships are allowed to have rail cannons as asteroid and debris defense.

Missiles

Missiles have fuel of their own and are located in clusters. The cost of missiles shows what each missile costs. Missiles are considered to be D-class weapons.

Ammunition Capacity of Ships

Generally, a ship has room for one spare "clip" per weapon, located near the weapon in question (with the exception for A-class ships). This clip is on an automated robotic feeding system called an autoloader, which automatically reloads the weapon system when empty. This takes about fifteen seconds. If the system jams (not breaks) due to damage, someone has to kick it into place. This usually requires a Brawn roll and it takes one to two minutes (reduction time 20 seconds). Jammed missile autoloaders and autoloaders for the larger weapons require the cooperation of up to four people or at least one PCR. It also requires four people or a PCR (or kinetic unit) to restock an autoloader. The Ability needed is Athletics or Repairs (whichever is highest). Cannons take 90 seconds to restock, while a missile cluster takes 90 seconds per 10 missiles to restock (avatars must have access to a PCR or a kinetic unit for missile restock). The reduction time is 10 seconds for both.

Installing Weapons: It is quite possible to illegally install weapons in a ship. These are usually hidden under extra layers of hull or disguised inside antenna arrays. A ship weapon which is installed normally (fired from the scanners or helm) is purchased for a normal price (or whatever the fence deems reasonable). It is possible to buy a rail gun or heavy rail gun which is manually operated, actually requiring a crew member to take the gunner seat located inside the ship, adjacent to the gun mount on the outer hull. These guns are fired using Attention + Scanners or Attention + Shooting. The price of these manual guns is reduced by 25%. The ship's targeting isn't added to the rolls of manual guns.

Spacecraft Scanners

Generally, ship scanners have a range of 50,000 kilometers. The greater the range, the harder it becomes to get an accurate read. All ships also have a deep scan mode on the signal scanner and LIDAR. These can pick up signals and shapes from across the galaxy, in theory, but it takes a lot of time for signals to travel, and with all the interference, these distant signals are very old.

Ship-to-ship contact and engagement usually occurs within the 50,000 kilometer range, which has been divided into eight ranges, from the shortest, *Dogfight*, to the longest, *Extreme Range*. An exact distance between the ranges isn't given, as it's easier to work with abstractions. When using normal propulsion, it takes a ship about six minutes to travel from one range to the next. So if a ship wanted to get four ranges closer (from let's say *Very Far* to *Close*), it would take twenty-four minutes (six times four). An Attention + Pilot roll can be made to achieve the perfect propulsion thrust. Each success shaves off one minute from the trip (minimum travel time is half the base time). The Speed trait of a ship is added to this roll.

The range modifier applies to scans as well as any ship weapon attack made at that range from the intended target. Beyond *Short* range, an actual visual can't be obtained and any attacks made are basically targeted at coordinates obtained by the scanners. The *Impact Time* is measured in segments and shows how long it takes for a projectile to reach its target from the given range. If it takes one segment, the hit will occur at the end of the segment following the actual firing of the weapon. Photon cannons hit directly at any range and the impact time doesn't apply.

In order to fire at a target beyond short range, the target must be targeted and locked upon by the ship's scanners. This is done with an Attention + Scanners roll, and the operator must decide which scanner he wants to use (LIDAR, Energy Scanner, Signal Scanner, etc.). A roll takes one segment for each scanner, so larger warships usually have one array specialist assigned to each scanner in order to make simultaneous scan sweeps. Firing upon a target is then done with Attention + Piloting or Attention + Scanners.

Distance Modifier		
Range	Modifier	Impact Time
Dogfight	-	0
Short	-	0
Close	–1	1
Medium	–2	2
Long	–3	3
Far	–4	4
Very Far	–5	5
Extreme Range	–6	6

LIDAR

The LIDAR (Light Detection And Ranging) is one of the most vital scanners used in crafts capable of flight. It sends out pulses, very much like a radar, but uses lasers instead of radio waves. The LIDAR gives off the range, size and shape of all objects within range in three-dimensional space.

Energy Scanner

The energy scanner located on ships isn't capable of determining the same details as a hand-held one, but they do distinguish types and ratio of energies. Information obtained with an energy scan combined with an adequate LIDAR scan can be fed into the ship's SAERS (Shape And Energy Recognition System) in order to get information on what type of ship (class,

Survey ships dispatched from their main C-Class ship and en route to an unexplored planet.

model, etc.) is targeted by the scan. A skilled pilot, navigator or engineer (or someone with similar ship knowledge) can make a Know-How roll using the readings if the SAERS is broken, in order to determine ship type. The energy scanner can also be used to determine if the ship's life support is active or not and at what capacity it runs.

Bio Scanner

These work a bit differently, and a ship must be within 500 meters of another ship in order to get a reading. The bio scanner can indicate if there is life on a ship, but it's extremely difficult to obtain exact information. If life-forms are few and scattered, it's possible that the scanner won't read anything at all.

Signal Scanner

A ship's signal scanner works exactly like the hand-held one, except the range is different.

Environmental Scanner

This has been developed especially for ships and is a combination of the radiation and atmosphere scanner. It only has a range of ten kilometers, and is often used to penetrate the atmosphere of a planet when in deep orbit in order to get a reading. It's also capable of measuring the approximate gravity of a planet.

Locking Action

This action is necessary when firing upon a target which is beyond *short range* and takes a segment to perform. In order to lock on to a ship, an Attention + Scanners roll must be made. The scanners used depend on the situation. In order to break the lock (with a lock break action), the pilot/scanner operator of the targeted ship must accumulate an equal number of successes. As mentioned, making a lock takes a segment, and if there's a gunner on standby, an attack can be launched in the same segment in which the lock was established.

In order to avoid being a target, it's prudent to execute a lock break action (Brains + Scanners). The lock break action

can be made in the same moment (in the same segment) in which someone has locked onto the ship, and the operator is allowed to make rolls every segment until the lock is broken. Each rolled success removes a success from the locking action. A scanner operator who is trying to break a lock can only concentrate on performing that one task. He is allowed to try to break multiple locks at the same time, using the same rules which apply to all other multiple actions. The same type of scanner that was used to make the lock is used to break it. As long as a ship has locked onto a target, their gunners are free to fire upon it.

Under most conditions (barring heavy disturbances), the ship's VIN will notify the crew when someone is trying to get a lock on them or when a lock has been established. The signal scanner is used for lock detection. The lock detection system uses an automated subsystem of signal pulses, and these can only be jammed for a short while, as opposed to jamming transmissions (see Actions That Need to Be Detailed). It is prudent to try to jam this system before trying to lock on to a foe who is unaware of an impending attack. This roll uses Brains + Scanners (signal scanner). The number of successes indicates the number of segments the lock detection system is jammed, and thus the length of time the in which ship in question won't notice a lock. However, the scanner operator in the ship being jammed will notice the jam, and he is free to roll using his Brains + Scanners (signal scanner). Each success will reduce the number of segments in which the jam is active. The scanner operator who tries to break the jam is free to roll for as many segments as he wishes. When the jam is gone, he will detect the lock, but the attacking ship is now free to try to jam him again, preventing him from breaking the lock. In many cases, it's a battle of wits. Most large warships have several array specialists running jams/counter-jams, a second group handling lock-on actions and a third managing the lock breaks. Keep in mind that signal scanners often get jammed by natural means, such as by space radiation and solar flares. So if not on patrol or expecting trouble, a jammed signal scanner doesn't make a pilot or array specialist automatically expect an attack.

Fooling Scanners & Running Silent

There are many ways to fool scanners; the simplest method is to turn off detectable sources inside the ship. Turning off the signal scanner and all internal radio communication will make it impossible for another signal scanner to detect the ship. Fooling a LIDAR can be done by two basic moves. The pilot can simply "hide" the ship behind an object or inside a cluster of debris, or if this option isn't viable, a scanner operator can actively try to jam the LIDAR using the LIDAR of his own ship. When the crew suspects that there might be another ship in the area and wants confirmation, they scan using the LIDAR actively for five segments. This means that a contested roll must be made: Brains + Scanners vs. Attention + Scanners. The one running the countermeasure uses Brains + Scanners, while the one making the scan uses Attention + Scanners. If the countermeasure succeeds, the hidden ship remain undetected by the LIDAR.

Fooling the energy scanner can only be done by running silently. In this mode, only life support and the belinium back-up systems are up and running. The engines stop, doors must be opened manually, low-energy lights kick in and only the most rudimentary systems (scanners, for instance) are online. Even the weapon systems are taken offline. The ship will maintain any speed it had before it shut down, but it can't slow down or turn. Switching to silent mode can be done in the blink of an eye, as all ships have this mode, requiring only entering a code in the Command Bridge or engineering bay. However, it takes the ship three segments to fully start up again. Running silent and running LIDAR countermeasures is a good way of keeping under the radar, so to speak, but it leaves the ship very vulnerable.

Evasive Maneuvers

There are many different maneuvers a pilot can try in order to become a harder target, everything from spins to loops and reverse thruster moves. In order to keep it simple, these are all considered "evasive maneuvers". A pilot who pulls off an evasive maneuver becomes a harder target to hit. An evasive maneuver can be performed at any time in a segment, as long as the avatar hasn't acted (or if he makes use of multiple actions). An evasive maneuver circumvents the highest initiative, like all defensive maneuvers. The roll is made using Reaction + Piloting (or Drive, if operating a ground vehicle), and the ship's handling trait is added to the roll. Each success imposes a −1 modifier to the attacker's next attack roll. The result of the evasive maneuver roll basically acts as defense during the segment. The negative modifier applies to incoming attacks to which the avatar is aware and can respond. It can also be used to cancel out rolled successes of an incoming attack that the pilot is aware of and tracking, such as a volley of rail gun fire or missile which takes some time to arrive due to the range. As a general rule, no one can avoid more attacks than his Attention score. Evasive maneuvers also make you harder to hit in a dogfight (see dogfight rules).

Example: Wei is hunted by three raiders in small fighters. He wants to avoid their fire and try to make a run for it. As he has an Attention score of three, he can keep up with them. He makes a Reaction + Piloting roll and scores three successes. This means that all three attackers will suffer a −3 penalty to their attacks during this segment. If a fourth attacker appeared, he would be free to fire upon Wei without any penalty, since Wei would have been too busy avoiding all the other attackers to notice him.

Example, Ship Combat: Hannibal, a C-class Osiris model GIC-registered ship operating with a skeleton crew, is on patrol. They have run into some trouble, so their LSA and ghost drive are offline. Things have been calm for days, but there have been reports of marls in the area. Suddenly, array specialist Angelina Daalk notices that their signal scanner is jammed. As the ship is on patrol, she notifies the captain, Janice DeSari, and the crew is put on high alert. She doesn't know if it's a natural jam or if an enemy is locking on, but she wants to find out. The player of Daalk makes an Attention + Scanners roll and the end result is two successes (she had a −1 due to the range). The jam was an artificial one made by a C-class marl freighter retrofitted for combat. The array specialist on the marl ship had only accumulated one success and Daalk managed to see through it. The whole process only took one segment.

In segment number two, Daalk runs a scan, using Attention + Scanners with −1 due to the range (which the player isn't aware of yet). She uses the signal scanner in order to locate the enemy. At the same time, the enemy tries to make a lock action. Daalk gets one success and finds the ship. It's at close range (all scanner and attack actions suffer a −1 as mentioned). However, the enemy manages to get a lock on them (and yielded three successes). Daalk has already made her action this segment and can't try to break the lock. Fearing an impending attack, she screams, "They got a lock on us!" The captain orders the pilot, Jacques Coretti, to perform evasive maneuvers. Coretti makes his Attention + Pilot roll and yields two successes. The marl gunner fires off a volley with his rail cannon with a −2 modifier due to Coretti's maneuver. The marl still manages to score two successes, but due to the distance, the volley will arrive at the end of the next segment, which means that

A group of raiders securing the site of a business exchange.

Corettis (who is aware of the incoming volley) can try to avoid the enemy fire one last time in the coming segment.

In segment three, Daalk makes an *Attention + Scanner* roll to lock onto the other ship. She trusts the skills of the pilot to keep them safe and she wants to blow the marls out of the black. She gets two successes. A lock! She yells out to the captain, "Captain, we got a lock on them! The captain barks out the order, "Fire forward heavy fragmentation missiles at will! Mr. Coretti, maintain your evasive pattern!" The player of Captain DeSari wants to make a direct strategy roll in order to aid the crew. The AI says that the situation calls for a *Cool + Strategy* roll. The player rolls and scores three successes. She assigns 2 points to Coretti and 1 to their gunner, Riley Shore. This will increase the chance of Coretti avoiding the incoming attack as well as make it easier for Shore to hit his target, as each direct strategy point adds +1 to the roll. Mr. Shore fires a missile using *Attention + Scanners*, while Coretti makes another evasive maneuver. Coretti scores an impressive four successes (more than the attacker's roll), while Shore gets two successes. Coretti makes a sharp turn, avoiding the incoming rail gun fire with ease. The missile Shore fired will hit at the end of next segment, due to the range.

In segment number four, Daalk wants to get rid of the lock. As this is a defensive maneuver, she acts first, regardless of Reaction score, if it had been relevant. She rolls for *Brains + Scanners* in order to perform a lock break action and scores three successes. This equals the marl lock and she breaks it. If the enemy wants to fire on them, they must make another successful lock action. "They lost the lock, captain!" Captain DeSari orders Shore to fire off a volley with the rail gun, and he asks the others to stand by. If the missile doesn't do as much damage as she wants, the volley will soften them up even more. The marl pilot hasn't made an evasive maneuver, so the missile Shore fired last segment hits now. Since Shore only got two successes, the missile detonates when it hit some debris at destructive radius from the marl ship. At destructive radius, a heavy fragmentation missile deals 8 + 1D damage. The hit causes a whopping

twelve points of damage! But the marl ship has an armor rating of six, scaling it down to six in damage. The marl ship's Hull Integrity Level has been reduced to Breached, which means that they're in very bad shape. The volley will hit at the end of segment number five.

Segment five has arrived and the AI decides that most of the marls on the ship are dead, and that the volley will destroy it utterly. The AI describes how the volley Shore fired hits the marl ship and blows it to hell. The players look very satisfied and are quite impressed with themselves, and they roleplay the mood of the crew. However, the happiness is short-lived. The AI tells them that four other ships of the same configuration have popped up. The player of captain DeSari gets into character.

"Turn 90 degrees starboard, then full ahead for ten seconds, then we go to silent mode! And miss Daalk, run LIDAR countermeasures." Coretti confirms, "90 degrees starboard, then full ahead for ten seconds before entering silent mode. Aye, aye, captain!" Daalk confirms as well. "Aye, captain. Running LIDAR countermeasures." The Hannibal turns 90 degrees, then they blast full ahead. Captain DeSari continues, "Silent mode in 7, 6, 5…" The AI informs the players that their signal scanner is being jammed. Daalk informs the crew. "They're jamming us, probably multiple locks on their way!" DeSari is unwavering in her command. "Steady, 3, 2, 1…go dark!" Everything stops and the low lights kick in. The Hannibal is now outgunned and outmanned, creeping along on silent mode in enemy territory. They have no way to call for help and can't make a quick getaway. It will take a daring plan to get them out of this situation.

Dogfights

Dogfights work a bit differently than long range space combat, and are generally conducted using an actual visual of the enemy, relying more on pure instincts and reaction.

These are intense and up close and personal. In order for ships to partake in dogfights, they must of course be within the *Dogfight* range. Only A-, B- and C-class ships can participate, as the larger classes are way too heavy and clumsy to accelerate and decelerate with enough efficiency. D- and E-class ships can still fire, if an aggressor flies by a weapon turret or missile cluster, but they can't perform evasive maneuvers, shaking/dogging, get into firing position or perform a break. However, a D- or E-class ship which is built for combat has several turrets and missile clusters spaced over the hull, and is capable of firing upon multiple smaller attackers each segment (disregarding the need for firing position, the weapon emplacements can fire and be fired upon). B- and C-class ships suffer a −1 on all rolls having to do with maneuvering when squaring off against A-class ships, as these have superior maneuverability.

Firing Position: If two ships are squaring off, they have to get into firing position before they can engage each other. This is simply done with a contested roll: Attention + Piloting vs Attention + Piloting. The winner will be able to engage the enemy. However, getting the upper hand on multiple hostiles is near impossible, as it requires multiple actions. The ship's Acceleration rating is added to the roll.

Targeting: This system works as long as the pilot/gunner has a direct line of sight to the target. All ships have a *Targeting* trait which is added to any attack roll, but it's possible to fine-tune it while maintaining a visual. This is done with a Reaction

+ Piloting roll. There are two ways this can be used: in order to get a better aim with rail gun and cannon attacks, or when firing missiles. If successful on the roll, all attacks made against the targeted enemy gain a +2 modifier. The same roll is made when targeting with missiles, but a successful roll only means that the missile can be fired, as it's near impossible (−5 modifier) to hit a target with a missile without an established lock. It takes one segment to target an enemy, and if the enemy gets out of the line of sight, the targeting system resets. Targeting works at the *Short* range as well as the *Dogfight* range, and the system is used by gunners on larger ships as well.

Evasive Maneuvers: These work as described above, but they don't get you out of the line of sight of a pursuer, they only make you harder to hit.

Shaking/Dogging: In a dogfight, the hunted aims to become the hunter. When you have a hostile on your ass, you want to shake him off and reverse the situation. While you're the one dogging an opponent, you want to stay on him. It's basically a simple contested roll: Reaction + Piloting vs Reaction + Piloting. The pursuer can either fire upon his target or try to stay on him, or try both with multiple actions. If the pursuer decides to just fire on his target, and the target is successful in his shaking action, the pursuer gets a −3 on his attack, but the target is then out of the line of sight (if not blown all to hell). If the pursuer manages to stay on the target, a new segment begins as normal. However, some ships have rear cannons and these can be fired at pursuers at will. The ship's Acceleration is added to the roll.

Break: Instead of trying to get into a firing position, or after successfully shaking off an enemy, a pilot can declare that he makes a break. This is done with a contested Attention + Piloting vs. Attention + Piloting roll. If a pilot has made a successful break, the position of the combatants is reset to default. The pilot is now free to flee or try to get into firing position. Making a break instead of competing for a firing position is often done in order to avoid a confrontation or to get out of harm's way. As the pilot just hauls ass to get out of a bad situation, his one roll can be pitted against up to as many pursuers as he has in Attention score. The ship's Handling is added to the roll.

Fleeing: If you want to put some distance between you and your enemy, effectively getting out of the *Dogfight* range, you must flee. You can only flee if you have made a successful break. Fleeing is an extended and contested roll. The first one who accumulates five successes is the winner. If the escapee wins, he's now out of the *Dogfight* range, free to continue his escape. If the pursuer wins, the escapee must make another successful break. The fleeing action is resolved with Attention + Piloting vs. Attention + Piloting. The ship's Acceleration is added to the roll.

Example: When on patrol in his Raven fighter, Wei sees three enemy bogies coming at him like bats out of hell. He feels that escape would be the best option here. The three enemies are trying to get into firing positions so they can engage him, and the AI rolls their Attention + Piloting score. The player of Wei tries to make a break, pitting his Attention + Piloting score against theirs in a contested test. The hostile fighters score 2, 2 and 1 success respectively. Wei manages to score 3 successes. If he was trying to get into firing position, he could only choose one against which to apply his score, leaving the other two free to fire on him. But since he just tries to get the hell out

of dodge, his score can be applied to a number of opponents equal to his Attention score (4). This means that he makes a successful one-eighty, avoiding their attempts to engage him. Next segment, he will try to flee. He saw a debris field a way back. He might just lure them in there, run silent for a while and pick them off one by one…

Ship Definitions

Type: Vehicle name and class.

Length, Width, Height: Length, Width and Height describe a ship's longest, widest and highest points. This is measured in meters.

Description: Covers uses, layout and a short history. Here, areas such as medbay and similar facilities will be described as well.

Speed: Gives a rating which is added to speed rolls. This value is added when speed is a factor in the long run. Speed is a very abstract stat. Some ships can fly well over mach 3 in an atmosphere, but writing the exact numbers down isn't necessary. The only thing that you need to keep in mind is that those with a higher speed rating move faster than those with a lower one and ground vehicles can never outrun space- and aircrafts. However, a ground vehicle can still outmaneuver a flying vessel at times, if the terrain is to its advantage (tunnels, covers, caverns, etc.).

Acceleration: When the actual shift in speed and short term speed come into play, this modifier is added.

Ghost Drive: This shows the advancement of the Ghost Drive, and the modifier which comes into play when performing ghost jumps, hiding or leaving the dragon tail or trying a *FMS*.

Handling: A rating added to ship handling rolls.

Scanners: A rating which is added to scanner rolls. Each type of scanner has a value of its own: Bio Scanner, Energy Scanner, Environmental Scanner, LIDAR, LSA, Signal Scanner.

Targeting: The modifier added when using the main guns and missiles.

Pods: This states the number of emergency pods available. There are several different kinds of pods. They can hold 1, 3, 6, 8 or 10 people, depending on size. Emergency pods can sustain the allotted people for three days. The pods have 10 minutes worth of thrusters, which are mainly used to rotate in a direction, thrust a short burst and glide toward the rescue (if lucky). The pods are cylindrical or round in shape. They have a signal scanner and a communications array, low-energy lights and waste outlet. They also contain five emergency beacons, one main and one auxiliary parachute, and crash foam which fills the pods if the parachute fails and works as an enclosing airbag. The thrusters can't be used to fly inside an atmosphere. There are some heating blankets and flashlights available as well (one per person) and four days' worth of fluids and nutrients per person.

The pods' specifications will indicate the number and type of pods available. So if it says 20 (3), 10 (8), it would mean that the ship has 20 three man pods and 10 eight man pods. Beyond the pods listed, every stasis tank can act as a one man pod. However, they only contain one hour worth of air, a parachute and a beacon, nothing else. The tubes are automatically ejected if there are crew members in stasis, and if a catastrophic event occurs which the crew won't be able to survive or prevent upon awakening. The stasis is interrupted the moment the tube is ejected.

AR: Armor Rating.
DHL: Damage Handling Levels.
Weapons: The ship's armament.
Spec: Special equipment or circumstances which are important.
Cost: Yeah, it will be steep.

Damocles Model,
C-class, Light Freighter
Length, Width, Height: 80m, 9m, 15m

Description: The *Damocles* model has been around for a hundred years and is a favorite among raiders and smugglers due to its low cost. It's rather fast, but is a bit clumsy when it comes to handling. Its size is about average for a C-class. The ship has four main decks. The second deck holds a small mess hall, kitchen and forward observation deck and some smaller storage rooms. The third deck consists of forward engineering and the reactor room. The actual cargo bay is a very large open space, which takes up about a third of the ship and is located in the aft.

Speed: +1
Acceleration: +1
Ghost Drive: —
Handling: –1
Scanners
Bio Scanner: –1
Energy Scanner: —
Environmental Scanner: —
LIDAR: —
LSA: —
Signal Scanner: +1
Targeting: —
Pods: 4 (6)
AR: 5
DHL
Immune: A, B, C*
Vulnerable: —
At Risk: D,E
Weapons: —
Spec: This model has several crawlspaces and removable panels with some room behind them in the freighter bay. These are quite good for smuggling.
Cost: 700,000

Gargon Model,
C-Class, Heavy Freighter
Length, Width, Height: 80m (+50), 20m, 15m

Description: This is one of the more popular ships used for hauling cargo within the core systems. The *Gargon* model is an extremely versatile vessel. The actual ship is 80 meters, but it comes with a 50 meter-long detachable barge, which is used to haul massive amounts of ore, ships or whatever material is being transported. The barge usually has no air, heat or gravity when transporting things such as metal and mining ore, but it can be configured in a number of ways. The bottom deck is an actual freighter/docking bay, and the ship has its own grav-cuff

emitters and room for eight A-class ships, or four B-class ships, if the hangar is empty and used for this purpose alone. When connected to the barge, all piloting rolls involving speed, handling and acceleration suffer a penalty. The barge is actually locked on to the front of the ship using the forklift-like front. The *Gargon* model can be flown within an atmosphere like all other C-class ships, but not with the barge. The numbers within the parentheses show the modified maneuverability when the barge is attached.

Speed: –1 (–2)
Acceleration: — (–2)
Ghost Drive: +1
Handling: +1 (–1)
Scanners
Bio Scanner: —
Energy Scanner: —
Environmental Scanner: —
LIDAR: +1
LSA: —
Signal Scanner: —
Targeting:
Pods: 1 (2), 2 (8)
AR: 6
DHL
Immune: A, B, C*
Vulnerable:
At Risk: D, E
Weapons:
Spec:
Cost: 900,000

Osiris Model,
C-Class, Light Hunter
Length, Width, Height: 60m, 15m, 10m

Description: Feared by many, this hunter and destroyer model has proven itself for the last seventy years. Fast, featuring a rather well-calibrated scanning and targeting system, it gets the job done. This is one of the most common models used by the Consolidated Fleet when patrolling areas within as well as outside the core systems. This ship has four decks, one of which is a flight deck which can hold six A-class ships or two B-class ships.

Speed: +1
Acceleration: +1
Ghost Drive: —
Handling: —
Scanners
Bio Scanner: —
Energy Scanner: +1
Environmental Scanner: —
LIDAR: +1
LSA: —
Signal Scanner: —
Targeting: +1
Pods: Pods: 10 (8)
AR: 7
DHL
Immune: A, B, C*

Damocles Deckplan

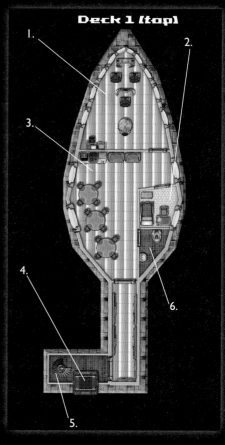

Deck 1 (top)

1.
2.
3.
4.
5.
6.

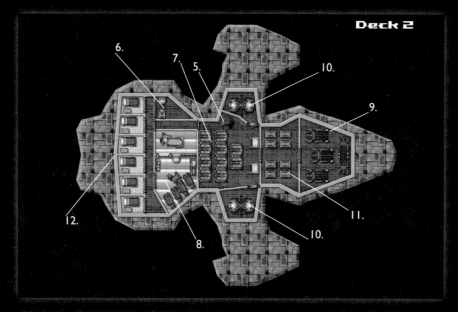

Deck 2

6.
7.
5.
10.
9.
12.
8.
11.
10.

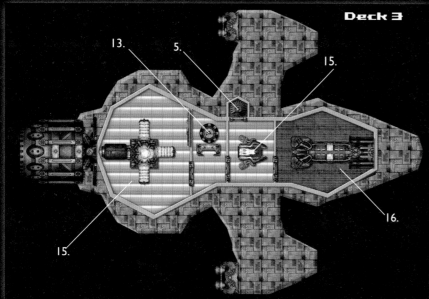

Deck 3

13.
5.
15.
15.
16.

1. Command Bridge
2. Captain's Cabin
3. Mess Hall
4. Airlock
5. Stairs
6. Bathroom
7. Stasis Chamber & Showers
8. Medbay With Med-Pod
9. Life Support
10. Escape Pods
11. Nutrient Storage
12. Crew Quarters
13. VIN Core
14. Reactor
15. Ghost Drive
16. Engineering Bay & Belinium Backup
17. Catwalk & Terminal
18. Cargo Bay
19. Ship-to-Ship Docking Access
20. Belly Cargo Shaft

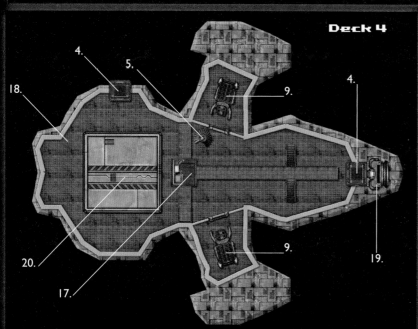

Deck 4

4.
5.
9.
4.
18.
20.
17.
9.
19.

Gargon Deckplan

1. Command Bridge
2. Captain's Cabin
3. Mess Hall
4. Airlock
5. Crew Lockers
6. Stairs
7. Bathroom
8. Stasis Chamber & Showers
9. Medbay With Med-Pod
10. Life Support
11. Escape Pods
12. Nutrient Storage
13. Crew Quarters
14. VIN Core
15. Ghost Drive
16. Engineering Bay, Belinium Backup, Reactor
17. Docking Control Room
18. Cargo/Docking Bay
19. Ship-to-Ship Docking Access
20. Belly Cargo/Docking Shaft

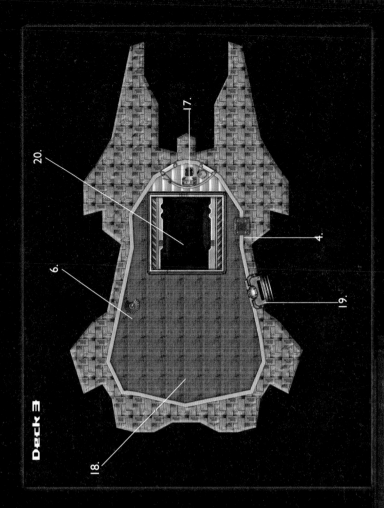

Deck 3

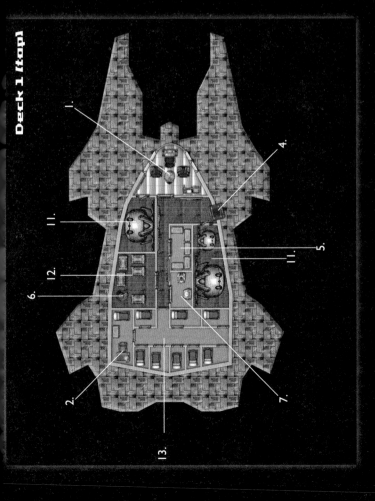

Deck 1 (top)

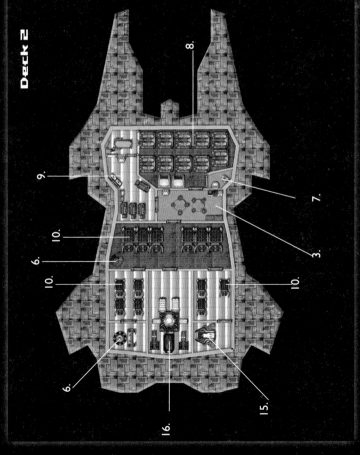

Deck 2

Cargon

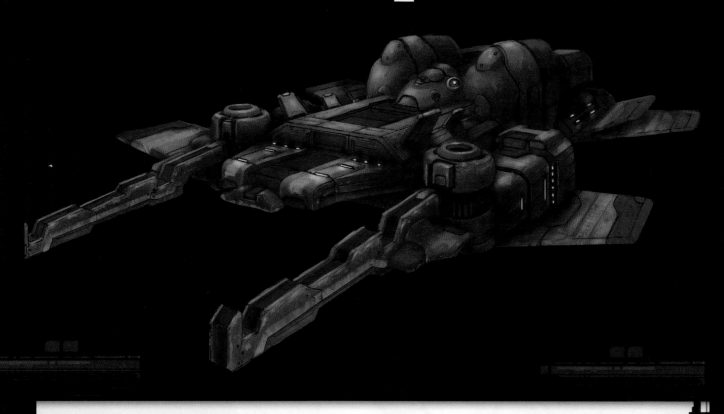

Vulnerable:
At Risk: D, E
Weapons
Front: Heavy Rail Cannon ×4, Heavy Frag Missiles ×40
Aft: Rail Cannon ×2
Top Hull: Light Rail Canon ×2, Frag Missile ×20
Bottom Hull:
Portside
Starboard:
Spec:
Cost: 9,000,000

Lexor Model, D-Class, Heavy Carrier
Length, Width, Height: 360m, 120m, 40m

Description: This ship has 3 to 5 decks if used as a freighter, while the passenger cruise model has eight decks. The Lexor model is one of the most common D-class models and has been used for almost ninety years. They work equally well as freighters. The bottom deck is split into two parts, forward and aft engineering, with the reactor core in the rear. The freighter models have an enormous amount of cargo space. In some configurations, the carrier model acts as a lesser mining ship. In this case the cargo hold has been split in half, the aft section working as a hangar bay capable of holding a dozen or so B-class ships or three Damocles model C-class ships that can be used to travel down to the surface with crew and equipment.

Speed: —
Acceleration: –1
Ghost Drive: +1
Handling: —

Scanners
Bio Scanner: —
Energy Scanner: —
Environmental Scanner: +1
LIDAR: —
LSA: —
Signal Scanner: —
Targeting:
Pods: 5 (6), 10 (3) 30 (1)
AR: 6
DHL
Immune: A, B, C
Vulnerable: D*
At Risk: E
Weapons
Front:
Aft:
Top Hull: Heavy Rail Cannon ×2 *(licensed as asteroid defense)*
Bottom Hull:
Portside
Starboard:
Spec:
Cost: 4,000,000

Titan Model, D-Class, Heavy War Carrier
Length, Width, Height: 400m, 90m, 60m

Description: This is one of the most effective and powerful D-class war carriers. It has only been in service for about ten years, but has proven itself time and again. It is fast, handles well and has a powerful arsenal. However, it does have some minor propulsion issues, making it slow to pick up speed. This is a terrible war machine indeed. It has a rather large medbay, which comes in handy during war situations.

Speed: +1
Acceleration: –2
Ghost Drive: —
Handling: +1
Scanners
Bio Scanner: —
Energy Scanner: —
Environmental Scanner: —
LIDAR: —
LSA: —
Signal Scanner: —
Targeting: +1
Pods: 10 (8), 20 (10)
AR: 10
DHL
Immune: A, B, C
Vulnerable: D*
At Risk: E
Weapons
Front: Heavy Rail Cannon ×4, Photon Cannon ×2, Plasma Hybrid Missile ×300
Aft: Heavy Rail Cannon ×3
Top Hull: Heavy Frag Missile ×300, Plasma Cannon ×4
Bottom Hull: Rail Cannon ×4
Portside: Rail Cannon ×4
Starboard: Rail Cannon ×4
Spec: Some of these ships also sport a front accelerated photon cannon; this substitutes for the two regular photon cannons.
Cost: Not available for purchase

Belenus Model, D-Class, Heavy Mining Ship
Length, Width, Height: 800m, 100m, 60m

Description: The Belenus model is a well-equipped mining ship with its own smelting facility, ore storage bay and docking bay. The docking bay can hold two Gargon models (with barges) or six Damocles models. These are used to transfer materials, crew and ore on and off the surface. The Belenus has a tram system on its middle deck, going from the front to aft. This is one of the most common mining ships around, and is used by midsized as well as large mining companies. This model has been in service for fifty years. They're a bit slow and unruly, but have a quite stable Ghost Drive.

Speed: –2
Acceleration: –2
Ghost Drive: +1
Handling: –1
Scanners
Bio Scanner: —
Energy Scanner: —
Environmental Scanner: +1
LIDAR: —
LSA: —
Signal Scanner: +1
Targeting:
Pods: 20 (8) 50 (10)
AR: 8
DHL
Immune: A, B, C
Vulnerable:
At Risk: D, E
Weapons
Front:
Aft:
Top Hull: Heavy Rail Cannon ×2 *(licensed as asteroid defense)*
Bottom Hull:
Portside:
Starboard:
Spec:
Cost: 40,000,000

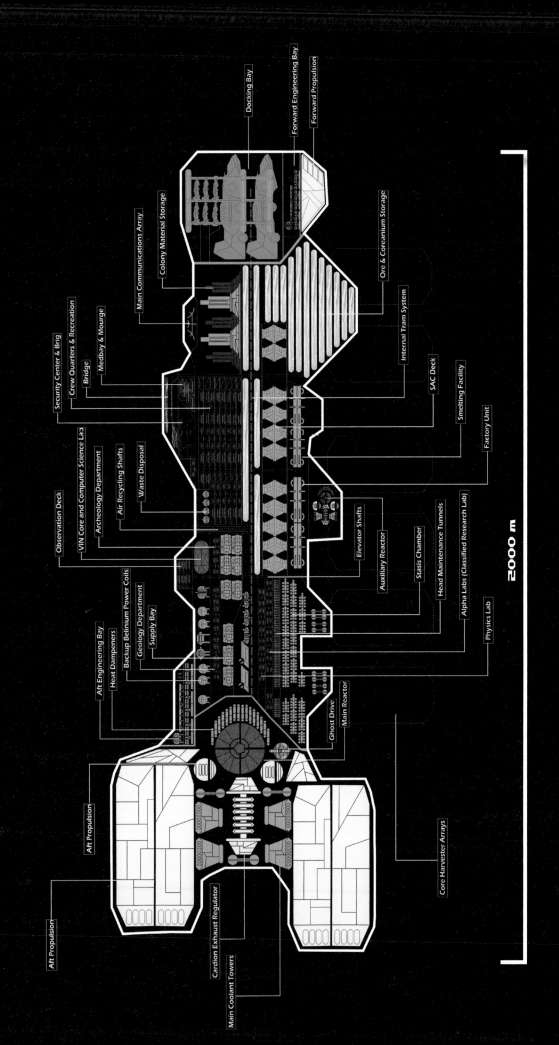

Aft Propulsion

Aft Propulsion

Main Coolant Towers

Cardion Exhaust Regulator

Aft Engineering Bay

Heat Dampeners

Backup Belinium Power Coils

Geology Department

Supply Bay

Observation Deck

VIN Core and Computer Science Lab

Archeology Department

Air Recycling Shafts

Waste Disposal

Security Center & Brig

Crew Quarters & Recreation

Bridge

Medbay & Mourge

Main Communications Array

Colony Material Storage

Docking Bay

Forward Engineering Bay

Forward Propulsion

Ore & Coreanium Storage

Internal Tram System

SAC Deck

Smelting Facility

Factory Unit

Alpha Labs (Classified Research Lab)

Physics Lab

Head Maintenance Tunnels

Stasis Chamber

Auxiliary Reactor

Elevator Shafts

Main Reactor

Ghost Drive

Core Harvester Arrays

2000 m

Thor Model, E-Class, Core Purifier
Length, Width, Height: 2000m, 500m, 250m

Description: The *Thor* model is the largest ship in existence. It's massive, bigger than many space stations. Most have been updated with the state of the art core purification array which uses electromagnetic fields, which don't require the standard core tube to be connected to the actual core. These colossal grav-cuffs are also used to pull out massive rock faces from the planet's surface during mining operations. The docking bay has room for thirty *Damocles* model ships, or three *Belenus* model D-class heavy mining ships. It has forward, middle and aft engineering bays, and a large tram system on the middle deck. Of course, it has an onboard smelting facility and ore storage facility. It has two reactors. The reactor in the aft powers the main engines, while the smaller reactor in the middle powers the core purification arrays, as well as functioning as a backup reactor when needed. These ships usually have a crew varying between two and five thousand, and in most cases remain out in deep space for months or even years at a time.

Speed: −3
Acceleration: −3
Ghost Drive: +2
Handling: −2
Scanners
Bio Scanner: —
Energy Scanner: +1
Environmental Scanner: —
LIDAR: —
LSA: +1
Signal Scanner: —
Targeting:
Pods: 300 (8), 100 (3) 200 (1)
AR: 8

DHL
Immune: A, B, C
Vulnerable: D*
At Risk: E
Weapons
Front: Heavy Rail Cannon ×2 *(licensed as asteroid defense)*
Aft: Heavy Rail Cannon ×2 *(licensed as asteroid defense)*
Top Hull: Heavy Rail Cannon ×2 *(licensed as asteroid defense)*
Bottom Hull: Heavy Rail Cannon ×2 *(licensed as asteroid defense)*
Portside: Heavy Rail Cannon ×2 *(licensed as asteroid defense)*
Starboard: Heavy Rail Cannon ×2 *(licensed as asteroid defense)*
Spec:
Cost: Not available for purchase

Icarus Model, E-Class, Heavy Destroyer
Length, Width, Height: 1300m, 350m, 100m

Description: According to public records, the Consolidated Fleet only has twenty of these monster ships. These are the most awesome destroyers in space and little can withstand them. Under normal circumstances, they hold two D-class *Titans*, ten flight squads (six crafts in each, a total of sixty ships) of *Raven* A-class fighters, and five B-class *Gabriel* model dropships on their flight deck. With military crew of about four thousand, these ships are flying military headquarters. According to rumors, MEC and CIM have been successful in infiltrating and actually stealing two of these by using a combination of covert agents, sabotage and years of planning. This is of course denied by the GIC.

Speed: —
Acceleration: −1
Ghost Drive: —

Handling: —
Scanners
Bio Scanner: —
Energy Scanner: +1
Environmental Scanner:
LIDAR: +1
LSA: —
Signal Scanner: —
Targeting: +2
Pods: 200 (8), 200 (6)
AR: 10
DHL
Immune: A, B, C
Vulnerable: D*
At Risk: E
Weapons
Front: Heavy Plasma Cannon ×8, Heavy Photon Cannon ×8, Accelerated Photon Cannon ×1, Plasma Hybrid Missile ×1000, Heavy Plasma Hybrid Missile ×600.
Aft: Plasma Cannon ×8, Heavy Rail Cannon ×2
Top Hull: Plasma Cannons ×10, Heavy Frag Missile ×250
Bottom Hull: Heavy Plasma Cannons ×14
Portside: Plasma Cannon ×20, Heavy Rail Cannon ×8
Starboard: Plasma Cannon ×20, Heavy Rail Cannon ×8
Spec:
Cost: Not available for purchase

Phoenix Model, 8-Class, Light Transport/Passenger Flight
Length, Width, Height: 25m, 5m, 4m

Description: There are two basic models: passenger model and cargo transport. The cockpit and staff area only takes up about five meters, so the rest of the craft is either filled with passenger seats or a cargo hold. In the cargo model, there's no crew area and only the cockpit, taking up three meters of space. The *Phoenix* can hold one hundred passengers, or has a storage space of about 200 cubic meters. The *Phoenix* is a very common sight in the core systems, as it is used to transport cargo and passengers between planets and adjacent space stations, and out of atmosphere shuttles as well as transport them between destinations on the surface.

Speed:
Acceleration:
Ghost Drive:
Handling:
Scanners
Bio Scanner: —
Energy Scanner: —
Environmental Scanner: —
LIDAR: —
LSA: —
Signal Scanner: —
Targeting:
AR: 4
DHL
Immune: A, B*
Vulnerable: C*
At Risk: D, E
Weapons

Front:
Aft:
Top Hull
Bottom Hull:
Portside
Starboard:
Spec:
Cost: 400,000

Site engineer training facility in orbit of Luna 2.

Gabriel [Military]

Type: *Gabriel* model, B-class, dropship.

Length, Width, Height: 14m, 6m, 3m

Description: There are two *Gabriel* types: military and civilian. The military ship has superior armor, and also has weapons. The ship is quite popular and used for shorter transports and deliveries, and is one of the most common B-class commercial crafts used for passenger flights in the form of air buses. The armor within the parentheses and the weapons are of course for the military version, as is the scanner modifier within parentheses. The ships can transport up to a heavy tank, or carry sixty people, and sports a two man cockpit.

Speed: +1

Acceleration: —

Ghost Drive: n/a

Handling: +1

Scanners

Bio Scanner: (+1)

Energy Scanner: —

Environmental Scanner: —

LIDAR: (+1)

LSA: —

Signal Scanner: —

Targeting: (+1)

Pods: 1 (2, ejecting cockpit)

AR: 3 (6)

DHL

Immune: A, B*

Vulnerable: C*

At Risk: D, E

Weapons

Front: Heavy rail cannons ×2, Frag Missiles ×16

Aft:

Top Hull:

Bottom Hull:

Portside:

Starboard:

Spec:

Cost: 300,000 (military grade, 1,200,000)

Gabriel Deckplan

1. Cockpit
2. Service Hatch: Access to Engine, Life Support and Scanner Arrays (crawl space).
3. Weapons Locker
4. Medical Trauma Equipment
5. Stairs
6. Airlock
7. War Roller Payload
8. Belly Staging Hatch
9. Officer Seating
10. General Cargo/Squad Area

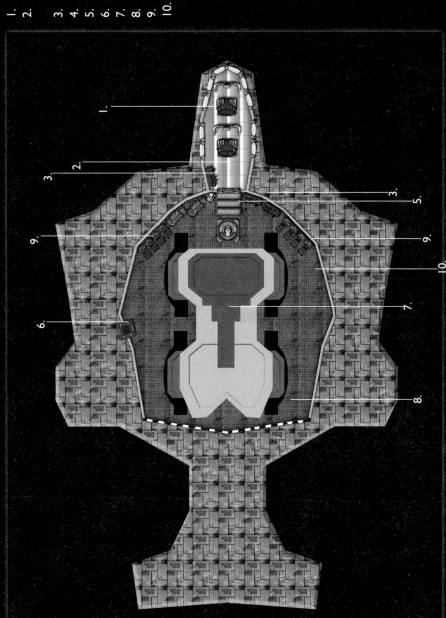

Archimedes

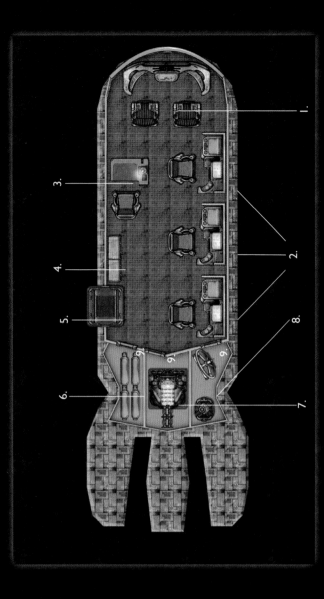

1. Flight Control
2. Scanner Controls & Computer Terminals
3. Scientific/Geology/Archeology Work Station
4. Lockers & Delicate Sample Storage
5. Airlock
6. Life Support
7. Engine & Capacitance Cells
8. Scanner Amplifier Array
9. Service Hatches

Type: *Archimedes* model, B-class, survey/science/repair craft.

Length, Width, Height: 7m, 3m, 2.5m

Description: The *Archimedes* model is a sturdy little craft. It has a two-seat cockpit, and the rear portion has been designed to be fitted with workstations. The ship is mostly used as a mining survey ship or a science vessel, collecting samples on planetary surfaces and the like. It has very advanced scanners and is pretty easy to handle, even if it's a bit slow. It has an airlock that can process two people at a time, which is handy when surveying in a hostile atmosphere.

Speed: −1

Acceleration: −1

Ghost Drive: n/a

Handling: +1

Scanners

Bio Scanner: +1

Energy Scanner: +1

Environmental Scanner: +1

LIDAR: —

LSA: —

Signal Scanner: —

Targeting: —

AR: 4

DHL

Immune: A, B*

Vulnerable: C*

At Risk: D, E

Weapons

Front:

Aft:

Top Hull:

Bottom Hull:

Portside:

Starboard:

Spec: It has a front tool array which holds a drill, plasma torch, plasma saw and ground-penetrating radar and two fine-tuned grappling arms. The tools have a reach of five meters, and the arms can lift 500 kilos each. It also has a forward sample compartment divided into ten slots.

Cost: 250,000

Raven

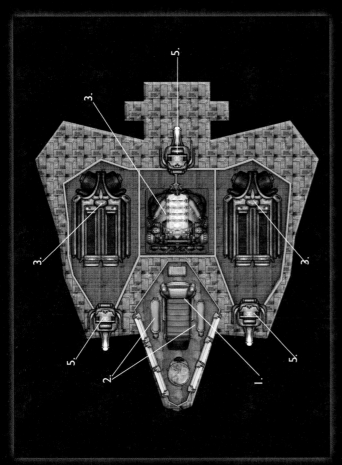

1. Cockpit
2. Life Support
3. Engines & Capacitance Cells
4. Missile Arrays
5. Rail Cannons

Type: *Raven* model, A-class, fighter.

Length, Width, Height: 5m, 3m, 2m

Description: In essence, this is a cannon and scme missiles with wings. The *Raven* fighter has no other purpose than to engage the enemy. It has a streamlined design and can navigate with ease inside or outside an atmosphere. It has a one man cockpit. The cockpit can serve as a one man life pod when ejecting.

Speed: +1
Acceleration: +2
Ghost Drive: n/a
Handling: +1
Scanners
Bio Scanner: —
Energy Scanner: —
Environmental Scanner: —
LIDAR: —
LSA: —
Signal Scanner: —

Targeting: +1
AR: 4
DHL
Immune: A, B*
Vulnerable: C*
At Risk: D, E
Weapons
Front: Rail Cannon ×2, Frag Missiles ×12, Plasma Hybrid Missiles ×6
Aft: Rail Cannon ×1
Top Hull:
Bottom Hull:
Portside:
Starboard:

Spec: The *Raven* has a boost system. Technically, it has eight boost points and can spend up to three at a time. Each point spent adds +1 to Acceleration and Speed on the next roll. When the boost is used up, the ship needs to refuel it in order to use it again.

Cost: 1,400,000

Dragonfly Model, A-Class, Personal Transportation

Length, Width, Height: 2,5m, 1,6m, 1,5m (typical)

Description: This is by far the most common craft. There are many different types and uses: sporty, extra storage, extra seats, family, etc. The *Dragonfly* is incapable of operating outside an atmosphere or in a hostile atmosphere. This model is used as taxis, LED-patrols and similar things. Only LED/military types have scanners, extra armor and a side-mounted carbine. There's also a small one man version. These resemble motorcycles without wheels. This version is very popular with the LED-traffic units, and these have a front-mounted carbine fired from the steering controls.

Speed:
Acceleration:
Ghost Drive:
Handling: Scanners
Bio Scanner: —
Energy Scanner: —
Environmental Scanner: —
LIDAR: —
LSA: —
Signal Scanner: —
Targeting:
AR: 3 (5)
DHL
Immune: A*
Vulnerable: B, C*
At Risk: D, E
Weapons
Front:
Aft:
Top Hull:
Bottom Hull:
Portside
Starboard:
Spec:
Cost: This depends on model and range from 5,000 to 150,000.

Ground Vehicles

PCR "Pecker" [Planetary Construction Rig]

Height: 2.4 m

Description: This is a walker built around an exoskeleton concept, using a combination of hydraulics and ionic polymer metal composites. The suit has a battery life of twelve hours, and a twelve-hour air supply if operating in a vacuum or dangerous atmosphere. The PCR has an array of tools and is used in mining, colony construction and when building ships and space stations. When on the ground, the PCR simply walk. For all intents and purposes, the vehicle is an extension of the pilot's body. When it comes to tools, the PCR has all manners of devices: fusion cutters, PSG, mechanical cutting tools, drills, plasma saws and whatever else a worker might need. In zero-g, these navigate using a thrusting system. Of course, they also have a standard kinetic unit. The PCR can move 15 meters per segment. It uses an augmented strength feeding off the

hydraulics, giving it a Strength of 10 when moving normally. While lifting slowly, locking into lifting mode, it can lift two tons mechanically. Drive or Piloting can be used to operate these walkers. They have no scanners, with the exception of a radiation scanner, but possess communications systems, a NavComp, front camera, navigation and front-mounted light array. It also has all shields up to level three, as it's used to work in hazardous environments.

AR: 4
DHL
Immune: A*
Vulnerable: B*
At Risk: C, D, E
Spec:
Cost: 15,000

Car

Length, Width, Height: 2,5m, 1,6m, 1,5m (typical)

Description: A capacitance-powered car, the standard means of transportation for surface-living civilians on worlds which have the technology level and resources. These come in all manner of shapes and sizes. Only military, mining vehicles and LED-vehicles have any kind of scanners; these are typically signal scanners, energy scanners and LIDAR. Prices and models vary; everything from motorcycles to large trucks to small sport cars are available, and the price is set after the model. Speed and acceleration may vary somewhat between the models. There are terrain models (sand hogs) with a six hour air supply (minimum van size) and a small airlock in the back. These are mainly for surface exploration of planets when constructing colonies.

Speed:
Acceleration:
Handling:
Targeting:
AR: 2
DHL
Immune: A*
Vulnerable: B*
At Risk: C, D, E
Cost: 2,500–100,000

Mammoth War Roller

Length, Width, Height: 7m, 3m, 2m

Description: This is a formidable tank. It has a running time of 12 hours, 12 hour air supply if used in a hostile atmosphere, and a back-end airlock that can process four at a time. It handles well and can hold a squad of eight inside. This is a favorite in the GIC Marine Corps, and is often the payload of the *Gabriel* model dropship.

Speed: –2
Acceleration:
Handling: +1
Scanners
Bio Scanner: —
Energy Scanner: —
Environmental Scanner: —
LIDAR: —

Planetary Construction Rig with open front hatch.

Signal Scanner: —
Targeting: +1
AR: 7
DHL
Immune: A, B, C*
Vulnerable:
At Risk: D, E
Weapons
Front:
Aft:
Top Hull: *Rail Cannon ×2, Heavy Plasma Cannon ×1, Frag Missiles ×20*
Bottom Hull:
Portside
Starboard:
PNR:
Spec:
Cost: 3,600,000

Facilities

Ships have some facilities on them worth mentioning. However, these are not standard in many civilian crafts (the AI must decide exactly what goes when acquiring ships). The system below is a simple way of keeping track of the most basic facilities on a ship, and the cost of upkeep.

> **Note:** *If this system is too much of an "accounting exercise", you can just skip it, but the AI should keep some kind of upkeep cost in mind if the avatars have their own ship. It does cost to keep a bird in the sky, and a lot of the money they make should pour right back into maintenance of the ship. Being without resources, food and other necessities will add to the grittiness of the gameplay.*

C-class Life Support and Nutrition

C-class is by far the most common kind of starship, since it's what private entrepreneurs can afford in most cases. A C-class ship has a limited supply of air, food and water. Generally, if fully stocked and rationed properly, it can last four months on its own. In reality, it's about half that, as crews seldom keep to exact rations until it's really a pinch. But the cost per person, per day is 50 credits (75 if buying air and not filling up for free in an atmosphere). This cost accounts for water, nutrition, clean CO_2 scrubbers and general living upkeep. So for a rough estimate, a crew member costs about 1,250 credits a month while aboard a C-class craft. That's about the same cost as maintaining bills, a small apartment and food in one of the core systems. This is why most crew members of private outfits seldom have a home other than the ship on which they serve.

Medbay

A medical facility on a ship contains a lot of equipment. In order to keep it simple, there will be a summarized cost for a fully-stocked medical facility. This contains everything except medical scanners, the aforementioned drugs, medi-tank, medpod and neuro-worms (all of which can be installed). The medbay has respirators, defibrillators, EKGs, surgical tools,

lesser pain killers, anesthetics, surgical facilities, and it has room for three to ten patients, depending on available space. A medical bay contains an amount of units that are used up (almost like a medi-tank). The units cost a certain amount of credits, and in turn different kinds of operations and treatments cost a certain amount of units. A fully stocked medbay of this size has 60 units. The medbay system can be applied for any kind of onboard laboratory as well, but the actions taken will be a bit different in nature.

Cost: A fully stocked, standard 3–10 patient facility costs 30,000 credits to install, while each unit costs 200.

Instance	Units
Dress a Scratch or any bashing damage.	0,1
Dress a wound on the Hurt or Injured level.	0,5
Stabilize an Incapacitating wound.	1
Perform surgery (fixing a critical hit).	7
Have a physically injured person in the medbay for one week.	10
Have a sick (bedridden and ill, poisoned, radiated etc) patient for one week.	10
Put together a medkit.	10
Perform lesser medical research/investigations (autopsies, bacteria cultures, etc) which takes no more than 24 hours.	2
Perform major medical research (viral studies, xenomorphological studies, etc), which takes up to one to two weeks.	10

Stasis Chamber

This facility is standard for C-, D- and E-class ships. However, they come in different sizes and it's necessary to have enough space to accommodate all travelers, if a crew wishes to travel through the ghost lines or use the RT-Drive. Below, you can find the standard number of stasis tubes that come with the different ships, depending on available space.

C: 5–20 tubes
D: 500–3,000 tubes
E: 1,500–15,000 tubes

Stasis tubes only cost 2000 credits each, as the tube itself is a pretty simple container which is hooked up to the ship. The actual stasis process (nanites and the like) needs to be replenished over time. The tubes are connected to a tank-like device about the size of a large moving box. This is the stasis cache. Each cache costs 500 credits and contains 15 cycles; each cycle can induce and end a period of stasis.

Engineering Bay

C-, D-, and E-class ships all have engineering bays. These are a combined engine room and mechanics station. Material and resources needed to make repairs are stored in the engineering bay. This is measured in repair units. The number of units depends on the class of ship. It's possible to increase the number of units available by ×1.5, but this will increase the size of the engineering bay by the same amount, requiring a rebuild. When there are no more units, the crew can only jury-rig broken parts of the ship. A whole unit is never used to fix small stuff such as a jammed door or broken corridor light; all such minor issues are part of the monthly upkeep. When

Engineering Bay

Repairs	Units, C-class	Units, D & E class	Units A & B class
Scraped	2	3	1
Dinged	5	10	2
Banged Up	7	14	4
Battered	10	20	6
Torn	12	14	8
Breached	15	30	10
Smashed	20	40	12
Fix a broken scanner	3	5	1
Monthly upkeep (without it all rolls get a −1)	2	5	1
Damaged transformer	2	2	1
Reactor leak	4	5	n/a
Broken coolant valve	1	1	n/a
Broken weapon system	2	3	1
A busted array of CO_2 scrubbers	2	3	1
Major blockage in water recycling system	3	4	n/a
Gravity cube surges in a section	4	6	1
Busted Ghost Drive	3	3	n/a
Damage to main propulsion system	6	10	3
Fixing busted up re-loader	2	4	n/a
Fix up a busted ghost net	2	2	n/a

fixing a ship's Hull Integrity Levels, all the associated problems are fixed as well. At times, things like firefights, explosions, accidents and sabotage inside the actual ship can cause damage to systems that don't really apply to the Hull Integrity Levels. In other cases, hits can cause more internal damage (like the effect of a blast wave) than hull damage. These effects are determined by the AI. This is an excellent way of sparing avatars when their ship is down to Smashed and continues to take damage. They will survive, but their ship will be even worse off. See examples and unit cost below.

Cost: C-class engineering 50,000; D-class engineering 200,000; E-Class engineering 1,000,000. Units cost 2000 each.

Amount of repair units according to class
C: 40
D: 60
E: 90

> **Hiring Help:** If you're incapable of repairing your ship on your own, it's possible to hire a repair shop to do it. The cost goes up considerably. The shops add 30% to 75% to the price. So if they use their own engineering bay, they will add this price to the cost of units, and if they use your engineering bay, they will simply add 50 to 75% of the unit cost for their time.

Ghost Net

Not a facility *per se*, the ghost net is an extension of the drive and is used to salvage objects. Salvage ships are usually of C-class size and can't stow away whole ships and large parts. Thus, they haul it after the ship in big bundles. This is no problem in normal space, but the debris (or whatever they're hauling) can't follow through the ghost. This is where the ghost net comes in. An electromagnetically-charged net, it is big enough to enclose a D-class ship. This device is attached near the back of the salvage ship. When the net is deployed, a jammer

or several must go out and physically enclose the debris. This can take everything from a couple of minutes to several hours (Attention + Know-How for jammers and site engineers, base time and reduction time are decided by the AI). The net feeds off the drive and will bring along the debris when the ship jumps, as well as tow it. Having a ghost net installed reduces the Acceleration of the ship by −1. Keep in mind that the reactor percentage loss goes up by an appropriate amount when towing large objects through the ghost.
Cost: 75,000

> **Note on salvages:** Players will engage in salvages, and this can become quite tricky as the AI must decide the value of debris salvaged. The worth of a derelict ship varies enormously. Most derelict ships have been badly damaged, and the materials can be worth as much as eighty percent of full price to as little as five percent of full price if the ship is in pieces and badly damaged. Usually, it ends up somewhere around twenty-five percent. So, after the salvagers have sold it to a broker (getting 25 percent of the price) and after taxes (which is 25 percent of what they sold the haul for), they get to keep what's left. As mentioned before, this is an eighth of what the debris was worth. Usually, you can just divide the money they received by eight to get their final cut. At times, it can be more cost-efficient to use spare parts to refill one's engineering bay, rather than selling them.

Chapter 13: The Cold & The Dark

The big empty is filled with obvious dangers, but there is more to it than that. There's a feeling of gloom which one can't purely define, a looming presence of something ethereal yet paradoxically tangible and foreboding. The rippers are indeed a thing that has made man scared of the dark once again, proof that there indeed are monsters out there. But beyond this there's more.

> **Warning:** *Spoiler alert! If you're not the AI you should stop reading.*

The Cold

Cold measures how rattled and afraid an avatar is and it gives the player a way to gauge his roleplay. The Cold is accumulated in an avatar when he's being forced to confront gruesome and harrowing situations.

When an avatar has reached level four or higher in Cold the AI may affect his actions somewhat (dropping items, accidental stress discharge of a weapon, faltering in logic). When Cold has reached six the person becomes completely frantic or passes out. Whenever an individual has been driven to level four or higher, more than once during a twelve hour period, (or passed out from fear at an earlier stage) he might gain a point of *The Dark*. To avoid gaining Cold the player can make a Cool test, the modifier depends on the situation. One success is enough to beat the effects of Cold.

When accumulated, Cold goes down at a rate decided by the AI but the avatar must have found some peace and safety in order to make it go down. Cold goes down by one point every 5 to 20 minutes that the avatar spends in a safe place (relatively safe in whatever situation he's in).

Be sure to roleplay the effects of the Cold. Look around frantically, breath heavily; let your voice reflect the anguish of your avatar when you act him out.

1: Rattled
2: Jumpy
3: Scared
4: Panicking
5: Terrified
6: Frantic/Unconscious

Cold Chart

There are a lot of things that can cause Cold. Everything from facing certain death, to finding a heap of mutilated bodies to encountering the horrifying unknown can scare a person. The Cold chart provides a guide by which you can estimate if a situation warrants a Cool roll. Every avatar reacts differently to any given situation. An archeologist might throw up or stagger if he finds a body riddled with bullet holes while the marine or operative wouldn't bat an eye as they're use to it. In essence, the AI has to use his reason when deciding when, and to whom, the Cool roll applies.

The modifier can range from +/- 0 to −5 for the most extreme situations. If the modifier exceeds the Cool score the avatar will automatically be subjected to Cold without a chance to even roll. These situations are deemed so horrible that the individual's psyche (without the aid of drugs that is) can't withstand them. The AI has to decide the modifier depending on the situation. There won't be any suggestions for modifiers attached to the situations since it varies depending on the circumstances and the avatar involved. But keep in mind that proximity and surprise can make things worse. Having a ripper jump down from a vent shaft and land in front of you is far scarier than seeing one from afar. Same goes for numbers, finding a heap of mutilated bodies is scarier than finding one. But don't roll all the time. Use tact in regards of this. Make rolls to add to the mood and when it's fitting not to halt the suspense. When a group of avatars have run across two bodies on a derelict ship there's no need to roll for the third (or even for the second at times as they're now expecting it). Something to remember is that even if an avatar passes his Cool roll he's still affected to certain degree and not unfazed.

Situation that might generate Cold in an avatar
Find a mutilated body
Facing a Ripper
Witness a Viscoutrope mutation
Facing a Viscutrope
Being tortured
Killing a human in cold blood
Nearly crashing

These are just a few out of thousands of situations that can instill Cold in an avatar. Things like hearing a terrible distress call from a loved one, or seeing horrible things in a video-log from the very abandoned ship you're on and currently investigating can cause Cold as well.

Example: *Science researcher Angela Ventress is walking to her lab when the power suddenly fails. She shrugs and takes out her flashlight. Short blackouts have been quite common in the colony as of late since the power stabilizers have been on the fritz. But as she enters her lab she immediately notices that something is very wrong. Equipment has been smashed, the walls are covered with voider glyphs painted in blood and there's a lot of blood on the floor as well. Her two lab assistants, Charity and Kurt are nowhere to be seen. Almost in a panic, she starts to back out and as she does she bumps into someone. Angela spins around and sees Charity. She's stained with blood, smiling calmly. In one hand she has a scalpel and in the other she has the severed head of Kurt. "They told me to find his inner self" she says and at this point the AI decides that it's time for the player of Angela to make a Cool roll for her avatar.*

The avatar has a Cool of 3, resulting in a dice pool of 6 as it's a pure Aptitude roll. But the AI decides to give her a −3 modifier. First off, the thing scaring her is right on top of her and secondly, a person she considered to be a friend has apparently murdered and mutilated another one of her friends. Normally, the −3 would apply to the roll and just reduce her dice pool of 6 to 3 but as this is a roll for Cold and as the negative modifier depletes her Cool the avatar's psyche is defenseless against the horror and gains a point of Cold (Rattled) automatically as she's not allowed to roll. The player acts out the horror, portraying Angela as she screams and runs towards the service hatch in an attempt to escape.

Effects

There are no direct effects stipulated from failing a Cool roll other than the accumulation of Cold and much is left up to the AI. The point is that the player should act out the behavior of his avatar. Does he freeze, run away or even throw up of sickening fear? It all depends on the circumstances. If you feel the need, as when a player basically ignores that his avatar is scared, you can impose a −2 modifier due to trembling hands or simply come up with an appropriate reaction. The main point is to leave the exact nature of the effects open so that you can adapt them to the situation and the avatar. As a general rule the effects become progressively worse as the Cold in an avatar gets higher. So if an avatar would go from a Cold rating of 1 to 2 as a result of an encounter that would paralyze him he might just be frozen for a moment before running away. If he would have gone from Cold rating 3 to 4 in the same situation he might have been frozen several seconds, needing a good slap in the face to snap out of it. And keep in mind that as long as the avatar has any Cold he is affected in one way or another even after the immediate effects have ended.

The Dark

The Dark is a measure of the psychological effects of being subjected to weirdness and horror in space, and the effects of voiders and viscutropes. The Dark instills a growing paranoia into the mind of the affected and then it makes him delusional. In the end the victim becomes violent and is driven insane. It takes on a certain expression depending on which powers that are close by. The Dark affects the roleplay and also allows

the AI to "fool" the player into acting out things with his avatar, which is a result of the paranoia.

The Dark is a much more severe problem and a more long term one as well than The Cold. It has a slower decline rate, and quickly becomes an ailment of some magnitude (see *Accumulation of The Dark* below). If it has reached stage five it doesn't go down at all if the avatar is in space (ship, space station or colony with fifty or less people). Only when spending time on a planet in a stable human community (with more than fifty people) or on a vibrant and safe space station with five hundred or more people on it does Dark go down by 1 per week. It is also possible to reduce the Dark by this rate while on a ship (station, colony or other non-terraformed environment) *if* the person gets enough human interaction and at least one hour of therapy per week (large ships have several medical officers specializing in the art of therapy). However, this is only possible if the afflicted hasn't reached level 5 or more. Also take into account that The Dark doesn't decline (or increase) during stasis sleep. If a person stays on level 5 or higher for more than three *waking* months he will become permanently insane, a permanent VPS victim.

At level 5 many people (4/8 if you want to make use of chance when determining this) finds an obsession. Often this is a twisted version of whatever they were sent to do (or what they do for a living, covet or believe strongly in) and their reasoning in connection to this is warped. A squad leader wants to complete the mission no matter the risk to his squad or

DECK
03

Once a vibrant workplace, the mining ship "Rivet" has been turned into a living nightmare of alien menace by an unknown artifact find.

anyone else and can even kill people for "treason" as they refuse to follow his insane and suicidal orders. An engineer can get fixated on increasing the power in the reactor in order to get the ship going again, not seeing that this might cause a reactor leak which can kill the entire crew. The person obsessed often sees his actions as something that will save or greatly benefit the group (or the whole of humanity), and when people try to tell him that it's pure madness or illogical his paranoia kicks in and he finds himself surrounded by "enemies" that wish to sabotage his efforts, harm him or outright kill him.

Mankind has dubbed the effects of The Dark as VPS. Whatever the MRG says, there really is no real classification of it. They have just come up with a name for that which we can't understand and fear so intently.

Levels of Dark

1: A bit less social.

2: A bit less social and a little suspicious towards people.

3: Spends a lot more time alone and is a bit socially weird and is generally mistrustful of others. Has some trouble sleeping.

4: As above but the victim often stares blankly out into space and can mumble to himself. The AI may provide small paranoid bits and hallucinations. The person often suffers from nightmares at this time and is often suffering from bouts of insomnia. Onsets of severe headaches are also common symptoms.

5: As above but the paranoia goes further and the avatar becomes a bit more delusional. This is regulated by the AI. Starts to have an aggressive disposition and often finds an *obsession*. Nightmares are thought of as being flashes of things that will come to pass if the individual doesn't stop them.

6: As above but can now start to sabotage for the others in a dangerous way led by delusions and paranoia. Is prone to self-mutilation and suicidal behavior. Hallucinations are worsened and the victim can at times suffer from violent outbursts.

7: Can become outright dangerous in the sabotages, intentionally harming others indirectly and at times directly.

8: Stark raving mad and can outright attack others or is very cogent but sociopathic, lulling people into a false sense of security before striking.

Other Effects: You can play around a lot with The Dark and its effects. When viscutropes are close by you can have the affected dream of them as their energy is linked to The Dark. The Dark can at times create group hallucinations, making the affected see the same things for brief moments which can lead to extremely dangerous situations.

Accumulation of the Dark

As mentioned under the Cold section, the Dark can be accumulated as a result of intense fear. But there are several other things that can affect it. Every waking month a person has spent in space (spaceship, small colony or station) beyond four months he has to pass a Cool roll. If unsuccessful he gains a point of The Dark. Every waking month beyond this gives a −1

on the roll. Botching on this roll will have dire consequences and the result is that the person immediately reaches level 7.

In order to reset the mind the individual has to spend at least one week in a large, safe and vibrant space station, colony or civilization located on a terraformed world. Of course, he has to socialize during his time spent in one of these locations as normal human contact is vital.

After this time he's free to spend another four months in space without having to make a roll.

Black Resonance: This permeates the entire universe and is what causes the Dark. This resonance varies in strength. In those places where it's extremely strong it can severely increase The Dark in all people in its proximity.

The Dark increases in different intervals, each one requiring a Cool roll from the affected to withstand. Every new interval imposes a −1 to the roll. Then there's the *Sphere of Influence* (just *Sphere* for short). This is the range the resonance has and it affects everyone within it. When the sphere is personal it adheres to anyone who uses the artifact (physically held it is enough, even with gloves, or spends time in the affected place) and remains within ten meters from it. Otherwise under sphere there will just be a range given. Everyone within this range will be affected by the black resonance as per Intensity. When venturing outside the sphere the person no longer has to make any rolls and the modifier of the Intensity roll decreases with one every three hours until it's nullified. If venturing inside the sphere again before the negative modifier has been nullified the modifier (whatever it has been decrees to) is in effect.

Talking to Ghosts: Being awake while traveling the ghost lines can be extremely detrimental. The ghost lines are very unpredictable and how fast the individuals will accumulate the Dark is random. Black resonance has a rather high intensity in the ghost. When relevant the AI should roll 1D8 and compare the result to the black resonance intensity chart. This will show the intensity for the ghost line in question.

Making more than one ghost jump per four days also imposes a threat. If this is done those exposed to it will have to make a Cool roll with −2 and a failure will give them a point of The Dark. Imagine the effect just one point of The Dark in every crew member on an E-class ship can have on events.

Example: Dr Ambuto Heath has been researching an alien artifact. What the player and his avatar are unaware of is that it radiates black resonance. The Intensity of it is Relentless, and the sphere has a range of five hundred meters. As long as he, or anyone else for that matter, stays within five hundred meters of the artifact, they have to make a Cool roll every third day.

If they fail they gain a point of The Dark. Every new interval they get a −1 modifier to the roll. But if they venture outside the sphere they don't have to roll and for every three hours their negative modifier goes down by one. So if the good doctor is about to roll for his third Interval he will get a −2 on the Cool roll (the first roll is normal, the second is done with −1 and the third will get a −2 as a −1 applies each new Interval roll.) But if he ventures outside the sphere the modifier will lessen for every three hours until it reaches zero. So if he stayed out for three hours and then came

The crew of "The Rivet" has been inexplicably driven irrevocably insane and murderous.

Blood, death, madness and fear is what is left to find on "The Rivet".

Intensity	Interval	Ghost Intensity Roll
Low	1 per two weeks	1–5
Severe	1 per week	6–7
Relentless	1 every third day	8
Overpowering	1 every 24 hours	-
Consuming	1 every two hours	-

back, his next roll would have been made with a −1 as the modifier decreased. But as long as he stays within the Sphere he will get an increase of the negative modifier to his Cool roll.

> **Extreme Cases:** *It is possible that there are even worse intensities. Holding a shard of, let's say, the arch (or something other of that sinister nature) in ones hand might incur a roll on initial contact and then one every minute!*

Environmental Circumstance Stress

"Self destruct sequence will initiate in 30 seconds". In space there can be a lot of different factors that can stress someone out. Being given three minutes to jury-rig a tiny breach in the hull before it blows wide open, and explosively decompresses the entire ship, can make a person a bit unsteady on the hand. When stress of this kind is involved, the avatar should make a Cool roll. The modifier can range from 0 to −4 depending on the nastiness of the situation. A failed roll will give the avatar a −1 to a −3 modifier to all actions until the imminent threat is fixed or no longer affect the avatar. This stress mainly affects actions that are in need of some concentration such as piloting, engineering and similar activities.

A Bit of Finesse

In the end it's the AI and the other players that have to make this come together. The information in this section can only go so far in helping you create the mood. The players have to act out the mindset of their avatars in-game, while the AI has to decide when to make rolls and when to let the horror creep up on the avatars without rolls. It's all a question of timing and subtleness. And above all, it's a joint effort. Cooperation between the players and the AI is vital. We're also talking about rattling the players, who are young adults or adults. This can't be done if the players won't allow themselves to be scared from time to time. And take into account that the system for the Cold and the Dark is prone to cause a downward spiral into fear and insanity for the avatars so be careful so you don't end up with a group of insane avatars too early on in a story (if that's not the main idea).

Lone survivor of the extraction team sent to "The Rivet" desperately tries to escape the very crew she was sent to save.

Chapter 14: Antagonists & Allies

Here some of the most common and probable antagonists of the avatars will be described, also the phenomenon of alien artifacts will be covered. There are some spoilers in this section which should be reserved for the AI's eyes only. Even though it won't ruin the game as such if a player reads it, it could take some of the punch out of the game further down the road. It's up to you.

> **Damage:** Types of damage is divided by a slash (/). For instance, if a creature has Claw 4/2 under its attacks it means that when using its claws it will inflict 4 in base damage and 2 in per success damage. If not stated otherwise, non-human antagonists use Brawn + Close Combat when attacking in close combat.
>
> **Note on health:** Human NPAs all have 14 plus Brawn in hit points. When they have lost half they get −2 and their movement is halved, when they have five left they get −3 and can only hobble about or crawl and when they are reduced to zero hit points they're dead or otherwise incapacitated and severely injured.

The Unimportant NPAs – It's a numbers game

There are a number of antagonists listed here that are ready for use, but what you won't find is an array of "normal" people such as marines, engineers and core system citizens. When you deal with unimportant NPAs you should have four numeric values named Poor 2, Okay 5, Good 6 and Pro 7. These represent total dice pools. Assign these when needed to whatever task they're trying to perform according to what you deem reasonable. Let's say that the avatars run across a marine that allies with them. They run into trouble and a firefight breaks out. Then you can simply deem that the marine is Good at shooting and thus you give him a dice pool of six in this (jot it down on a scrap piece of paper). Later, they run across a door that has to be busted down and the marine helps. You deem that his ability to break down doors is Okay and he can pitch in with 5 dice. After a while you will have jotted down a lot of his stats and actually created an NPA during play without a hassle. The hit points and movements of these can always be placed at a mediocre, 16 hit points and a movement of 22 (sprinting), and their defense is usually 2. If you want to have pre-planned and important NPAs you should sit down and create them using a full interface as these will play a more important part. And at times an unimportant NPA becomes important and you can translate your scribbles into the more detailed system.

Animals

Basically, most the animals that exist today exist in the world of C&D. However, there are a lot more as well and some are extremely weird and alien looking. Some are huge monster-like and carnivorous while others are gigantic herbivores. This is a result of genetic engineering as well as the belinium radiation. An icy planet that seems dead could have been a belinium mine decades or centuries ago and now the animals left behind from the settlement have mutated and spawned. Take it upon yourself to create as many weird animals as you can. There are some examples given of weird and dangerous types of animals that exist in the universe of C&D.

Special Animal Traits

Aptitudes: The Clout of animals mostly measure how they interact with each other. Their Brains show their cleverness and ability to solve problems and learn new things.

Pounce: This attack requires a Brawn + Athletics roll and if it hits it counts as doing claw damage +1 to base damage and the victim will suffer −2 on all his actions in the current and the following segment. The victim also has to pass a −2 Quickness roll or fall down on the ground.

Ram/Impale: This special attack can be used to rush and knock down or impale an enemy. The attack requires a Quickness + Close Combat roll −3 and if it's successful the victim suffers 10 points worth of damage.

Alphas: The top "dog" of a pack or heard has the same basic traits as his followers but gains +1 to Brawn and Clout. He also gains a rank 2 in Strategy which he can use in the same way humans can and allocate Strategy points or create clever ambushes (within the limits of the intelligence of the animal in question) when leading his pack.

Large Dog, Wolf, Cougar

Attention: 5
Brains: 3
Brawn: 4
Clout: 3
Cool: 2
Gut Feeling: 4
Quickness: 4
Reaction: 3
Defense: 3
HP: 12

AR:
Attacks: Bite 3/2, Claw 2/2, Pounce
Movement: 30
Abilities: Athletics 4, Close Combat 2, Search 4

Large Herbivore (Ox, Wildebeest, Bison)

Attention: 2
Brains: 2
Brawn: 7
Clout: 2
Cool: I
Gut Feeling: 4
Quickness: 2
Reaction: 2
Defense: I
HP: 20
AR: I
Attacks: Impale/Ram, Kick 4/2, Standstill horn slash 3/2
Movement: 25
Abilities: Athletics 2, Close Combat I, Search 4

Tundra Cephalopod

It's unknown why or how these monsters came to be, but some speculate that they were a GIC military experiment gone awry. They can measure up to fifteen meters in length and weigh approximately two tons. These fleshy tentacle beings can only be found on icy worlds. They burrow tunnels under the tundra and hunt by vibrations. They break through the ice and attack their prey with their many arms. They have six extremities; each and every one of them has a large spike which they can use to impale their victim. The adrenaline gland of this creature is considered to be a great delicacy and aphrodisiac among high-end society in the core systems and can fetch a good 10000–25000 credits depending on its size. The rest of the meat tastes disgusting but is nutritious and packed with proteins.

Attention: 4
Brains: 5
Brawn: 9
Clout: 3
Cool: 3
Gut Feeling: 4
Quickness: 3
Reaction: 2
Defense: 0
HP: 40
AR: 2
Movement: 20 under the ice (or deep snow), 15 above the ice.
Abilities: Search 2, Stealth 2
Attacks: Can perform 2 Impale attacks per segment (damage 6/3 fatal), or 2 normal tentacle attacks which cause 5/2 bashing. It can also try to grab its prey with a –2 Quickness + Close Combat roll. If it has managed to grab the victim it inflicts 3 bashing points of damage each segment due to crushing damage (armor does not apply).
Spec: It only ingests victims after they have died (or after it believed that they have died). It has no teeth and the process of digesting food is slow. If someone were to be eaten

alive and has a large bladed weapon or a gun he can shoot/carve his way out, killing the beast simultaneously.

The Tundra Cephalopod is never found in an environment where the temperature goes higher than –25 Celsius. It hates strong sources of heat such as fire and plasma and has to pass a Cool –2 roll to come any closer than 5 meters of these. If damaged by fire or plasma it also has to pass a normal Cool roll. If it fails it flees and stays away for a couple of minutes or even hours. The creature is immune to critical hits.

Armadillo Wolf

This animal is in all likelihood the result of belinium radiation mutation. Basically it's a large canine covered with thick jointed leathery armor plates. Beyond this, the creature can change texture and color pattern like a chameleon.

The Armadillo Wolf can be found in any climate and they usually run in small packs. The animal can be tamed if captured and trained before it has reached a year of age. LED TARGET

units often use the animal as part of its K-9 unit.

Attention: 5
Brains: 3
Brawn: 5
Clout: 3
Cool: 4
Gut Feeling: 5
Quickness: 3
Reaction: 3
Defence: 2
HP: 16
AR: 4
Attacks: Claw 4/1, Bite 4/2, Pounce
Movement: 30
Abilities: Athletics 2, Search 1, Stealth 2
Spec: All attempts at spotting the animal when it hides using its camouflage are done with –2. Not even IR can spot them as their plating isolates their bodies and has the temperature of the local environment.

Rippers

Rippers are the stuff nightmares are made of. It's as if they have been designed by some of our most primordial fears, roused from a feverous nightmare best left undreamt.

The origins of this enormously dangerous race have never been established. A home planet has never been found, neither is it known exactly how they managed to get on the *Doppelganger* all those centuries ago.

What is known is that rippers are an alien race that seemed to have hailed from insect- and reptilian-like creatures. They're extremely aggressive and cunning. Rippers are driven by four basic needs and nothing else: Survival, feeding, reproduction and colonization. But in doing so, they leave no room for anything else. Some xenomorphologists speculate that the rippers are a flawed race or a designed bio weapon as it seems that they eradicate all life wherever they go. This, in the end, will lead to them being left without a way to reproduce or feed, paradoxically at odds with their basic instincts. But there are some other factors that make it possible for them to survive indefinitely without any nourishment. They seem to be immune to radiation, most poisons and known pathogens.

There have been five types of rippers encountered. Burrowers, Prowlers, Spawnlings, Drones and Queens.

Ripper Acidic Cloud: When a ripper is killed there's an emission of an acidic cloud of gas. Burrowers only spray a spatter of acid 1 meter around them when they die which burns for three segments while Prowlers and Spawnlings produce a cloud of 2 meters in every direction, Drones a cloud of 2,5 meters in every direction and Queens a cloud of 3,5 meters in every direction. These clouds last for three segments and the acid continues to burn during one segment after a victim has left the cloud. Ripper acid starts out as Harsh, and goes up one level for every segment while it's in contact with the victim/object until it reaches Incinerating. When they sustain an injury that penetrates their exoskeleton a splash of the acid is released (about 90 degree spray radius with a reach of two meters). This will burn for two segments with the same strength as the gaseous cloud.

Ripper Nerve Stem: Only Prowlers and Drones have this. Hitting it is done with a −3 modifier (if the ripper is standing rather still that is) and if you manage to inflict 7 points of damage (after the armor has been factored in) the ripper dies without expulsing acidic gases or sprays.

Burrower

A two foot long centipede-like creature. It is very fast and has a rotating scolex. It can burrow into the flesh of a living creature. At the same moment it has fully entered it releases a stimulant which releases endorphins and synchronizes the victims mind with the survival instinct of the ripper. The victim won't be remembering the attack as painful and horrifying. He will protect the thing while it gestates, defending it and regarding it as something "wonderful" that has entered him. He will hide it as best he can from others. The victim will also hide the fact that his body is getting sicker and sicker as he is consumed from within. Burrowers have to make a Cool roll if they're confronted with fire or flee uncontrollably.

Attention: 3
Brains: n/a
Brawn: 1
Clout: n/a
Cool: 2
Gut Feeling: 2
Quickness: 4
Reaction: 3
Defense: 3
HP: 8
AR: 2
Movement: 15
Abilities: Athletics 3, Close Combat 3, Search 2, Stealth 2
Special: When bitten by a Burrower the victim has to pass a −2 Brawn roll. If successful the poison will give the avatar a −3 to all further actions and reduce his movement by 15. Each new bite will add another −1 to the Brawn roll. If unsuccessful the victim is completely paralyzed. The poison

is short lived though and all effects will pass after one minute. A burrower only needs about ten to twenty seconds to fully enter the body.

Drone

If Prowlers are the foot soldiers the Drones are the centurions. A Drone is about two and a half meters tall and weighs about 120 to 140 kilos. They are extremely fast and strong and due to their claws and spiny growths they can rip a foe to shreds in close combat within seconds. Drones are capable of running on walls and ceilings on all fours. The creature is immune to critical hits.

Attention: 4
Brains: n/a
Brawn: 6
Clout:-
Cool: 3
Gut Feeling: 3
Quickness: 4
Reaction: 4
Defense: 1
HP: 20
AR: 4
Movement: 30
Attacks: Claws 6/2, Bite 7/2, Spines 6/2 (See Ripper Acidic Cloud above), Pounce.
Abilities: Athletics 2, Close Combat 1, Search 2, Stealth 3

Prowler

These are fast and vicious creatures. They're about one meter tall when standing on their hind legs, but in most cases they run on all fours. Prowlers only weight about twenty-five kilos, as they have been created from about that amount of dead flesh. The Hive regards Prowlers as very expendable and uses them as cannon fodder when in need. They are perfect for this as the dead bodies of mammals can be used to produce more Prowlers. Like Drones, they're capable of running on walls and ceilings. Small though they may be they do have one advantage over the drones. They're capable of spitting forth their acidic blood on command (using Attention + Athletics to hit). The attack has a reach of 10 meters. They can perform one such attack per segment and a total of fifteen such attacks during a twenty-four hour period. *This will burn for two segments with the same strength as the gaseous cloud.*

Attention: 4
Brains: n/a
Brawn: 3
Clout:-
Cool: 2
Gut Feeling: 3
Quickness: 4
Reaction: 3
Defense: 3
HP: 12
AR: 2
Movement: 30
Attacks: Claws 3/1, Bite 4/2
Abilities: Athletics 2, Close Combat 2, Search 2, Stealth 3

CASE FILE: 938-039
BRANCH: MRG, DOX2
ID: Dr Ellen Rainsworth
SUBJECT: Ripper main physiology

All ripper types have an enclosed high-tensile carapace and a body that's divided into sections. This allows them to survive in a vacuum fully mobile for up to twenty minutes. They can store atmospheric gases within and make use of them when deprived. It's unclear exactly what a ripper can and cannot breathe. They seem to be fully functional in our atmospheres but have been found to breathe (using tracheas, small tubes all over their body, instead of lungs) methane, nitrogen and several other gases without any problems and they're able to withstand heat and cold extremes. If they're wounded and their carapace is punctured, the damaged section is closed off. This will continue to keep them immune to the vacuum. This also means that they are unaffected if limbs are shot off. The only way to take down a ripper is to shoot it to shreds or hit the nerve stem which is located just below their throats beneath their carapace and muscle tissue. It's roughly the size of a tennis ball. Their carapace can be hard to penetrate as its composition is about as strong as light ceramic armor plating. Their extreme resilience is probably a result of their remarkable ability to shed and replace their molecules. They can switch from carbon, sulphur to silicon in order to adapt to different environments as these substances are tailored to suit different atmospheres. Their natural resilience extends to the Burrower eggs and Prowler chrysalis as well. As does their uncanny capacity to withstand radiation, toxins and pathogens.

Their blood and tissues are ammonia based rather than water based. This in combination with presence of sulphur in their system will produce a corrosive agent when their carapace is penetrated. It's recommended to keep at least a five meter distance when shooting at rippers since the corrosive is capable of wearing down a COG and eat away at exposed flesh if not properly shielded. This corrosive is related to fluorine, but it's unknown how the rippers own tissues and physiology is unaffected by it.

They have the ability to enter a state we have dubbed "multibiosis". There are several forms of biosis found in nature, which entails a state of hibernation (freezing all the liquids within in order to survive extreme dehydration indefinitely or chemibiosis which renders a being hibernated but immune to atmospheric toxins). This multibiosis makes them capable of hibernating indefinitely until conditions change (atmosphere changes, prey and reproductive chances comes within reach). They awake within minutes as the conditions change. In theory, this means that a whole colony of rippers can lie in multibiosis for millions, or even billions, of years on an otherwise dead planet until something that ensures their survival rouses them. The multibiosis is of great interest to our stasis sleep research.

They're capable of climbing on walls and ceilings without any trouble. When doing this they crawl on all fours. Otherwise they shift, running equally effective on either all fours or their hind legs.

Burrower

DNA Analysis

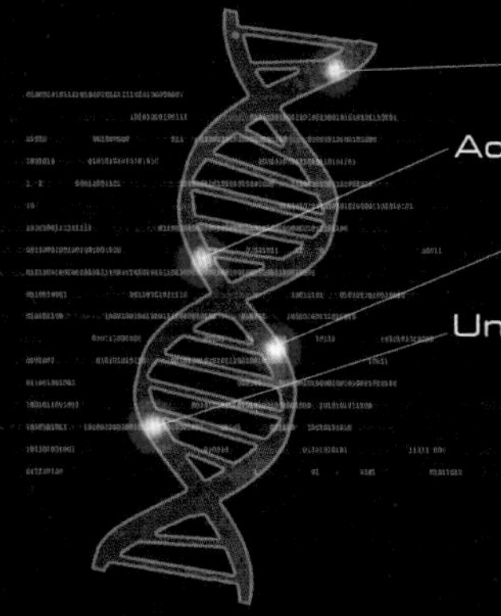
Anomalous Nucleotide Configuration
Accelerated Cell Division Markers
Mutation Indicator
Unknown Genetic Aberration

Ripper Drone Basic Profile

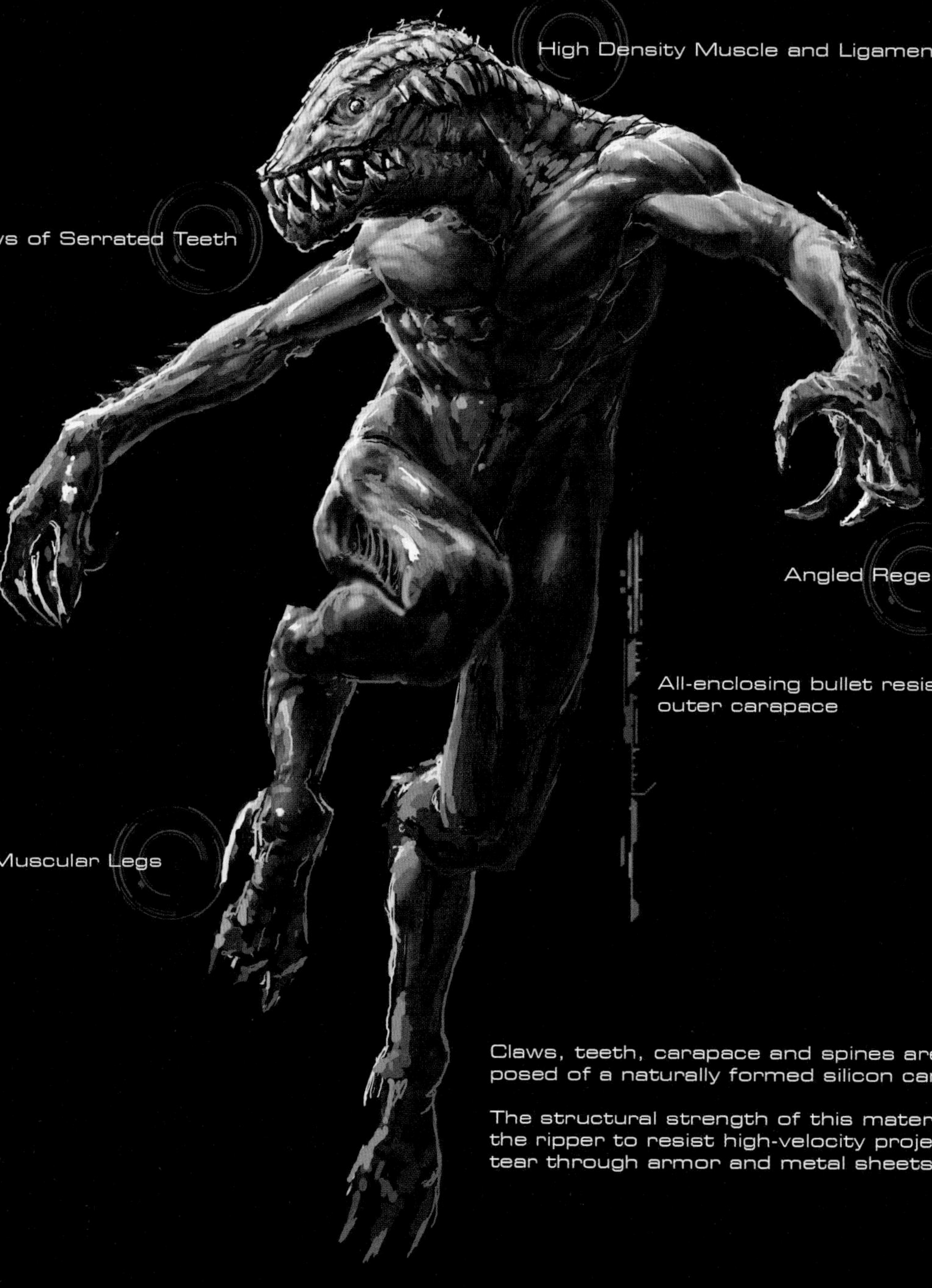
High Density Muscle and Ligament Clusters
Dual Rows of Serrated Teeth
Sharp Retractable Spines
Angled Regenerating Claws
All-enclosing bullet resistant flexible outer carapace
Powerful, Muscular Legs

Claws, teeth, carapace and spines are composed of a naturally formed silicon carbide.

The structural strength of this material allows the ripper to resist high-velocity projectiles and tear through armor and metal sheets.

CASE FILE: 938-040
BRANCH: MRG, DoX2
ID: Dr Jerico Kurokawa
SUBJECT: Ripper neurology and behavior

The creature is extremely hostile. If they don't have a hive they will hunt down and kill every large mammal they encounter, often starting with humans or Gerions as they (by genetic memory) know them to be the largest threat. If they're small in numbers they use cunning and stealth tactics, but if they're great in numbers they overwhelm the opposition. If they have a Queen they try to capture their enemies and bring them to the hive where they keep them for "impregnation". They often stack dead bodies in one hidden location if not having a queen, where they keep them for nourishment and possible hosts for Prowlers in the event that a Queen would show up.

Rippers do not have a brain, only a central nerve stem. Their head is only used to feed, for the placement of sensory organs and as means of attack. The "eyes" of a ripper, aren't eyes at all. These organs function as sonar, vibration sensors, LUX sensors, heat sensory organs and sense of smell. These are crystalline and hard to the touch.

CASE FILE: 938-041
BRANCH: MRG, DoX2
ID: Dr Ellen Rainsworth
SUBJECT: Ripper genetics and reproductive cycle.

There are four (spawnlings are only the early stage of two of the types) known types of rippers and these are Queens, Drones, Prowlers and Burrowers. These four require three distinct different methods of "conception". Drones and Queens are dependent on two things to come into existence: A Burrower and a living animal (it has to weigh at least 25 kilos). The Burrower attacks the host and burrows inside it. Usually it goes for the back where it's hard to reach. The whole process takes about twenty seconds. As it attacks it injects a highly potent paralytic agent which renders the victim completely immobile. After about a minute the host is free to move around, the Burrower releases a protein in its wake which closes the wound. After insertion, it moves on the outside of the organs within the ventral cavity, without damaging the host. It also releases a series of signal substances of an extremely complex nature which we haven't been able to deconstruct or replicate. These make the victim bond with the creature inside on a psychological level. The host will experience the "impregnation" as a blessing and hide it and protect it from all others, except those in the same condition.

While this is going on the creature gestates inside, merging with vital organs. The ripper takes over the role of life support (heart function, breathing) as it takes the place of the organs. The host will become sicker and sicker. First pale, then clammy and cold to the touch. In the end they will have a hard time with fine coordination, blurred vision and uncontrollable shakings and perspiration.. Still, the host sees the invader in his body as a blessing (hosts have often stated that they're "becoming"). He will protect it at any cost and if someone wishes to examine him he will avoid it and if someone tries to force him he will respond violently. The substance causes a mild dementia, making the host somewhat forgetful and disoriented at times. It also blocks the pain center, making them unaware of the pain (and immune to all other pain). In general, hosts isolate themselves. If working they call in sick and stay as far away from people as possible. Some even go AWOL and hide until the "birth". However, there have been cases where the victim has kept his faculties, fully aware of the horror being afflicted upon him. It is unknown why some victims are unaffected by the substance.

The gestation period ranges from six hours up to five days. Why the time differs is unknown, perhaps it's connected to the hosts DNA, but on average it takes twelve hours for the ripper to be "born". After a period of four to twelve hours it's impossible to remove it without great risk to the host and all the major organs has to be replaced. This requires an extremely complex surgical procedure that takes about ten hours to complete. After the four to twelve hour timeframe it's impossible to save the host.

Seconds before the creature is born the substance release halts, which enables the host to realize what has happened to him. About 90% of the organs and tissues of the ventral cavity has been replaced by the ripper. During the first four hours the ripper merged with the organs, and after six hours it has mutated into the early stage of a Queen/Drone "spawnling", using the tissues in the host as nutrition and raw materials. When born, it rips itself loose violently. This is extremely painful for the host. The entire ventral cavity explodes and the creature emerges. The body is split in half and the host dies. Luckily it's over within seconds so the suffering of the host is short.

The "newborn" (spawnling) Queen/Drone looks like a small and not fully developed version of the fully grown animal. If having access to a food source (in most cases other living creatures) it can be fully grown within twelve hours. It needs about 120 kilos of food in order to be fully developed (Queens need 400 kilos). Queens are very unusual; about 1 out of 1000 becomes a Queen.

Rippers have a remarkable genetic structure. Prowlers seem to be less advanced but Queens and Drones take on favorable genetic aspects from their hosts. Rippers that spring from a four legged predator have a tendency to run more on all fours, pounce even more when they attack and so forth. If sprung from an herbivore species they develop means of attack and defense, or movement patterns, from these. We studied a case where a Drone that came from a bovine had developed hornlike ridges which made it even more adapt at rush attacks.

In the case where the host is human the Drones or Queens develop the uncanny ability to understand and interact with technology, though only rudimentary. They can never control or use advanced technology (weapons, tools and such) but they understand that tearing out wires can cut the power, or that doors are opened by interacting with an NIS and what kind of damage a gun can inflict. This, of course, is if the host knew this. Otherwise they, as humans, are quick to learn these things.

The Prowler is a much smaller creature and is also born from a Burrower, but a Prowler is born out of dead flesh. The Burrower crawls into a dead body or carcass. The host cannot have been dead for longer than a month (if not preserved) and can't be in a state of severe decomposition. For every 30 kilos of dead material within the body a Prowler is born (as before, the Burrower mutates). So a corpse weighing 90 kilos would spawn three prowlers weighing little less than 30 kilos (a Prowler always weighs this much and it takes a whole 30 kilos dead flesh to spawn them). The host's body is turned into a chrysalis after about four hours after infection. The soft tissues are centered into a lump while every last scratch of bone and cartilage is turned into an outer protective crust. After 6 hours in the chrysalis stage the Prowlers are born. If Drones are present, they usually transport these chrysalises to the hive if one is within reach, or hide them away in clusters. Burrowers spring from the eggs laid by the Queen.

Queen

The queen is a big and nasty ripper. She is stronger and bigger and she's capable of laying eggs with Burrowers inside. The drones construct an incubator tube which they attach to her, and she can then produce eggs. She is however capable of producing the incubator herself if needed. The creature is immune to critical hits.

Attention: 3
Brains: n/a
Brawn: 9
Clout:-
Cool: 4
Gut Feeling: 4
Quickness: 2
Reaction: 3
Defense: 1
Movement: 25
Attacks: Claws 6/3, Bite 7/3, Spines 6/3, Tail whip 5/2
HP: 50
AR: 7
Abilities: Athletics 2, Search 2, Stealth 1, Impale

Spawnlings

These are the rippers that just has busted out of a body. They're about the same size as a small Labrador. They have the same basic capabilities as a full grown Drone but are weaker. Basically they're miniature versions of their larger counterparts. Spawnlings try to stay hidden and out of harms way until they're fully grown, only performing blitz attacks on single individuals in order to feed.

Attention: 4
Brains: n/a
Brawn: 3
Clout: —
Cool: 2
Gut Feeling: 3
Quickness: 3
Reaction: 3
Defense: 3
HP: 12
AR: 2
Movement: 30
Attacks: Claws 3/1, Bite 4/2, Spines 4/1
Abilities: Athletics 3, Close Combat 1, Search 2, Stealth 4, Pounce

> **The Hive:** Rippers build hives when having a queen or smaller nests if alone in order to store bodies. They secrete a resin that is comprised of a mix of silicone and carbon, it hardens within seconds after being produced. The rippers use their clawed hands to form it into structures, using whatever other material that lies about. A ship that is infested with rippers will in all likelihood have several nesting areas which will be covered wall to wall with bizarre insect-like patterns. Rippers are virtually indistinguishable from the grayish color and patterns of their hives, and create small burrows in which they lie when not on the hunt. Spotting a ripper (if knowing this and looking for one) in a burrow is done with a −4 Attention + Search roll.

CAV (Cave)

The Caliphrian Aggression Virus is a very dangerous contagion. No one knows where it came from, only how it spreads (to a certain degree) and what it does. The known cases have been transmitted through introducing infected tissue into the blood stream of a healthy individual. A scratch or bite that breaks the skin, blood in the eyes, mouth or in open wounds is enough. Someone who gets infected will succumb to the virus within 10 seconds to 1 minute if not inoculated. If inoculated it takes five to nine hours before becoming infected. There have been cases where someone has been carrying the CAV strain latently for days (running a fever and having severe flue symptoms) before succumbing to it. It is unclear how these individuals were infected and how the process of latency works. Victims who have been infected and killed rise within minutes as Cavers. During the first outbreak it took a lot longer for the virus to take effect and it's speculated that it wasn't as potent then, that it has mutated. In essence, CAV kills the host and reanimates him.

Caver

Cavers are, as we understand it, dead. After cellular death, the virus provides a jolt and promotes bioelectrical activity. This process effectively suspends cellular degradation, which allows Cavers to exist for decades if undamaged. They don't require food or air. No definitive proof have been found, but it's speculated that they can transfer energy from objects into themselves, thereby fueling their movements. There have been incidents where a derelict ship filled with dead frozen bodies has been turned into death traps after a salvage crew turned on the heat. As the dead bodies really were Cavers they thawed out and started to slaughter everyone they got their hands on. Cavers attack every living thing within sight (except other Cavers, Viscutropes or permanent VPS victims). They have lost all linguistic and reasoning abilities and the people they once were are gone. They can use objects and tools as melee weapons, but that's about as far as their sophistication goes. Only by complete bodily dismemberment, decapitation or the total destruction of their brain (separating the brain from the body will also do just fine) can they be stopped. They feel no pain and have no fears whatsoever. They only exist to infect the uninfected. If a person has been inoculated and then infected they can be saved if given the antivirus before they have changed. The sobriquet Cavers is used because it's simply very fitting as the illness first of all is pronounced Cave and the fact that the infected revert to a kind of primal caveman state has made the nickname Cavers stick. The creature is immune to critical hits (not counting the head).

Attention: 2
Brains: n/a
Brawn: 4
Clout: —
Cool: —
Gut Feeling: —
Quickness: 3
Reaction: 3
Defense: 0
HP: 30 (for total dismemberment) 10 (called head shot)
AR:
Movement: 20
Attacks: Bare hands 2/1 (Bashing), Bite 2/1 (Deadly), improvised weapon (wrench, pipe, etc) 2/2 (Deadly/Bashing), fire axe 5/2.
Abilities: Close Combat 1, Search 2, Stealth 2.
Spec: A horde of cavers are capable of pulling off parts of a COG in order to get at their foes if these are heavily armored. It might take some time but eventually they will get at a downed armored enemy through this method.

CAV Inoculation and Serum: Most people who are born within the core systems (or in a civilization which has a modern medical facility and ample supplies) are inoculated against CAV at birth. An inoculated individual who has been infected becomes sick and will as stated turn within five to nine hours. However, if given the serum within four hours the individual will be cured and immune to the infection for twenty four hours. The reason why marines and other personnel who risk infection don't shoot up before they deploy into a hot zone is the fact that humans, if not infected, will start to develop immunity to the serum if injected. Each dose costs 500 credits and modern medical facilities have access to them. Marines and medical personnel usually have one to ten shots of serum as part of their standard gear, depending on the situation.

Marls

These space faring savages were once human, but their generational exposure to the radioactive downfall caused by belinium mining has mutated them. Most people who are exposed to the radiation die, but with the Marls something was different. Scientists blame the atmosphere processors on old marl, while others blame the gene therapy the work crew went through in order to cope with the environment down on the planet. In truth no one knows.

The mutation has made these people extremely aggressive, prone to self mutilation and they lead an almost tribal cannibalistic way of life. But the mutation has also left them with an extremely robust immune system, the ability to regenerate and withstand certain amounts of radiation. They also have an extremely high pain threshold. Marls look like humans but they adorn their COGs with remains of their enemies, engage in savage scarification and bodily dismemberment. As they are virtually immune to infection and have the ability to regenerate rather fast they often push metal objects under their skin or drive them right into their bones. This can give them a sort of "natural" subdermal armor and an array of bladed weapons attached to their bodies. Marls are intelligent but extremely impulsive, they are driven more by instinct than their rationale. They can fix and maintain technology (however, it's all busted up and is in a sorry state). A Marl ship can easily be spotted as it's adorned with war paint, bodies and has metal pikes welded to the hull. Radioactive scanners will pick them up rather quickly. As Marls are immune to a certain degree of radiation they're prone to let the reactor containment stay busted when it falls apart, this also means that they often burn an excess of cardion gas, leaving a heavy blackish pillar of smoke from their burners.

Their bodies are tougher than that of a normal human and this has led to a very special way of flying. As they can withstand enormous amounts of g-force and are fearless, their way of piloting is erratic and borders on the suicidal. For example, they can cut thrust mid spin when entering an atmosphere and letting their ship "fall" through it, only to get it up and running a couple of hundred meters above ground.

Marls operate out of the Rykos system and most people are very careful in this region, but marls do jump to other systems. They raid smaller ships and colonies, taking ships, supplies and provisions. They take the women as they use them as breeders and kill the men, desecrating the bodies and even engage in cannibalism. To most people in the core systems marls are nothing but wild space farer tales. But to those who travel the reaches they're all too real.

Marl Raider
Attention: 2
Brains: 2
Brawn: 4
Clout: 1 (4 when intimidating)
Cool: 3
Gut Feeling: 5
Quickness: 3
Reaction: 2
Defense: 2
HP: 18
AR: 2
Movement: 23
Abilities: Athletics 2, Close Combat 3, GLC 2, Navigation 2, Piloting 3, Repairs 2, Shooting 2, Search 2, Stealth 2.
Attacks: As by weapon, but about 50% of the Marls can inflict 3/1 fatal damage with their bare hands as they have all manner of sharp metal objects grafted to their limbs.
Spec: Marls register pain but can get no more than a −2 in negative modifiers as a result. They can ignore any type of radiation except Severe, from which they lose 2 hit points per interval when exposed. The inside of their ships are usually exposed to Concentrated/Mild or Concentrated/Hard radiation and the marls themselves give off a ten meter radius of Mild/Mild radiation. They are immune to most viruses and infections (not CAV though) and regain one lost hit point every half hour. Marl Chieftains have the same basic traits as raiders but they gain +1 to Brains and have a score of 3 in Strategy.

The Unknown Threats

The following threats have not yet been discovered. They have affected mankind, but no one has seen the connections or laid eyes on the creatures and lived to tell about it. The above threats will keep the players occupied for quite some time, but when you want to really crank up the horror and the weird you can introduce more of the elements below. The *Voiders* and their artifacts do affect us all the time through VPS, but it's unknown to the scientific community that this is in fact what's going on.

Voiders

These were, and in a sense very much still are, an ancient race. Perhaps they were one of the first to develop sentience. When they reached a certain level of sophistication they were able to construct technology using a material (dubbed by humans who found the artifacts) called biometal. The technology they created was linked to the very essence of the Voiders. The race was widespread.

At some point in their evolution they transcended the need of flesh and they managed to convert themselves into energy. They became a part of the universe as one single energy cluster. Not sentient as such, but on some level aware and capable of affecting things to a certain degree. This energy does indeed consider the very planets, nebulas and systems as parts of it.

Marl

As mankind harvest planets the balance is disturbed and as a means to defend itself the Voider energy invades the minds of those who use their technology, or stay to far out in the reaches of space. This is what causes VPS. They can affect humans through some of their relics and artifacts left behind and by sheer force of will if humans stay too far out or in the ghost lines for too long. Even CAV is a result of the Voider energy. By a fluke the black resonance mutated a common flue virus in an archeologist. Her name was Hanna MeHarec and she worked onboard the *Injiro* harvest ship, she had found pieces of an artifact during a dig and she had kept them from the crew, wishing to sell them for her own gain. However, she fell ill and her prolonged exposure to the black resonances made the virus mutate. She also had some genetic abnormalities which enabled this to happen. She became a caver and within a couple of hours the contagion was a fact.

As the Voiders are connected to many of their artifacts, the presence of artifacts can influence people with black resonance. The mere presence of voider glyphic writing can actually influence individuals. There is no way to measure this energy. The MRG and some of the corporations suspect a connection but as of yet they haven't found any quantifiable evidence even if their experiments suggests as much. This information is strictly classified and kept from the public.

Permanent VPS Victims

Permanent VPS victims' (beyond 8 points of the dark) loath mankind as they are influenced by the Voider energy. Permanent VPS victims are not attacked by cavers as they share the same Voider energy. This makes for a very dangerous combination. A ship infested with cavers can be navigated towards colonies filled with people by a VPS victim. They have the same intellect they always had, but it's now warped. Most permanent VPS victims are much calmer than your standard raving lunatic, they can act in a calm and calculated fashion, basically they become sociopaths guided by the voiders and their own obsessions. But keep in mind that a VPS victim is alive. He needs to feed, breathe and is just as susceptible to injury like anyone else. But the pain threshold and physical strength is heightened due to adrenaline. Basically, a VPS victim has the same stats as the NPA/avatar who is afflicted but you may add a +1 to Brawn and count pain modifiers as one less. Some are connected to the Viscutropes, worshipping them like gods. However, the Viscutropes don't discriminate as cavers do and kill permanent VPS victims as they would other creatures. The VPS victims usually accept it, believing they will ascend to a higher existence. If an avatar becomes a permanent VPS victim he is lost and the player has to create a new avatar.

> *Voider Glyphs: Those who suffer from the Dark (level three or higher) has a tendency to dream of Voider glyphs and often scrawl them down. In places where VPS has broken out on a larger scale it's not uncommon to find ritual-like configurations of glyphs painted in blood, crayon or whatever, often surrounded by candles and the like. Whispers and eerie sounds are often reported to be present at these scenes as well as weird communication interruptions and rolling blackouts. Some scientist claim that these "ritualistic" setups on occasion can worsen the effects of the VPS in those in the proximity but nothing has been proven…*

Viscutropes

So what are the Viscutropes? There isn't a clear cut answers to that. They originally came from the Arch, a large Voider artifact. The Arch seems to hold a very strong black resonance as well as the strange structure holds a form of mutagenic virus trapped inside very resilient spores. Is the Arch perhaps a biological weapon created by the Voiders and left behind? Is it a form of medical library or genetic altering device, or is it just a piece of art which components are deadly to other forms of life? In any event, the artifact is extremely dangerous and should never have been unearthed.

The Fate of Orion and a Spark of Death: The Orion, the IMC core harvester and mining ship that disappeared without a trace in 490 IT, was the main factor in bringing back the Viscutropes. During their early surface scans they detected that a rather large construct of some kind was buried under the surface. There could only be one conclusion to be made, it was an alien structure. They decided to go down with several mining ships and a science vessel to drill for the construct.

During the dig numerous incidents occurred. It took them four months to get down to the structure during which time a substantial amount of crew members were killed. Some died in what seemed to be fluke accidents, while others committed suicide or were murdered by colleagues who had gone insane. In the end they found what they thought to be an alien artifact. It was an object shaped like an arch. It was thirty meters high and ten meters wide at the base. It was covered with advanced Voider glyphs. The Arch is indeed a powerful device, its main function unknown to those who discovered it. What was also unknown was the fact that the specific biometal contained a mutagenic genetic strain. When the biometal of the Arch is introduced into a living creature, it kills them, mutates them and re-animates them. In a way it's similar to CAV, but is much more advanced.

The Arch also emitted black resonance that eventually drove the crew of the Orion insane, in the end prompting them to kill each other and themselves. The battles that broke out led to the destruction of one of the auxiliary reactors, sending a powerful explosion through the cargo bay. This is where the Arch was kept and the blast was powerful enough to chip off pieces from the bottom section of it, creating thousands of small shards. Most of them were expulsed during the decompression before the emergency doors shut and somehow manage to slip into a ghost line, spreading into space. Some of the shards got released in the Orion, infecting some of the crew. And then the mayhem really began. The ship is now lost, it travels the ghost lines holding the Arch and thousands of Viscutropes. The Injiro is a living ship, a hybrid of dead infected flesh, biometal and alloys.

And thousands of shards holding the deadly strain and dark resonance has landed on several planets. The odd ship have been infected as the Orion at times have slipped out of the lines in order to release infectors that managed to slip onto ships or debris that has been picked up by gear jammers. As of yet these vile creatures have gone undetected and haven't reached a planet with a larger population, only existing in some ships that are still adrift in the black and the odd far out mining colony.

The strain is hellbent on destroying all human life first and foremost and then all other life. They have no regards for a continued existence after that. The universe shall be left void of all life.

Infection and Infectors: Cutting oneself on a shard from the Arch will result in infection. This patient zero will become ill, as if suffering a flue. He will progressively become worse and die after a week. Seconds after his death he is mutated into six or so infectors.

This ganglion-looking and extremely fast creature can produce short lived spores which it has to inject directly into the spine or brain stem of a corpse. This spore holds a replica of the Arch mutagenic strain but it's a weakened state, only capable of mutating and re-animate dead flesh (it can't break through an active immune system like the strain contained in the Arch). Within a couple of seconds or so the corpse has been mutated into a Viscutrope. At times a corpse is turned into three infectors instead of a combat ready viscutrope. The process of mutation is a violent and perverse affair. In a spray of gore the body contorts, rips and basically turn parts of itself inside out. As it only takes seconds it's like watching a reconstructive demolition of the flesh.

CRAFT ID: D-class mining ship
SHIP NAME: Rimtur
DATE: 4th November, 498 IT
LOGGED BY: Tatiana Goreman, kitchen staff.

I don't know how many of us that are still uninfected or alive. As far as I know I might be the only one. I have no idea what happened. We responded to an emergency beacon, it came from a c-class cargo freighter. I don't know the details but I think the captain decided to bring the ship into our dock. After a close examination we concluded that the ship was empty. According to the security logs I managed to read they found a lot of blood in the ship but no bodies. It also seemed that something had trashed the main controls and crudely rerouted the wiring. What they had plugged it into I don't know. The log states that the wires were hanging loose over a pool of blood in front of the controls. The life support system was offline. Apparently Captain Fletcher decided to keep the ship and sell it as salvage.

I'm convinced that these alien beings were hiding on the ship, maybe inside the ducts or even on the outside of the ship, inside the turbines as these were shut off. It seems that they are completely unaffected by the cold and the vacuum. It's my belief that they can generate heat as a means to stay mobile and avoid being frozen.

From the first attack it only took them about four hours to overrun the entire ship. Something had tapped into our communication which made it impossible for us to contact base. They killed everyone. Somehow those who were killed came back to life, but not as...neat as in the case of CAV. They changed, they mutated into more of these things. They're at my pressure door now. Good bye.

CRAFT ID: E-class core purifier
SHIP NAME: Agnes
DATE: 23d June, 500 IT
LOGGED BY: Ivy Chen, Xenoarcheology.

There was no way to get to engineering through the ITS. They had sabotaged it, crafty bastards I must say. My chances of survival are next to none. All the emergency pods were launched before any of us got to them. Probably by the aliens. The only thing I can do is to hold up in the security room and describe these entities as best I can in this log. Before I set out to do what I intend in order to kill them off, I'll flush this data out an airlock attached to a short range beacon. Maybe someone will come close enough to it one day and pick up the faint signal on a scanner. All long range communication has been taken out as well. I have no idea how they managed it.

Well from what I have learned these creatures are extremely hard to kill and cannot be reasoned with. I have chosen to call them Viscoutropes. Viscu for the Latin term for flesh and Trope as in "commonly used theme". I thought this was quite appropriate as they always use our dead flesh to... reinvent themselves and increase their numbers.

I won't even pretend to know where they come from originally. All I do know is that they showed up shortly after we picked up those artifact shards from the planet. The Viscutropes decimated the entire crew within hours, the security team's guns didn't seem to help that much. I discovered that their torso is extremely resilient, which is quite a nifty contrived biological construction as the torso makes out the largest target for attacks. I have encountered two types of Viscutropes so far. I've named these two Infectors and Reapers.

The Infector is a small creature that seems to be put together of a cluster of ganglions with a central proboscis. This creature injects something into the spine or the brain stem of corpses. These then mutates into Reapers. Infectors are very resilient for their size, and extremely fast.

The Reaper is much larger, composed of a reanimated mutated corpse. Their upper chest has merged with their lower jaw and turned into a large orifice filled with bony spikes comprised of molded ribs. Their upper jaw has sprawled out in a cone-like downward shape while bone from the scull have created a tight row of bone spikes here as well that act as teeth. Their hands have been formed into several bone pikes, resembling bird wing skeletons in their distribution. These are extremely efficient in close combat.

Reapers are very strong and they have no fear and they feel no pain. As these beings are "dead" and capable of generating heat they can move perfectly well in the cold reaches of space. They are crude and animalistic, not capable of much higher thought. At least not what I've seen and this is a small comfort. But this leads me to believe there is another type, something that can interact with our technology as they managed to sabotage the ship. Not that it matters much now though.

I will try for the reactor core, maybe I can make it reach critical mass and blow these bastards to hell. I don't know if I'll make it there though, if going straight there's about one point two kilometers to main engineering. And I have to stay alive long enough to get there. I got a pistol with five shots in it, a plasma saw and a fusion cutter I managed to convert into miniature flamethrower that will be good for five or so bursts. Setting them on fire seems to disorient them and damage them somewhat. It's possible that all of the crew, all 9236 of them, have been infected. Killing them by blowing them up is my only chance. They cannot be allowed to reach civilization. May my essence be pure as it reaches the Great Stream. Praise the infinite. This is Dr Ivy Chen, head researcher of xenoarcheology aboard SES core purification craft Agnes, signing off.

Reapers

These are the most common and simple types. Basically, they have contorted the body into a piece of weapon. Their lower jaw fuses with the chest. The ribs are formed into huge spikes which point upward. Their hands fuse into jagged spikes (similar in shape to that of bird wing skeletons) which they use to tear their victims to shreds. Viscutropes can be killed by depleting their hit points to zero and the creatures are immune to critical hits.

Attention: 2
Brains: 1
Brawn: 5
Clout: n/a
Cool: n/a
Gut Feeling: 2
Quickness: 3
Reaction: 2
Defense: 2
HP: 23
AR: 0
Movement: 25
Attacks: Bone spikes 5/2, Bite 4/1
Spec: They only sustain a quarter of the damage from hits that strike the torso. As with cavers, dismemberment is a good way to go when bringing them down. However, all viscutropes can function for several minutes without their head, slashing wildly. Fires and corrosives do full damage and is an excellent method of dealing with them.
Abilities: Athletics 2, Close Combat 3, Search 1, Stealth 2

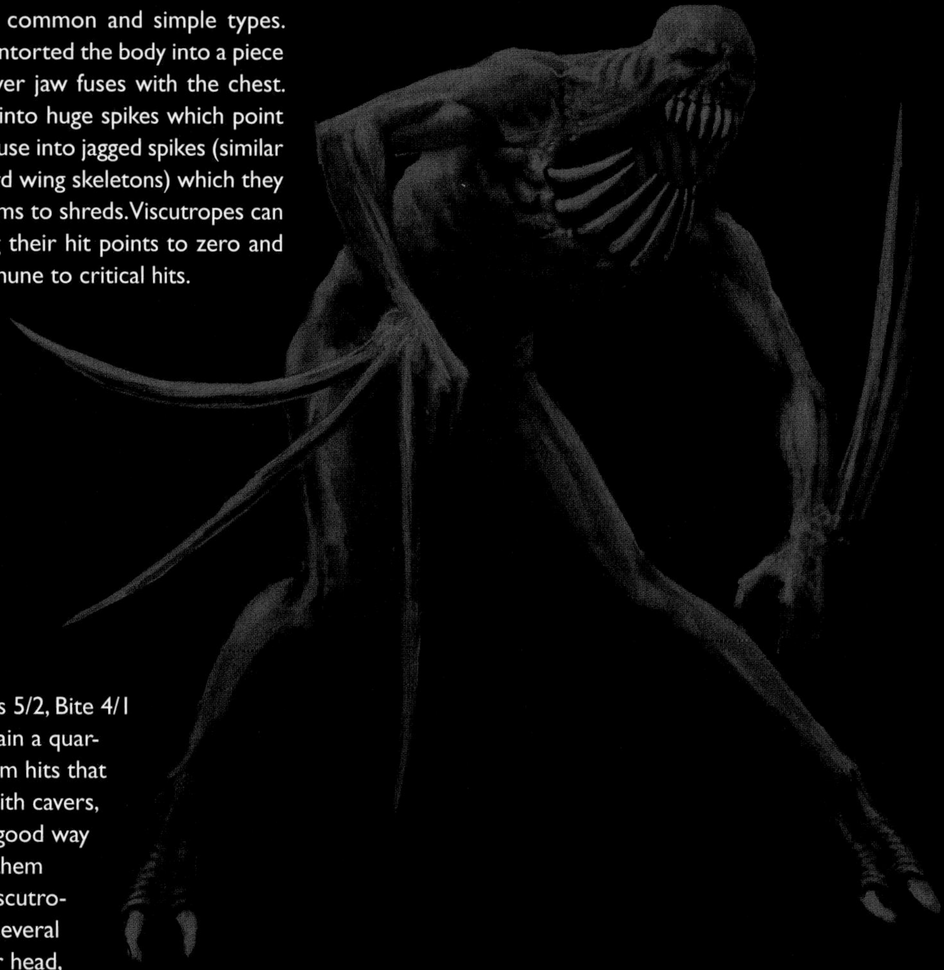

Reaper

Steel Seeker

Maws

Maws have been mutated into lumbering massive forms and often requires two corpses (in most cases it occurs when one corpse is mutated while lying on top of another). The larger parts of their bodies consist of a perverted elongated wormlike body with a huge and grinding maw. This viscutrope is slower than the reaper but stronger and presents a bigger threat. They regenerate in a fast pace and the only way to kill them is to sever the neck. All other body parts, including the head, will regenerate within seconds after it has been blown off and the creature is immune to critical hits. It is possible to burn them to ash, submerge them in acid or freeze them and smash them into bits.

Attention: 1
Brains: 1
Brawn: 6
Clout: —
Cool: —
Gut Feeling: 2
Quickness: 1
Reaction: 2
Defense: 1
HP: (Neck 15, called shot)
AR:, Movement: 15
Attacks: Bone spikes 6/1, Bite: 7/2
Abilities: Close Combat 2, Search 1, Stealth 1
Spec: Regenerators
Viscu-Grafts: *Keep in mind that the four types of Viscutropes above are but a small part of the forms they're capable of producing. They can Viscu-Graft (basically twist, merge and mutate) dead flesh into just about anything. Be creative and bizarre when designing Viscutropes of your own.*

Steel Seeker

These have merged with technology. This gives them an Armor Rating, power tool weaponry and the ability to hook up to computer networks and technology and issue simple commands. They are a horrid combination of abnormal mutation of dead flesh melted together with wires, metal plates and alloys. The ability to use technology as they do makes them extremely dangerous. In order to use technology (piloting, hacking, etc) they make simple Brains + Repair rolls and they have to be merged with the technology in question. Steel seekers are used to pilot infested ships.

Attention: 2
Brains: 2
Brawn: 4
Clout: —
Cool: —
Gut Feeling: 2
Quickness: 3
Reaction: 2
Defense: 1
HP: 25
AR: 4
Movement: 18
Attacks: Metal spikes 4/2 (armor piercing, count armor as −2), power tool 6/2
Abilities: Athletics 2, Close Combat 2, Repair 3 Search 2, Stealth 3
Spec: The creature slitters across the floor like a metallic snake with cables and strands of flesh trailing behind it. It takes the Steel Seeker about a minute to hook into a system. They are capable of lashing out with their cords and wires. These have a reach of five meters. They usually have 1D + 1 number of wires which they can use to attack their foes. The wires can be used to cause 3/2 lethal damage, ensnare an enemy or to distribute a Mild electrical current. Feel free to experiment with these creatures: Some might have merged with firearms and plasma torches. Maybe some even have a self-destructing device…

Infector

These are about three feet high when forcing themselves up to an erect position. Infectors are basically a lump of sinewy muscled tissue with small bone spikes woven in. In the middle of it all they have a proboscis which they use to inject the spore into corpses. They are extremely fast and slither about using their appendages. The creature can infect 200 corpses per 24 hours. As one might imagine, the infection rate is staggering.

Attention: 2
Brains: 1
Brawn: 3
Clout: —
Cool: —
Gut Feeling: 2
Quickness: 4
Reaction: 3
Defense: 3
HP: 15
AR: 2

Infector

Attacks: Bone spikes 3/2
Abilities: Athletics 2, Close Combat 2, Search 2, Stealth 3

Year: 490 IT
System: Sylvian
Planet: Y-34
The Arch is being unearthed by the crew of the Orion.

REPORT SUBJECT: Increase of Energy
DATE: 13th August, 500 IT
RESEARCHER: Dr Ambuto Heath
DEPARTMENT: Artifact Dimensional Research, IMC

As you know we have been requiring a lot of energy lately, but we need even more. As we calibrate the artifact and get more precise dimensional jumps it requires more energy. The whole thing is in fact incredible. If we could figure out how it works and how to decrease the energy input after we have fine tuned it it's possible that we might be on the verge on discovering teleportation. This technology would be worth billions of credits. But as I said, for now we need an increase of energy down in beta labs.

I would also report that we had an alarming rate of researcher displaying early symptoms of VPS according to our psychiatric technician. I think its stress. We are under a lot of pressure as the time schedule is narrow, and working on a non-sanctioned project in a hidden lab under the surface of a dead planet in the guise of a mining operation isn't exactly helping the crew to relax. When on this subject, I would like to request a new assistant. My current one is...indisposed. During a blackout caused by a power drain during our last test run of the artifact he panicked and attacked one of the junior researchers with a scalpel. Luckily security managed to take him out using a stunner so no one was hurt, but he's currently under house arrest and sedated. If (and I would like to stress the word if) there is any real VPS here my old assistant is the only real case according to me. Otherwise things are going well but in order to continue we need more energy routed down here. Please see what you can do.

LOG: Biometal
DATE: 3rd January, 478 IT
RESEARCHER: Dr Clair Mattsson
DEPARTMENT: Artifact Composition, IMC

There has been some buzz about my disposition in regards of the artifacts. But I'm not going to change my opinion: Most artifacts are dangerous. We have never been able to, and I do believe that we never will, fully understand the inner workings of biometals. We can only replicate and maintain the energy levels in the same composition at times and use glyphs as geometrical mappings to simulate the main function. But everyone seems to forget what all our known research shows. And everyone in the scientific community knows this but keeps quiet about it. All artifacts show signs of life when put into a bio scanner. The metal is alive.

We have run every conceivable test known to man on the damn things and have yet been able to classify it. It does not exist on the periodic table. How can we fool around with something this powerful when we don't even understand it? Wouldn't it be much more, in lack of a better word, "sane" to understand it before we meddle with it? Sure, many of the artifacts have shown to be quite safe and led to great discoveries, but others...you know what they can do. No one really wants to talk about the connection between some artifacts and VPS. I think we all are walking willingly blind into this for the profit. What is to say that VPS or even CAV isn't a direct result of our meddling around with the artifacts? Why is the board so unwilling to even look into this? It's the researches on site who take all the risks. I recommend that we form an independent research group that investigates the hazards and collate with MRG. Who knows what dangers we can avoid by...

Artifacts

All the artifacts found have been created by the Voiders before they went away. The bio-metal in the artifacts act as a conduit to their very essence and bio-metal is in away a living thing. So when the nature of the Voider energy changed so did most of the artifacts. There are many artifacts that remained unchanged, why is uncertain. It's quite possible that it has something to do with a different form of construction. It's ironic that Voider tech is the source of core harvesters, the very thing that the Voiders are trying to prevent.

A lot of the artifacts have become very useful as they have been back-engineered. Others that have been found have never been understood. Most artifacts are covered with strange glyphs of a varying nature. A few can be deciphered by archeologists, while others remain a mystery. The Voiders crafted these artifacts for thousands of years, in the millions using many different languages. So artifacts found can differ greatly in shape, size, markings as well as function.

It's strictly forbidden to handle non-sanctioned artifacts. If a person finds one he is bound by law to report it to the GIC. Scientists and archeologists can be given grants to experiment with artifacts, but whatever comes out of it goes to the corporation or GIC branch that handles the cash flow, also they own the artifact. Corporations have to apply for research licenses with the GIC if they find an artifact, GIC science investigators look into it and determine if the nature of the research and the artifact isn't of a martial nature. If it is they will confiscate the material. Needless to say, black market sales and illegal corporate and civilian research runs rampant. Even if many of the artifacts have been put to good use and back-engineered the scientific community as a whole have no idea of how the inner mechanisms of the things work. They can only make use of some of the traits by replicating energies and building clunky versions using human technology. The main thing with many artifacts is that they can affect the mind and the body in a way that's not possible with human technology. Some are just straight off powerful weapons.

There are a lot of rumors (many true) surrounding artifacts. Some say that certain ones are capable of opening portals to other dimensions where nightmarish beings live. There is no telling how the resentful Voider energy will react, or what it can do. The more powerful an artifact is, the more likely that it will teem with Voider energy and black resonance. Biometal is a dark hard material with a hue of reddish brown and green in it.

Available Artifact Technology

Here a couple of devices developed from artifact technology that are legal and available to the public will be described. The artifacts are suggestions that may act as a guide when creating your own.

> **Note:** *Artifacts that are back-engineered only uses human technology (marked be) while others are hybrids (marked h) that uses parts of or the whole artifact combined with human technology in order to make it work. Hybrid technology is always much more expensive since there are so few of them. Weapon technology that has been created from artifacts is a well kept secret and these devices seldom leave the safe confinement of their well protected holding areas in the labs.*

Lingosphere [be]

This device is roughly the size of a golf ball and is a chromed device filled with glyphs. While held, the user can talk and understand all the languages that have been programmed into the device. The device comes with one language and then costs 400 credits. Each new language (maximum three more) costs an additional 50 credits.

Ability Node [be]

This star shaped ridged device is about five centimeters across and about five millimeters thick. It can be programmed to slightly amplify an already existing Ability (avatar needs at least a score of 1 in the actual Ability and gets +1 in it when wearing the artifact). The device is placed over the neck where the arms of it attach themselves to the skin. It can be pulled off at any time and it feels about as much as pulling off a small piece of scotch tape. Only one ability node can be worn at a time and the node can only hold the one preprogrammed Ability.
Cost: 1500 cr

Dreamer [h]

This device lets a person decide the theme of his dreams before going to bed. If the theme chosen was something that is soothing and very pleasant to the avatar he will get a +1 to Cool for about four hours after waking up (have to sleep at least six uninterrupted hours for the modifier to kick in). There are places called dream shops where people come to sleep, renting a Dreamer in house (1 credit a minute) when power napping after lunch (usually available in larger cities, stations, colonies and ships). Even if this doesn't give them a boost to Cool as the period is to short they often wake up in a very good mood after dreaming of their theme of choice.
Cost: 5000 cr

Intimizer [h]

This device is worn on around the neck, usually disguised as a necklace. It's about the size of a small marble. When worn it makes the wearer more attractive to anyone who's sexual orientation would make it possible (a gay man wouldn't be attracted to a woman and a gay woman wouldn't be attracted to a man, etc). In order for it to work the person has to be within four meters from his "mark". The device doesn't override the will of the other person or make them do anything they don't want to. It simply makes the person who wears it more appealing. In game terms a wearer gets +1 to Clout when using charms, looks or similar methods to woo someone. Couples who can afford it often wear these to enhance the sexual experience and to keep the attraction level high between them. A known combo is to use a dreamer to have erotic dreams then get it on with your partner when both are wearing the Intimizer.
Cost: 6000

Unavailable/Illegal

Most of the unavailable artifacts are quite powerful, and often have offensive capabilities and applications. You have to decide which one that might have reached the black market. Two useful but very dangerous artifacts will be described. There are no known prices for these, but their worth a fortune.

Bioforce Gauntlet (h)

This is a dangerous weapon, there are only twenty or so around so far in the entire galaxy. The gauntlet is rather large and cone-shaped. When used it covers the entire forearm. By will alone the user can fire a powerful wave of plasma. It has a reach of hundred meters and does 8/3 in damage. It can fire fifteen shots before it needs to recharge. It does so by assimilating ambient energy and trace gases for five minutes. Then it's ready to fire again. But the gauntlet is unsafe. After it has been fired fifteen times the user has to make a roll for Cool. A fail will lead to the gauntlet merging with the user, actually growing into his arm. Every ten shots after the first fifteen shots will impose another Cool roll with a cumulative -1. After it has merged the black resonance goes from Overpowering to Consuming. A merged gauntlet has to be surgically removed but it's very dangerous. For every point of Dark accumulated after the forth point the wearer changes appearance. The artifacts seem to grow roots into him, dark wires that spreads under the skin. And for every point beyond four in the Dark the wearer also gains +1 in natural Shock armor. For every point above five the user also gains +1 to Brawn. As you can imagine, a VPS victim with an obsession wearing this is a very unpredictable and destructive force.
Intensity: Overpowering.
Sphere: Personal, 20 meters.

Severer (h)

A severer is a device that can sever the consciousness from a body. This is a rather large artifact and resembles a black table filled with strange and eerie runes. For it to work, the subject has to be naked. As he lies on the table the biometal reshapes itself, becoming soft so the person sinks down into it. It moulds around the body. After this the runes start to glow. After about one minute the persons perception can travel anywhere within 5000 kilometers. No walls or other barrier stops him and he can travel in an instant. He can hear, smell, see and sense everything in the place his "soul" frequents. He can monitor up to his Attention in amount of places at the same time. In a world of secrets this is a very powerful tool.

Every time the person uses the device he has to make a Cool roll. A failure will give him a point in the Dark. Each time he uses it within a week he gains a -1 on the roll. His obsession will be to know it all, which will make him stay longer in the fluid world of the soul, neglecting his physical self. After a while he will think of the physical world as a mere shadow of reality. In the end if no one helps him he will die of malnourishment. While he uses the artifact he is completely unaware of his surroundings close to his physical self and can't travel within ten kilometers of his own body.
Intensity: Overpowering.
Sphere: Personal, 100 meters.

The Gerions

If measured by human standards the Gerions really are "alien" when it comes to appearance. At least their bio-suits are, humans have no idea what they look like underneath. Their bio-suits are rather imposing and somewhat disturbing in appearance. They look as if they have been modeled after some predatory sea creature that has evolved to move on land as well. Those that have been sent to us have been trained for

both inter species relations and combat if needed. The template below doesn't represent all Gerions as such, but are the most common type that avatars might encounter. Their suits are armed with two plasma emitters which are quite powerful. These are as located on two of their back appendages.

When Gerions die they do indeed turn into ash which makes it impossible to see what they look like inside their suits.

Gerion Soldier/ Body Guard

Attention: 4
Brains: 3
Brawn: 7
Clout (Imposing): 4
Cool: 6
Gut Feeling: 4
Quickness: 3
Reaction: 5
HP: 22 (+8 for the suit, which heals back at a rate of one every hour)
AR: 6 (shock armor)
Attacks: They can perform two close combat attacks at the same time without penalty using their appendages. These do bashing damage: 6/2. Their plasma emitters have a range of 200 meters and do 8/3 in fatal damage. These have a ROF of 4 and have 40 rounds each. They can fire both weapons simultaneously at different targets without any penalty.
Abilities: Athletics 2, Close Combat 3, Fringewise 2, GLC 5, Interrogation/Information Gathering 2, Politics (human relations) 2, Piloting 2, Scanners 2, Search 4, Security 3, Shooting 3, Strategy 2
Spec: They have sensors in their appendages which effectively gives them 360 degree field of vision ranging 100 meters. Of course they have an array of vision modes available (basically anything that can be found in the optics of a COG). Count them as having the highest shielding against corrosives, radiation and all other hazards. They can breathe in most atmospheres for days if there are some trace gases and survive up to twelve hours in complete vacuum.

Gerion Emissary

Attention: 3
Brains: 5
Brawn: 5
Clout (Imposing): 6
Cool: 6
Gut Feeling: 4
Quickness: 3
Reaction: 3
HP: 18 (+6 for the suit, which heals back at a rate of one every hour)
AR: 3 (shock armor)
Attacks: They can perform two close combat attacks at the same time without penalty using their appendages. These do bashing damage: 4/1. The emissaries have no plasma emitters.
Abilities: Computers 4, Fast Talk 4, GLC 3, Interrogation/ Information Gathering 3, Know-How (human Gerion interaction) 5, Navigation 2, Politics 5, Rhetoric 4, cience 3, Search 2, Void Lore 2, Xenoarcheology 2, Xenomorphology 1.

We have no idea where they come from and they refuse to explain it or their disappearance and return. According to the history files they knew all known human languages when they arrived on Earth the very first time. I speculate that they use some kind of voice modulators when they speak. All of their voices are dark, metallic and generally unsettling. As is the structure of their bio-suits. I believe that all this is planned. It seems that it is in their interest to keep us on our toes. Their suits and their voices paired with their, in most cases, mild-mannered behavior and helpful nature, create a very unsettling paradox.

Gerions are strong, in most cases stronger than humans. This we gathered after a taxi shuttle crashed in Claret City. One of those whom witnessed the accident was Ordos, one of the Gerion emissaries appointed to the Forum. He quickly moved in and using four of his six back positioned appendages he ripped the craft's door from its hinges and pulled the two survivors out from the burning wreckage and got them to safety before the craft blew up. As how much physical damage they can withstand I don't know as we have never seen them attacked, nor does the files from old Earth contain any information on this. But it would stand to reason when taking their strength, and their ability to use it, into account that they can withstand at least slightly more than humans, at least when wearing their suits.

Regular people on the street seldom see them as the Gerions mostly resides in the Inner City or stay in their ships when not engaged in helping us with our research or listening in on our political debates. In most cases the average Joe only gets a look when the Gerions appear on The Circuit as a part of research infomercials or scientific debates.

When it comes to their DNA we have no clue as to how it's put together. They have never allowed us to take samples as such, but we have tried obtaining these from transfer on objects they have touched but come up zero. They do shed cells, but what they shed seems to be subjected to a biochemical incineration. All we're left with is ash. It wouldn't surprise me if they are completely turned to ash upon death, hindering anyone from seeing what they look like. It would also make it impossible to perform an autopsy. The suit also seems impervious to X-ray scans as well as medical scans due to the bioelectrical composition of the material.

We know very little about their technology, other than that it's very advanced and most likely entirely based on bio-technology and activated by their very DNA. This is indicated by their ships as these respond to their very presence. The only hostile acts from their side have been "committed" by their ships as these activate their weapon systems when armed humans comes within vicinity or when unarmed humans comes within five meters of them. The Gerions have warned us of this and their docked ships are kept isolated and under ISA and LED guard so that unwatchful and unauthorized individuals don't come close and get harmed. The creatures themselves are possibly unarmed, but two of their back appendages seem to be of a more metallic nature, at least the tips, with an opening. These might be some kind of firearms directly built into the suit (plasma?) which would mean that they are armed all the time.

No one has ever seen them eat, drink or ingest anything (their suits don't have a mouth). And they probably ingest nutrition when on their ships, outside their suits. Nor have we seen if they need to sleep. And as their ships have no visible openings or windows we have no way of telling. But I have to say that it's quite remarkable to see their ships open, it's like the material melts open and merges closed again. As they are much more advanced than us and that they seem to only help us the only thing we can do at this point is to accept the circumstances, but I recommend that we keep an eye open.

The Gerions

If measured by human standards the Gerions really are "alien" when it comes to appearance. At least their bio-suits are, humans have no idea what they look like underneath. Their bio-suits are rather imposing and somewhat disturbing in appearance. They look as if they have been modeled after some predatory sea creature that has evolved to move on land as well. Those that have been sent to us have been trained for both inter species relations and combat if needed. The template below doesn't represent all Gerions as such, but are the most common type that avatars might encounter. Their suits are armed with two plasma emitters which are quite powerful. These are as located on two of their back appendages.

When Gerions die they do indeed turn into ash which makes it impossible to see what they look like inside their suits.

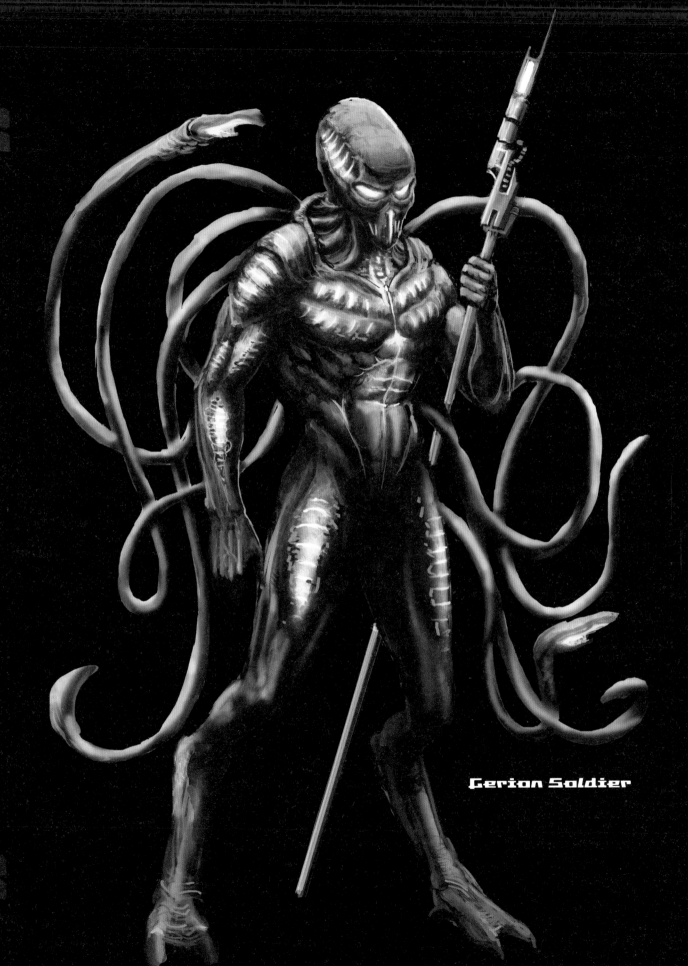

Gerion Soldier

Spec: Every emissary is always accompanied by one or two guards and all emissaries have +2 extra points of credibility. Their bio suit has the same vision, shielding and breathing capabilities as the guard suits.

The "Creators"

The voiders were an extremely advanced race. They managed to integrate their very DNA and essence with highly advanced alloys, creating biometal. This astonishing material reacts to different energies and bio signatures. The material can even hold the will of a voider, an echo of a purpose long since forgotten by the voider who transcended into energy. The ability to craft and use this material was the fundamental core of the voider technology and way of life when they were at the peak of their physical stage in evolution before they ascended.

With their superior knowledge of genetic engineering combined with their ability to craft biometal they fashioned a sort of slave race at the end of their bodily existence. The end result was a hybridization of biometal and cloned genetic material. It was a scientific marvel of biomechanics. These creatures were unaware of their own existence and simply performed the tasks they were given. The voiders used them to perform what little dangerous and physical labor that remained.

After a millennium (a very short span of time to the voiders) when the ascension drew near the voiders decided to terminate their handcrafted living tools. It was a simple matter of recalling them from all the corners of the galaxy and extract and separate the genetically engineered material from the biometal. In the beginning they heeded the call, but some of them stayed silent and hidden away. This was worrisome. But not wanting to hinder the ascension the voiders sent out a signal to the biometal integrated into the creatures. The signal activated the biometal integrated into the bodies of their creations. It virtually burned any living material it was attached to into cinders. This was a pre-planned failsafe if anything ever would go wrong. Assured of the final destruction of their creations all of the voiders ascended. What they didn't know was that several of the creatures had evolved during the years. Timeless as the voider's physical forms, sprung from their DNA and attached and integrated into biometal, it was only a matter of time until some of them gained sentience. This fact was something which the voiders in their arrogance couldn't even imagine.

The beings that had managed to gain sentience had become extremely advanced. They were able to use and communicate with biometal as their masters could. However, they also knew that they were viewed as nothing but tools to be discarded so they hid and waited as they were far less powerful than the voiders. During this time they forged enormous bio-ships and installations hidden away deep beneath the earth on remote desolate worlds. After the ascension they intended to emerge, free from the bonds of the voiders. Incapable of reproduction they intended to seek out other worlds and use hosts which they could reshape. In their ships they had managed to create bio-pods. These were pods of biometal (cylindrical in shape about a meter high) which held several simple living seeds containing their genetic structure and a complex recombinant strain. This enables the seed to form biometal upon being introduced into a living sentient being and reengineer the host on a genetic level. The final entity would be based on the host's basic bodily appearance (but integrated with biometal and genetically upgraded) and hold the mind and genetic memory of the slave race. It would be stronger and deadlier than the host species due to the integration of biometal. Through this method they planned to carve out their own corner in the galaxy and maybe even the universe. But as the signal came to incinerate the slave race they all died and their ships were severely damaged. Their ships buried, silent, empty…but the bio-pods remained. The living seeds are in stasis, ready to spring to life when a suitable host approaches. They are still holding the memory and unchanged agenda of the slave race. When a seed has fully taken over a host the creature will work towards one goal: Getting the bio-ship to the home world or worlds of the host, releasing the seeds in the atmosphere, infecting billions. This will effectively replace the host species in the end.

The last couple of hundred years the bio-ships have begun to come online. They have slowly repaired themselves over the eons. And the ships themselves hold the echoes of the slave race. They have begun to receive and transmit signals. They have received everything they need to know about humans: Our curiosity, nature and collective history. They're sending out signals to random locations all over the galaxy. These signals are affecting some of the buried bio-metal artifacts and voider ruins, actually changing them via instructions. The glyphs and depictions on these are now telling a story, the story of the origins of man. If the bio-ships can't come to us they will lead us to them. The ships are not powerful enough to simply call us over and the process of reconfiguring the bio-metal over thousands of light-years is an arduous process. And then one must understand that the ships don't really comprehend the received transmissions as we would. They absorb knowledge (in way not explainable in human terms) and then they filter it out to the artifacts. Some artifacts hold identical pictograms while others hold our genetic code written down in the glyphs or even woven into the metal. The pictograms make out starmaps (hard to interpret) which shows distant worlds near the dark rim which are in place to guide us to them while the presence of the human genome is there to peak our interest: *"Have these been left by our Creators? Might this be a map which will lead to our very beginning?"*

None of these artifacts have been found yet. But as soon as some of them are found it won't take the scientific community that long to put it together if they communicate, and someone will launch a scientific mission. If alien artifacts (predating old Earth) bearing our genetic code and identical starmap pictograms would to be found thousands of light years from each other any scientist would jump at the opportunity to investigate it. Hell, anyone would! The Church of Infinitology, which constantly search for our origin and already believe that a higher intelligence did indeed create us, would support such a mission fervently.

Warning: The Creators are best used as part of a long and epic campaign and their use have potential world ending consequences. Think long and hard before you use them as it might lead to you having to reboot the entire C&D universe. If you decide to use them it's recommended that you weave them into the myth. It all might begin with the avatars finding a similarity between the energy signature or genetic makeup of the CAV-strain and some artifacts (voider involvement). This might put them on the trail of viscutropes, leading to ancient far away worlds where they find artifacts never before seen. Artifacts containing our genetic structure…

The Bio-Pods

It may take some time before the pods become active. They have slumbered for eons and will slowly respond to the presence of human bioelectrical signatures. It may take minutes, hours or even days.

The pods contain the seeds. In appearance, the seeds are similar to large black slugs in shape and texture and each pod holds six seeds. They're about a foot long. When a pod is dropped in the atmosphere all the seeds basically vaporize and a single nano-particle is enough to start the infection in an individual.

The seeds themselves can move as an animal. They can slither quickly and actually attack an individual. As they do they slither towards the head and upon contact they dissolve into a gelatinous mass. The process is painful to the victim; the seed actually merges with the skin, flesh and bone with an acidic effect. The first minute or so the victim will suffer from severe convulsion and a web like network of black striations similar to veins will spread under the skin. But after about a minute has passed the victim falls into a coma and there's no sign whatsoever of the traumatic event. Medical scans will not turn up anything unusual. After a couple of hours the victim will wake up feeling fine. But he is infected and his body will soon begin the change. This is irreversible. If anyone makes skin contact with the seed while it's merging with the victim (when it's turned gelatinous) the area of the body which made the contact will be locally infected.

If someone manages to grab an active seed (maybe as it slithers) it will simply dissolve into the gelatinous state and merge with the hand and locally infect the lower arm. Seeds can burn through any COG within seconds when in their gelatinous state (disregarding all shields). Once they have turned gelatinous they either manages to infect a victim or dies (a victim might be able to discard his helmet before the seed eats through it). Seeds can only move fast for short bursts of time. In other cases they crawl slowly and will wither and die within twenty four hours if they haven't found a host. Only in a sealed bio-pod can they survive indefinitely. A medical examination of a seed will conclude that it shows traces of biometals and human DNA and a barrage of other genetic strains which a doctor barely can make heads or tails of.

The Bio-ships

These ships are huge and located under ground. They're completely forged out of biometal and it's near impossible to identify them as ships while inside.

On the inside these ships appear as giant biomechanical caves. There are no visible controls or screens. Most of them are accessible through natural cavern systems. They're sealed, but when a human stands in front of a main door (which is covered with glyphs) it will open. About a hundred meters in, the atmosphere is inexplicably breathable no matter the planet's atmosphere. The main room of the ship's upper deck is gigantic and in it sits a huge human hand and it gently clasps a detailed miniature version of old Earth. This is in fact the biometal which has adapted itself in order to be looked upon favorably by humans, lulling them into a false safety. The room also contains about fifty biopods. They're filled with glyphs. If interpreted they will simply tell a tale of an exogenesis corresponding with the first signs of life on Earth. This is of course an after construct as well. In the bottom of the ship (completely sealed up) are millions of bio-pods located.

Only when a host has been reengineered into an early stage creator and entered the ship will it start to power up and open a door which will lead to an enormous hall. In the middle is a mould, perfectly shaped to suit the new creature. This is the cockpit. It is surrounded by a free floating starmap. On it, the course to every human world can be seen plotted out.

After the Creator has entered the cockpit it will only take the ship a couple of minutes to start up fully, after which the ground (actual part of the Creator's docking bay) will open and the ship will leave. It will start slowly, hovering for a full five minutes before it jumps. The Creator uses a whole different jump method and it's approximately thirty times more effective than the ghost lines. As you can imagine, it will only be a matter of weeks before every planet has been infected. Game over.

The Infection

If infected directly by a seed which reached the head the process is irreversible. After awakening from the coma the victim feels fine. But after a couple of hours he will notice that he feels hot, as if running a fever and soon after he will notice black spots appearing in the eyes. Some hours later his hair will start to come out and he will become fatigued, barely able to stand. He will remain like this for a few hours after which black veins will appear under the skin of his face and head. They will spread through the entire body with a growth rate of ten centimeters per hour. When they cover the entire body the victim will start to convulse all the while his eyes turns pitch black. The victim's mind is now taken over by a Creator (the avatar or NPA is no more).

Someone who has been infected in a part of their body will experience the progression of the infection differently. To begin with, the area will only hurt and be raw and red as if it has been scolded but there is no real damage. A medical examination won't reveal a thing. Some twelve hours after, a dark patchwork of veins will appear. They will spread at the alarming rate of approximately one centimeter per hour in every direction. During this time the victim will run hot and perspire off and on. When half the body is covered the victims hair falls out and he will become very weak. When the entire body is covered he will slip into a coma. After twelve hours in the comatose state the victim will wake up in a fit of violent convulsions. His eyes will turn black and he is taken over by a Creator. However, someone who has suffered a local infection like this is left with an option. If possible, he can always cut off the infected area. Keep in mind, this infection perforates the bone and marrow. If he's successful he will be saved from the infection.

Those infected by the airborne version will suffer the irreversible progression that follows when a seed manages to merge with the head of a victim.

The Creator

At the same moment the victim's mind is gone another shocking transformation takes place. In an instant, some of the biometal (the black veins) will push their way through the skin, creating a subtle but protective patchwork over the now gray colored skin. The victim gains fifty centimeters in height and his muscle mass increases with fifty percent. At this stage he will gain +5 to Brawn and an additional 10 hit points. He also gains the ability to regenerate 5 hit points per segment and all damage he suffers is decreased by a third and he is counted as having level two shielding (all shields). The metal gives him the ability to cause fatal damage barehanded (damage 4/2). And he can breathe in the harshest of atmospheres and survive for over an hour in a vacuum. He's not yet fully a Creator in body, only in mind and he has to get back to the ship in order to complete the transformation. If he manages to get back to the ship (either to the main hall or the cockpit) he will siphon biometal from it (in a matter of seconds). When all is said and done he will have the following total increases. Brawn +7, hit points +20, regeneration 5/segment, damage reduction ½, barehanded fatal damage 5/3, level three shielding (all shields). The Creator is born. He will not attempt to communicate (they can't communicate vocally), he can't be reasoned with. His only motivation is to save his people by taking them to the human home worlds.

Archeologist discovering luminescent alien glyphs.

Chapter 15: Game Design

Now you have this whole bunch of background information and game mechanics. What you need to do now is to use these building blocks and start designing your game world and the levels, chapters and stories you wish your players to experience. This section will provide you with some additional tools that you can use when designing your own unique game. This entire book, the game mechanic and upcoming products can all be viewed as a design kit in which you're given game world facts, physics engine and the plot tools you need to design your very own fine tuned version of the game. Sure, this is a ready to play game but once you take on the role of the AI it becomes *your* game and every gaming group will have its own style, gameplay and feel. After you have read this through you should discuss with your players what kind of stories, moods, and themes they're interested in.

Responsibility and Role of the AI

The AI is the arbiter of the rules and the one who creates the levels, chapters and the overall story. He represents the game in a way and as the voice and state of play of the game he's not the adversary of the players. His function is to create a game that is fun to play. This incorporates coming up with all the story hooks, enemies and allies and balancing the difficulty as to best suit the players and the capability of their avatars. The avatars can surely die, but even though players want a game to be challenging they want to make it to the end of the levels and campaigns they're playing. But the players have to work with the AI and vice versa, both sides have the job of making it work.

Counting Time

As the AI you have to regulate and narrate the time flow in the game. When a fight breaks out everything is counted in three second segments, when the avatars goes into stasis in order to sleep for months you simply describe how they fall asleep and how they wake up after a couple of months. Longer travels and waiting periods are simply called downtime and are usually narrated quickly. So it's your job to compare, guide and adapt the flow of time and tie it to your narration.

Tell Me a Story

Levels

The avatars of the players need places within which they may move around and act. These are known as levels. A level is represented by both a physical place (s) and an activity (s). Some times the activities are closely tied to the place and at other times they're not. A level has a clear beginning and a clear end. They shouldn't be to long or to short. And the players should always be aware of how many levels there are and when they have begun a new one and when they've cleared it. Keep in mind that levels should have multiple ways by which they can be completed. The end result is the same in most of the cases, but the exact nature of how players go about clearing a level should be made as open as possible.

Example: This example will show how to plot out three very short and simple levels. This is just to show the general idea of a beginning and an end of the levels. The avatars, Dorn (Medical Tech), Teagan (Freelance Pilot), Spook (Scout) and Nadja (Site Engineer) have just crashed into the docking bay of the core harvester Madden after their grav-cuffs failed and rammed them into the side of the outer hull, ripping their left aft engine clear off (also smashing their long range communication, of course). They're a bit banged up but alive. They have failed to get an answer from the Madden crew and the docking bay is empty. They're part of a rescue team that just happened by when they got a distress call from the Madden. After a quick look Nadja determines that their ship is grounded until they get their engine up and running. Teagan (who is the captain of the ship) says that she and Spook will sweep the docking section and look for any crew while Dorn and Nadja stay with the ship, Dorn assisting Nadja best she can on the continued diagnostics and repairs.

The AI has decided that the docking station and one of the adjacent cargo holds are the two places to which they have access at the moment. To gain further access they have to find the cargo master (who they will find dead in the cargo hold stuffed in a locker) and use his access code. The information on the cargo master can be found in the docking log up in the docking office overlooking the bay. There are also ten VPS victims in hiding armed with pipes and plasma tools. Defeating these, investigating the area, finding the code and get a full diagnostics of the ship makes up level one. If not dragging it out to much, this will take an hour or two for the players. The first VPS victim will attack up close and personal but the others will come at a distance and Teagan and her crew is armed

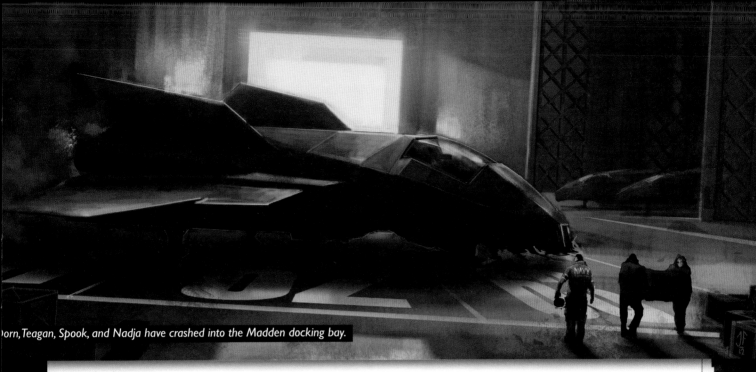

...orn, Teagan, Spook, and Nadja have crashed into the Madden docking bay.

with pistols and SMGs so the adversaries shouldn't present a real threat as the level is designed in favor of the avatars. When they have gained access to the next section of the ship (ore processing) the next level will begin. Here they will experience some horror elements (whispering voices) and they also have to make a Cool roll to withstand the Dark (there's an artifact on board radiating black resonance) and they will be presented with some additional resistance in the form of more VPS victims. The ore processing area is big and it seems that some kind of explosion has messed it up, virtually turning it into a maze of twisted minerals and machinery. During their walk they will find some eerie messages here and there, scribbled in blood talking about the end of humanity. The diagnostics they did on their ship showed what spare parts they needed in order to fix their ship and they're now on their way to the ITS to get them there. The door on the other side will be jammed and Nadja has to open the panel and cut the hydraulics. This will take some time and as she starts there will be a small onslaught of the VPS victims that has to be kept at bay. When they have moved on to the next area the third level will begin, which will involve meeting some sane crew members and getting a bit of background of what's going on (see Cut Scenes) as well as hacking the security network to access schematics and getting the tram back on line.

Chapters

Chapters consist of three levels and are used to keep track of things. A game session usually has one to a maximum of three chapters (depending on the length of the levels). Chapters should have a name that shows off a bit of what they might be about. For example, in the level example above the three levels would make out a chapter. A fitting name for this chapter could be *Dead in the Water*, which pretty much sums up the general situation at the beginning of the game session.

Story Mode Campaign or Single Chapters

When running Single Chapters there's no real overarching plot or story that ties one series of chapters in one game session to the ones in future sessions. Sure, there will be reoccurring NPAs and whatnot but there are no meta-plots or similar things tying it all together. Story Mode will string together several chapters

through several game sessions, creating a campaign consisting of a long term story and plot. Usually, it takes a Story Mode Campaign two to four game sessions (six to twelve chapters running three chapters per session) to complete. Throughout a Story Mode Campaign there's a single thread that runs through all the chapters, leading to the final resolution whatever that might be.

Example: The AI wants to create a Story Mode Campaign for the players portraying the avatars of Teagan and her team, starting with them crashing into the Madden. It's a short campaign, only requiring six chapters to complete. The AI models it as follows.

Game Session 1
Chapter 1: *Dead in the Water*

They get a whiff of the emergency beacon, crash and have some run-ins with the VPS victims.

Chapter 2: *The Living and the Dead*

Still on the Madden, they learn of the artifact and that it in fact has created CAV victims of some of the crew. The only way to "de-infect" them (the AI created her very own breed of Cavers) is to find the artifact and hurl it into space. This they have to do before getting access to the parts they need as the Cavers block their way.

Chapter 3: *Everyone Dies Alone*

They now have to fight their way back to the docking bay with the parts and fix up the ship.

Game Session 2
Chapter 4: *Nothing Is Simple*

The avatars get back to Claret City and they discover that the artifact they blew out into space belonged to someone very powerful. They don't know who, but this person has sent operatives after them hell-bent on taking them in for "questioning".

Chapter 5: *Make it Happen*

They found out that it was a research team belonging to SES who was out to get them. They've learned that a similar artifact exists and that the only way to survive is to get it and deliver it to the SES team. They get a hold of it. But the GIC got a hold of the avatars and arrested them for illegal artifact smuggling.

Chapter 6: *Deliver Nothing, Die for Everything*

The GIC offered them a deal. Make the artifact drop to the SES team as a part of a sting operation. If they do they'll be granted reduced sentences (just serving a couple of months of jail time and a year or so of probation instead of four years). How will the avatars act and how will it end?

Keep in mind that the players have their own free will and that you never can predict how they will shape a story, but you can write quick notes as those above as if you already played through the campaign just to keep track of the structure and main idea of the story. Play one session at a time and then amend your notes after any unexpected outcomes. This is a good way of keeping the campaign on point without taking away the will and choices of the players. It's also made quite easy by using the level/chapter structure.

One Shot Mode

This mode uses avatars that the players only will portray once. It's often used when the AI or the players want to take a break from their regular campaign/avatars, when they want to try something new or when using *story framed cut scenes*.

It doesn't really matter if the avatars in One Shot Mode die as they were only meant to be used once. At times their deaths might be part of the overall story. You can even play out the avatars against each other as part of the game session, having them off each other even as the players have their regular and long term avatars safe and sound. Here you have the chance to experiment freely.

Story Framed Cut Scenes

These are used when engaging in a bit more advanced type of level designing. Here the players will use their regular avatars but also get limited access to one shot avatars. These are used to play a part of a parallel story. A classic example is what we call the aftermath scenario:

Example: *The players portray their regular avatars and they arrive at a seemingly derelict space station. There are signs of violence and horror of all manners. As they progress they will find logs and clues and at times when doing so they will get to actually "see" what happened. They're then handed a one shot avatar with a short background story and the players get to play them in the "before time". The levels involving the one shot avatars are much more limited and "rail road like" than those of the regular avatars as the catastrophe (whatever it was) has to happen so that the regular avatars can experience the aftermath. So using this method you can create very sleek parallel stories in where some of the choices of the one shot avatars (if from a before time that is) will affect the choices of the regular ones. If the one shot avatars choose to strip the power cells from the backup generator instead of that of the tram this will greatly effect the logistics and repairs the regular aftermath avatars have to deal with. This is a very powerful tool if mastered.*

Cut Scenes

Normal cut scenes are in most cases used in the introduction of a chapter, especially the first one. Here the players get introduced to their current situation. Where are they and why? Cut scenes are generally used to introduce important parts of the story, such as background information and similar things. This system is mainly used for the benefit of the AI as a way of keeping track of key elements. They can involve things as placing the avatars on a ship heading for a rescue, at a crime scene or any other suitable situation at the beginning of the story. For example, when Teagan and her crew (above) started out they had already crashed into the Madden as a part of a cut scene which laid out the situation and circumstances at hand.

Story Arc

Levels and chapters are a good way of keeping track of the narrative. But they all have to fit into your overall story arc. If you boil down storytelling to its simplest component it's about placing the one taking part of the story in one emotional state and then taking him from that state into another. This is the core of telling a story, the emotional rollercoaster. That's why most people love underdog tales. We feel for the underdog, at times we squirm when we see and feel his degradation and pain. But when he finally rises and knocks down the opposition we cheer and feel a sense of justice and relief. Again, the story made us feel one thing and then made us feel another; the emotional journey triggers us. But in order to feel anything the story has to be credible and well planned within the context of its presentation. Always keep this in mind. Which feelings do you want your players to experience, what triggers them?

That Which Is Missing

Sure, there's enough information in this book to start playing, but there's still something missing. A lot in fact. For instance, how does it look when someone is shopping for clothes in Claret City? Is it just like today or do they have special NIS mirrors through which the shopper can see himself dressed in a variety of combinations of clothes available in the stores. Or does he stand inside a NIS and get a 3D rendering of the clothes wrapped around him? This is a small detail but it can make the whole difference to the players when it comes to immersion. You have a lot of material but there are a lot of minor details that aren't described. Why? Simply put, it would take up way to much space to detail all the particulars of a fictional society. Every game and game media has its limitation. But you still need to figure these things out to a certain extent in order to put a personal touch on your world and your levels. In order to help you we will provide some areas you might want to elaborate on. Basically there will be an open text with some questions on design. Answering some of these questions might help you with your personal blueprint over the C&D world. For some, a lot of this is already clear, the genre and sources of inspirations being what they are. But there's always room for total redesigns and personal twists and add-ons. How you describe the world is in most cases balanced with your *Setting* (see below).

ORBITAL RATE | CODE ACCEPTED | INTERCEPT

ORBITAL LOCK =
DUAL PHASE SHIFT SIGNAL DECAY =
LSA AMPLIFIER =
DIGITAL IMAGE SCRUBBER =
PLANET IDENTIFICATION =
SIGNAL DUAL SHIFT MODE =
ECHO SOUNDER =
SATELLITE =

TARGET UPDATE FOCUS TRACK

2500 M (2734 YD)
TOTAL: 5.529 KM

HYPSOMETRIC TINTING PRESS

Ship Design: You get some illustrations, texts and stat blocks. That's it. But what does the controls feel like when you grab them, what kind of noises do you hear when walking down the corridors of an E-class harvester and how is the lighting? Is it stark but limited, cones of light coming down from the ceiling leaving all else in shadow? Or is it a soft light mostly comprised of floor lights? Or is it ample light which makes everything pleasant and fairly bright (until the power drains and the red emergency lights kick in).

A lot of ships in this genre have a dark and foreboding design. Metal, rust and narrow spaces. Some wonder why the hell would anyone design a ship like that, or let it deteriorate. Well, in a world where spaceships are as common as boats are today it's not so strange. Have you seen the inside of a worn oil tanker or freighter? Or the cargo hold of a freighter aircraft for that matter? But even so, you don't have to follow this standard. What if all the crew quarters, small as they may be, are very homely? They have wood panels, brass handles and NIS screen for windows which gives them a lake view. Stepping outside into the dark corridor will then present a very stark contrast which can be very effectual. And when things go south the effect of a bloodstained crew quarters will be even more powerful as these represented a safe place of serene and bright design. These behemoths of the void might just as well have a layout of vast halls of chains, forged steel and five meter fans that rotate rather than spin. Everything resonates with an almost gothic design and medieval melancholy.

Techno Speak and Moving Parts: The ship has broken down. But exactly *what* is broken? You should let the players create their own techno speak and give them some free reign with this as long as it keeps the mood of the game. So if the ship has suffered some damage which affects the steering the player portraying the engineer could come up with something fitting on the top of his head to describe the damage when acting as his avatar. *"The third angle propulsion module is shot to shit. I need to reroute the core guidance circuit in order to fix the damn thing. It's gonna take a while…"* The player just pulled the lingo out of his ass, but it suited the situation and gave off the illusion that his avatar knew what the hell he was talking about. This applies to most technology and even to some everyday situations. Let the players decide how they talk about things in the world and encourage it. This will only make your game universe evolve and come to life. Call it user generated content if you will.

Clothing: Sure, space travelers wear COGs but what kind of design does everyday clothes have? How does their equivalent to a designer suit look like? Is it the same as today or has the merging of ethnicities, space travel and the passage of time changed things radically? And it ought to be a difference between people living on the fringe and those living in the cities in the core systems. Take this into consideration as well.

Everyday Pleasures Made Sci-fi: Take something mundane as a digital game and transfer it into the world of C&D… picture it. Yep, it can be made pretty awesome and extreme. Players can step into a NIS which senses their movements and these in turn control game characters in a fighting ring. Shoot 'em ups can actually be contained to a large physical area where the nanites in the NIS build the environments, simulate hits and the players actually run around. Combat training and FPS will in many cases be the very same thing. How about surfing the circuit? Is there full size 3D movies? How about a movie directed by a VIN in which the viewer can actually participate as a character and affect the story? How you use this and which way you go with it will often decide how the world you present is viewed. The main idea isn't to make it all "Star Treki" with holodecks and such. The technology in C&D is gritty and there will be no doubt that the graphic presented on a NIS is just that, graphics. Of course, you can go either way but in general the game is designed to be high-tech but in a gritty and kind of clunky way.

Alien structure discovered on undisclosed planet.

Other Worlds

There is a myriad of other established systems and worlds out there other than those shown on the starmap though the worlds on the map are the GIC approved ones. There are also a lot of systems that have been destroyed by planet harvesting. If you wish to have your players discover new worlds you can simply make them up or use a simple randomization method for generating the conditions on a planet.

Use the following classifications: *Harsh Conditions, Civilization, Hostility, Resources* and *Rule*. Roll 1D for each classification. The higher the result the more "dense" the classification is.

Harsh Conditions indicates how well a planet has been terraformed and how hard the terrain is to traverse. A result of one would indicate a totally terraformed planet with rather pleasant terrain while a result of eight would indicate an unterraformed world with high/low gravity compared to Earth norm also featuring some kind of solar windstorms or volcanic activity.

Resources can mean anything from actual minerals to salvage or job opportunities depending on the circumstances.

Civilization simply indicates how many people that have settled on the planet. A result of one to three generally means that there is no settlement while four to eight means that there is a population (the higher the result the more people).

Hostility indicates just that. But if it's rippers, local fauna or the local population (if any) is up to you to decide. A number of one would mean none or very low hostile creatures while eight would indicate that most encounters will be of a hostile nature.

Rule decides if the planet is ruled or controlled by a centralized power. The higher the result the higher the chance that one or two powers have the planet under its sway. This can mean everything from a company owning the mining rights to a local chief clan controlling the population of a primitive and disenfranchised world.

This system doesn't present anything in detail but it will help you with the randomization process should the need arise. Also, it doesn't really represent a realistic curve for discovery as odds are that most worlds would be void of life but flying around discovering all empty and useless worlds wouldn't be all that fun.

Setting

There are many ways that you can present and play this particular branch of science fiction. Some settings are pitch dark in an "all hope is lost" kind of way. Others are a bit lighter and humorous, while still being serious at their core. It's also possible to start with one type of setting and gradually let it become another one. But try to keep it simple and make changes in a controlled and planned fashion. Jumping from one to the other sporadically will only make for a game design where it feels like the game (and the gameplay) is unsure of what it's trying to be and achieve. When it comes to settings and the mixing of them, less is often more if not very smoothly planned, balanced and executed. Talk to your players and see which settings they would like to experience when you play. Below some examples of settings suiting to the genre will be presented.

Cowboys and blues in space

"I'll be goddamned, haven't seen one of you GIC boys this far out on the fringe in a long while. Why don't you sit a spell?"

There are a lot of fringe planets on which life has become a weird mix of high- and low tech living. The laws of the GIC only apply at times out on the fringe of the core systems (and not at all further out). Here, there are a lot of injustices that actually can be solved with enough bullets flung in the right direction. The technology doesn't have to be primitive as such, it has a lot to do with the presentation of it and how it's used. And of course, style is everything. A Merc doesn't come walking down the street in a polished up and glistening COG, he wears a tattered one, over which he has a long black coat. The LED-Officer in the area wears a badge that says "Regulator" or "Sheriff" and he even has bullets in his gun belt. The technology is presented dirtier, more waste spewing and grimy: *A layer of low-tech over all that high-tech if you will.*

A Site Engineer is covered in grease and fixes up the motherboard with a pair of pliers and a screw-driver, after which he hurls a mouth full of tobacco spit on the rusty deck. The crews Delegate is a smooth talking, tattered suit wearing, conman who loves a good poker game, his blues guitar and of course, the ladies…preferably married ones. This style often swings between seriousness and comic relief. Stagecoach (stage… skimmer?) robberies, train robberies, duels and all that which we love about the wild west genre fits perfectly well in this setting. It's possible to take a darker road, making it all about Old Testament vengeance on the avatar's part, or make them into black hearted desperados.

Dead in the dark

"I...I don't know where they came from, they just appeared and... they killed everyone! They did something to the dead...changed them into something else. Oh god, we will never get out of here! All the emergency pods have been ejected. There's only one thing left to do..."

In and of itself, space is a very (unfathomably so) scary, dangerous and lonely place. You don't need monsters, mental instability or anything else really to feel exposed and scared out of your mind when all alone in the big empty. But if you add these ingredients...well, let's just say it won't be pretty.

Dead in the dark is survival horror in space, pure and simple. There are a lot of tools in C&D that you can use to make this come alive. But true survival horror stands and falls on two elements: Resources (rather lack there of) and exposure. Take five marines armed to the teeth, pit them against one ripper within a clearly lit space station and have their dropship wait on the platform outside (sentry guns in place). No one would break a sweat. But take away their weapons, their dropship and have the station suffer constant power drains and blackouts...and cut their communication. The ripper just became the most dangerous thing they ever encountered and the station has now turned into their worst nightmare. And by the way, did somebody just say VPS? *You all have a wonderful day now, you hear.* It's very easy to create survival horror stories using the tools above. And this being space, odds are that you won't be having trouble with avatars running away. Good luck catching a ride when you're a thousand light years from anything resembling civilization.

Survival horror can be done in many different ways. Some only involve insane individuals while other types include monsters of the dark. Many use both. If you wish, you can put an almost supernatural spin to it: *People that have gone insane by VPS, worship the Viscoutropes as if they were gods, creating altar rooms and sacrificial chambers on the derelict and broken down ship.* Weird artifacts are always an easy tool that you can employ. An acute sense of paranoia, not knowing whom to trust and the feeling of being beyond help and redemption are very powerful emotional themes. Put them to good use in order to scare the crap out of your players.

Just using the human aspect, isolation and desperation is also very effective. A crew trapped on a ship with broken down drives, shot communications array and failing life support is enough to create a claustrophobic and paranoid nightmare. No monsters needed. Under these circumstances humans can be driven to commit monstrous acts upon each other.

Rebel Scum

"Sure, the parts of the cities we see look all shining and nice, and the infomercials portray the GIC like some goddamn salvation. But I have seen the truth. The corruption that eats away at the GIC core, the work camps and I know of the human experiments. You best stay quiet though or else you might end up missing..."

How true and just the GIC is to its people is actually regulated by the AI. Is it really a fair government or is it in fact a dictatorship coated in the sleek and PR friendly veneer of democracy and choice? In this setting the GIC is an unforgiving administration that will stop at nothing when it comes to uphold the façade of a stable and democratic society. The MEC and CIM are portrayed as soulless, greedy and fanatic terrorists by the GIC (while they in this setting in fact are freedom fighters, granted they often resort to violent actions that hurt civilians at times). The GIC are conducting unlawful genetic experiments on unwilling subjects, those who don't conform often disappear and every circuit search, conversation and transaction is closely monitored. In the cities big brother is always watching. The GIC aren't necessarily evil, but as an organization they tend to have "very bad micromanaging skills" and only look at the big picture, quashing that which is perceived to stand in the way of the "greater good". And of course, people within the power structure will have their own greedy goals and agendas. Many times one arm has no idea of what the other one is doing. Backwater planets are used as sources of cheap labor and these settlers are sometimes left to their own devices in a new colony, often ending up starving to death. Here the avatars fight against the GIC, having their own personal reasons for doing so. They can be members of the MEC and CIM coalition or freelance agents, acting as rather grim and relentless Robin Hoods.

This setting can get very dark and cruel in its nature and revolves around classic questions such as "does the end really justify the means?". Sacrifice and loyalty often comes into play as well.

Another way to do it is to let the avatars play the part of the GIC henchmen and politicos. They hunt down rebels, undesirables and crush any resistance to the greater good before it results in any serious acts of sedition. A very important thing when running the setting this way is to make the players believe that what their avatars is doing is indeed the right thing. Maybe later they will realize (but not necessarily) that they are in fact nothing more than an extension of a violently corrupt and misguided organization, making a dictatorship possible. Often the avatars have lived a sheltered life within the nurturing arms of the GIC, their perception of reality formed by the infomercials and GIC controlled learning centers. When first confronted with the reality of things they will in most likelihood react with both horror and disbelief at first. And then there's the third option: The avatars are evil greedy bastards that will stop at nothing from keeping the population in check in order to line their own pockets and keep the GIC strong. *All hail the great steel clad empire of prosperity!*

Sci-fi Noir

"You got me tied to this chair and you've beaten me for the last hour in hopes of getting more information out of me. Look, I'm not being cocky, but I would like to have a cigarette before you beat me some more and before I have to start lying to you. Hey, I don't want to lie but the bottom line is this: I don't know a thing but if you beat me long enough I'll tell you that I'm the chairman of the GIC if you ask. Screw this, kill me or let me go."

Noir is a very charming (in a stark kind of way) and often grim setting that you can use as well in science fiction as anywhere else. When running Sci-fi Noir the focus is often on the personal and emotional drive of the avatars and the overall drama. Every avatar has a personal reason behind his actions and a background filled with betrayal and dark twists.

When employing this setting, recurring NPAs and places are *very* important. As is the avatar's emotional ties to the world around him. This setting is more about discovering the motivations of other people and solving harsh mysteries than the exploration of new worlds and places. But combinations are possible. How would a detective agency look like in the world of C&D? A missing person's case can get really complicated and intricate when the one missing has a whole galaxy to hide in.

Noir often benefits from being run in a city (seedy space station or colony) as it's easier to structure a network of contacts and antagonists for the avatars to tangle with. But travels are still on the table. Going from one dark city to a seedy gangster run space station can be very rewarding and fun for the players. Violence, lost love and betrayal are common and important elements. In this setting being in space is mostly another twist while the focus is on the personal stories. You can even decide that the clothes have a 1940s cut and style and the ships can even sport some of the design from that era. This will lead to a very fanciful 1940s style science fiction world. Who knows how the styles and fashion will be like in about half a millennium?

Semper FI!

"Hey, quit your bellyaching. Rippers aren't that tough. Oh yeah? Well put ten of those roach fuckers in a space station and drop me and my Spreadshift AC .50 caliber high powered carbine with em and I'll show you just how fucking tough they are!"

This setting is a classic within this genre and is fairly simple to manage. The player's avatars are military or at least work as a military unit. What's usually simple about it is that they get a mission. *Go there, kill this and bring this back.* Of course, it's much more to it than that and a lot of things will happen during a mission, but it's seldom a problem getting the players and their avatars motivated. This setting is often surrounded by a certain amount of dark comic relief as well as heart breaking loss and sacrifice. Setting aside differences (or let them jeopardize the team) when the pressure is on is a common theme as well. Elements of on site investigation (where are the colonists?) and suspense before the shit hits the fan are also a common ingredient. Levels often start out very clear cut but if the squad loses their commanding officer and gets separated from the command as a whole, well then things can go to hell in a hand basket pretty damn fast. Do they respect the chain of command? Do the mission come before the survival of the squad? Add to this some VPS and you will have a very interesting (and possibly tragic) military story. But remember that kicking ass and shooting the crap out of the enemy (come get some!) is a VERY important part that most players who like this type of setting wants to experience.

The Vastness of It All

"Even with our science and all our knowledge no one knows where we come from. Who is to say what God is like or if he even exists. The Ghost Storm? I know very little, but one day the great void might bring us an answer."

Traveling in space, discovering new life forms and worlds has a great impact on religion and belief in general. This setting center on the greater questions and the journeys the avatars take will both be physical and spiritual ones. Things like the origin of man, the truth of life after death and what's

beyond the black rim will come into question. Avatars will often explore and find traces of old civilizations that will question the world as they know it.

The setting is riddled with deep mysteries and might even border on the supernatural/occult. Some of the avatars should be believers (Jewish, Jesuits, Infinitologists or be part of any other religion) while some are not. This will lay a good foundation for conflict and discussions when they encounter different phenomenon and mystifying puzzles.

True insight and insanity walk hand in hand in this setting, which often makes it impossible to get a clear version or understanding of the truth whatever it might be. In all this, space is regarded as more than a place. Space itself, its planets and stars boarder on something that is actually alive and at times this should become part of the mystery. Definite answers and explanations don't have to be presented. There is no definite truth or answer to the question: *What is the meaning of all existence?*

Artifacts that are conduits to the divine (but can actually be weapons of some kind making the user believe he's in connection with God or the universe, in fact making him dangerous and crazy instead) are classic tropes. If this setting would be presented in a movie there would be no background music, only the murmur of the engines, eerie transmission echoes or the quiet of the big empty.

> *Core Blanket Setting: Dead in the Dark is the Core Blanket Setting of C&D. It can of course be run on its own in which case everything is dark, industrial and horrific. Even the designs of the spaceships and the environments are menacing. It being a blanket setting means that it always wraps itself around any other setting when the horror factor creeps up on the game.*
>
> *Let's say that you're playing using the Cowboys and Blues in Space setting and it takes place in a mining colony located in an asteroid belt. In the middle of the story some miners come across an ancient chamber containing all manner of old alien relics. Soon, the inhabitants begin to act strange. They even start to look sickly. Shortly after, several of them disappear. Some days later the avatars discover what looks to be already hatched human-sized cocoons hidden away in a decommissioned mining shaft. The number of cocoons correlates to the number of missing colonists. Then, something begins to stalk the avatars and the unaffected colonists. It takes weeks to get a signal through out here and the next supply shuttle isn't due for a month. The Dead in the Dark setting has now wrapped itself around the stylistic design of the Cowboys and Blues in Space setting.*

Opposition and Conflict

Without opposition and conflict there could be no game. Without these there would be no challenge. Within a roleplaying game these two arise from two things: The rules and the levels. Whenever a roll is required there's an opposition, an actual obstacle to be overcome by the player as well as there is a conflict, the player vs the task at hand. Here we have a challenge. Then there will be opposition and conflict that stem from the levels based on the story. Avatars will

There are many unknown and deadly forms of alien life in the Sirius Galaxy.

face different enemies, choices and situations that will present these things as well.

Players want to be challenged. Running into opposition and conflict (may it be rule- or, plot or drama based) is the main reason why they're playing. Being presented with a task that they can succeed with is a motivator, but only if there's also a chance that they may fail. Imagine a game where everything the player did would be successful and he would always come out on top. This would hardly count as a game, it would rather be some form of activity with which most people would grow tired rather quickly. As the AI you have to manage the difficulty curve.

The difficulty curve will change and also needs to change as the avatars Ability/Aptitude score increases (as well as their equipment improves). The players will also become more used to the world and its dangers, making them wearier of certain situations. The first time they play (and if they don't have all the facts) you might fool them into switching on the heat in a ship filled with dead bodies before they have secured the corpses or know that they're not CAV victims. The next time around they won't make the same mistake. So you have to come up with new ways to challenge them story and drama-wise.

Mortal NPAs: A lot of the opposition can be experienced through hostile NPAs. Their numbers, intelligence and capability make all the difference. When you play hostile NPAs it's very easy to make them into mindless killing machines in fights: They and their companions will keep coming no matter how many of them that dies and with no regard for their injuries. You might think that some might do this all the time by their very nature (rippers, Cavers and VPS victims) but they don't have to. Most sane human NPAs will in all likelihood flee if they're too hurt, outgunned or outnumbered. So don't have them keep coming like storm troopers no matter what. This would be unrealistic and frustrating for the players. But of course, some will be insane and gung-ho. Limiting the death wish and craziness of human NPAs will make for a much

better impact when one of them go all combat-psycho and death defying. When the avatars meet a human NPA that will come at them like a rabid dog even with his arm shot off they will be quite freaked out.

When dealing with the more monstrous enemies you should make these behave differently at times as well. Cavers are quite mindless and aggressive but you can have them learn that running straight toward someone sporting a carbine is a bad idea. Having these seemingly mindless creatures learn from their mistakes and actually begin to think tactically (though limited) will be scary as hell. Now the avatars (and players) will have to reroute their way of thinking. In a way one can say that they will be facing a whole new enemy. Main thing is to mix it up a bit from time to time.

> *Encourage roleplay:* First off you should try and keep the players (and yourself) immersed as much as possible in the game when it comes to dialog, and also try to direct players towards them. A player can say "My avatar asks the raider if she knows where Mr. Fawkes is" but you should encourage him to ask the raider through roleplay with the voice and mannerism of his avatar.
>
> Secondly, you should also encourage spontaneous bursts of roleplay and personal scenes that the players create between their avatars. The questions asked under the Fleshing it Out bit in avatar creation will often be of great help for players as the avatars can have different/similar views on things or shared experiences which they can discuss or even argue about. Later on they will have a lot more to talk about as they will experience things together.

Gameplay: What's Your Focus?

When you design levels, you need to talk to your players about what kind of experiences they would want their avatars to encounter. With their help you can decide what type of activity(s) that will be the focus of your upcoming gameplay. This makes it easier for you to design levels, chapters and campaigns as well as it will please the players since they had a chance to influence the upcoming type of gameplay. In order to give you an idea of gameplay focus there will be some examples listed. In many cases there will be instances featuring parts of the following focuses in most game sessions, but the gameplay usually only has one primary focus. The focuses listed are examples and in reality things tend to become more detailed than this, but this will give you an idea of how to handle things when it comes to gameplay. Remember, the focus is basically independent of the setting.

Challenge/Adversarial: This is one of the most basic and primal focuses. The avatars are presented with an open and personal adversarial/challenging situation. It can be as simple as a race for prize money, to the crew competing with another firm about the same juicy delivery contract under SES. It can also be a bloody thing which has to do with revenge and life and death. Managing this focus is quite simple. The avatars have a goal and the adversaries either have the same goal (and only one party can achieve it) or they wish to stop the avatars from achieving their goal (or the other way around, hell maybe both).

Examples of Challenges/Adversaries: Prisoner escape, assassinations, collecting a bounty, an actual warlike situation, political competitors, treasure hunt.

Creation/Destruction: This can take many forms and is about creating something lasting or destroying something important. Building something can be extremely fulfilling and inspire a drive and a sense of pride. But it often takes time, effort and stamina. Destroying something can be equally satisfying. Both of these are dependant of it being obstacles in the way of success. Often the Creation/Destruction can be symbolic as well, having to do with ideals or spiritual matters. While the Challenge/Adversarial focus almost has a clear cut win/lose resolution this focus is a bit more blurry at times and it often takes a lot more time to ascertain if the avatars have been successful or not. Also, there are usually more people involved in this kind of thing which leaves more room for betrayal/support. Time limits are something that can spice things up and put pressure on the players.

Example of Creation/Destruction: Build a military base, destroy a political agenda, create a company, build a ship, destroy a criminal organization, establish a new colony, annex and fix up a derelict space station.

Exploration/Discovery: Okay, space is an excellent place to do some exploration. There are thousands of systems that are just begging to be found. Exploration is about finding new places, objects and people. Both the destination and the actual journey are important. This is a classic "space adventure" focus that, depending on setting, can be as light or dark as you choose. But exploration doesn't have to be as far reaching as new planets, abandoned space stations or systems. A city has a lot to offer in the ways of discovery as well. The dirty reaches of Below in a city is more than enough to keep a crew busy discovering for a lifetime. As the AI, you have the

ample opportunity to sit down and come up with all manner of breathtaking environments and discoveries.

Example of Exploration/Discovery: Finding the remnants of an ancient civilization, exploring a forgotten old space station, searching for secret labs and hidden technology down Below in a city, searching for bizarre animals in a dense and unexplored jungle.

Gathering: Many people like to gather things. The lust and need to gather has been with us since the Stone Age. The focus of gathering can have to do with personal goals and agendas on the avatar's part, or it can be a necessity that has arisen as a result of a particular circumstance. Gathering also imposes the risk of losing that which has been amassed. In many cases the gathering has a limit in the form of an amount of units (of whatever) gathered. And of course, there are always obstacles in the way of the gathering of things and the risk of losing them.

Example of gathering: Reaching a mineral quota in a mining operation, save up credits in order to invest in a particular thing, gather ship parts in order to get the ships life support back on line, acquire a number of scientific samples, find and round up certain people, find different pieces of information.

Roleplay: Ok, it is a roleplaying game but when the focus is on the actual roleplay the focus is also on the social interaction. Everyone that play these games roleplay, but some like to do so with more immersion than others. This is not for everyone and is often dependant on the person's willingness to really act out and play the part. There will of course be a story when focusing on roleplay but most things are played out through dialogs and by acting with a minimum focus on the rules. This will give everyone involved a chance to really get to know their avatar and keeping as much as possible in-game is vital. There are no examples of this that we can provide as it has to do with the player's ability to play a part rather than actions and instances in the game.

Structuring Gameplay

The three basics of gameplay that should be stressed is that it challenges, entertains and captures the player. These three in a well balanced mix will ensure that the player feels motivated by the challenge, keeps his drive and interest up as a result of the entertainment and comes back for more because of the capturing nature of the plot and gameplay. In a computer game there is a whole team of specialists that works hard in order to get this right. Here, all this is on you.

Choices

Player choices are the Alpha and Omega when designing your gameplay in order to achieve the above mentioned mix. The biggest difference between games and other entertainments such as books, movies and the theater is that the player is an active participant in a game, he can affect- and is the focus of the story. To maximize the potential of this you as the AI have to give the player a lot of choices with varying degrees of consequence in order for the story to be inspiring.

However, there are a lot of different types of choices and they come in handy in different ways. These have been divided into three categories:

Vital: These are crucial and span from life and death situations to those almost as serious and the consequence of these decisions have a profound impact on the avatars. The consequences are in most cases rather immediate. Of course, by chance (and unlucky series of Piloting rolls in a dogfight) these choices can pop up, but you should always have some structured up beforehand as part of your game design.

Examples:

- *Stay and fight inside the ghost line or perform an FMS?*

- *Decompress the ship to ensure that all rippers are flushed out and trust that the emergency air will be enough for you to survive until the rescue comes or trust the dinged up scanner (that says there no rippers onboard) and go inside and wait for the rescue?*

- *Use the experimental anti CAV serum (that might kill you) or hope that the Medical Technicians will find you in time to use the real thing before the infection spreads from the bite you received?*

Basic: Not as important as Vital, the Basic choices still has to be made. The consequences of these have a rather large impact at times while not so much at other times but they never determine life or death situations and the consequences often have a delayed or roundabout way of affecting the avatars. At times these choices need to be structured beforehand.

Examples:

- *Upgrade the targeting or the handling of the ship when you only can afford one?*

- *Should you sell the contraband to your old friend that is in need of the supplies right now or should you sell it to your new fence that is ready to pay double?*

- *A Gear Jammer can jury-rig your ship with ease in a pinch and get you out of hot water but a Site Engineer can probably make some upgrades and long term fixes but isn't as good in a pinch. Which one do you hire as a mechanic?*

Negligible: The consequence of these types of choices can affect the avatars direct or indirect, but the effects are small or next to nil. These seldom have to be structured beforehand,

if not used for something as a planned comic relief situation or for in game downtime entertainment.

Example:

- *You're playing balls and cups with a street entertainer and the bet is one credit. Under which cup is the red ball?*

- *What will you name your new fraxnse delivery service?*

- *Do you want to hire the cook that makes Italian food or the one who makes Cajun food?*

Keep in mind that it really matters what basis the players form their decision on. You have to regulate this depending on the situation at hand. The example with the ball and the cup above shows a situation where the choice is made arbitrarily. In this situation it's quite alright since there are no real consequences. This was after all a negligible choice. But look at the example with the CAV serum (under vital choices) you would have to give the players some more information. What are the odds of them dying if they test the new serum and what are the odds that the medical technicians will find them in time? When the choice is as important as this (actually deciding life or death) you *must* give the players some information so that they can analyze the situation and take an informed decision. Forcing players to make these kinds of choices arbitrarily (basically flipping a coin that will decide if their avatars will live or die) will piss the players off and doesn't make for a good design at all. If the avatars go down as a result of an informed decision it's easier to swallow since they had some insight of the odds and risks, and if they went with the riskiest, well that was indeed their informed choice. The bottom line is: *The more important and vital the choice is the more information about the potential consequences should be relayed to the players.*

Then you can design choices to tap into different aspects of you players and avatars. Creating a choice where one of the avatars will have an emotional tie while the other only has a rational tie will also create some great scenes and chances of intense roleplay.

The Game Engine and how to use it

The game mechanics is there for a reason and mostly it's used to resolve conflicts and determine what an avatar can do and what he can't do. But it's also in place to keep the players as well as the AI in check in a way. Every person is different in this regard. A classic example is the Cold/Dark (fear, sanity, or what have you) mechanic. Some gamers think that such a mechanic will halt the roleplay as it imposes a reaction and behaviors in their avatars rather than letting the player choose a reaction. And in one way they're absolutely right.

If a player has no problem playing out the negative effects that Cold/Dark has on his avatar and the behavior is suiting there's no need to impose an exact behavior on the player. But if a player has an avatar who is scared out of his mind but still plays him gung-ho then you should impose the behavior. This is an example on how a game mechanic can be useful.

Never forget that you as the AI control the modifiers, which means that you basically decide when there will be an automatic success in non-stressful situations. Use this to advance and add to the story. Don't have the players roll for every little thing when it doesn't add to the story or suspense. And never make them roll in order to find vital clues and similar things that are necessary to move the story forward. If an avatar with the right Ability (which you hopefully planned for) is in the right place and says that he uses this Ability you should let him find the vital clue (or whatever that's needed) that lets the story progress. Who benefits if the story comes to a standstill? No one does. The players will be frustrated and you won't get to use the rest of your chapters.

Crunch is Optional

The mechanics used in C&D can be put into play with the crunch valve turned way up, utilizing every rule and chart to their fullest extent and on the other hand the mechanics can be used without so much as looking up a single chart. The main goal of the mechanics is to create a cohesive system in which there are solutions for the most common encounters and situations. Some just glance at the charts once and then use their judgment to come up with modifiers based on the mechanics while others like to compare every chart in order to add and subtract the exact modifiers. So basically run the game in a way that you and your gaming group find entertaining. If, for some reason, there is a dispute over modifiers and rules when running the game in "low crunch mode" the charts and rules give you something to fall back on.

Blueprints and Such

As the AI you should be prepared to create maps of important locations. At times they only have to show an overview and at other times they need to be more detailed. There are some examples of overview blueprints provided in the book that you can use on the fly or as inspiration to create your own.

You can use the environment in order to create levels, chapters and stories. This is a classic theme within the dark sci-fi genre. When a D or E-class ship has broken down it can take the avatars hours to get around as bulkheads are sealed, the ITS is offline and entire decks are filled with a vacuum. In many cases they have to get to a part of the ship that is far away in order to fix something that's rather close. When the ITS and the logistical system is offline it gets a lot harder to transport spare parts and at times it becomes complicated to complete the most rudimentary tasks. But be careful as to not make the whole thing stupid or too farfetched. Also, do *not* create mazes or labyrinths. These will only generate a series of frustratingly arbitrary choices for the players that only act as a filler in lack of crafty level design. If you for some reason feel the urge to use these things do so with finesse, create an actual puzzle system by which the players can navigate. Players would rather use their intelligence in order to generate informed choices than arbitrarily have to choose between "left, right, or straight ahead" over and over again.

Rewards and Punishment

This is very important and as with many other aspects of the AI's job this boils down to balance. The chance of being rewarded inspires most people and in this case the players will be inspired if their avatars stand a chance of being rewarded. They love being rewarded and hate being punished. So with that in mind you should be focusing on, and emphasize the rewards while using the threat of punishment more than the actual punishments (all punishments and rewards are of course an in-game factor). For when push comes to shove, if you do it the other way around the players will be utterly bored and maybe even a bit ticked off.

But this doesn't mean that you should shower them with praise and treasure. What stipulates a reward is relative and a larger reward obtained after a period of being subjected to harsh trials while also being threatened by punishments tastes all the sweeter. The old saying *anything worth having is worth fighting for* illustrates how to best handle the reward and punishment bit.

You should also take into account that there are many types of rewards and punishments. A reward or punishment can come in the form of actual usable resources or loss of them, but at many times they are even more powerful if they tap into the emotional side of the player using his avatar. Taken to its core one can say that punishments/rewards that come in the form of humiliation/vindication (for the avatar) in all likelihood will engage the player more so than gear and trinkets that their avatar may obtain.

For example, if the ship the avatar is on is likely to explode at any moment the player will probably do everything he can to get his avatar off the death trap. Even if taking a chance might bring him a lot of cool gear he probably wouldn't risk the life of his avatar. But if the information the avatar needs in order to find his archenemy who killed his wife and child is on the ship, the player will probably be willing take a bigger risk with the avatar (as well as the avatar would be more inclined to take a risk). The threat of punishment (certain death in this extreme example) is the same in both scenarios, but the reward has to do with mere profit in the first scenario while tapping into the personal and emotional in the second scenario. This clearly illustrates how tapping into different aspects of your player through his avatar will have a profound effect on his decision making in most cases (if the player is immersed in the game that is).

Story Seeds

Here are some examples of story seeds common to C&D. It's quite easy to come up with ideas in general but these might give you some inspiration.

Dogs of War: Way out, far from the core systems, the CIM and GIC are butting heads out in the black as well as on the surface of planets and both sides are in dire need of good pilots, soldiers, scouts and anyone that can aid them in the ongoing conflict. It doesn't matter which side the avatars are on, either way they will be involved in sabotage missions, all out space combat or recon runs behind enemy lines. The winner of the conflict will gain control over a large amount of belinium and be able to establish themselves in the region.

Ghastly Rituals: A strain of ritualistic style murders have occurred out in a small but lucrative mining colony. The avatars are hired to investigate and get to the bottom of things, preferably without disturbing the work or make the investors nervous. As of now the killings have been labeled as accidents as the mining company don't want to get their funds cut. Preferably they even want to keep most of the workers out of the loop so the avatars might go in undercover to solve the mystery.

Lost Station: A far out research station went quiet and after a month of silence they sent out a distress call. It was an automated distress beacon which only stated that they needed help. Not knowing what to expect the corporation funding the station sends out a mixed bag of professionals and here the avatars come in. They're sent to find out what has happened to the station, save survivors and retrieve research data. It might just be a busted LSA or the whole damn station might be overrun by rippers. Needless to say, they have to be prepared for anything.

Political Hay: The aide of a senator is very keen on his boss winning the reelection and to ensure that this happens he needs some dirt on the competition. At first he just wants the avatars to perform surveillance and monitor the subject's bank accounts for suspicious transactions. Later the competing politician heads off to Stoneshade as part of his campaign trail and the avatars are asked to follow. While there during a speech the politician is assassinated. For a rather ridicules amount of money they're asked to sabotage the investigation of the murder. It's a no questions asked dirty and dangerous job…but the pay is VERY generous…But what is to say that the avatars aren't being used as pawns in this high stakes game?

Quarantine: A brutal serial killer and sex offender has managed to escape to the core system where he's looking to seek vengeance on the judge, prosecutor and jurors involved in the trial that led to his conviction. As this wasn't enough, the killer is the carrier of an experimental slow working strain of CAV (the GIC used him as a guinea pig before his planned *cool burning*). It will take weeks before he's turned but he can still spread it through the transfer of bodily fluids. The avatars are hired to bring him back, stop a possible outbreak and to keep the whole thing out of the eye of the public.

Raiders: Simple, the avatars are hired to raid a specific commercial ship in one of the core systems and deliver the goods to a preordained meeting spot. However, they encounter a lot more resistance than their client told them there would be and when they arrive at their meeting spot an ambush is waiting for them. What the hell is going on? Someone seems to really have it in for them.

Spy vs Spy: A rather small new outfit has hired a large lab section in the Steeple in the Berion system. They're conducting cutting edge research involving energy focused weapons. The avatars are hired to do some industrial espionage. How they do it is up to them as long as they get data and keep a low profile. The problem is that the employers of the avatars have competitors and they have also sent in a group to do some digging around. And on top of this, the company they're spying on also have their security people in place. The whole thing is soon turned into a deadly game of cat and mouse as billions of credits worth of research data are at stake.

The Find: The avatars are on their way home from a period of work (prospecting, mining, raiding, etc) and are slumbering as they travel using the RT-Drive. Suddenly the VIN wakes them. It tells the crew that it noticed a strong transmission some days travel from their location. The transmission resembles a commercial emergency signal but there are some slight differences. The VIN has also picked up a strong bio-signature from the location, as if bio-signs had been focused and transmitted as well. The signal comes from a small asteroid field and originates from a downed C-class mining ship. As the avatars board the ship they find the crew dead, apparently from explosive decompression. However, they also find a monolith shaped artifact covered with glyphs and it can probably be sold for a small fortune. Soon after they have taken it onboard their ghost drive is activated, seemingly by itself (though the bio-energy seems to spike in the artifact as it does). The crew has no choice but to go into stasis. Is it possible that an artifact has a will of its own and the power to affect its surroundings? If that's the case, where is it sending them and what does it want?

A Ripper going through an unknown mutation.

Cold Cash: *So how much does a freelance crew get paid for their services? Well it all depends on the circumstances. If the employer wants a freelance pilot and his crew to travel a couple of months through the ghost, jack a shipment from someone and then go back he has to be prepared to pay a lot. The ship will need maintenance, the stasis sleep costs, the reactor also needs to be maintained. When all that is covered the crew need food and spending money when it's all said and done. It's hard to say exacts, but the cost of gear and the prices of living should enable you to come up with suitable fees and payments, and of course they're always up for negotiations between employer and employee. As a general rule, which is accepted under normal circumstances by serious employers, freelance contractors take a fifteen percent "startup" charge when they take on the mission and keep it whether or not they complete their assignment. Trying to skim this startup charge from employers, not actually doing the work, is a dangerous thing indeed and those who get caught are often killed or black-listed. The unwritten law is that the captain of the ship (if a private enterprise) takes the payment. Spends what's needed on repairs, medical, crew living costs and whatnot. The captain then takes what's left, takes a 10%-35 (depending on the crew size) cut and divides the rest as evenly as possible. In a perfect scenario the crew members get a 10% cut of the final loot while the captain keeps 25%. Few people squabble over this extra cost since the captain is the one responsible for any additional repair costs and bribes most of the time. In a way, crew members have it pretty good if their captain is fair. They get food, shelter and medical and whatever money they get is theirs to spend. But as a general rule, crew members are responsible for maintaining their own gear such as weapons and COGs.*

A smart captain gives out bonuses from time to time, and if he does it right it doesn't need to cost that much. Entertainment, a meal cooked from real raw materials can go a long way to heighten moral out in the black, often more so than cash. Keeping some stakes, potatoes and real greens preserved can be a life-saver when crew moral is low. Most captains see this as "crew maintenance" and it comes with the job.

Upgrade Points

As the avatars progress they will become more skillful. This will be reflected in the form of UPs (Upgrade Points). Every chapter the players will receive one to three UPs. A regular chapter with just minor dangers will give them one UP. More dangerous chapters will give them two and the most dangerous chapters will give them three. These can be used to upgrade the avatar. Some gaming groups want the upgrades to be "natural". If an avatar wants to upgrade his Shooting he'd better practice or be involved in some shootouts in the chapter in question. While other groups prefer to just buy stuff without these prerequisites. It's up to the group, but the AI has final say.

Below you can see how many UPs it takes to buy one extra dot in the different areas.

Save Points: 2
Aptitude: 8
Fourth or Fifth dot in Aptitudes: 10
Specialty: 4
Ability: 5
Fourth or Fifth dot in Abilities: 6

Resources can never be bought using the upgrade system as they have to be obtained/lost during play. And if you wish you might have a bonus system that will reward a player for things such as exceptional roleplay or if he thought out a particularly clever solution to an in game problem. But the recommendation is that you stick with an even spread of points as integrated in the system above and use in-game rewards if you wish to encourage some particular aspect (avatar courage, roleplay, etc.).

Or...just wing it!

Yep, might seem a bit paradoxical after all this rhapsodizing about choices and structures that we're just going to tell you to wing it. But if you have your basic building blocks in order, a beginning and an end (and an okay grasp of the system) you can probably start a game session with very little preparation, especially if you know the avatars. And no matter what, you'll have to wing it quite often anyway since the story has a way of changing and evolving a lot during play.

The planet Bedos.

COLD AND DARK

Basic Info

Player:_____

Avatar:_____

Package:_____

Variation:_____

DoB:_____

Age:_____

Stasis Time:_____

Aptitudes

Brains ●OOOO   Carrying Capacity____

Brawn ●OOOO   Credibility____

Clout ●OOOO   Run/Sprint_____

Cool ●OOOO   Defense_____

Gut Feeling ●OOOO   Save Points OOOOO

Quickness ●OOOO

Reaction ●OOOO

Attention ●OOOO

COLD OOOOOO

DARK OOOOOOOO

Health

Bashing

Bruised (-)   OOOOOOOOO Beaten(−1)OOOO Broken(−2) OOOO Inc (−3/Out)OOOO OOOOO

Fatal

Scratched(−1)OOOOOOOOO Hurt(−2)OOOO Injured(−4) OOOO Inc (out)OOOO OOOOO

Abilities

Administration OOOOO	GLC OOOOO	Search OOOOO	**Specialities/Bonus**
Athletics OOOOO	Interrogation OOOOO	Security OOOOO	_____
Close Combat OOOOO	Know-How OOOOO	Shooting OOOOO	_____
Computers OOOOO	Navigation OOOOO	Stealth OOOOO	_____
Driving OOOOO	Politics OOOOO	Strategy OOOOO	_____
Explosives OOOOO	Piloting OOOOO	Void Lore OOOOO	_____
Fast Talk OOOOO	Repairs OOOOO	Xarcheology OOOOO	_____
Fringewise OOOOO	Rhetoric OOOOO	Xmorphology OOOOO	_____
First Aid OOOOO	Scanners OOOOO	_____OOOOO	_____
Forensics OOOOO	Science OOOOO	_____OOOOO	_____

Weapon	DMG	PSD	Range	ROF	Clip
_____					
_____					
_____					
_____					
_____					

Resources

_____OOOOO

_____OOOOO

_____OOOOO

_____OOOOO

_____OOOOO

_____OOOOO

_____OOOOO

COLD AND DARK

COG_____

COG Armor Config: Lean O/Shock O
AR:_____

Other Armor Config: Lean O/Shock O
AR:_____

Main Circuitry OOOOOOO

NavComp O ISS O Nexus O Mag Boots O
Breather O

Total Durability:_____ Current:_____

Total Durability:_____ Current:_____

NAP Location	Device	Level
Array ( )		O O O O
Array ( )		O O O O
Array ( )		O O O O
Array ( )		O O O O
Array ( )		O O O O
Augmentations ( )		O O O O
Augmentations ( )		O O O O
Augmentations ( )		O O O O
Augmentations ( )		O O O O
Augmentations ( )		O O O O
Expendables ( )		O O O O
Expendables ( )		O O O O
Expendables ( )		O O O O
Expendables ( )		O O O O
Expendables ( )		O O O O
Shell ( )		O O O O
Shell ( )		O O O O
Shell ( )		O O O O
Shell ( )		O O O O
Shell ( )		O O O O
Visor ( )		O O O O
Visor ( )		O O O O
Visor ( )		O O O O
Visor( )		O O O O
Visor( )		O O O O

TCI NAPS	Level
	O O O O
	O O O O
	O O O O
	O O O O
	O O O O
	O O O O

Stealth Module O O O O
Forensic Filter O O O O

Capacity
/
/
/
/
/

Mission Log

_____
_____
_____
_____
_____
_____
_____
_____
_____
_____
_____
_____
_____
_____
_____
_____
_____
_____

Additional Gear/Loot

_____
_____
_____
_____
_____
_____

Credits:

UPs:_____

COLD AND DARK

Ship Name:
Ship Class and Model:
Color/markings:

Length, Width, Height:

Main Stats

Speed: ____
Acceleration: ____
Ghost Drive: ____
Handling: ____

Scanners

Bio Scanner: ____
Energy Scanner: ____
Environmental Scanner: ____
LIDAR: ____
LSA: ____
Signal Scanner: ____

Targeting: ____
Pods: ____
AR: ____

DHL

Immune: ____
Vulnerable: ____
At Risk: ____

Reactor
Type:
Percentage:

Stasis Units
Number:
Total Cycles:
Spent Cycles:

Facilities
Life Support/Nutrition:
Medbay:
Engineering Bay:
Other_____:
Other_____:
Other_____:

Cannons

Weapon	DMG	PSD	Range	Clip		Notes

Missiles/Other Weapons

	Weapon		Weapon		Weapon
	DMG___		DMG___		DMG___
	PSD___		PSD___		PSD___
	Range___		Range___		Range___
	Clip___		Clip___		Clip___
	Ground Zero___		Ground Zero___		Ground Zero___
	Devastating___		Devastating___		Devastating___
	Destructive___		Destructive___		Destructive___
	Blasting___		Blasting___		Blasting___

Sections A B C	Damage
O O O	Scraped
O O O	Dinged
O O O	Banged up
O O O	Battered (−1)
O O O	Torn (−2)
O O O	Breached (−3)
O O O	Smashed (−4)
O O O	Demolished

COLD AND DARK
Avatar Interface

INFO

Player: _____

Avatar: _____

Package: _____

Variation: _____

DoB: _____

Age: _____

Stasis: _____

APTITUDES

Brains ● ☐ ☐ ☐ ☐   Gut Feeling ● ☐ ☐ ☐ ☐

Brawn ● ☐ ☐ ☐ ☐   Quickness ● ☐ ☐ ☐ ☐

Clout ● ☐ ☐ ☐ ☐   Reaction ● ☐ ☐ ☐ ☐

Cool ● ☐ ☐ ☐ ☐   Attention ● ☐ ☐ ☐ ☐

Save Points ☐ ☐ ☐ ☐ ☐

Run/Sprint: _____   Carrying Capacity: ___

Defense: _____   Credibility: ___

HEALTH

	Bruised	Beaten	Broken	Inc
Bashing	OOOOOOOOO (-) OOOOO	OOOO (-1)	OOOO (-2)	OOOO (-3/Out)

	Scratched	Hurt	Injured	Inc
Fatal	OOOOOOOOO (-1) OOOOO	OOOO (-2)	OOOO (-4)	OOOO (Disabled)

COLD OOOOOO
DARK OOOOOOOOO

ABILITIES

Administration OOOOO	GLC OOOOO	Search OOOOO
Athletics OOOOO	Interrogation OOOOO	Security OOOOO
Close Combat OOOOO	Know-How OOOOO	Shooting OOOOO
Computers OOOOO	Navigation OOOOO	Stealth OOOOO
Driving OOOOO	Politics OOOOO	Strategy OOOOO
Explosives OOOOO	Piloting OOOOO	Void Lore OOOOO
Fast Talk OOOOO	Repairs OOOOO	Xarcheology OOOOO
Fringewise OOOOO	Rhetoric OOOOO	Xmorphology OOOOO
First Aid OOOOO	Scanners OOOOO	_____ OOOOO
Forensics OOOOO	Science OOOOO	_____ OOOOO

BONUS SPEC

_____

_____

_____

_____

_____

_____

_____

WEAPONS

Weapon	DMG	PSD	Range	ROF	Clip

RESOURCES

_____

_____

_____

_____

_____

Credits: _____   UPs: _____

COG

NAP Device	NAP Location	Lvl	Capacity	Special	Lvl
		OOOOO		**Stealth Module**	OOOOO
		OOOOO		**Forensic Filter**	OOOOO
		OOOOO			
		OOOOO		**TCI NAPs**	
		OOOOO			OOOOO
		OOOOO			OOOOO
		OOOOO			OOOOO
		OOOOO			OOOOO
		OOOOO			OOOOO
		OOOOO			OOOOO
		OOOOO	**GEAR**		
		OOOOO			
		OOOOO			
		OOOOO			
		OOOOO			
		OOOOO			

SHIP

Ship Name:
Ship Class and Model:

Color/markings:
Length, Width, Height:

Reactor:
Type:
Precentage:

Facilities/Units

Stasis Units Number: /Total Cyc: /Spent Cyc:
Life Support/Nutrition:
Medbay:
Engineering Bay:
Other/ :
Other/ :
Other/ :

Main Stats

Speed: /Acceleration: Ghost Drive/ Handling:

Scanners & Targeting

Bio: /Energy: /Environmental: /LIDAR: /LSA: / Signal:
/Targeting:

OHL

Immune:
Vulnerable:
At Risk:

Additional Ship Notes

Section			Damage
A B C			Scraped
O O O			Dinged
O O O			Banged up
O O O			Battered (-1)
O O O			Torn (-2)
O O O			Breached (-3)
O O O			Smashed (-4)
O O O			Demolished

Weapons

Type	DMG	PSD	Clip	Range

Index